LABRADOR

THE COMPLETE OWNERS GUIDE

Essential facts tips and information about keeping Labrador's including; Feeding, Health, Housing, Training, Care, Grooming, Breeding and much more.

LEN PACKWOOD

AUTHOR NOTE

If you are reading this information as an experienced dog owner, then parts will already be familiar to you. Having said that, the information is intended for everyone and I am sure that even the experienced dog person will find a lot of new facts and information.

It is not my intention to patronise the reader and to tell you how you should read a book. However, unless you are an experienced dog person and are confident enough to skip certain sections, I would highly recommend that you thoroughly read all of the contents before you begin to implement any of the instructions. You may wish to take notes as you go or re-read the book a second time noting important steps to give yourself an action plan.

Also, please note that the use of 'he' or 'him' will be used throughout the text and is simply for ease of reading. It is generally intended to refer to both sexes. It is not meant to indicate a preference by the author of one sex over the other. 'She' or 'her', may also be used specifically where it is more appropriate to indicate the female (bitch) as opposed to the male (dog).

Please also note that throughout the book you will come across website links. At the time of press, the web links were working. However, from time to time, pages get changed, deleted or a supplier goes out of business. If you find these do not work, please go to the route .com or .co.uk web address. Again, the author takes no responsibility for the availability of any of these, when you the reader come to access them.

TABLE OF CONTENTS

CHAPTER ONE:

UNDERSTANDING LABRADORS

The Labrador is considered by many to be the ideal, all round, adaptable, perfect, all purpose companion dog. It is therefore no surprise that they are popularly thought of as excellent family dogs. In fact if Kennel Club registrations are an indicator of how popular they are, they have been the most popular dog according to the UK Kennel Club, since 1990. Similarly according to an AKC report dated 21st March 2017, The American Kennel Club stated that the Labrador had yet again held top spot for a 26th consecutive year. Other global kennels clubs have also reported similar statistics.

The Labrador versatility has traditionally allowed them to be outstanding and capable gundogs, but also retaining the temperament and sociability to get on with everyone. However, as well as being competent Gundogs, their versatility has enabled them to excel at a number of other occupations. This has included involvement in drug detection, search and rescue, detecting land mines, therapy dogs in homes and hospitals, in some cases hearing dogs for the deaf and of course as guide dogs for the blind.

1.) AN OVERVIEW OF THE LABRADOR

TYPICAL CHARACTERISTICS

You will commonly hear the Labrador being referred to as follows: keen, affable, kind, responsive, enthusiastic, biddable, friendly, good natured, loving, affectionate, playful, happy, versatile, easy going etc etc. Once again, the Labrador is unsurprisingly a very people oriented breed. But this also means they have relatively high affection needs. They are also not necessarily known as loyal, one person dogs as they make friends with anyone.

They are generally a confident breed, but some dogs have been known to be timid requiring gentle handling and early socialisation for confidence building.

Labradors are alert as watchdogs and will 'alarm bark' to warn of intruders, but they are not typically known as excessive barkers, if at all. They may bark if someone rings the front door bell, but many more do not bark at all. They are generally not considered as suitable guard dogs as most are more friendly than suspicious. However, some are known to be quite territorial and this to be one of the few times they may become relatively aggressive.

VITAL STATISTICS

The Labrador is considered a medium to large breed. Depending on whether he is a 'working' type or a 'show' type (we will talk more about this as we go), he can be bulky, stocky and muscular or relatively lighter and thinner looking. He has what is often referred to as an 'otter like' tail. Similar to many water retrievers, he has webbed feet enabling him to be a strong swimmer.

Typical dimensions are as follows:

Height

Female: 21 to 24 inches (55 to 60cm)

Male: 23 to 25 inches (57 to 62cm)

Weight

Females: 55 to 70lb (25 to 32kg)

Males: 65 to 80lb (30 to 37kg)

Puppies at 8 weeks of age weigh on average 10lb and generally somewhere between 9 and 12lb

In terms of size the North American and British bred dogs also tend to differ in size and bulk. For example the North American type Labradors tend to be slightly taller and more muscular.

Coat colour

Black, yellow and chocolate

Coat type

Short, straight, dense, double coated weather resistant outer coat and a soft undercoat. There is no feathering or waves. In terms of shedding hair, they tend to shed at a moderate level and heavily shed (blow the coat) seasonally, twice per year. However, this has usually been a common occurrence for dogs that live most of their lives in outside kennels. You may therefore find that a dog living in centrally heated accommodation during colder spells will moderately shed all year round without necessarily having copious seasonal sheds. Incidentally, having a relatively thick double coat, do not be surprised if he decides to sleep on a cold hard floor. This will be particularly desirable for him when he wishes to cool off during warm weather or when the heating in your accommodation becomes too much.

Longevity:

11 to 15 years

YELLOW, BLACK AND CHOCOLATE LABRADOR TEMPERAMENT DIFFERENCES

PLEASE NOTE: Traditional Labrador colourings have always been either yellow, chocolate or black. However, a number of breeders have started crossing Labradors with Weimaraner's to produce a so called 'designer dog'. Such breeders tend to sell these puppies with the 'unique selling point' of them being silver, charcoal, champagne, white, pink, green, blue or white chocolate Labradors. Once again they are not true Labradors and if you are serious about the Labrador breed, I would avoid breeders who are selling them. At the time of press the breeders listed in the book were only engaged in the sale of the yellow, chocolate or black Labrador and it is doubtful such breeders will divert from this practice. However, the author accepts no responsibility for changes that a breeder may make.

Having said that, the following will give you some idea of how the three different coloured Labradors differ temperamentally

Black Labradors

Potentially, all 3 colour variations can occur within the same litter where the sire and dam are black Labradors.

However, two yellow Labradors will always produce yellow puppies.

Opinions will again of course differ, but black Labradors tend to be more active than the yellows, therefore requiring more exercise. Most 'working/field' type Labradors are black, which perhaps explains why many black Labradors have a higher energy level. Black Labradors have also generally dominated field trial competitions. The black colour is the original colour of the 'St John's Water Dog' (a descendent of the Labrador), and technically the genetically dominant colour of the Labrador.

Yellow Labradors

Yellow Labradors have a slight tendency to whine or bark, more so than the others. However, on the whole, yellow Labradors tend to be more easy going than for example black Labradors. The yellow is also arguably the most popular colour as a family pet. However, some yellow Labradors can lack confidence and in some cases display more aggression than the other colours, (Cases of aggression can and do occur, but this is rare. Some yellow Labradors have also been noted to be more domineering than the black. This can manifest itself with displays of disobedience, although these are in isolated cases. Many temperament problems relate to irresponsible breeding and puppy farmed dogs).

Chocolate Labradors

The colour of the chocolate Labrador, is considered to be a genetic mix of yellow and black. In terms of temperament, the chocolate Labrador can be either extreme. Either calm and placid or boisterous, excitable with a tendency to want to make contact by running into people etc. They have in the past been the rarer of the three, but have become increasingly popular over the years.

Most Labradors, regardless of the colour are what trainers refer to as having high pain thresholds. This is unsurprising as they are naturally conditioned to tolerate harsh weather conditions and for example entering icy water. Unfortunately some trainers in the past have resorted to rough handling, this is never acceptable, but most Labradors seem to be insensitive and unaffected by this.

EXERCISE NEEDS FOR A LABRADOR

Opinions differ, but being a relatively high energy breed, daily exercise should be somewhere between 1 and 2 hours. These dogs are unlikely to refuse several hours of exercise per day. Remember that as a Gundog, this breed has the stamina to go all day if necessary.

This exercise may consist of two 30 to 45 minute minute off lead runs per day, preferably with either playtime from you or the opportunity to play and chase with other dogs. Walking on a leash alone will not be enough as he needs energetic outlets to burn off excess energy.

However, some road walking will be very beneficial to keep his nails short and his pads hardened.

He will enjoy long walks, but off lead runs, playful games and of course retrieving ideally needs to be provided. The Labrador can also be quite active indoors, becoming restless if not given sufficient exercise. However, they are generally, a lot more well behaved, more accepting and less inclined to problem behaviours such as destructiveness that can afflict some high energy breeds.

Please remember that their playfulness and exercise needs means they are less suited to less active owners.

TYPES OF ACTIVITIES TO CONSIDER

Being a retriever, games of fetch are an excellent way to provide exercise provided you have a large garden, yard or access to a local park or field. Such retrieving games never seem to bore these retrievers. There are a number of relatively cheap devices you can use to help you with retrieving games. Traditional gundog training dummy launchers, launch dummies approximately 100 meters or more and are a great way tire a dog out. However, they do require a cartridge which makes a noise similar to a starting pistol. A good alternative is to use a relatively cheap tennis ball launcher [please do a Google search using a search term such as "ball launcher"]. These range from free standing and gun type dispensers that fire approximately 10ft to 80ft, depending on the type, to hand held types which launch as far as you can throw, to catapults which fire approximately 200ft. Using these devices are also excellent if you do not have access to a large field or park for off leash runs. They also mean that you personally do not have to trek miles and can literally give your dog the milage as you stand still.

However, please be aware that the Labrador intelligence can lead him to become bored of certain routines. In this respect it is important to keep him interested with a variety of games and activities.

If you are a regular gym user, but are limited for time otherwise, it is advisable to think about alternative forms of exercise that involve your dog also. These could include speed walking, jogging, running, cycling, bikejoring/urban mushing, hiking etc etc. Also remember that these dogs excel at obedience, agility working tests, field trials, Gundog training and many dog sports.

The Labrador loves to swim and historically they were originally bred as assistants to fisherman. In this respect any chance they get to associate with water, they will gladly indulge themselves. Trips to rivers, lakes, the seaside etc will not need any encouraging from their owner before the dog is diving in. However, a word of caution is needed here; fitting a lifejacket and attaching a long line, before allowing them access to any form of water is highly recommended, particularly when they are young. Please remember that sea tides and river currents can be quite strong and overpowering. Also be careful of anywhere he may not be able to climb out of, such as swimming pools or canals. In this respect, always supervise such activities.

PLEASE NOTE:

Once again as this breed is relatively slow to mature, growing puppies should avoid high impact exercise to prevent damage to growing bones and cartilage.

A final note: some owners will insist that no one should consider owning a Labrador unless they are prepared to provide a minimum of 1 to 2 hours walking, or the equivalent off leash runs and playing, per day.

Accommodation and exercise needs

Although not ideal, the Labrador could adopt to living in a flat/apartment situation. However, this would only really be acceptable if they were given sufficient daily exercise per day.

POSSIBLE BEHAVIOUR PROBLEMS:

Behaviour problems will be detailed towards the end of the book. However, for now by way of a summary, the following behaviour problems have been noted in some Labradors. Also much of what follows will go against the general descriptions you will read for most Labradors but cases have occurred:

Possessiveness, resource guarding, jumping up, digging, destructive chewing (particularly during the puppy years and adolescence) etc are all possibilities. Aggressive, nasty behaviour has also been noted in certain puppy farmed dogs or through other irresponsible breeding practices. Similar problems can occur with temperament, behavioural issues of puppy farmed dogs such as biting, aggression towards other dogs, people, territorial aggression etc. Such dogs can also be prone to timidity, fearfulness, submissive urination fawning and grovelling.

Bad, irresponsible breeding has also unfortunately resulted in dogs with health problems and shortened lives.

Labradors can also be moderately excitable, although not to the extent that this would be deemed a problem.

However, enthusiastic mouthing and licking of hands and faces often occurs, particularly as a puppy and adolescent. Although again, exuberant behaviour can occur due to boredom and lack of exercise. In such cases, you may also find a dog that refuses to come back on off leash runs. Therefore providing plenty of exercise and training a reliable recall is a must.

Being relatively jowly, can lead them to being slobberers. As carrying objects in their mouths is a regular occurrence, it is advisable to therefore provide plenty of toys and other objects that you do not mind covered in spit. He may also be inclined to chew items other than his toys, so you will need to be mindful of what items you leave lying around.

Also expect toys or other items to be carried, presented to you or otherwise dropped everywhere.

Labradors tend to be glutenous, so strict diets are a must as ad lib feeding will see a dog quickly becoming overweight, particularly if he does not receive adequate exercise.

A condition known as 'pica' (ingesting non food objects), is also common as many vets will bear witness to.

Labradors can be one of the 'velcro breeds', wishing to be by their owners side. This along with pestering for attention can be annoying for some people.

Although generally considered to be attentive and alert, some can also be easily distracted by scents etc, whilst out on walks. Their strong scenting ability can also lead them to wander if they pick up an interesting scent. It is therefore imperative that off lead exercise is only carried out in safe areas, away from busy roads. In this respect, early training for control and obedience is a must. As an extra safety precaution, attaching a long training or tracking line will at least allow you to quickly stop him should he suddenly take off running, and refuse to stop. A secure fenced yard or garden is also a must as he will be inclined to escape and wander given the chance.

Lead pulling, and the dog taking the owner for a walk, can also be an issue if the dog is not taught basic obedience (heeling) to prevent this.

AS A WORKING GUNDOG

The field or working Labrador is arguably considered to be the ultimate, supreme retriever. They are relatively easy to train, well behaved and have a hardy, rugged constitution to tackle most if any terrain and the harshest weather conditions. In fact it is said, if you fail to train a Labrador you are likely to fail with any dog. In other words they are generally considered to be extremely easy to train. Some would say far easier than most other gundog breeds. However, the Labrador is considered by experienced owners to be more than merely a 'retriever'. They are very capable hunting dogs at scenting, tracking, quartering, stalking, flushing, in some cases pointing (a skill they are not popularly renowned for) etc, and all without ever receiving any training. It is just that they have been relegated or relieved of those duties in favour of other breeds considered to be better at certain specialist skills.

It is also amusingly said that Labrador's are born half trained and Spaniel's die half trained. They are usually the most recommended 'gundog' for the first time handler. They have such a calm easy going disposition that some unfairly refer to them as boring in comparison to certain manic spaniel breeds. To give you an example of how cautious (and apparently boring) a Labrador is in comparison to a daredevil Spaniel consider the following in relation to the task of 'flushing' game. Labradors are a lot more cautious about entering undergrowth (flushing) than the daredevil Spaniel. The Spaniel will dive in without a second thought, whereas a Labrador will have to convince itself there is actually something there.

Labradors are experts at the 'marked retrieve' (the dog sees and memorises the location). With their highly developed scenting ability, tracking a 'blind retrieve' will pose little problem to them.

Working and show bred Labradors tend to be considerably different in terms of energy levels. In this respect a show type Labrador will be a lot more manageable in the house. This isn't to say that a working bred Labrador will be impossible, but the working type Labradors tend to be more exuberant, excitable and potentially clumsy indoors. Gundog trainers will also insist, that if you want a Labrador as a gundog for hunting or field trials, you should aim for one with proven bloodlines in these disciplines and avoid show or pet bred Labradors.

SHOW AND WORKING TYPES

The Labrador is currently one of if not the most popular 'working' Gundogs. However, they are also commonly associated with the show ring. Once again, in a similar way to other Gundogs, the working and show Labradors are very dissimilar. Many working bred Labradors as well as being black, yellow or chocolate are also coloured a deep red, similar in shade to a red fox. This darker colour, will generally be indicative of a dog coming from a working/field line. Again this means the dog will be more active and therefore require more exercise and mental stimulation.

Opinions also tend to differ as to the physical appearance of the working as opposed to the show Labrador. Some assert that Labradors bred for show are usually bulkier with broader heads, thicker coats and tails. Others will state that this is the appearance of the working type. It is also sometimes the case that the coat of the working type is relatively thinner than the show type, in some cases almost single coated. However, many working or field types are usually taller and lighter in build with thinner heads and longer muzzles than a typical show type (there are links to working type Labrador breeders in the chapter on where to buy. You will see many of those Labradors do in fact appear tall, thin and athletic. Not your typical overweight looking Labrador). What is fair to say is that the working type will not follow the strict standards laid down by the Kennel Clubs, as their working ability is deemed as far more important than what they look like. In other words, you are likely to encounter more variation in a working Labrador than you will in a show type.

Although the kennel clubs make some provisions in their respective standards to accommodate statistics of the working Labrador, they are less common as 'duel champions'. In other words an individual dog that excels in field trials and the show ring. Duel champions are far more common among breeds such as German Shorthaired Pointers. Incidentally, the chocolate Labrador is not as common as the yellow and black as a working type.

LABRADOR TRAINING

We will go into more detail in the two chapters on training later. However, for now the following will give you a brief introduction as to what you can expect.

Being intelligent, Labradors are generally quick to learn, biddable and therefore considered to be easy to train, this includes housetraining.

They are very responsive, alert, active, and adaptable. They have a good memory, meaning that repeating of training commands is generally not necessary.

However, in some cases they have been known to be quite wilful, singleminded and with a stubborn streak.

Once again, although the Labrador has an excellent reputation as a friendly, good natured dog, it is still vital that he receives early socialisation and initial obedience/toilet training. If this is not forthcoming, it can easily lead to an adolescent and adult that that is bad mannered, aggressive, destructive, hyper, mouthy etc. Please remember, the Labrador has an excellent reputation as a well behaved dog, but they are not necessarily born that way and therefore have to be taught good manners.

An untrained Labrador will certainly push boundaries in an attempt to get his own way, particularly when young. Early obedience training is therefore necessary to maintain a calm well mannered house dog. You will need to be patient and determined with his training initially as he can be easily distracted by his surroundings.

RETRIEVING AND CARRYING OBJECTS

The Labrador loves to retrieve and carry objects, often presenting them to you as a mark of his affection towards you. To some, he may seem obsessed with carrying objects. This is a typical characteristic of retrievers who were originally bred for that purpose.

Many owners encourage their dogs to carry objects and toys, perhaps his leash, whilst out on walks, giving the dog a sense of purpose and satisfying job to do.

THE BREED STANDARD

The breed standard is simply a set of statistics of a breed, that determines what the dog should ideally look like and how they should ideally behave. For show purposes the breed standard and the quality of your dog to accurately match it, will be very important in terms of potentially winning shows. The breed standard is also highly important from a breeding point of view in terms of producing high quality dogs that not only have

the best appearance, but also possess optimum health and temperaments. However, for the majority of pet owners, the breed standard will only really be useful to you as a pet owner, to give you a general overview of the dog, and to provide useful information such as his size in relation to how big a crate you need etc. Some books replicate the breed standard in its full. The breed standards are not replicated here, but links to the breed standards are provided at the end of the book in the resource section.

THE IDEAL LABRADOR OWNER

The perfect owner would themselves be; affectionate, sociable, active, outdoors, sociable, energetic people. In other words, someone who ideally matches the personality of the Labrador. So an owner, prepared to provide long walks, off-lead runs, training routines, playing games. Preferably a sporty, keep fit type person who likes to run or jog, obviously taking the dog with them. Perhaps someone interested in canine sports such as flyball, agility, field trials, working tests and of course Gundog training. Someone who wishes to share their lives with a companion by their side most of the time.

Unsuitable owners include:

Relatively inactive, sedentary, couch potato, unsociable, house-proud, allergy sufferers.

A BRIEF HISTORY OF THE LABRADOR

The Labrador that we know today is considered to be a relatively newly developed breed. This new breed is said to have emerged during the late 19th century England.

However, the descendants of the modern day Labrador are thought to date back to 16th century Newfoundland, Canada. Newfoundland was considered as a hub of activity for European fishing and trading ships.

The original purpose of these canine descendants was helping fisherman with their nets (gundog training came much later). They were basically trained to plunge into water, either from boats or from the shore line, retrieve the floated ropes of fishing nets, whereby fisherman would then hall the nets back to shore. They would also retrieve fish escaping from nets. Unsurprisingly the Labrador loves to retrieve and swim. However, they are more commonly known today as a retriever of game.

These original Newfoundland dogs were thought to have been brought over to British shores by Newfoundland fisherman. In turn the Europeans were responsible for introducing various retrievers, setters and spaniels to Newfoundland.

The Lesser Newfoundland, otherwise known as the St John's Water Dog (sadly rendered extinct in the early 1980's) is one of the original breeds considered to be an ancestor responsible for the development of a number of breeds including the Labrador, and thought to be native to Newfoundland during the periods in question. However, it is also speculated that the St John's Water Dog, (Incidentally, St. John's is the largest city and capital of the province of Newfoundland and Labrador), was originally known as the St Hubert's Hound, of French descent. The St Hubert's Hound is said to have been brought to England during the 16th century, and during the same period English fisherman are thought to have transported these dogs to Newfoundland.

Despite this, once again the modern Labrador was largely developed in Britain. There is no documented evidence to indicate exactly when the descendants of the modern day Labrador arrived on British shores. But, it is speculated this is likely to have occurred during the mid 18th century. One of the earliest, actual documented references appears shortly after this period. Col. Peter Hawker in a letter dated 1814 describes two dogs having arrived from Newfoundland, one of which he refers to as 'the Labrador or St John's dog'. He furthermore referred to the dog as being 'by far the best for every kind of shooting'. This was taken to imply that at least as far back as 1814 the dog in question had by then been trained as a gundog. The 10th Earl of Home was also said to have had imported descendants of the modern day Labrador from Newfoundland during the 1830s.

Another one of the first 'purchasers' of these dogs was The Earl of Malmesbury who in a letter dated 1870 referred to these dogs stating 'We always call them Labradors.' However, it wasn't until the late 1800's that the Earl of Malmesbury, Earl of

Home and the Duke of Buccleuch collaborated in a breeding program set to develop the Labrador that we know today.

Along with the St John's Water Dog, other breeds considered part of this breeding program and the Labrador heritage include: The now extinct Tweed Water Spaniel; Curley Coated Retriever, Flat-coated Retriever and some have suggested the English Pointer.

In 1903 this new Labrador Retriever breed was officially recognised and registered by the Kennel Club UK. 1917 was the year the American Kennel Club officially recognised and registered the Labrador. Many Labrador breed clubs have emerged since these dates. Once again, their popularity has grown to the extent that they have remained the most popular breed of dog in many countries for over two decades.

THE LABRADOR NAME

There seems to be some confusion between the Labrador and Newfoundland dog and their respective names and origins. Although named after the region of Canada known as Labrador, the Labradors origins are actually Newfoundland. Again the descendent of the Labrador was the St. John's Water dog also known as the Lesser Newfoundland. When these dogs were first imported to England they were said to have been referred to after Labrador the geographic location, but also Labrador Retriever, in relation to the dogs retrieving from the Labrador sea. It is also thought that they were named Labrador to simply distinguish them from their neighbour, the larger Newfoundland dog.

The irony of this is that the early descendants of the Labrador originated in the areas of Newfoundland and Labrador, and the large wooly mastiff type Newfoundland dog we are familiar with today, originated in the geographical location of Labrador.

HOW IMPORTANT IS IT THAT A WORKING SPORTING/GUNDOG PUPPY IS FROM A PROVEN WORKING LINEAGE?

You may already be aware that although the Labrador is known as a loving family pet, they have also been known and still are, as a traditional gundog. The reason I wanted to touch upon the subject at the beginning of the book is because this may well have an impact on your choice of puppy. If you have fallen in love with this breed, you may only be wishing for a new family addition as a pet only. You may perhaps have a desire to have a top show pedigree pup, that you could potentially enter into shows in the future. If however, at the back of your mind you are thinking that you may wish to involve yourself in field, working trials or traditional hunting and specifically shooting game, then there are a number of fundamentals that you should be aware of. We will go into more detail throughout the book, but it is important to remind you that there are 'working' gundog Labradors and 'show' Labradors and in some cases, 'dual purpose'. This is very important as although they generally look identical, they are quite often different in both ability and energy levels. Opinions differ but it is generally considered that a show dog will not be suitable as a gundog and vice versa. This is not entirely true, as pedigree show dogs have been known to be very good natural, instinctive hunting dogs. However, show dogs generally demonstrate much less ability in working trials. This will therefore have an impact on the choice of breeder you approach. However, you may have no interest whatsoever in a working gundog or gundog training. But you are strongly advised to consider some level of gundog training whether your new friend is a show type or not. The instinct to hunt and retrieve will be present in both types to differing degrees. The important thing to be aware of is that your puppy has a heritage as a gundog, and will therefore benefit greatly from the gundog training discipline. This will more than likely prevent any serious behavioural issues as your dog will be engaging in what he was originally bred for.

Most if not all experienced Gundog handlers will confirm that it is vital that a puppy intended as a Gundog has to come from a long line of proven working Gundogs and not show dogs.

For this reason, many gundog trainers have been known to refuse to train a pedigree show dog, because of the difficulty and consequent frustration of the task.

Working dogs are usually selected in a similar way to pedigree show dogs, from proven field trial winning dogs.

Selective breeding aims to produce the very best natural characteristics and temperament required of a successful Gundog.

Again, this is not to say that a dog that doesn't have a proven track record in field trials would not make an excellent Gundog.

It is just a question of probability, i.e. the probability or likelihood that the puppies from proven parents are more likely to have the same ability of the parents.

WHAT MAKES THE BEST WORKING SPORTING/GUNDOGS?

An excellent gundog whether working type or not, will display an excellent aptitude for retrieving, taking commands, be bold and courageous working in water and cover etc.

Mentally sensitive dogs usually make the best working Sporting/Gundogs in terms of sensitivity to noise, sight, scent stimuli etc. This ensures they readily respond to stimuli you want them to react to but also enables them to choose to react to or ignore the selected stimuli. The key is to have a dog that doesn't instinctively react to and act upon all available stimuli.

In addition to this, the best working types interact well in social situations involving people and other dogs as well as with activities they are involved in.

Puppy farmed or isolated kennel reared dogs are likely to be the most problematic in this case as they will probably have had very limited exposure to sufficient stimuli and social experiences during their critical period socialisation period.

CHAPTER TWO:

A GENERAL OVERVIEW OF THE RETRIEVER AND SPORTING/GUNDOG:

The Labrador along with other gundogs has a heritage as a working hunting dog.

The following is not intended to get you interested in hunting and shooting. It is merely intended to give you an overview of the Retriever and therefore the Labrador, and how they fit into the general Sporting/Gundog breed group.

The gundog as a group is more or less noted for their energy, cheerful personalities, but most generally requiring large amounts of daily exercise. This should include off leash runs in a safe area. In this respect these breeds are not for everyone.

In general this group would therefore suit active owners who like to get out and about. They are reasonably active indoors but more active outdoors. By the same token they will probably be unsuitable for sedentary, couch potatoes who would be more suited to a less busy, active breed.

Originally and currently the gundog was bred to find, flush and retrieve on land or from water, injured or killed game. Sporting/Gundogs in general have varying degrees of size, energy, stamina and drive, which makes most, but not all of them unsuitable for small flat/apartment living, or again anyone unable to provide a sufficient daily outlet for pent up energy if not given sufficient exercise.

Certain gundog breeds including the Labrador, have extremely acute senses of smell and strong hunting drives which can be a problem with obedience, particularly when off lead runs are given. In this respect the prey drive can take over as they single-mindedly pursue a scent. So, Sporting/Gundogs should only ever be let off leash in safe areas away from nearby roads/traffic.

Their actions tend to be reasonably vigorous and forceful, particularly when exposed to highly motivating, typical hunting country terrain.

Unsurprisingly, most of the breeds tend to interact very well with other dogs and people. They also tend to lean more towards submissive behaviour rather than displays of dominance with other dogs and people. The group in general additionally, tend to be very good with children.

The individual breeds within the group, but not generally, are commonly afflicted with several behaviour problems including: Barking, Howling, Soiling in the house, Jumping up, Restlessness, Escaping and Roaming, Gluttonous, Scavenging or stealing food, Fussy/picky eaters, Destructiveness, Biting (fear or otherwise), Snoring. With the exception of food related problems, most of these behaviours are simply a symptom of boredom, lack of mental stimulation and a lack of exercise.

This is a perfect example of matching the dogs needs with the owners lifestyles. If the prospective owner is unable or unwilling to provide adequate time to exercise and train a Sporting/Gundog breed, then this is probably reason enough to choose a less demanding breed.

A BRIEF HISTORY OF THE WORKING DOG;

The overall objective of the gundog was and still is to hunt, capture and retrieve game.

The large variety of Gundogs evolved and developed, through years of selective breeding, to meet the differing terrain and game. Certain breeds then became more specialised and suitable for these specific needs.

The very early hunting dogs would hunt and kill independently of the handler. Hunting then became more sophisticated whereby dogs would be trained alongside the hunter who would use falcons, snares and nets.

Although firearms existed during the 16th Century, it wasn't until the mid 1700s that the double barrelled shotgun akin to modern shotguns became available for hunting purposes. Modern hunting gun dogs that we are familiar with today proliferated from that point.

CATEGORISING HUNTING DOGS

Originally sporting or hunting dogs, where categorised into several groups.

The first group were essentially Sighthound type dogs, such as the Greyhound and Saluki, who relied on their acute visual sensitivity to motion, chase instinct and peripheral vision as well as speed to chase and kill game.

Scenthound types such as Beagles and Foxhounds, comprised the second group which again would pursue and kill game, but obviously utilising their strong scent abilities.

These first two groups would work remotely, often in packs, independently and often at distance from the hunter.

Obviously the sight and scent hounds are not what we consider as Gundogs, but again they served a similar purpose.

The third group consisted of Pointer type dogs, again using scent, but these were trained to not chase game, but to merely indicate their presence with their natural instinctive pointing ability.

A forth group consisted of flush and retrieve type dogs. Groups 3 and 4 would typically work in close proximity to the hunter and most importantly taught not to kill the prey.

Essentially the group divisions were indications of the differing hunting styles of each breed,

further divided and developed for specific hunting needs. In other words the dogs performed specific jobs for the hunter dependent on the game hunted and the environment they hunted in.

These last two groups, 3 and 4, are obviously what we consider in modern terms as Sporting/Gundogs.

AN OVERVIEW OF THE RETRIEVER

Retrievers: which technically included (although not necessarily classified as Gundogs) Poodles and other dogs such as the Portuguese Water Dog, are specifically used to locate and retrieve shot game on land or water.

The most popular of the Retrievers include; Labrador, Golden, Chesapeake Bay, Flat Coated, Curly Coated, Nova Scotia Duck Tolling etc. Primarily they retrieve but can also be taught to function in much the same way as Spaniels.

A retriever will be most suitable on shoots that involve the gunman remaining static whilst a line of beaters flush the game. In fact most situations which involve the retriever sitting still for prolonged periods such as hunting from hides, will suit the retriever. Labradors and Goldens are especially suited to this, particularly during colder spells where their thicker coats and larger build helps them to keep warm.

The Labrador and Golden is also much calmer and placid whereas Spaniels, for example are in general fussy bundles of energy who like to be constantly active, darting about and would certainly not like to be still for too long. Think in terms of how effective and reliable Labradors and Goldens are as guide dogs for the blind. Incidentally, Spaniels also feel the cold much more than a Labrador or Golden, so prolonged wet, cold conditions will not suit the Spaniel as much.

Typically, retrievers were, and in many cases still are expected to have patience to wait for their masters command to retrieve and have the hardiness to work in all terrain types including extreme cold weather conditions, sometimes having to plunge into icy waters.

Although they are a tough tolerant breed they should never be exposed to harsh training methods or harassment by children.

Originally bred for tolerance of gun fire and to generally stay calm has ensured they have the same quality of noise tolerance, such as dealing with a noisy household.

Noises likely to affect certain reactive breeds such as thunder or fireworks will probably have no effect on Retrievers.

Although there are exceptions, hostility and aggression are unlikely traits in these breeds. Again the objective of selective breeding was and still is to develop breeds that were/are able to work closely and harmoniously to their handler as well as other dogs. There is a strong possibility that a dog with a hostile and aggressive temperament is the product of puppy farm or similar breeding.

Commonly known for: Being overly enthusiastic; chewing, mouthing, jumping up, pulling on the lead, in these cases they therefore need to be taught self-control.

Ideal household: Regular daily exercise and training.

Supervision within the house will be necessary for the first year or so.

How game hunters make their choice of suitable gun dogs

Again the following would only apply if you had a serious interest in hunting.

As indicated previously, a deciding factor as to the most suitable type of dog, will be the type of terrain and birds whose habitat you wish to frequent.

You should know what you need the dog for; what its purpose will be. Is it as a retriever of waterfowl for example? Predominantly small or large game or a mixture of both? Does your choice depend on the specific function of certain breeds, such as the specialist Pointer, flushing or retriever?

For example, if the terrain you frequent is predominantly dense cover, then a flushing Spaniel will be far more productive than a Pointer.

It is important that the temperament of the dog is friendly and should certainly never show any kind of aggression to people or other dogs.

It is obviously desirable that the dog has natural ability and trainability or demonstrates traits, such as pointing, that cannot really be taught. These will have been bred into the dogs from proven generations displaying such traits.

A dog that is too head strong, stubborn and independent is likely to be difficult to train and consequently difficult to control.

A well trained dog is a valuable asset, whereas a badly trained dog is likely to run riot, be more trouble than it is worth and is therefore a liability to have around on the shooting field.

CHAPTER THREE:

Is a Labrador the right pet for you?

Owning a dog should never be discouraged and having a dog can have a profoundly positive influence on a family or individual, to the extent that many people cannot imagine life without one. Anyone who has ever owned a dog will tell you they are truly mans/womans best friend. You will undoubtedly never experience affection, friendship and loyalty like it.

However, it is very important that you educate yourself and find out all you can about looking after a puppy, long before you make the commitment. It is very important not to rush into buying a puppy, then finding out what type of care and training will be involved, not to mention the time you will need to actually do this.

For example you need to know facts such as young puppies being very curious and wishing to explore and learn. This will involve biting, chewing, digging, barking etc. Until he is fully house-trained it will also mean he may go to toilet anywhere in and around the house. These are natural behaviours for a dog and it is up to you to educate him into what you expect in terms of how he has to behave.

You will not be able to take anything for granted or assume he will know. He has to be taught and this involves being patient and never becoming angry, certainly never hitting him, no matter how frustrated you may feel. You want him to explore and do his thing safely but without causing havoc. He is not some wilful uncontrollable monster. He will want to please you, but just like a young child, they have to be taught and shown how to please you, by you.

The following is not intended to put you off dog ownership. The intention is to give you some idea of the pros and cons of actually looking after a dog. Hopefully it will convince you one way or another whether this is something you want to commit to.

1) Labrador basic needs

On a daily basis a dogs basic needs will include:
- Exercise and playtime
- Initial house and obedience training (obviously this is not ongoing once he is trained)
- Cost and time to feed and water him
- Cleaning up possible toilet accidents
- Muddy feet and hair shedding can have an impact on household cleaning
- Regular grooming, both time for you to do it or the costs of paying a professional groomer
- Time and cost associated with visits to the vet.
- Dog walking/sitting service costs if you pay some one to exercise and take care of your dog, perhaps if you work all day

In a nutshell, you will have to compromise time, money, cleaning issues, disruptions and generally considering your dogs needs on a daily basis

2) So you think you want a Labrador?

For some people, having owned a dog previously as a child perhaps, is better than never having owned a dog, but it does not make you an expert or even particularly educated in dog behaviour. It is necessary to either study books, videos or take part in classes to gain an advanced knowledge of caring for and dealing with potential behaviour problems. Your childhood memories are usually of the rose tinted glasses variety, or you probably never had to care for the dog and may not fully appreciate now what looking after a dog entails.

People decide to become guardians to a dog for a number of reasons, but have you really considered why exactly?

Have your children been pestering you to get a puppy, but deep down you really do not like the idea? If so, do yourself and the dog a favour and please consider a less demanding pet.

A) Are you prepared for the following:
- A puppy that chews your best shoes, in fact all of your shoes given the chance. This is avoidable with suitable chew toys and simply keeping such items out of the dogs reach.
- When you have spent hours training him and it all goes out of the window when your friends come to visit and he jumps all over them and generally disobeys you.
- Mud that gets pawed all over your clean kitchen floor or carpets.
- During a frantic play session, his food and water gets scattered all over the floor, or he knocks into a coffee table with the contents ending up all over the carpet.
- After spending weeks, sometimes standing out in the cold or rain waiting for him to do his toilet business, just when you think you have toilet training down, he comes back into the house and does his toilet business or vomits on your carpet.

The answer is to expect such eventualities may occasionally happen. However, many such cases are easily avoidable by correctly teaching the dog self control through basic obedience training, which we will cover later. Above all, be prepared to give time, patience, forgiveness and love and if that is not possible, again please consider another pet.

B) BENEFITS OF DOG OWNERSHIP

- Sense of pride and achievement at a well trained, well behaved dog that is a pleasure to be with.
- Their positive zest for life can give you hours of fun, joy and laughter.
- They are a positive influence on any family and are fun to have around the house.
- They will put a smile on your face, lower your blood pressure and stress levels as well as raise your spirits.
- They give you a tremendous sense of purpose and responsibility as they depend on you for their care.
- They will love you unconditionally, forgive you, never judge you, be a loyal devoted companion and be your number one best friend.
- They will comfort you when you are depressed, stressed, lonely, ill or any other personal problems.
- If you are a sociable type, a dog will get you out and about socialising with other dog walkers.
- Exercise needs of the dog will give you a reason to exercise more.

C) POSSIBLE DRAWBACKS TO DOG OWNERSHIP

- Your lifestyle may dictate you being away from home all day. This could mean you have to arrange for a professional carer, friend or neighbour to look after their daily needs such as letting them out to do their toilet business, exercise, feeding etc.
- Do you work long hours, or spend most of your leisure time in activities that leave you with very little time to do much else, especially looking after a dog? Have you therefore considered the time necessary for daily walks, playtime, training,

regular grooming, feeding, clearing up accidents etc?

- Your social life can suffer as again you have to take care of their needs; a similar situation to baby sitting
- Do you travel a lot and cannot take the dog or provide alternative accommodation for him? If you are away a lot, why would you want a dog anyway?
- Vacations need to be taken into account: Do you find holiday accommodation which accepts pets, but means you can't travel abroad? Do you arrange for the dog to stay with friends, relatives or board them in kennels for the duration?
- Daily ongoing costs not to mention potentially expensive veterinary bills. Are the financial costs of owning a dog now or in the future likely to have a bearing on you being able to take care of them?
- Do you have the patience and time for obedience training or do you pay a professional?
- Ultimately do you have the time on a daily basis for their basic needs such as feeding, toilet business, training, play time, exercise, grooming etc?

If you have doubt about any of the above, please do not consider a dog unless you have family, friends, pet sitter, walker etc, who you can rely on to take care of them.

3) REASONS FOR NOT TAKING ON A LABRADOR:

A) NEVER BUY A DOG BASED ON IMPULSE

It is far too easy these days to purchase a puppy from a puppy farm agent via free ads or whatever. It is also just as easy to drop the dog off at a rescue centre when the novelty wears off or the dog becomes an inconvenience. What this implies is that a dog is just like any other disposable modern day consumable with limited value. Dogs are not a possession or object of amusement that can be switched on and off when it pleases you.

Under no circumstances should you buy a puppy or even an adult dog, as a surprise gift for either a child or other adult. For obvious reasons

13

this implies that the adult or child in question will have the responsibility to take care of the dog. If you know with certainty that they really want a dog and that they or someone will look after the dogs every need, then fine.

Quite often dogs are bought on a whim because one of the children has decided they want a dog. Remember the slogan, 'dogs are for life, not just Christmas and birthdays'? As well as teaching responsibility, a dog can be a great educational experience for kids as they learn about caring for another creature as well as the unconditional love a dog can provide.

On the other hand, children as well as adults can be very fickle, wanting the latest fad and can soon become bored and move onto the next thing. There is no way that you can rely on a child who pesters you and promises to take care of the dogs everyday needs.

If any of the following is likely to apply then you are strongly advised against a dog that will probably end up facing the prospect of being re-homed.

You fall in love with a breed you saw in a film, commercial, TV show or the latest fashionable breed: This is similar to impulse buying and indicates the necessity to properly research the breed. It is too easy to get caught up in the latest fad, and a few months down the line, become bored, lose interest and move on to the latest fad.

B) Because you feel sorry for it; or for their adorable cuteness

An unfortunate statistic occurs whereby as the puppy grows, it quickly loses its cuteness, starts off relatively small, but grows much bigger.

The reality of looking after him day in, day out then overwhelms the new owner, the dog is then either abandoned or given up to a rescue centre.

Unless you know a particular breed's temperament and behaviour, please do not choose a puppy/dog based mainly on what the dog looks like and how cute and cuddly they appear.

C) Getting a dog so your children can learn about being caring and responsible:

Children can learn a lot about responsibility by helping you to look after a dog; but ultimately

you have to be solely responsible.

If you are feeding, walking and generally taking care of his daily needs, and they are helping you do this, then they can learn a great deal by observation and example.

If there is no one guaranteed responsible person then the following is likely to be the case:

Feeding, training, grooming, exercising, play time, affection will all be neglected. The dog is then seen as an inconvenience, suffers as a consequence and at worst, abandoned whether this is to a rescue organisation or otherwise.

Under no circumstances should you expect a child to be solely responsible for the total upkeep of a dog.

The Whole Family Decides:

Ideally it is important that every family member is in favour of getting a dog. The dog does not want to face any hostile objections from anyone. Preferably everyone will help to take care of him, but again, at least one person needs to be the reliable carer for the dog.

D) Breeding for money.

Breeding requires a responsibility that you don't just match the first available stud dog with a bitch you may intend to breed off. Responsible breeders choose sires and dams who have excellent, sound temperaments. They also carry out genetic health testing for hereditary conditions and defects that the dog or bitch may have a predisposition for.

If you then decide to breed a litter, you face the risk of whelping complications that could result in expensive cesarean surgery for example. A first litter is likely to consist of a less than average number of puppies. If you get this far, you will have to spend a minimum eight weeks ensuring that as well as extra caring of the mother, the puppies will require a considerable amount of attention to care for their needs. This will include general supervision and ensuring your house is safe and puppy proofed; adequate socialisation needs to take place; keeping to a strict feeding schedule when the puppies are ready to wean; extra cleaning and sanitising the living area; house training; grooming as they grow; regularly weighing the puppies to ensure they are gaining weight; worming and possible vaccination; the time needed to find suitable homes etc. Breeding should ideally be undertaken for reasons of genetic improvements, not as an extra or sole income stream. There are far too many unscrupulous breeders of dogs, namely puppy mills/farms, with a sole interest in exploiting dog breeding to make money.

E) OTHER REASONS FOR NOT GETTING A DOG:

It is vital that you are aware of the instinctive drives and energy levels of this breed. There is no point in assuming you can change a dogs temperament or natural characteristics. You can change and modify their behaviour through training, but ultimately their natural instincts will always be there.

It is also far better to conduct research on breeds objectively and impartially rather than meeting a litter of pups that you instantly fall in love with, without finding out first what these cute, adorable puppies will actually become as adults.

For anyone thinking that this is a cold and heartless way to select a breed, think about how the poor dogs feel who end up in rescue centres simply for instinctively acting the way they were bred to act.

Are you house proud, and have you considered the prospect of having the house disrupted by dog hair, furnishings and clothes strewn about, potential toilet accidents etc?

4) THE IDEAL PERSON

Someone who above all else wants to care for a dog and is prepared to do whatever it takes.

A dog should be viewed first and foremost as a loyal respected friend and companion. Never as toy or an object that gets our attention when we feel like it. People rush into marriages and get divorced as quickly. Obviously nobody has a crystal ball, so we make decisions in life to the best of our ability and sometimes relationships do not work out. But the relationship you have with a dog should never be viewed in the same light. A dog will be loyal, devoted, loving and consistent, and does not expect much in return! They truly are man's/woman's best friend.

A dog lover is someone who accepts their companion warts and all. Serious behaviour problems should never be tolerated but in the vast majority of cases are easily remedied. But minor annoyances or behaviour issues, such as shedding, drooling, digging, barking, jumping up or the occasional toilet accident are also easily remedied and not the end of the world. If they are to you, then again a dog is probably a bad choice for a pet.

Like every aspect of life there are pros and cons and it is up to the prospective dog owner to decide whether the advantages outweigh the disadvantages. Looking after and caring for a dogs needs is for 7 days per week for 365 days of the year, multiplied by up to 15 years or more. In total that's approximately 5,475 days or 780 weeks over the dogs' lifetime. It's probably best to not think of it like that, but for the next 15 years or so, you will make plans and live your life not counting down the days or weeks. But the reality is, the same commitment you give to 15 years of your life, or bringing up a child, has to also apply to your dog. Obviously with a child as they grow they become independent and eventually leave to fend for themselves. Unlike street dogs left to scavenge, the domestic dog relies on you for almost everything.

The best thing you can do if you have the slightest doubt about owning a dog, is to consider fostering one. There are no long term commitments with this, but the drawback is that most cases will be adult dogs and not puppies. You may also find that volunteering at a local dog rescue centre or even borrowing a friends dog for a few weeks will give you a tremendous insight into dog ownership.

Chapter Four:

What to Know Before You Buy

Now that you understand the basics about the Labrador breed you should have a better understanding of what the Labrador will be like as a pet. As well as obtaining a good understanding about the breeds characteristics etc, it is also important to consider other specific aspects of owning a dog.

This chapter will look at a number of considerations such as: whether to buy a puppy or adult; a male or female; whether they are suitable for children or other pets; is it best to keep one or two?; additional details such as licensing.

This section will also look at the costs associated with keeping your dog. We will look at the likely cost in terms of both initial one off costs as well as ongoing monthly costs. Please do bear in mind that this is a guideline only. The costs illustrated are a good indication of the likely costs. However, it will be necessary to confirm the exact costs once you research your local area as well as shopping around. But the important intention is to get you thinking about the costs. Dogs are often given up to rescue organisations, or worse still abandoned, simply because their owners failed to consider the actual cost of keeping their dog.

1.) Do You Need a License?

A.) Licensing Labradors in the U.S.

There are no federal requirements regarding the licensure of dogs in the United States. Rather, these requirements are made at the state level. Before you buy a Labrador puppy or an adult Labrador you need to apprise yourself of local dog licensing requirements. Most states require dog owners to license their dogs and, in order to obtain a license, your dog must also be up-to-date on rabies vac-

cinations. Some jurisdictions encourage the spaying and neutering of dogs. For anyone providing proof of this, certain states charge significantly lower fees. Obtaining a license for your dog is not difficult. Simply contact your local council . For example, if you were resident in Arlington County, Virginia, the following link will provide details of their application procedure:
https://taxes.arlingtonva.us/dog-licenses/

Even if your state does not mandate that you license your Labrador dog, it is still a good idea to do it anyway. When you license your dog you will need to provide contact information for yourself. If your dog gets lost and is still carrying his license, whoever finds him will be able to use that information to contact you. Obtaining a dog license requires you to fill out a simple form and to pay a fee around $25 (£19.45 currency rate at 12/05/2017). You must renew your license each year, although you may have the option to purchase a three, five-year or a lifetime license in some states.

B.) Licensing Labradors in the U.K.

Licensing requirements for dogs in the U.K. are a little different than they are in the U.S. Dog licensing in the UK was abolished in 1987.

Important Update 2016:

Please note that as of 6th April 2016 it is compulsory for any dog owner in England to microchip their dog. Scotland and Wales were working towards compulsory micro-chipping by April 2016. To confirm whether this applies to you, please check with your vet.

Failure to comply may result in a fine of £500. What this means is that you as the owner of a non micro-chipped dog, will be served a notice of 21 days to comply. If after 21 days of non compliance, the owner will face a £500 fine.

Please have a look at the following web link for further information.
http://www.bva.co.uk/News-campaigns-and-policy/Policy/Companion-animals/Microchipping/

At the time of press, the link was valid. If the page gets removed please use a Google search term such as [compulsory microchipping dogs]

For a general overview of global licensing, have a look at the following link:

https://en.wikipedia.org/wiki/Dog_licence

2.) HOW MANY LABRADORS SHOULD YOU KEEP?

Again, the Labrador is very much people-oriented and requires a lot of attention from their owners. In this respect they have a relatively high tendency towards separation anxiety. For this reason, it is not recommended that you leave your Labrador alone for long periods of time. If you do, he may develop the condition, or begin chewing household furnishings or worse still, electrical cables. If you work a full-time job and are away from home for long periods of time, it could be beneficial to get two Labradors so they can keep each other company in your absence. That said, two dogs will not necessarily prevent a dog experiencing separation anxiety, but they can alleviate some of the stress. A pair of dogs generally play, interact and bond. It is also easier on the conscience because you are not leaving a dog completely alone whilst you are at work or socialising. Incidentally certain rescue shelters purposely look to re-home dogs that are already an established pair.

Having said that, a pair can be difficult to handle if they form a pack like mentality and become reactive on walks and in the home. All dogs have individual personalities so the way that a pair of dogs react will really depend on the nature of each dog. Although Labradors are generally amiable, friendly dogs, two dogs can develop the pack mentality and become a hustle of growling and barking excitement on walks. If you are looking at puppies though, taking two from the litter is not usually a good idea if you yourself want to be an integral part of your dog's emotional life.

Puppies that are taken from the same litter will be very bonded with each other and as they reach adolescence one of two things can happen. Firstly they may only focus on each other making them difficult to train and control. Secondly they may begin to compete, causing friction between them. That said, the pair could just as easily settle down and be happy together but it is important that you are aware of the risks. If you want two Labrador dogs because of all of the positive points of a bonded pair, then you can either look for a pair in rescue or bring one dog home, spend a few months getting to know the dog, socialising him or her perfectly, then look for another dog to join your family a few months later. This is an approach that will work well with dogs of all ages. You may find that one Labrador dog and a dog of a different breed get on really well together instead of a pair of Labradors. Raising one Labrador puppy can take a lot of time an energy so you should think carefully before bringing home two of them. If you work a full-time job and are not home a lot during the day, the Labrador might not be the right breed for you. Having a second dog to keep your Labrador company might help but it will not be a substitute for the level of human interaction this breed craves.

Having said all of that, experienced Labrador owners will tell you that this is a very high-maintenance breed. The Labrador has a friendly personality and an even temperament but they require a lot of attention and exercise. Raising one Labrador puppy can take a lot of time and energy, so you should think carefully before bringing home two of them. Don't forget, the Labrador is a very social breed but he tends to prefer the company of people to that of other dogs.

Your Labrador will form a very strong bond with you and he will want to follow you around the house, getting as much attention as you are willing to give. If you work a full-time job and are not home a lot during the day, the Labrador might not be the right breed for you. Having a second dog to keep your Labrador company might help but it will not be a substitute for the level of human interaction this breed craves.

Does the sex of the two dogs matter?

Opinions differ as some people insist that two dogs of the same sex can potentially disagree and at worse have a dog fight, but this depends on sibling rivalry or whether the breed has a predisposition to fight. But opposite sexes are probably less likely to fall out. The only problem then is when the bitch comes into season.

3.) Do Labradors Get Along with Other Pets?

The Labrador is good with other pets, friendly towards strangers and unfamiliar dogs, although at first they may act cautiously.

Even though the Labrador is typically used for hunting and has very well-developed protective instincts, he usually gets along well with other household pets and with children. This breed is primarily used for fowl and upland game hunting, so it may retain a tendency to view pet birds as prey, but other household pets should not be a problem. In order to ensure that your Labrador gets along with other pets, dogs, and children you should socialize your puppy from an early age. Raising your Labrador around other pets will help to make sure he gets along with them.

For the most part, Labradors get along well with other pets. However, your best bet for making sure that your dog gets along with other household pets is to bring the puppy up with those pets. If raised from puppies, with smaller pets such as cats and rabbits, they tend to bond and become good friends.

Proper socialisation and exposure from an early age will again ensure that your Labrador dog gets along well with other dogs and household pets. However an older, perhaps rescue dog may view birds or small animals as prey due to the Labradors natural prey instinct. You will therefore need to supervise him with any birds and pets such as

rabbits, guinea pigs and cats initially. An adult dog may well chase, attack and potentially kill anything unusual to them. Hopefully your Labrador will soon get used to other pets as a part of the family. But certainly in the early stages, they should never be left unsupervised with other animals.

4) Do Labradors Get Along with Children?

Labradors are good natured, playful and affectionate, so ideal companions for children. They are generally patient with children of all ages. Although an excitable, exuberant Labrador may be too boisterous for young infants or toddlers.

His constant wagging tail is one of his endearing qualities. But be mindful of his potential to whip small children or knock valuable objects from low level tables.

They are not known to snap at children. However, this does not mean they will stand for prolonged abuse or harassment from a child who has not been taught how to respect and behave with the dog.

Most Gundogs, including the Labrador, because of the inherent need for them to be friendly towards everyone, are generally good with children. However, it is important that you socialise your Labrador puppy with children as soon as he comes into your home. Children should be taught to respect and care for the puppy and told to never tease or hurt them. They are not a toy and should never be treated as such. Failure to ensure this could result in the puppy becoming mishandled by young children. In the early stages, please do supervise children handling and playing with the new puppy. Everything will be strange to the puppy including excitable, energetic children, but they will soon get used to each other and accept each other as part of the family.

Most dogs that have been brought up with children, manage really well in a family environment. However, it is worth remembering that if an adult dog, perhaps rescue dog, has never encountered children, he may find them worrying. Children do, after all, move and sound differently to adults.

If you have a dog that is worried about children, it is really important that you make your pet feel safe and secure when there are children around. And for both the dog and child's sake never take any risks. You can get children to give the dog treats, otherwise completely ignore him. He ideally needs to get used to them in his own time.

Dogs that are considered to be good with children and good overall as a family pet will generally be very tolerant and friendly. However, a dog that is labelled 'good with children' is not meant to indicate a dog that will tolerate a mischievous terror, who will pull its ears and tail and potentially mishandle, tease or torment a dog.

Selective breeding has ensured that dogs, such as Gundogs, are more likely to tolerate a lot of pestering and harassment from a child. However, the potential is always there for the dog to snap if sufficiently provoked.

Breeds generally considered to be good or very good with children are also usually from reputable breeders who focus on breeding excellent temperaments. Un-reputable puppy farm breeders are likely to have no concern as to whether a breed's temperament is good or not. In fact many Labradors behavioural problems have been identified as deriving from puppy mill dogs.

Never under any circumstance, leave a dog with a young child. There are too many cases of dogs attacking children. Dogs can be unpredictable, and children do not have the awareness that an adult has in being able to read signals that the dog needs to be left alone.

Provided children are taught that dogs are not playthings to be roughed about, dogs can be an excellent influence on a child. Dogs considered to be compatible with children, can benefit a child by teaching kindness, patience, responsibility, care etc. Research has also shown that dogs teach a child to be more sociable, confident, friendly and outgoing, than children not brought up around dogs.

5) MALE (DOG) OR FEMALE (BITCH)

Many dog breeds can differ considerably between the male and female. However, Labradors of both sexes are temperamentally very similar, with the main difference being that the males are generally larger and heavier than the females.

A lot of prospective dog owners choose a female as they wish to breed from them at some point. However, if this is something you are considering, please don't be tempted to breed with her on a continuous basis. It is always good to have one litter to keep the generation of your beloved pet going. However a common potential draw back with never breeding from her is the potential for developing pyometra later in life. This is a uterine infection, that requires the removal of the female reproductive system. However, pyometra can also occur in bitches who have had litters, particularly as they get older. This again is a very good reason why you should have your dog spayed as soon as possible.

When deciding upon a male or female, it sometimes comes down to the preference of the owner or the personality of the dog. Two dogs of the same breed and the same litter can have completely different personalities. But sometimes, dog owners who have always had dogs for years simply prefer either a dog or a bitch. However, the dogs of most breeds including Labradors, tend to be more boisterous than bitches. But, where a dog and a bitch are present, bitches commonly become the dominant of the two.

To help you, the following offers a general guideline and what many breeders and dog owners have found to be true between the sexes.

Please note however that the following is not necessarily typical of all breeds or gender as opinions and findings often differ. This again is intended to give you a general idea of what you may encounter.

There are misconceptions that males are aggressive and females gentle, which can be the case but not necessarily as a rule. However, in general females are considered more docile than males. In this respect they are less likely to be aggressive, hostile or to get into fights with other dogs.

A) TYPICAL FEMALE TRAITS

Labrador bitches can be demanding, independently inclined, territorial, moody and stubborn.

A bitch will come into season twice a year and may be problematic during those periods. A dog however may be problematic all year round in terms of wandering or escaping, particularly if there are many bitches in the area.

Again this is debatable but females are generally considered to be easier to train than males. One reason for this may be because the male of certain breeds are known to be more problematic in terms of ignoring the owner and pleasing themselves whereas the females will be more attentive to the owner.

Many female dog breeds perhaps because of a maternal instinct are usually more caring and considerate towards children.

Opinions differ but it is not necessarily true that males are harder to house/toilet train than females. Females to a certain extent have also been known to be hard to house train. However, generally females tend to be moderately easier to house-train than males

Females can also affect the appearance of a lawn with urine spots that appear like bleach stains.

B) TYPICAL MALE TRAITS

Probably due in part to dogs being slightly larger and bulkier, they are considered to have more strength and stamina. Labrador dogs also often have greater exuberance than bitches.

Certain specific breeds are prone to roam, but in general this trait is not very frequent, and again this typically occurs if a bitch is in season. Generally however, Labrador dogs are not inclined to roam or wander.

Males have a tendency to display more sexual behaviour than females in terms of urine scent marking, mounting other dogs as well as people.

Males can also have a tendency to scent mark any object that takes their fancy which can leave stale urine smells if not disinfected.

From a guarding point of view, although females can be excellent in this capacity, males are generally considered more protective than females. However, in certain cases you will find hardly any difference between males and females.

Males can be more boisterous, appear more domineering, and can be more aggressive to other dogs (particularly other males), and people, than females. But unless as a breed they are inclined to be aggressive or fight this is not very frequent. However, intact males can become aggressive towards other males if there is competition for a bitch in heat. Males in general have much more of a tendency towards attempting to dominate their owner.

Again exceptions of both sexes can occur. The following provide additional information of differences between male and females dogs:

- In terms of excitability, very little difference is noted between male and females
- Males tend to be moderately more active than females
- Males have a moderately greater inclination to snap at children than females
- There is hardly any difference between males and females in terms of whether they will excessively bark or not
- Males tend to be slightly more playful than females
- Males tend to be moderately more territorially inclined than females
- Females tend to have more of a demand for affection than males
- Males tend to be moderately more destructive than females

6) A PUPPY OR ADULT?

Raising a puppy is a lot of time consuming work including; supervising toilet training every hour or so; regular daily exercise; basic obedience training; cleaning up after them; generally supervising them to ensure they have not managed to find a dangerous object to chew on; preparing their meals four times per day etc etc. Obviously a number of those points applies to an adult dog also. The following is presented to you in a 'pros and cons' format which will hopefully cover all probabilities.

A) PUPPY PROS AND CONS

In comparison to other Retriever breeds Labradors have a tendency to mature at a later age. However, this applies more to the show type, generally not working type who have a tendency to mature at a relatively early age. In fact it is often the case that some Labradors as young as 6 months old are working on shoots when other dogs are still going through their basic training. Bitches usually mature by 1 year of age, males by 2 years. Before 2 or 3 years of age they can be quite boisterous and exuberant, becoming much calmer as they mature.

Pros

- Puppies are cute, cuddly, entertaining, lovable and adorable, which makes it very easy for us to want to look after them.
- A puppy is a blank canvas and much more impressionable, flexible and adaptable than an older dog. Because you are starting from scratch, you have a fantastic opportunity to mould, develop and nurture him into a perfectly well behaved dog. But obviously it is your responsibility to make this happen through correct training and maintaining this every day thereafter.
- Another training advantage is the ease by which a new puppy will accept every member of the household including other pets.
- The bond will be much greater with your puppy as opposed to an adult rescue dog for example.

Cons

Although some adult rescue dogs have never been house-trained, most have. All puppies however, do not come into the world house-trained, and therefore need to be trained. Obedience and toilet training require time and patience to be successful.

There will also be a considerable time commitment needed for adequate socialisation, which ideally needs to happen before the 'critical period' ends at approximately 14 to 16 weeks of age.

Although it is not necessary to provide your puppy with 24/7 undivided attention, for the first few weeks or so however, they will need frequent supervision throughout the day. If you think in terms of toilet training for example, a young puppy will need to relieve themselves every half hour to an hour. If you do this properly then someone will need to let the puppy out. They also need feeding about four times throughout the day, so as well as first thing in the morning later in the day, they will also require two feeds, in between, during the day.

Be prepared for the pup to become bored and feel the need to chew things

B) ADULT DOGS

They tend to be relaxed, easy going, calm, sensible, gentle, sensitive, kind, friendly, eager to please, devoted and dependable.

However, being typical Gundogs, many Labradors retain a juvenile, playful, puppy enthusiasm even as mature adults.

Older dogs can be very adaptable and will, given sufficient time, bond to a family. However, this depends on their upbringing and possible mistreatment. They may consequently have baggage that affects how they respond to people. For example if they have been mistreated they are likely to be mistrustful, and although you are likely to gain their trust to a certain extent this will probably never be 100%. Obedience and house training may be limited or nonexistent, which can be worked on with success but may take longer than a puppy. In general however, an adult dog will be more stable and settled.

D) ADULT PROS AND CONS

Pros

- An adult dog that has been raised in a household and is without any obvious behavioural issues, will probably have been house-trained and received some sort of obedience training and adequate socialisation.

- An adult is likely to be more independent and emotionally stable than a puppy, and may therefore not require the same level of attention and supervision.
- With an adult dog, what you see is what you get. You can also never be 100% sure on how a puppy will develop in terms of temperament and potential behaviour problems.
- Senior dogs can be excellent, trouble free companions for anyone, but in particular people who cannot get out and about very often. They will be more easy going and not require the same demands or level of exercise that a puppy would.
- An adult rescue centre dog will be available to try out. If things do not work out, a good centre should be happy for you to return the dog.
- Some rescue dogs may have behavioural issues, but with an experienced person or someone prepared to put in the time, it is possible to rehabilitate them.
- Many well trained and well mannered rescue dogs who because the previous owner was unable to continue their care, simply need a good home.
- Contrary to popular belief, it is possible to teach an old dog new tricks, it just takes more time and patience to achieve.

Cons

- An unknown dog can be a risk in terms of health problems and behavioural baggage such as barking, chewing, chasing, digging etc.
- Sometimes a seemingly friendly amiable dog can become different again once you get them home and introduce them to your family. This can involve possible aggression and hostility to dogs and other pets you may have. It may not be obvious until the dog is exposed to a particular trigger or stimulus.
- Habits, behaviour and manners of an older dog, two years plus will be pretty much moulded and set in their ways.

- A puppy will be young enough to adapt to any household whereas an older dog might not accept or be problematic around your house and family.
- An adult rescue dog may or may not have been properly assessed in terms of behaviour problems they may have.

7) EASE AND COST OF CARE

Another very important factor you need to consider before bringing home a Labrador, adult or puppy, is the cost associated with their care. You also need to ensure that you can adequately cover these costs. Owning a dog is a big responsibility and it is up to you to provide for your dog's every need. Not only does this include shelter, but it also includes food, veterinary care, grooming etc.

The overall cost of owning a dog over its lifetime can be quite considerable, and it is certainly a major aspect of dog ownership that any prospective owner should be fully aware of.

Ongoing costs such as food, accessories, grooming etc can be predicted to a certain extent, as well as one off costs such as spaying/neutering over a dogs lifetime. Other costs such as occasional veterinary visits are not so predictable, and can sometimes run into thousands. You therefore need to be certain you can afford ongoing variable costs as well as potentially costly veterinary bills

In this section you will find a list of initial costs and monthly costs associated with Labrador ownership as well as an overview and explanation of each cost.

A.) INITIAL COSTS

PLEASE NOTE: The following is offered as a guideline only, as costs can vary depending on where you are located, where you buy from, the time you are looking etc.

The initial costs for owning a Labrador include those costs you must cover to purchase your dog and to prepare your home for his/her arrival.

Initial costs

Certain items bought for a puppy will probably need updating/replacing as they get older or grow to adult size:

- Collar and leash (probably needs updating as you generally need a smaller collar to start)
- Suitable puppy bed (may need updating if you buy a smaller bed to start)
- Food (initial puppy food)
- Water/food bowls (may need updating if you buy smaller bowls to start)
- Micro-chipping (one off cost)
- Vaccinations (vital initial cost for puppies, ongoing subject to titre testing)
- Chew and other toys (initial cost then ongoing as and when needed)
- Training classes (initial for obedience and socialisation).

Below you will find an overview of each expense as well as an estimated cost range:

Purchase Price – The initial purchase price for a dog is potentially a big chunk of money. However, caution should be exercised when assuming that you get what you pay for. The cheapest option is obviously free to good home, the next being a rescue dog whereby you pay a nominal fee to cover basic costs to the rescue centre.

Prices will then vary depending on the breeder and pedigree of the dog which can again vary depending on whether the dog is a standard pet or show quality. A high price may indicate a superior show winning pedigree, but it could be from a breeder motivated by money and using misleading promotional marketing. Again certain breeders will charge inflated prices for 'average' pedigree puppies simply because they are either greedy, cleverly marketing the breed by promoting so called 'unique' features, or both.

We will go into more detail in the 'purchasing a Labrador' chapter.

USA

Labradors in the USA typically range between $1,000 and $5,000 or more for a champion show type.

UK

Labradors in the UK typically average around £1,000, for a non-show type, some will be more, some less.

A more popular and recognised Labrador breeder will have more expensive puppies, especially if of show winning quality, and good representatives of the sire and dam are used. You are also likely to find that this type of breeder will not advertise and therefore only come via word of mouth or through organisations such as AKC or KC UK.

Wherever you purchase, always try and ensure that your Labrador has a written health guarantee against hereditary and congenital defects. In other words the parents should have been health tested. Again you need to see evidence of these, which you should check with the organisations who carried out the tests.

Crate – Having a crate for your Labrador puppy is very important. Not only will it be instrumental in house-training, but it will give your puppy a place of his own in the house where he can retreat if he wants a nap or just needs a break from people. If you intend to buy a crate that will be large enough for a full grown Labrador make sure the measurements are at approximately 40 inch in length x 26 inches wide x 28 inches high. It is also preferable if you can buy a crate with an adjustable partition option until your puppy grows to full size. Alternatively if you are DIY inclined you can make your own partition and adjust this as your puppy grows.

You will need to upgrade your puppy's crate as he grows, but to start with, a small crate should only cost you about $35 (£26 exchange rate May 2017) for a relatively inexpensive one. Although some are hundreds of $/£.

Spay/Neuter Surgery – Having your Labrador puppy spayed or neutered is incredibly important, especially if you do not plan to breed your dog. There is much debate about when is the ideal time to spay or neuter a dog. Traditionally between 6 months and a year has always been considered ideal. Some vets recommend that you spay or neuter your puppy around 6 months of age to reduce the risk of certain types of cancer developing. Spaying a female dog before her first heat is considered to significantly reduce your dog's risk of developing mammary cancer as well as ovarian and uterine cancers. Incidentally, the Labrador usually receives her first heat around

6 to 11 months of age. The ASPCA points out that the traditional age to spay is 6 to 9 months. However, they also suggest dogs can be spayed before 6 months of age. To find out more, have a look at the following site; https://www.aspca.org/pet-care/general-pet-care/spayneuter-your-pet. According to 'Blue Cross' they advocate spaying or neutering before the age of 6 months, but for larger dogs this should be after the first heat. The Blue Cross further asserts that there is no benefit in delaying spay surgery until after their first season. They also suggest that certain health benefits are reduced if you wait until after the first season. More information is available at the following https://www.bluecross.org.uk/pet-advice/neutering. Others will assert that the dog should be fully mature and developed, consequently carrying out spay surgery in between the first and second season. Always discuss this with your veterinary surgeon.

Spay/neuter surgery can be very expensive if you go to a regular veterinarian. But there are plenty of low-cost clinics out there that offer affordable spay/neuter surgery options. If you go to a clinic or shelter, neuter surgery will very likely only cost you $50 to $100 (£38 to £76 exchange rate; May 2017). Spay surgery with a private vet can be quite expensive and generally costs anywhere between $100 to $300, in some cases more. (£76 to £228). Incidentally, castration is usually cheaper than spaying.

I am all in favour of breeding at least one litter of pups in order to keep the generation going of your beloved pet. If you do not wish to breed with your dog, or only intend to breed one litter, you may wish to consider the benefits to your dogs health of spaying or neutering. However, please be aware that if you intend to show your dog, most organisations insist on the dog being intact (not spayed/neutered). So if showing dogs is something you are likely to be pursuing, please do research any show limitations relating to a spayed/neutered dog.

Is it beneficial to castrate a dog?

Contrary to popular opinion, castration for dogs does not guarantee that behavioural problems will be eliminated. Many cases of castration however, have indicated a significant effect. An adult dog which has serious behavioural issues

and is then castrated is likely to either show a rapid reduction or a gradual reduction of the behaviour. It also seems to be the case that castrating before or after puberty doesn't make a significant difference towards altering behaviour. It is also said that castration will probably not make a dog less destructive, calmer, less active or more tolerant of children.

The possible effects of castration:

- Decreased aggression towards other dogs, particularly males.
- A reduced tendency to dominate
- Reduced scent/urine marking
- Less inclination to mount dogs, people and other objects
- Reduced inclination to escape and roam
- Can still however show sexual interest after castration

Spaying a bitch

Spaying is effectively the removal of the female reproductive system. An intact (un-spayed) female will come into season twice a year, in some cases once. Spaying is also thought to increase body weight of between 5 and 10 percent as a result of a loss of certain hormones. However, it is thought that the intake of too much food and not enough exercise would probably have more of an effect than spaying.

Problems associated with a bitch coming into season include:

- The dog being more vocal
- More active and fidgety
- Can be more nervous than usual
- Urine and vaginal secretions attracts any other male dog

Benefits of spaying:

- Sexual behaviour such as mounting can occur but is unlikely
- No twice yearly oestrus and consequent male attention
- Reduces the risk of her contracting certain cancers connected with her ovaries, mammories etc. Also prevents pyometra which is a life threatening disease similar in humans to appendicitis.

Neutering a dog or a bitch is commonly highly recommended by veterinarians and rescue organisations particularly to reduce the millions of abandoned dogs each year as well as for a number of health reasons.

The other obvious implication of Neutering a dog or a bitch is that doing so will negate the ability of either breeding. Although this book does not cover breeding, if this is something you are interested in please consult the following:

For further reading and information on breeding, I would highly recommend 'Book of the Bitch' by J.M. Evans & Kay White.

Vaccinations – Vaccinations are not necessarily a one off cost as you may continue vaccinating, subject to titre testing, each year.

Before your Labrador puppy turns one year old, he/she will need to get certain vaccinations. However, this is generally completed before 3 months of age. If you buy your puppy from a reputable breeder the pup may already have a few of these vaccinations taken care of by the time you take him home. Speak to your veterinarian about a vaccination schedule for your puppy and plan to spend up to $100 (£76) for your puppy's vaccinations. Although you will find cheaper options by shopping around

http://www.akc.org/content/health/articles/puppy-shots-complete-guide/

A UK example can be found at the following link, although obviously you will need to price for your specific location:

http://stannesvets.co.uk/current-pricelist.html

Micro-chipping – Not only may you need to have your puppy licensed, but you should also consider micro-chipping as well. Again dog licenses are usually worn on a collar around your dog's neck but a microchip is implanted underneath the skin so that it cannot be lost. The procedure does not hurt your dog and it only takes a minute or so to complete. You should be able to have it done at your local animal shelter for as little as $15 (£11.50) or around $50 (£38) for a veterinarian to do it. Once again, check your location, as for example microchipping in parts of the UK was compulsory from April 2016

Other Accessories – In addition to your dog's crate, you will also need certain accessories. These accessories will include a food dish, water dish, collar, leash, grooming tools, and toys. What you spend on each of these items is up to you and the cost will vary depending on quality. You should expect to pay about $100 (£76) for these accessories, though you could easily spend $200 (£152) or more if you purchased high-quality or designer items. Again many of these items may need replacing at some point, but are not considered an ongoing monthly cost.

B.) MONTHLY COSTS

Part of being a responsible dog owner is meeting the ongoing needs of your dog. If you cannot comfortably cover the initial costs and monthly costs described in this section you should not purchase a Labrador dog.

The monthly costs for owning a Labrador include those recurring costs you must cover on a monthly ongoing basis. Monthly costs include the food and treats, veterinary care, grooming, license renewal, insurance and other costs.

Ongoing costs

- Daily food needs (beyond initial puppy food)
- Pet insurance
- Vaccination boosters, again subject to titre testing
- Veterinary visits: (you may decide to put a contingency fund aside to cover costs not covered by pet insurance)
- Parasite control such as worming, Flea, tick treatment etc (ongoing cost)
- Grooming costs
- Doggy day care
- Pet sitting/walking services
- Possible kennel costs for holidays etc

Below you will find an overview of each expense and an estimate:

Food and Treats – For a medium to large sized Labrador your food costs will not be too high. It is difficult to provide an accurate average cost here as it depends on whether you feed raw, dry, home cooked or a mixture of both. However, it is not recommended that you shop by price. The quality of the food you give your dog has a direct impact on his health and wellbeing, so do not skimp. If for example you were feeding a quality dry food,you should plan to spend about $30 to $50 (£23 to £38). on a large bag of dog food that will last you about one month. In addition to food, you should budget an extra $10 to $20 (£7.50 to £15) per month for treats, especially when you are training your dog.

Pet Insurance - Again this depends on the type of plan you take out and a number of other variables. The variables can make a considerable difference depending on the type of dog, the dogs age and where you are located. In the UK for example the average monthly cost if you lived in the North of England would be £30 approx. However, in London this would double to £60. Until you shop around with your specific details you will not be able to establish an accurate cost. However, on average you can expect to pay approximately £30 more or less

https://boughtbymany.com/news/article/dog-insurance-cost/

In the USA the following link will give you an idea of what you can expect to pay.

https://www.petinsurancequotes.com/petinsurance/cost.html

Again it will depend on a number of factors, but you could expect to pay about $40 per month

Booster Vaccinations - Booster vaccinations are supposed to be administered every year. However, opinions differ as to whether this is necessary. Titre testing is a reliable way of determining if a vaccination is necessary. However, for argument sake, if you assume you need all vaccinations jabs again we will use the same figure for the initial vaccination of $100 (£76). This will average out at $8.30 (£6.40) per month.

Veterinary Care – In order to keep your Labrador in good health, you should plan to visit the veterinarian about every 6 months. Your Labrador puppy may need more frequent visits during the first year for vaccinations, but after that, two visits per year should be adequate. You should expect to spend about $50 (£38) per visit which, with two visits per year is $100 (£76), and averages to about $8.30 (£6.40) per month.

Parasite Treatment - This will obviously depend on the product you use. You will at least be looking at a general flea/tick treatment and wormer. On average you can expect to pay about $40 (£30) for 3 doses of flea/tick treatment working out at about $13.30 (£10) per month. For a good all round wormer expect to pay about $10 to $20 (£7.50 to £15 Exchange rate May 2017) for a 3 monthly treatment. Which works out at about $3 to $6 (£2.30 to £4.60) per month

Grooming – The Labrador is so easy to groom on a weekly basis, that this is unlikely to be a cost you will have to incur. Although professional grooming costs will vary, you should expect to spend about $50 (£38) per visit. You may however, decide to make an annual visit, just to get a professional to check him over.

Dog walking/care services: - It is difficult to put an exact price on this as it depends on what you need. For example a service may include sitting for up to an hours approximately $30 (£23). Walking for 30 minutes or so could cost $20 (£15). A 12 hour overnight service could easily cost $50 (£39) to $70 (£54). Transporting your pet within a 10 mile radius could cost $20 (£15), typically with a $1 per mile extra charge. Again you really need to decide if these are services you may need, which ones and how often. If so please do check your local area and shop around. For this reason the table is left blank.

Kennel costs for holidays

Once again this is a cost that you may not need to factor in. It is subjective depending on how long you are away. Different providers are likely to have different rates if it is 1 night, a weekend, 1 or 2 weeks, how many dogs etc. Again this is really something you need to decide as a potential cost, and if so search your local area and shop around.

License Renewal – (Again, this does not apply to every country or even U.S. state) License renewal is not a major expense. You only need to have your dog's license renewed once a year and again, it generally costs about $25 (£19.45 currency rate May 2017) which averages to just $2 (£1.50) per month.

Other Costs – In addition to veterinary care and grooming costs, there are other costs which you may need to cover once in a while. These costs may include new toys, replacement collars as your Labrador grows, new grooming tools, cleaning products, and more. To be safe, you should budget about $15 (£11.55) per month for these additional costs.

CHAPTER FIVE:

PUPPY MILLS

Before we look at the options for buying a puppy, the following two chapters are intended to highlight two very important subjects to be aware of at this stage. The intention of this short chapter, is to therefore alert you to the seriousness of puppy farmed dogs. You will soon be starting your search for your ideal puppy and the one thing you will hopefully avoid is a puppy that has been bred by an unscrupulous puppy farmer. The following will provide you with warning signs and traps to avoid.

1) BEWARE OF THE PUPPY FARMER!

The opposite side to an ethical breeder is the 'puppy farmer'. Unfortunately not everyone with Labrador puppies for sale is a good, honest and ethical dog breeder. In actual fact some care very little about the dogs in their charge.

This is a trap that most people fall into when looking for a puppy, thinking that every breeder is reputable. It's actually hard to believe that people would farm dogs in this way, but it happens and if you are looking for a puppy, you can be sure that at least some of your available options will puppy farmed dogs.

The pet store puppy is usually from a puppy mill, as are those sold in big sized litters through classifieds. This is not to say that buying puppies from classified ads is a bad thing. Some excellent puppies are available this way, and often this is the most convenient way a reputable 'hobby' breeder can find potential puppy parents. However, please take note of the warnings that follow, if you are considering a classified add puppy or adult dog. Although all puppies look the same, usually healthy, clean, fluffy and with that addictive puppy scent, the farmed puppy is very different indeed.

The puppy mill is a harrowing place. It is much the same as a factory farm for pigs, cows and chickens. Dogs are kept in small pens, rarely cleaned up after and bred from, each time the dog comes into season. The Mother dog is stressed throughout her life and often puppy farmed dogs never go for a walk. They rarely, if at all, receive veterinary attention.

They are also rarely handled and are fed on cheap food. As you can probably imagine, bacteria thrives in this type of environment and stress levels are high. With the ever increasing link between low quality commercial food and illness, a puppy born and whelped in this type of environment will have a very poor start in life.

Studies are increasingly showing that the presence of stress in a pregnant mother dog can lead to flighty and fearful puppies with the behaviour only showing up in the dog's adolescent and adult life. So how do you recognise a puppy farmer or a puppy that has been bred for money alone?

The signs of a puppy farmer are quite easy to spot when you know what to look for. The important thing to remember with this type of dog breeder is that the most important thing to them is money, and the way that they act will betray this.

It may be tempting to buy a puppy from this type of breeder anyway and see it as a sort of rescue attempt. This is highly inadvisable because the puppy farmer only exists as a result of people buying their puppies. Therefore to buy a dog in this way is funding the cruel practice of puppy farming. The risk of genetic and environmental health problems caused by bad care of the parent dogs and their offspring from pregnancy onwards, is greatly increased when buying any puppy from a puppy farmer.

http://www.dailymail.co.uk/news/
article-2515297/Foreign-gangs-rabies-
appalling-cruelty-The-sickening-truth-
cute-Christmas-puppies-sale-internet.
html

2) KEY POINTS ABOUT PUPPY FARMED DOGS:

- Dogs are very often kept in cramped, cold, filthy conditions with little chance of fresh air and exercise.
- Mothers are relentlessly bred every time they come into season, and then disposed of when they can no longer reproduce.
- The puppies will probably have been separated at far too young an age from the mother and litter mates.
- Puppy mill puppies are unlikely to have received sufficient, if any adequate socialisation.
- There is a strong risk that the puppy will have inherited a debilitating disease.
- Puppies will be transported, long distances, in cramped, unsuitable conditions.
- Avoid pet shop puppies as there is a strong likelihood they did not come from reputable breeders and quite possibly from puppy mills.

Also avoid kennels or individuals advertising numerous breeds rather than one. Agents for puppy farms commonly pose as legitimate families in a normal family home and act as if they only have one litter for sale. However they will commonly use the same telephone number and perhaps a different name to advertise multiple litters.

When calling anyone that you are not sure about regarding a litter of puppies they may be advertising, ask the following: 'Hello, I'm phoning about the litter of puppies you have advertised'. If they seem vague or ask which litter, you are probably talking to a puppy mill or an agent of one.

The breeders are only interested in money and have no interest in the health, welfare or quality selective breeding of their dogs. Therefore be wary of anyone who is more interested in talking business, rather than finding out if you are a suit-

able candidate for the puppy.

Avoid at all costs anyone wanting to meet you in a lay by, car park or offering to deliver.

The general advice is to always insist on seeing at least the mother, preferably both parents. But how do you know you are seeing the genuine parents even though they look like the breed? Admittedly, agents for puppy farms could have parent dogs living with them but will not want the hassle, particularly if they are selling multiple litters, so its easier for them to make excuses as to their absence. Fake Kennel Club papers exist and its probably possible to be looking at fake health test certificates should they be available. Unfortunately as fraudsters get more sophisticated, this could possibly happen. The sad fact is that there are no 100% guarantees, and it is a shame that you have to go to these lengths. But if you are aware of how these people operate then you can at least go some way to avoid dealing with unscrupulous people intent on scamming the unsuspecting.

Classified ads have a bad reputation for being the preferred choice of puppy mill agents who prey on the unsuspecting and people who buy on impulse. This is a very good reason why you should never buy on impulse.

One of the reasons why puppy mills or their agents are a popular solution and consequently thrive, is that they provide such an easy option to buy. They will never make you feel bad that perhaps you haven't thought things through. All they want is your money. You should never expect any written guarantee that you can return the puppy for whatever reason. Or if you do get offered some sort of written contract, it will probably have untraceable contact details, and in general be unenforceable and therefore not worth the paper it is written on.

Please remember that puppy farms and other un-reputable breeders have no interest in health testing or whether the dam or sire has a bad temperament. So if you hear a breed described as good with children, placid, easily trained, this refers to a dog that has a sound temperament and has been well socialised. Through sheer luck, a puppy farmed dog may be temperamentally and genetically sound. But you can be pretty certain that they will not have been health tested or their temperament assessed for soundness. They will most probably not have received adequate, if any, socialisation or early toilet training. In the same respect, the puppy is unlikely to have received any initial vaccinations, worm or flea treatment.

A lot of agents for puppy farmers are very good at having answers ready for questions you may ask. But be very wary if they make excuses why you cant see the parents, such as 'my husband/wife has just popped out with them'. Any excuses or refusal to answer questions should have alarm bells ringing as to their validity. Please make sure you ask questions for the points raised in this section.

We will go into much more detail in the following chapters, about questions to ask, and what a reputable breeder is likely to ask you.

CHAPTER SIX:

LABRADOR RESCUE DOGS

Unfortunately year after year, far too many dogs are given up for adoption/rescue, because of unrealistic expectations from dog owners. There are many reasons, but these mainly revolve around the unsuitability of a particular breed to the life-style of a particular individual. Additionally, such prospective owners are left ill equipped with either a lack of knowledge, ability or both, necessary to address the day to day care of their new family member. The lifespan of the average dog is approximately 12 to 14 years and it is difficult to plan ahead with any certainty what the future holds. Major upheavals can and do happen such as the loss of a job or having to move away, perhaps to another country. Admittedly these are considerations that for the majority of people we cannot possibly predict and therefore have no real control over. What we can do however, is to address our current lifestyle and give some thought as to possible events in the future, which could have an impact on dog ownership.

This short chapter is therefore intended to briefly explain the rescue dog situation and perhaps prompt you into looking at adopting one as a viable option.

1) ADOPTING A LABRADOR RESCUE DOG

Unless you specifically have your heart set on a Labrador puppy, you may be able to find an adult Labrador at a local animal shelter or Labrador rescue. There are many benefits to adopting an adult dog versus buying a puppy. For one thing, adoption prices are much lower than the cost of purchasing a puppy from a breeder. Adoption rates typically range from $100 to $200 (£77 to £154 exchange rate at 15th May 2017). Furthermore, when you adopt an adult dog it may already be house-trained and have had some obedience training.

Whilst raising a puppy is great, it can take a lot of time and commitment and it can be a challenge. If you do not want to deal with a puppy having accidents in your house or if you want to avoid the whole teething stage, adopting an adult dog may be the right choice. Furthermore, when you buy a puppy from a Labrador breeder you do not know what its temperament and personality will be when it grows up. If you adopt an adult dog, what you see is what you get.

2) WHY DOGS ARE ABANDONED:

No one can predict with any certainty what they will be doing in 5, 10 or 15 years time! A lot of people take on a dog that is relatively high maintenance. But at that time they have the time and the inclination to take care of above average exercise needs etc. Then perhaps something happens in their lives, e.g. a divorce, career commitment, losing a job, moving house, disability, illness, births, deaths or marriages etc. The inevitable outcome is that the owner is simply no longer able to care for the dog. These are obviously stressful times for you, but they will also be stressful for a dog that needs to feel emotionally secure. It is at such times when we have to prioritise and it is so easy for our dogs to become neglected as a result.

Although many people genuinely experience unforeseeable, life changing events that throw everything into chaos, too many more, use certain 'excuses' for deciding they are no longer able to commit to looking after a dog. You again, therefore owe it to yourself, a potential dog owner, to properly research and decide whether owning a dog is something you can commit to.

Properly weigh up all the pros and cons and be as near to 100% certain as you can be, that for the next 10 or 15 years you will be able to take care of your dogs needs.

Many excellent global animal welfare charities do not have unlimited financial resources to cope with the demand of abandonment. The tragic implication of this is that on an annual basis, unwanted dogs face euthanasia simply because suitable homes cannot be found. An annual stray dog survey conducted by the Dogs Trust in 2015 recorded over 100,000 dogs handed over to local authorities. Approximately half were claimed by their owners, the rest remained abandoned with over 5 thousand having to be euthanised. This is an ongoing issue that the new UK micro-chipping law brought out in 2016, hopes to address to a considerable extent.

https://www.dogstrust.org.uk/news-events/news/over-47-000-people-heart-lessly-abandoned-their-dogs-in-one-year

In the U.S.A. according to a Washington Post article in 2014 an estimated 7.6 million animals, mainly cats and dogs end up in animal shelters on an annual basis. Approximately 2.7 million of those will face euthanasia.

https://www.washingtonpost.com/local/shelters-destroy-millions-of-animals-each-year/2014/11/28/1759aef4-702c-11e4-ad12-3734c461eab6_story.html

Cesar Millan lists 10 typical major reasons why dogs are abandoned to rescue centres.

https://www.cesarsway.com/get-involved/rescue/reasons-dogs-end-up-in-shelters-rescue-series-pt1.

Again, one of the main reasons why dogs are turned over to rescue centres is that the owner was simply unaware of what was involved in caring for a dog.

In addition, please take time to view the following links for other reasons why people have abandoned their dogs.

http://www.dogingtonpost.com/real-life-idiotic-reasons-people-have-aban-doned-their-dogs/

http://www.animal-rights-action.com/pet-abandonment.html

http://www.peta2.com/blog/why-peo-ple-abandon-animals/

http://prime.peta.org/why-people-aban-don-animals

http://www.vetstreet.com/our-pet-experts/by-the-numbers-10-reasons-puppies-and-dogs-end-up-homeless

http://www.noahsdogs.com/m/advice/view/The-Most-Common-Reasons-for-Returning-or-Abandoning-a-Dog

http://blog.theanimalrescuesite.com/the-real-reasons-animals-end-up-in-shelters/

https://www.petfinder.com/pet-adop-tion/dog-adoption/pets-relinquished-shelters/

Pet statistics from the ASPCA
http://www.aspca.org/animal-home-lessness/shelter-intake-and-surrender/pet-statistics

In all cases, a dog simply wants to be loved, respected and cared for, and in return reciprocate with such unconditional love and devotion that most humans would find hard to match. There is no wonder then that dogs are left bewildered and heartbroken when through no fault of their own their owners give up and abandon them. There is no big secret, dogs have certain needs and if these needs are not met, they will suffer. If they do not receive these needs, behavioural prob-lems arise. It is usually at this point, that in most cases of abandonment the dogs become too much trouble and the owners decide they can no longer cope. These needs are much the same as ours. Love, Companionship, Warmth, Comfort, Shelter, Food, Water, Exercise, Play, leisure time, Mental stimulation etc.

Ask yourself what you would do? Would your first thought be to abandon your dog to a rescue organisation? It is important that you are honest with yourself and can confirm that you have con-sidered and given a lot of thought to whether you can commit to looking after a dog.

3) THE RESCUE CENTRE DOG

Rescue dogs end up at rescue centres for many of the aforementioned reasons. Sometimes they are abandoned on the street and picked up by dog wardens. In many cases dogs end up being abandoned simply because the owner didn't take the time to find out that the small adorable puppy would grow into something much larger with greater than expected needs.

If a dog has been used to home comforts and pampering, they often find it difficult to cope with suddenly being made to live in rescue centre kennels. There is no excuse for failure on the pro-spective owners part to do their homework in terms of finding out about the breed and consequently their suitability and compatibility to adequately take

care of their needs. Ultimately avoiding becoming yet another rescue centre statistic.

A lot of rescue dogs also end up at the centres simply because the previous owners found them-selves unable to provide the time necessary to train and generally care for the dog. They found that the dogs developed behaviour and temperament problems, but again this mostly occurs because of a lack of adequate exercise, training, mental stimulation or socialisation. In the majority of cases the owners probably didn't know how to train them, or it became too much trouble. The dog is then left to its own devices, unsupervised with a lack of exercise. The owners then wonder why the dog misbehaves, rebels and generally acts up.

A typical scenario

In their frustration the puppy will start to chew household items or do their toilet business inside. In some cases the dog is expected to hold it in all day. Some owners see a solution to this problem, or as punishment, by making the puppy live outside in a kennel. This will be unsettling for a dog that has been used to living indoors. They will suddenly feel even more isolated, experience separation anxiety and other behavioural problems such as barking or digging in an attempt to escape, will manifest.

After this punishment, the puppy is perhaps once again permitted inside. The puppy will be so happy at this prospect that they will find it difficult to contain their excitement. They are likely to bark enthusiastically, jump up to greet everyone, run around possibly knocking things over, and soon find themselves back outside. It becomes an avoidable vicious circle, and all because of a lack of training and consideration for the dogs needs.

4) LOCAL ANIMAL SHELTERS AND SPECIFIC LABRADOR BREED ORGANISATIONS.

Local animal shelters often have a variety of breeds, either purebred or crossbreeds. However, there are usually a number of specific breed rescue organisations in different countries. You may have to travel some distance, but do not rule these out as they are a viable option that you should consider to find a Labrador.

Puppies are sometimes available, but usually dogs range from around 6 months old upwards to senior. There are usually conditions of adoption such as a requirement to have the dog neutered by a certain date. Specific breed organisations will often know the history of the dog, often via micro-chipping, whereas general animal shelters often take abandoned dogs, knowing nothing of their history.

A) VISITING A RESCUE CENTRE

Viewing will be either on a drop in basis or by appointment. The best time to visit a rescue centre is during the week as weekends and school holidays etc are likely to be busy times. Spend as much time as you can and try to be objective with your choice as it is too easy to become emotionally swayed by a sad looking dog that may be perfect in itself, but could also be totally unsuitable for your household. Most if not all centres will insist on a home check, where they visit your home to assess the suitability of your accommodation. You may or may not have to fill in a questionnaire or be asked a series of questions at the centre.

Things to think about, and questions to ask

- What if you are faced with a dog with behavioural problems? This is a possibility and this could be the reason they were relinquished in the first place. But it is unlikely that a rescue centre will allow an inexperienced owner to take such a dog anyway.
- Again although a detailed history of a dog may not be available, you should still ask questions about the background of the dog. This could be limited to the rescue centre assessment or a foster home assessment. Questions could include the following:
- How long has the dog been at the centre? If the dog has been there a while, you need to know why. It could be because of a behavioural issue, or a serious health condition etc.
- Is the dog known to be good with other pets and children?

- Importantly, check if it will be possible to return the dog, for any reason. Some centres will only allow this under certain circumstances.
- Make a shortlist of potential dogs, you like the look of.
- Make sure you have the opportunity to spend time with the dogs so that you can interact and gauge how friendly and easy going they are.
- Ideally the dog should be friendly, interested and happy to be with you. Any signs of aloofness may not be a problem, but if the dog seems fearful or aggressive and hostile, then you are probably best to avoid that particular dog.

If you are thinking of adopting a Labrador rescue dog, the following links will give you a few choices to start your search:

B) U.S.A LABRADOR RESCUE CENTRES

ASPCA
https://www.aspca.org/adopt-pet/

Last Day Dog Rescue.
http://www.lastdaydogrescue.org/

SOS Labrador Retriever Rescue
http://www.soslabrescue.org/

Labrador Retriever Rescue of Connecticut
http://www.labrescuect.org/

New Orleans Lab Rescue
http://www.nolalabrescue.org/Available-Labs.html

The Dallas Fort Worth Labrador Retriever Rescue Club
http://www.dfwlabrescue.org/

Central Indiana Lab Rescue & Adoption
http://www.cilra.org/

Labrador Retriever Rescue of Florida (LRROF)
http://lrrof.org/

Greater Dayton Labrador Retriever Rescue
http://www.gdlrr.org/

Southern Skies Labrador Rescue & Adoption (SSLR)
http://www.southernskiesrescue.org/

Safe Harbor Lab Rescue
http://www.safeharborlabrescue.org/

Central California Labrador Retriever Rescue
https://www.cc-labrescue.org/

The Labrador Retriever Club
http://www.thelabradorclub.com/sub-pages/searchrescue.php

The Rocky Mountain Lab Rescue
http://www.rockymountainlabrescue.com/

Labs4rescue
http://labs4rescue.com/

The Labrador Retriever Rescue of Fresno (LRRF)
http://cclabrescuecvc.org/

Golden Gate Labrador Retriever Rescue (GGLRR)
http://labrescue.org/labsavailable.html

Atlanta Lab Rescue
http://www.atlantalabrescue.com/

Lucky Lab Rescue & Adoption
https://www.luckylabrescue.com/

Save A Lab Rescue
http://www.savealabrescue.org/

American Lab Rescue
http://americanlabrescue.com/

Lab Rescue
https://www.lab-rescue.org/

The following link is a comprehensive list of breed rescues throughout the USA, some which may have already been listed previously.
http://www.8pawsup.com/labrescues/

c) UK LABRADOR RESCUE CENTRES

Blue Cross
https://www.bluecross.org.uk

Dogs Trust
https://www.dogstrust.org.uk/

Battersea
http://www.battersea.org.uk/

Oldies Club
http://www.oldies.org.uk/
The Kennel Club Retriever (Labrador) Breed Rescue (contains an extensive list of links (at the time of press 35) to Labrador Retriever Rescue organsiations)

https://www.thekennelclub.org.uk/services/public/findarescue/Default.aspx?breed=2048

You may find even more Labrador Rescues by doing a search for Labrador rescue dogs [home town]

In addition to the above, please check your local RSPCA / ASPCA and any local dog rescue centres, by doing a Google search such as the following: 'Rescue dogs [home town]

Chapter Seven:

Purchasing a Labrador Puppy

Once you have decided that a Labrador is the right dog breed for you, your next step is to find a reputable Labrador breeder to purchase from. Finding a breeder is not a task that you should take lightly. You need to find a quality breeder that takes great care with selecting healthy breeding stock and then raises the puppies properly. If you buy your Labrador from an inexperienced or hobby breeder, you may end up with a Labrador that has some kind of congenital defect or other health issues. In this section you will find tips for selecting a reputable breeder as well as advice on what to look out for and avoid. There is also information on buying a Labrador in the U.S. and in the U.K.

1) Labrador Breeders

Choosing which breeder to deal with, is just as important as deciding which breed to get. Buying from poor sources such as puppy mills and back-yard breeders is a bad choice, and contributes to the continuing overpopulation of pets, and even

to large numbers of dogs surrendered at shelters today.

PLEASE NOTE: I am bound to be repeating myself here, but if at all possible, purchase a puppy whereby the parents have been health tested. We will talk later about health testing.

The only exception I would ever make to only purchasing a puppy from health tested parents is adopting a rescue dog. I have rescued a number of dogs that I had no idea about their historical pedigree or health test history. These dogs were exceptionally healthy and only ever had minor ailments. Perhaps I was lucky, but in a lot of cases these rescue dogs are desperate for loving forever homes. I would certainly take a rescue dog any day, regardless of possible health issues. However, the choice ultimately has to be yours.

A) The reputable breeder

The only dog breeder to consider is the one that has a conscience. This is the type that loves the breed and only breeds one or two litters. They will also carry out all of the testing required before making a decision to breed a litter. This type of breeder knows about puppy socialisation. They also know about genetic health, and dog welfare is at the forefront of their minds.

The good dog breeder has a list of people wanting the puppies before they even allow the parent dogs to mate. They are extremely interested in finding the correct puppy home, and are not afraid to turn people away. The good breeder does not have to use classified sites, Facebook or newspapers to advertise their puppies. They are not cagey about the parent dogs and they will always, without fail, allow you to see the puppies with their Mother in the home environment.

The reputable breeder will be keen to ensure you are very keen on the welfare, care, happiness and long term health of the puppy. They are therefore likely grill you with questions. You may even feel interviewed, on your initial phone call. This may not make you feel comfortable, but it will certainly affirm that they have the dogs best interest at heart. You can at least be certain you are enquiring about much loved and well-bred Labrador puppies. These puppies will undoubtedly be wormed, health checked, vaccinated and at least eight weeks old before they leave their Mother.

B) SIGNS OF A REPUTABLE BREEDER

They will have been established enthusiasts of this specific breed for at least several years.

They are more than likely registered with one of the Kennel Clubs as well as specific breed or training organisations.

Some reputable breeders are enthusiasts of two breeds, but certainly not a kennel that breeds lots of different breeds. Kennels who make their living this way will probably be more interested in the business of making money, keeping costs down etc. This is not to say that some kennel bred dogs are not impeccably looked after with regular veterinary visits and health tests. But puppy farms for one, will only ever look at such costs as eating into their profit margins.

Reputable breeders will be very keen to find out about you as a suitable home for the puppy. They will also be keen to take the puppy back if you find you are unable to take care of him properly.

They will be knowledgeable and be prepared to talk about the breed particularly in terms of training and exercise needs, potential behaviour, temperament and health issues associated with the breed. They will probably offer to help with advice about their upbringing or any problems you may have.

They will volunteer or at least go into detail if asked about the pedigree of the litter, i.e. parents, grandparents etc and preferably have health test certificates to back up their claims of these being clear of diseases being tested. They will also be happy to show you verified health test/screening results.

The reputable breeder will endeavour to disclose problems they have encountered. This may include selective breeding they have undertaken and are undertaking to eradicate genetic health and temperament/behavioural problems.

So be wary of breeders who tell you they have never had any problems with dogs they have bred in terms of genetic health problems or temperament.

The breeder should also have his veterinarian available to answer any questions you may have about the health history of the puppies, and the breeder's adult dogs.

If your Labrador breeder is reluctant to give you any information related to veterinary care or previous buyers, this should raise a red flag, and you are probably best to look elsewhere!

They will never make you feel pressured to take the puppy, such as 'this is the last one', or 'they have a few people interested'. Perhaps genuine, but a tactic often used by agents for puppy farms.

A well-respected Labrador breeder will usually be able to give you a list of references. This list should contain the names of people that have bought puppies from that breeder over the past few years.

In summary, the breeder should not be defensive, evasive, insincere etc, but be open, friendly and forthcoming with information. You will get the impression that they desire to find the best homes for their puppies. They will check that you have the knowledge, sense of caring, responsibility and maturity to look after a dog for its whole life, not just until the novelty wears off. They will probably ask you what accommodation you will be providing and give their opinion as to your suitability for this breed of dog.

C) SELECTIVE BREEDING

The following is intended to give you a basic idea of how and why reputable breeders selectively breed their dogs. Again this is something the puppy farm or un-reputable breeder is unlikely to have the slightest interest in.

Reputable breeders generally breed selectively for a particular temperament, show or working potential. This is usually based on the temperament, show and working line or pedigree of the sire and dam of the litter of puppies.

Be aware however that an amiable, placid temperament or show winning looks, is not always necessarily the aim. For example what the dog looks like is of far less importance to the person wanting a highly competent Gundog.

D) THE BREED STANDARD AND SELECTIVE BREEDING

The breed standard is simply a set of statistics of a breed, that determines what they should ideally look like and how they should ideally behave. For show purposes the breed standard and the quality of your dog to accurately match it, will be very important in terms of potentially winning shows. The breed standard is also highly important from a breeding point of view in terms of producing high quality dogs that not only have the best appearance, but also possessing of optimum health and temperaments. However, for the majority of pet owners, the breed standard will only really be useful to you as a pet owner, to give you a general overview of the dog, and to provide useful information such as his size in relation to how big a crate you need etc.

AKC, Kennel Club UK or other global kennel club's, link specific dog breeds with their breed standards which again contains general or ideal traits/characteristics.

A breed standard is very important for show dog purposes, as it offers the blue print by which reputable breeders adhere to as they selectively breed potentially show winning dogs.

However, there has always been the potential risk of inbreeding pedigree dogs. This carries potential associated health problems, within a very small gene pool in order to maintain what are considered to be 'ideal' show winning standard dogs.

This can be problematic in terms of genetic and inherent health problems that have plagued the pedigree dog breeding world for decades.

Subjective interpretation of breed standards by show judges can also have an impact on future selective breeding.

E) IRRESPONSIBLE BREEDING & THE BAD BREEDER

Irresponsible breeding is the main reason for unwanted and sick dogs in the Western world today. When genetic testing is not carried out; the temperament of the parent dogs is not considered. If the puppy is not socialised from as early as birth then as the pup matures to adulthood, the dog may well have problems. If you buy a puppy from an irresponsible breeder, the dog is at risk of health or behavioural problems, or maybe even both, at any time in his life.

F) SIGNS OF A BAD BREEDER
- There is a strong probability that the following will apply:

- No contract
- Nothing in writing about claims they are making. There will probably be no proof of worming, vaccination or veterinary checks.
- No Kennel Club paperwork or the possibility that such paper work is forged
- No certificates of health testing even if they say they have health tested
- Puppies show obvious signs that no adequate socialisation has taken place; such as being fearful, wary, submissive etc
- The puppies show obvious signs of ill health such as bad skin, discharges from the eyes, nose, rear end etc
- The puppy may be quite cheap.
- The puppy will be younger than eight weeks old when it is sold.
- The breeder will ask very few questions about the home you are offering.

A bad breeder is likely to attempt a 'hard sell' pressuring you into making an instant 'you must act now' decision. This can include them telling you other buyers are on their way as you speak or that this will be their only litter for the foreseeable future.

Excuses are made as to why the parents are not present or a dog is present that shows signs of not knowing the puppies and vice versa. A lot of agents for puppy farmers are very good at having answers ready for questions you may ask. But be very wary if they make excuses why you cant see the parents, such as 'my husband/wife has just popped out with them'. Any excuses or refusal to answer questions should have alarm bells ringing as to their validity.

G) ARE BACKYARD BREEDERS A BAD CHOICE?

Backyard breeders should not be confused with the hobby breeder. The hobby breeder is likely to take a proactive interest in the furtherance of the breed including working towards the eradication of inherent health problems.

The backyard breeder may well be a dog lover with one or two dogs. However, the likelihood is they may have no interest in showing, training, dog sports etc. They may also not be members of a breed organisation or respective kennel clubs and they will therefore have little if any knowledge of breed standards. They may have no idea about or interest in health testing.

H) TRAPS TO AVOID

Be aware that selling puppies is big business and unfortunately there are many unscrupulous people out there taking advantage of unsuspecting buyers

- Always be wary of buying off the internet or classified ads
- Always meet the breeder at their home with the litter and mother present. Meeting the mother, or at least the genuine mother of the puppy will generally not be possible if you are dealing with a puppy farm agent.
- Always ask to see the puppy in the whelping environment. If this isn't available, the chances are the litter has been bred and raised in a kennel.
- Avoid buying from a kennel breeder, in other words a dealer selling many different breeds
- Run a mile if a seller suggests meeting at a car park/motorway service station etc
- Avoid pet shop puppies as they have generally been associated with 'puppy farmed' puppies
- Avoid at all costs any puppy you suspect has come from a puppy farm

2) HEALTH TESTS AND TESTING

Health tests are not a Kennel Club or legal requirement for the Labrador, or any other breed. Certainly in the UK, but other authorities may have certain requirements. However, many breeders do believe in using the tests available because they have a strong ethical belief in the care and welfare of the breed. If at all possible, only deal with those breeders who carry out applicable health tests.

A) WHAT IS HEALTH TESTING?

Health testing simply means that the parents or grandparents have been tested for common hereditary diseases. The tests will confirm either a positive or negative result at the time of testing. If several generations have been tested as clear

of the disease, then there is a strong probability of the puppy being clear also, but again this is in no way 100% guaranteed. Certain parental health tests such as vWD with a negative result usually means that the puppies will be clear. Unfortunately other health tests are not as conclusive.

Incidentally, it is possible for a dog to carry the gene for a genetic disease, without it affecting them. However, a predisposition to a disease does not mean your dog has the disease lying dormant or will probably get the disease, it just means statistical incidences of the disease have been noted historically.

Without the tests however, you are relying on luck and the possibility of a puppy that may develop a serious disease that a health test would have indicated. In addition, there is nothing remotely pleasant in seeing the life of a puppy or relatively young dog, cut short because of a horrendous disease.

B) HEREDITARY DISEASES AND THE NEED TO HEALTH TEST

It is very important to find out as much as you can about heredity conditions that are common or have been noted with a significant level of frequency with the breed in question. You will then be able to establish, with proof from the breeder, that the parents have been tested for e.g. Hip Displaysia, Eye conditions or whatever disease the breed has a predisposition for.

Certain breeds are unfortunately afflicted with several. Some of which can be either life threatening or very expensive if you need corrective surgery such as for hip dysplasia. Reputable breeders will genetically health test both parents and only breed a litter if they are clear. This is why it is very important to establish and see proof that health testing has taken place.

Through inadequate, careless breeding practices over the years by unscrupulous breeders/ puppy farms, many breeds have predispositions to inherent diseases as well as temperament problems.

In contrast reputable breeders will carefully select and annually health test parents for such congenital diseases known to affect the breeds. These correct practices not only endeavour to eliminate the disease but ensure that only the dogs with the best temperaments are bred with, again cancelling out potential behavioural problems. Once again, there is no 100% guarantee that carrying out such breeding protocols will completely eliminate the chances, but they will certainly be considerably reduced.

c) Health tests you may come across

Please note, not all diseases and disorders can be reliably health tested:

Common health test reports may include the following terminology:

- OFA, GDC, PENNhip
- Hips /elbows/patellar luxation, craniomandibular, copper toxicosis, congenital hearing disease, craniomandibular osteopathy, all indicated as normal
- CERF eyes indicated as normal
- BAER hearing indicated as normal
- vWD negative; indicating no presence of von Willebrand's Disease.
- Other indicators are Hips Clear, cardiac tested, normal thyroid function
- When interpreting hip scores for example, the report will indicate a set of numbers between 0:0 being perfect and 53:53 being dire.

d) Establishments offering health tests

The Orthopedic Foundation for Animals (OFA) in the United States offers health tests, and reputable breeders will for example have OFA certification having tested their dogs for Hip Dysplasia (HD). Other diseases commonly tested for include; Craniomandibular Osteopathy (CMO), Osteochondritis dessicans (OCD) etc.

http://www.ofa.org/

The Canine Eye Registration Foundation (CERF) offer similar health testing for eye disorders. Eye testing is of particular importance for many gundog breeds.

http://www.tctc.com/~maplerg/cerf-.htm

In addition, you may find the following links useful. This is a selection and you may find many more examples by searching [health testing dogs], or a similar search term. The author is not rec-ommending any in particular. You are therefore advised to do your own research and judge for yourself:

https://www.vetgen.com/

http://www.animalgenetics.us/Canine/Canine_Index.asp

https://www.optigen.com/

https://www.pawprintgenetics.com/

https://www.caninehealthcheck.com/

http://www.akc.org/dog-breeders/bred-with-heart/health-testing-requirements/

http://www.antagene.com/en/antagene/about-us

For information on UK health testing, please access the following links:

http://www.thekennelclub.org.uk/health/

http://www.thekennelclub.org.uk/health/for-breeders/dna-testing-simple-inherited-disorders/

http://www.aht.org.uk/cms-display/genetics_canine.html

http://www.animalgenetics.eu/Canine/canine-index.html

http://www.laboklin.co.uk/laboklin/GeneticDiseases.jsp?catID=DogsGD

https://www.bva.co.uk/Canine-Health-Schemes/Eye-scheme/

e) What you should be aware of when contacting a breeder or other source, regarding health testing

When reading an advert or contacting a breeder for litters, it is very important that it is noted health tests have been carried out.

A major drawback of buying a dog cheaply, whether this is from free ads or rescue centres is that it is unlikely the parents were health tested.

Again, the only exceptions are rescue centres where you will at least not be helping the puppy farms, but probably saving a dogs life.

However, it is equally important that you insist on seeing the actual certified results of applicable health tests for a stud dog used as well as the mother of the litter.

Ideally you want to know that a breeder has tested over several generations all of which have been negative for the disease tested.

There is an obvious cost of having health tests carried out, and certain breeders who only have an eye on profits will be reluctant to incur this cost. However, the cost factor of such tests is negligible when you consider the value this has to the puppy and to you avoiding the heartbreak of seeing a sick puppy as well as costly vet bills.

You should never accept excuses from breeders who insist it is an inherent breed disorder, and nothing can be done about it.

3) FINDING A REPUTABLE LABRADOR BREEDER

Other than the 'where to buy' links and suggestions that follow at the end of the section, you may find the following pointers useful:

As with many things in life, personal word of mouth recommendations are usually the safest way forward.

Other points of contact include:

- Dog shows; You may be able to meet and talk to specific dog breed breeders
- Specific breed clubs/societies; They will probably have details regarding current or future litters. There are some links to these at the end of the book.
- Local professionals such as vets, rescue centres, behaviourists, trainers and training organisations etc.
- Breed enthusiast/hobby breeders who are actually interested in the breed and health testing and not focused on making money are a good choice. These

may advertise in classifieds, but again, always check that the puppies have been health tested.

4) ADVICE ON PURCHASING A WORKING SPORTING/GUNDOG

Professional gun dog trainers occasionally breed litters, if not they are bound to know of excellent sources. You will no doubt be able to find local trainers by doing a Google search for your surrounding area.

In general what you may find when looking for a working dog, is a predominant availability of older puppies of eight or nine months or more. This can be a good option if you wish to bypass the early puppy training stage. An additional advantage is that the older puppy is likely to be partly trained and well behaved.

The surprising thing with older puppies is that they are still very adaptable to training to the extent that you could start again from scratch, going over basic training.

This will not only be good for the puppy as a refresher, but also you as the handler, to ensure that you can be certain that your older puppy is completely trained by you now and as you progress with more advanced training.

However, a disadvantage you may find with an older working puppy is that the close bond that you get when rearing a young puppy will not be as great, but most adult dogs soon bond to their new owners.

In addition you need to be careful that the puppies are not being sold because they have developed certain behaviour problems or have not demonstrated the quality of working ability you require.

Having said that, if the dog has proved to be an excellent worker with lots of potential, then you have taken away the risk associated with buying a puppy that you have no guarantee of their future working ability.

A) WHAT DO THE ABBREVIATIONS ON A WORKING LABRADOR PEDIGREE MEAN?

We will briefly touch upon here what to look for when viewing the pedigree of a working dog.

FTCh indicates Field Trial Champion which is important if you want a puppy from proven working parents.

However, it is recommended that unless you intend to dedicate your leisure time to field trials, a dog with the pedigree showing all FTCh is likely to be too high energy for the average person.

Ch (Champion) and Sh Ch (Show Champion) are likely to have nothing to do with the pedigree including working breeds in the lineage.

Having said that, a lot of HPR pedigrees consist of a mixture of FTCh, Ch and Sh Ch.

5) WHERE TO BUY LABRADOR'S

By now you should be aware that buying a Labrador puppy is not necessarily as simple as stopping in to your local pet store. You need to be very careful about where you buy your puppy to ensure that it will be healthy. In this section, you will find details for finding 'health tested' Labrador puppies for sale from breeders in the U.K. and in the U.S.

Apologies if you are based elsewhere. But please be aware that you simply need to make contact with similar organisations listed here, but for your specific location. Additionally, a Google search for [Health Tested Labrador for sale, [your area/country]], or similar search term, will doubtless provide appropriate results.

PLEASE REMEMBER:

You should not necessarily buy the first Labrador puppy for sale that you come across. You need to do your research and make sure that you are purchasing from a responsible breeder. Again, a responsible Labrador breeder will be careful about selecting healthy breeding stock and they will keep detailed records of their breeding practices. If the breeder does not appear to be experienced with the Labrador breed, or with breeding dogs in general, you should look elsewhere.

Probably, THE most important thing to consider when buying any dog not just a Labrador, is the health of the puppy. The following will give you a lot to think about in terms of choosing a reputable, preferably highly recommended breeder, and consequent health testing etc.

PLEASE NOTE: The following offers as much information as I am aware about pitfalls and potential problems you may encounter with certain breeders. However, I need to add at this point that a Kennel Club certificate does not necessarily guarantee that the dog you have bought is the same as the pedigree suggests. As unbelievable as this may sound, some unscrupulous breeders have been exposed and prosecuted for selling puppies with false KC registered papers. In some cases the puppies have not even been the breed they were supposed to be and at worse, had major health problems or potential physical defects.

Unfortunately in this day and age of scammers and fraudsters, some un-reputable breeders have been known to pass on puppies with falsified papers. You can also do all the checks you like on a breeder that is registered with the KC and has council approval, but your research and investigations should not stop there. The Kennel Club (UK) for example, does have their 'assured breeder scheme', which was set up to protect dog purchases. AKC offers similar assurance. Effectively they list breeders who have been checked and verified by the Kennel Club. You can search this at the link at the end of the paragraph. When you click on a breed, it gives you the following message, that if there is a green tick beside the breeder that 'This Symbol indicates that a breeder has had a successful inspection carried out to standards assessed by the United Kingdom Accreditation Service (UKAS). These standards were formally introduced in January 2013 and only Kennel Club Assured Breeders that have completed a successful visit since that date are issued with a UKAS Certificate'

http://www.thekennelclub.org.uk/services/public/acbr/Default.aspx

However, in addition you may also find the following link enlightening:

http://pedigreedogsexposed.blogspot.co.uk/2013/12/the-discredited-breeder-scheme-kennel.html

Please do research as much as you can. It is a good idea to visit and speak to as many Labrador breeders as possible.

A.) BUYING IN THE U.S.

When it comes to buying puppies in the United States you have two main options; a pet store or an independent breeder. Unfortunately, many pet stores receive their stock from puppy mills. Again, a puppy mill is a breeding facility where dogs are kept in squalid conditions and forced to breed until they are no longer able. They are then ruthlessly disposed of. The puppies that come from puppy mills may be inbred or bred from unhealthy stock which means that they, too are likely to be unhealthy. Buying from a pet store is generally not a good option unless you know exactly where the puppy came from and you can confirm that it is from a reputable breeder.

When you buy a puppy from a reputable breeder you are assured that the breeding stock is in good health. Once again, most reputable breeders put their breeding stock through genetic testing before breeding, to ensure that they are not going to pass on congenital conditions such as hip dysplasia or progressive retinal atrophy. Responsible breeders also know a lot about the breed and can help you to decide whether it is a good choice for you.

The following information is intended to give you a good starting point for researching potential breeders.

PLEASE NOTE: The following, to the best of my knowledge are all good, reputable breeders who at the time of press, where actively health testing the parent dogs. However, I am in no way connected/affiliated to them, nor am I endorsing/recommending anyone in particular. I urge you as always to do a thorough research of all possibilities, consider all options and make your own mind up.

Your decision as to who you buy from may well be based on who is closer to you. However, please check that your chosen breeder regularly health tests the parents of the puppy. You should also ask to see the certified proof of this.

Some Labrador breeders who at the time of press carried out health testing are as follows:

Show & Pet Type Labradors

AKC Marketplace; have a list of registered breeders at the following link:
http://marketplace.akc.org/puppies/labrador-retriever
Wisconsin Labradors
http://www.wisconsinlabradors.com/index.html

Bel Amour Labradors
https://www.belamourlabradors.com/home.html

Prairie Rose Retrievers
http://www.prairieroseretrievers.com/home-.html

Endless Mt. Labradors
https://emlabradors.com/

Mabry Labrador
http://www.mabrylabrador.com/

EverOak Labradors
https://www.everoaklabs.com/home

Daisy Mountain Labs
http://foxredlabradorretrieverpuppies.com/

Idlewild Labradors
http://www.idlewildlabradors.com/

Working Type

Please note, the following are examples of breeders of working type Labradors. If you enquire, you will have to check with them whether or not they currently health test their dogs.

Deep Run Retrievers
http://www.deeprunretrievers.com/puppies.shtml

Southfork Retrievers
http://www.southforkretrievers.com/puppies.php

British Labradors
http://britishlabradors.com/

Loves Labradors
http://loveslabradors.net/

You may also find the following links of interest (however, please do check again that litters or adults dogs have been health tested):

The gundog Breeders site lists Labradors as well as other hunting dogs. It is again important to research possibilities whereby the parents have been health tested.

http://www.gundogbreeders.com/

http://www.gundogbreeders.com/breeders-by-breed/labrador-retriever/

http://www.gundogcentral.com/

https://gundogcentral.com/hunting_dogs_for_sale.php?breedID=22

B.) BUYING IN THE U.K.

Purchasing Labrador puppies in the U.K. is very similar to buying them in the U.S. Always do your research before buying Labrador puppies in the U.K. to ensure that the Labrador puppies for sale have been bred properly. As always, health tested parents are of paramount importance. On the next page you will find a list of breeders with Labrador puppies for sale in the U.K.

AGAIN PLEASE NOTE: The following, to the best of my knowledge are all good, reputable breeders. However, I am in no way connected/affiliated to them, nor am I endorsing/recommending anyone in particular. I urge you as always to do a thorough research of all possibilities, consider all options and make your own mind up.

Show & Pet Type Labradors

Davricanby Labrador Retrievers
http://www.davricanby.co.uk/

Rivermeadow Labradors
http://www.rivermeadowlabradors.co.uk/index.html

Marchstone Labradors
www.marchstonelabradors.co.uk/

Jimjoy Labradors
http://www.jimjoylabradors.co.uk/index.html

Afinmore Labradors
http://www.afinmore.co.uk/

Llanstinan Labradors
www.llanstinanlabradors.co.uk/

Aidens Labradors
http://aidenslabradors.co.uk/

Woodmist Labradors
www.woodmistlabradors.co.uk/

Rowanbrow Labradors
http://www.rowanbrowlabradors.co.uk/about-us

The Kennel Club; Find A Puppy

Do not automatically assume that all litters listed are from health tested parents. It is therefore important that you check this for yourself.

https://www.thekennelclub.org.uk/services/public/findapuppy/Default.aspx?id=Retriever+(Labrador)

Kennel Club Assured Breeders (KCAB)
https://www.thekennelclub.org.uk/services/public/acbr/Default.aspx?breed=Retriever+(Labrador)

Champdogs is a useful site listing most dog breeds. Please access the following link and apply filters applicable to what you are looking for. The most important filter should be 'health tested' only, which are highlighted in red. You can also search for 'show', 'working' or 'duel purpose'.

https://www.champdogs.co.uk/breeds/labrador-retriever

Working Type

Mordor Gundogs
**https://mordorgundogs.com/breeding.
html**

Mekoro Labradors
**http://www.mekorolabradors.co.uk/
index.html**

Camelwood Labradors
**http://www.camelwoodlabradors.co.uk/
our_dogs.htm**

Wylanbriar Labradors
http://www.wylanbriar.com/

Fenway Labradors
http://www.fenwaylabradors.co.uk/

The Gundog Club; lists a number of Labrador breeders, which you may wish to consider.
**http://www.thegundogclub.co.uk/Refer-
ence/Directory/Breeders/labradors.htm**

Champdogs link of breeders and who health test. You should find listed breeders of working and/or dual purpose puppies.

**https://www.champdogs.co.uk/breeds/
labrador-retriever**

**https://www.champdogs.co.uk/breeds/
labrador-retriever/breeders?ht=1&wk=1
&wk=3&tx=&pc=&distance=**

6) MAKING CONTACT WITH A LABRADOR BREEDER

Follow the steps below to choose a reputable breeder:

Visit the website for each breeder, if they have one, and look for important information such as photos of the facilities, the breeder's experience.

Contact each breeder by phone and ask them questions about their experience with breeding and with Labradors specifically. If the breeder is hesitant to answer your questions, or if they do not seem knowledgeable and experienced, move on to the next option

Evaluate the breeder's interest in learning more about you. A reputable breeder will not just sell his puppies to anyone, they should be eager to ask you questions to see if you are a good fit for one of their puppies.

Narrow your list down to two or three breeders that seem to be a good fit and visit the facilities before you make a commitment to buy a puppy.

Ask if it will be possible for a tour of the facilities and look to make sure that the dogs are kept in clean conditions and that they appear to be in good health.

Make sure you see the breeding stock for the puppies that are available to make sure that they are in good health and good specimens of the Labrador breed.

Ask to see the puppies that are available and make sure that they are kept in clean conditions. Remember that the puppies should be kept with the mother until at least 8 weeks old.

Choose the breeder that you feel is the most knowledgeable and experienced, and not just the one that has puppies available. You will also probably get a gut feeling as to whether they are a reputable breeder or not.

Ask about the process for reserving a puppy. You will probably have to leave a deposit by way of a down payment. In addition, ask what the price includes (vaccinations, worming etc).

A reputable breeder will offer some kind of health guarantee on the puppy as well as information about the parents to certify its breeding.

The puppy or litter should be with the mother at the time of viewing, if not, ask why not

Reminder for the type of questions to ask
- How long have they been breeding?
- Ask them to explain the bloodline including strong and weak points
- Ask where the litter was whelped? (it is important from a socialisation point of view that the puppies where raised in a home exposed to many sights and sounds, rather than isolated in a garage/ basement/kennel)
- Ask if genetic health tests were carried out on the parents and ask if it is possible

to see the proof?

- Ask how old the puppies will be when they leave the litter? Be aware that puppies should be at least 8 weeks old before leaving the litter.
- Have the puppies themselves been health checked? Again ask to see the proof.
- Confirm whether the puppies have been wormed, flea treated and possibly initial vaccinations started. If so make a note of the start dates and work out when they are next due, unless of course the breeder provides this information anyway.
- Do they offer a contract and any kind of guarantee?
- Ask if the puppies have been or will be Kennel Club registered
- Have they been micro-chipped?
- Is insurance included?

Questions a reputable breeder may ask you?

They will be interested to know about you and your suitability. This will include them asking questions such as 'have you looked after a dog before'?, 'are you aware of this breeds energy levels and again exercise needs'? etc.

Typical questions a breeder may ask include:

A caring breeder will be keen to know that you will look after and be able to manage the dog. They may therefore ask questions such as the following:

- Why are you interested in this particular breed? (if you haven't already found out warts and all, all there is to know, then a good breeder should be only too willing to fill in the gaps). If you get the feeling that the breeder is trying to put you off the breed, then they may have good reason to believe this breed is probably not for you.
- Have you been a dog owner previously and are therefore aware of generally taking care of them, including training and exercising
- Are you aware of how much time is needed to care for a dog, and do you have this time available on a daily basis? If not will you be making arrangements

for someone to provide this care?

- Do you have local access to parks and safe open fields?
- Do you work full time, in other words are you away from home most of the day. If so, who will look after the dog during this period?
- What is your family status? Single? Married with a young family etc?
- Do you have young children or children regularly visiting you? They will be keen to know that the dog will be treat with respect and consideration. This will also imply that the dog will not be put in a position to possibly attack a child.
- Do you have other pets that the puppy may not have been socialised to?
- What is your accommodation situation? In other words, can you offer a suitable home? What type of accommodation do you live in, house/flat etc? Do you have a reasonably sized garden/yard?
- Have you ensured your house is hazard free and your yard/garden escape proof?

Contracts and guarantees

They will more than likely have a written contract which will probably include the following:

A neuter or spay clause which may insist on this taking place as soon as the puppy reaches the appropriate age; it may include the option of you agreeing to one litter only.

A statement or guarantee by the breeder that they will deal with certain health issues that may arise. A breeder who gives you a word of mouth guarantee that you will never encounter any health problems should be avoided at all costs.

A returns policy is an excellent way of indicating that a breeder is highly responsible and has the puppies best interests at heart. Generally a returns policy affirms that the breeder will take back a dog at any age or under any circumstance.

You should properly read such a contract as it could imply co ownership, which is not advisable. Some people do not like the restriction imposed of having to neuter in case they may wish to have at least one litter later on. The obvious reason for neutering or spaying is to limit the chances of adding to the unwanted dog statistics.

CHAPTER EIGHT:

SELECTING A HEALTHY LABRADOR PUPPY

Once you have located at least one reputable breeder with puppies available, you will need to view the litter to hopefully choose your puppy. Before actually viewing the litter, it is important to observe and take note of the breeders facilities.

Please note: It is important that when viewing a litter of puppies that they are at least 5 or 6 weeks of age, actively moving about on their feet.

1) WHAT TO LOOK FOR WHEN VIEWING A LITTER AND THE BREEDERS FACILITIES

- Do the breeders facilities as well as their home, appear clean, healthy and well maintained?
- Look for signs that the puppies live in the house such as a play pen, toys, food and water dishes, beds etc.
- Ask whether the puppies have started to receive house-training as well as other basic obedience.
- Find out to what extent the puppies have been socialised, with appliances, other animals, people of all ages etc. Do you notice evidence of this?
- Do they or other family members play interactive games with the puppies?
- How often has the breeder handled the puppies per day from the puppies first week of age?
- If the puppies are kennelled outside, is the facility clean (no faeces or stale urine smells), dry, warm, fresh clean water available, chew toys etc?
- Can the breeder offer a back up service if you need to ask questions or get advice?

2) VIEWING A LITTER OF PUPPIES

When initially viewing a litter, taking your children or someone with you can be useful to get different opinions, but try to keep an objective, impartial view yourself. Do not be swayed to pick a puppy for the wrong reasons. If you have the pick of a litter or at least a few, you are bound to be drawn to one in particular. You ideally want a puppy who is friendly and approachable to you. The whole family will of course eventually need to be present when actually choosing a puppy.

If it is possible to spend at least an hour observing the puppies, you will see how they react to their normal surroundings. You are likely to see what they attempt to chew, and what they do when needing to do their toilet business. Again an indication as to whether they have been toilet trained or not. If you can, watch the puppies being fed as well to make sure that they have a healthy appetite. A puppy that does not eat is likely to be sick.

The breeder may admit that the puppies have been contained in a large play area which has sheets of paper or some form of litter, allowing the puppies to toilet where they please. At least you will know that your toilet training will have to start with a similar arrangement, because that is exactly what they will do when they start living with you. If the puppy has been used to that arrangement up until 8 weeks you will have to be patient as it will take time for them to get used to your house-training routine.

The following assumes that you have the pick of the litter or at least more than one puppy. If not, then you may still be able to use most of the guidelines to determine the temperament of the puppy.

For this next part you are advised to have a note book and pen to take down notes of observations.

A) OBSERVING THE LITTER AT A DISTANCE

Firstly observe the litter from a distance without any interaction. Also try to view the pups in a confined area as well as running freely outside and notice if they react differently.

Observe how they interact with each other. Take note of their traits such as ones that are timid, boisterous, domineering etc, as such traits may be an indication of how the puppy may behave when older. Are they generally alert and curious, responding to what is going on around them? The more assertive or bossy types may be more difficult to manage and train, the more easy going ones, less so.

- Notice the overall size of the puppies and whether some are larger than others
- Do they move with any apparent defects, limping, awkward gait etc?
- Do you notice any discharges from their, eyes, nose, anal area etc. The eyes and nose should look bright, clean and clear.
- Do you see any diarrhoea or vomit in the play area?
- Notice whether they run up to you, run away, appear fearful, bark, attempt to play and interact, dominant or bullying of litter mates, appear curious, confident etc.
- Are the puppies active, playful and lively or lethargic because they are ill or maybe they have just been fed?
- Ask whether the breeder has designated certain puppies as show and some as pet quality, and what are their reasons?

B) INTERACTING WITH THE LITTER

After the initial observations you should interact with the puppies

Ideally the puppies mother should be present and should be in good health and confident and friendly towards you, and certainly not hostile or wary. This is a very good indication of what the puppies will be like. Introduce yourself to her first then approach the puppies.

- Sit or kneel down to greet them as they will feel more at ease and more likely to approach you than if you are looming over them. Ideally they should be confident and not shy with you.
- Spend a few minutes engaging with each puppy. Play with a toy to gauge the puppy's activity and try petting him to make sure he doesn't respond with fear or aggression.
- When you first make contact with the puppies, notice which one makes first contact and whether they stay close to you and interact. A 6 to 8 week old puppy will not have had chance to learn any polite etiquette when greeting you. So expect them to gallop over to you, jump up or attempt to chew your hand. This is all quite natural, confident behaviour and certainly not an indication of a future problematic, aggressive dog. A timid, shy, fearful puppy on the other hand may be a sign that insufficient socialisation has taken place. Again this is not the end of the world for a puppy. It just means that his 'rehabilitation' to bring him out of his shell will take longer than the confident puppy.
- Ask the breeders permission if you pick one up and only do so when you are sitting/kneeling close to the ground. Be very careful as some can wriggle and are easily dropped.
- You can usually calm him by gently stroking him along the ridge on the top of his head, between his eyes. You can also try gently massaging his ears, chest or around the jaw where it hinges.

Are they happy to let you handle them or again do they show fear, or attempt to wriggle and bite your hand? They should ideally be happy and relaxed and not wriggle too much. Try and handle all of the puppies and use this time to inspect the puppy. You will notice straight away whether a puppy is familiar with being handled once you attempt to pick one up. If they run away or struggle, then it is likely that this aspect of their socialisation has been neglected.

- Again check their eyes and ears closely for traces of a discharge. The eyes should be clear and bright with no cloudy, opaque appearance. Certainly not inflamed or showing signs of discharge or weeping.
- The nose should look clean and bright, again with no discharge or dry crusty skin.
- The ears should be clean and free from any discharge. The puppy should have good hearing and be responsive and alert to sudden noises, which they may be shocked by, but show no signs of fear.
- There should be no signs of breathing difficulty such as wheezing or unusual panting and certainly no coughing.
- The mid section should show no obvious rib protrusions, tummy or naval swelling.
- Make sure there are no unusual lumps anywhere. Check that their paws look healthy and the pads are free from any cracks. The nails should not appear split and should be trimmed. Take a look in the puppies mouths to see if it is pink and not pale. Being pink is indicative of a healthy mouth.
- The coat should look clean and soft with a pleasant odour. The fur should look groomed and un-matted. If you part the fur, there should be no signs of parasites or black specs indicating parasite faeces.
- The skin should look healthy and be free of flaking, disease or inflamed lesions.
- The anus should not look inflamed or generally unclean. There should be no signs of stained hair possibly indicating a discharge.

C) ASKING QUESTIONS ABOUT THE LITTER

Again a note book and pen will come in handy. Have questions pre-written, for you to then write down the answers.

Has basic obedience taken place? You can quickly check whether the puppy has received any obedience training. Either issue the commands of sit, come, down etc, or ask the breeder to demonstrate these. Again, its not the end of the world if they haven't, but it will be further indication of the good, reputable breeder you ideally want to deal with

Check that the parents have been health tested for hereditary diseases and ask for proof/certification now.

Have the puppies been wormed and vaccinated, if so when, or when will they be?

If you decide to take out insurance, can the breeder provide free temporary cover. Again a reputable breeder will be keen to have their own insurance cover whereas a puppy farm is less likely. You may be able to get free temporary cover anyway from a number of insurers, with no obligation to take out full cover with them.

Can the breeder offer a back up service if you need to ask questions or get advice? Will the breeder, for whatever reason, be prepared to take the puppy back? A lot of breeders actively engage in contracts with written guarantees to confirm their willingness to take back a puppy. Check what the contract implies, as certain breeders impose conditions such as not being permitted to breed from a bitch and so forth.

D) TEMPERAMENT TESTING

Opinions differ as to whether temperament testing a puppy is a reliable indication of what a puppy will be like as an adult. It is up to you whether you wish to proceed with this when you greet the litter. It could be a valuable indication of what the puppy will be like as an adult. However, it could prove to be completely inaccurate.

Within a litter of puppies there will exist many similarities that make each puppy have roughly the same characteristics. However in the same way that children from the same family can have very different temperaments, so too will a litter of puppies. The individual puppies are likely to have different unique genetic combinations to each other. So although they are all likely to look very similar or the same, their personalities are likely to differ to varying degrees.

There are a number of temperament tests that you could perform that indicate whether a puppy is currently of a dominant or more compliant nature.

For example, when you pick up a puppy the more the puppy consistently struggles, bites, vocalises could be an indication that a puppy has a dominant tendency. A normal puppy may struggle initially but calm down and accept the situation. A submissive puppy may not struggle at all, panic and appear fearful or even submissively urinate.

Tossing an object to gauge the puppies reaction has a similar effect. The average puppy will chase, play with, return with the object if you call and allow you to take it. A submissive puppy is characteristically likely to shy away from the game, perhaps showing fear. The dominant puppy is likely to take the object away, perhaps jealously guard it with growls if you attempt to take it back. A puppy with a strong aptitude to retrieve should at least show an interest in going to pick an object up and carrying it, whether they return it to you or not.

Encourage a puppy to come to you, again by kneeling down, clapping your hands and softly calling the puppy. This will again elicit typical displays of dominance, submission or normal behaviour. The dominant puppy will either ignore you or boldly charge at you. A submissive puppy again will either run and hide, or warily approach you, perhaps rolling over onto their side. With normal behaviour the puppy should confidently trot over to you showing no extremes of the other two.

It is debatable whether these behaviours continue into adulthood as a group of puppies may have had limited social contact, but will display either extreme. Shy puppies may be more timid and sensitive and if they remain so to a certain extent will no doubt suit a sensitive, quiet, thoughtful person. A gregarious, loud, brash sort of a person needing a bold guard dog will have an ideal dog in the dominant characteristic. The average person wishing to have an easy going, happy, confident dog would obviously be best suited to the normal, average temperament showing neither extreme.

For the purposes of a Labrador, particularly as a working dog, the normal middle temperament would probably be the best choice. Shyness isn't a big concern as the puppy can easily develop into a very confident adult. A confident dog is ideal.

The shy or dominant puppy may take longer to train. A dominant, independent nature is also not ideal for training, as the dog is less likely to obey commands.

E) HAS ADEQUATE SOCIALISATION TAKEN PLACE?

Socialisation is extremely important during a puppies first 6 months, and equally so in the first 8 weeks. A reputable breeder will ensure the puppy has been exposed to everything going on around the house. This ensures that the puppy has no fear of the similar sights, sounds and smells around your house. Even kennel bred puppies should be exposed to household experiences and therefore brought into the house a number of times per day.

Daily handling should have been started by the breeder and should continue once the puppy comes to your home. The handling should take place by as many different people as possible. Not only members of your family, but strangers also, who are likely to want to greet and pet a new puppy anyway. This handling should always be gentle and never rough. Children especially should be taught how to carefully and respectfully hold, pet and play with the puppy.

Handling should not just take place when a puppy is walking or running about. At the neonatal stage, a puppy is barely able to see, hear or walk. But they can feel and have a developed sense of smell. They are also at a sensitive and impressionable age. So being handled at this stage is very important and can do so much good.

In this respect it is important to ask the breeder in a general sense, how the puppies have been socialised. They should hopefully say that they have been handled throughout their neonatal period. You should also hear that this has happened several times a day, every day, by adults, children and occasional strangers. It is worth asking, how many different people have been involved. As the puppies grow it is important that these interactions have included play time.

Regardless of what you are told, you will soon find out once you handle the puppy yourself. Whilst they are on all fours, gently hold and restrain them. As mentioned previously, they may struggle or wriggle a bit, but if the puppy shows signs of distress at this, they have probably not been handled very much, if at all.

You can also test how much Socialisation a dog has received by how quickly they recover from a sudden noise. Always ask the breeders permission before you attempt this, and explain what you are about to do.

If you clap your hands and a puppy recoils with fear and terror it is likely Socialisation has been relatively nonexistent. You can also test by talking loudly, or make sudden laugh, shouting, crying, hissing, whistle sounds etc. Always have a food treat to hand to tempt the puppy back to you and for reassurance that you are friendly.

You ideally need to be sure that the puppy has been exposed to loud, sudden noises, shouting, screaming, crying, all domestic appliances, loud music, TV etc.

Under socialised dogs who react with fear in this way, as adults can compensate with aggression, which needs correcting with remedial rehabilitation. This usually involves gradually exposing an affected dog to the very thing they fear.

3) QUALITIES TO BE AWARE OF WHEN CHOOSING A WORKING PUPPY

Natural ability and trainability are traits that cannot really be taught, but bred into the dogs from proven generations displaying such traits. 'Pointing' is an obvious example. However, not all dogs are quiet and soft mouthed and hard mouths and vocalising such as whining can be hereditary.

When viewing the litter are the parents relatively placid and easy to handle? It is important that the temperament of the dog is friendly and should certainly never show any kind of aggression to people or other dogs.

Are they relatively slow and steady or live wires? A dog that is too head strong, stubborn and independent is likely to be difficult to train and consequently difficult to control.

4) CHOOSING A HEALTHY LABRADOR PUPPY

Whilst you are spending this time interacting with the puppies, you should be able to gauge which puppy is a good personality match for you. Hopefully the preceding advice will have confirmed which puppy you will choose. Quite often you instinctively choose the puppy you like the look and personality of. If the puppy appears to be physically healthy and does not show any behavioural warning signs such as aggression, excessive fear, or lethargy, then he is probably a good buy.

You may at this stage decide this is the breeder you are happy with, choose your puppy and leave a deposit. If so, then it will be advisable to take care of a few preliminaries before the puppy finally comes to live with you:

Obtain a diet sheet or at least information regarding the diet the puppy has been weaned on and will be eating once he comes home with you. You will then need to check your local pet suppliers, unless the breeder can recommend one, to ensure you will be able to have this ready for the puppies arrival.

If possible visit the puppy as often as you can so that they get used to you as a familiar person. Check to see if the breeder will allow you to leave an old blanket, 'vetbed' or other bedding that the puppy and litter mates can personalise. This will be comforting for the puppy as it will have the scent of his mother and litter mates when he comes to live with you.

It is also very important to check the pups inoculation status. In other words has the puppy received any vaccination jabs as yet? If not then you need to contact your vet, giving the pups date of birth and to then start the course of vaccinations as directed as soon as possible after you take ownership.

Ask the breeder about transferring Kennel Club ownership. If they haven't already done this, contact the Kennel Club and ask for the relevant forms to fill in and send them off.

5) NAMING YOUR LABRADOR PUPPY

Once you have finally chosen the puppy you want, now will be a good time to decide on his name. You can then ask the breeder if they can start calling him by that name. Don't worry if this is not possible as dogs quickly get used to their name. This even applies to rescue dogs that already have a name, they soon get used to the new one. You probably already have ideas yourself, but if not, please make the name short and sweet. Something like, Daisy, Tess, Max or a name that relates to his appearance such as Patch.

Naming a dog is usually based on personal choice, but some names are more suitable than others. Short names of no more than two syllables make it easy to use when calling them. Be aware however that some names may sound similar to a cue/command word e.g. 'Stay' (similar to May, Jay, Jane etc) 'Sit' (similar to Brittney or Brit, Kittie or Kit, Fitz etc). It is not a big problem, but you do not want to confuse your dog unnecessarily. It is also important to never use his name for anything negative or your dog will try his hardest not to respond when he hears it.

6) Leaving his mother and litter mates

This is likely to be an anxious, confusing time and will not be an easy transition for a puppy used to living with his mother and litter-mates, to then be suddenly separated without any warning. Which is why it is important to make this easier by providing him with familiar objects or scents whilst still with the litter.

Once he comes to live with you, another useful product that you may wish to consider, is known as DAP (Dog Appeasing Pheromone). DAP is a synthetic product based on the natural Pheromone the bitch gives off during birth which acts as a comforter to the pups. It is also effective for older dogs, again acting to comfort them and alleviate the stress of a new situation. These or similar devices usually plug into an electrical socket and diffuse the chemical in a similar way to an air freshener. If you use one, try and plug this in a day or so before the puppy arrives. Choose a part of the house where the puppy will sleep or spend most of their time resting. Pheromone is also useful for dogs that get anxious of certain events such as car journeys and if you can get this in spray form it is worth a try.

Chapter Nine:

Necessary Supplies and Equipment

In this chapter you will learn the basics about making a home for your Labrador including tips for setting up his crate, other habitat requirements as well as an essential shopping list of all the initial supplies and basic accessories you will need.

1.) Habitat Requirements for Labradors

a) Should you keep your Labrador in an outside kennel?

Opinions differ as to whether to keep your dog in your house or outside in a purpose built kennel/compound. Some people do one or the other or a combination of both. Traditionally many Gundog handlers believed it essential to house Gundogs in an outside kennel. The argument is that the dog will be happier to see you, keener to work and to please you during training. Conversely the house dog who has seen you a lot more during the day and has perhaps become bored is likely to be less keen and enthusiastic. If the dog in question is naturally double coated i.e. soft downy under layer and thicker, courser top layer, living in an outside kennel is a feasible option. The Labrador has a relatively thick double coat. In this respect he could technically thrive outside, provided they were in a good, well insulated kennel.

If the dog predominantly lives as part of the household there will certainly be a greater bond between handler and dog. My personal preference is that the dog should ideally live as part of the family, but with the option of an outside kennel on the odd occasion that it may be needed. It will certainly be useful to train him, get him used to both situations, for the following reasons:

- If you go away on holiday, it will be less traumatic if the dog has been used to spending some time in kennels at some point.
- You may have to vacate the house for major building work etc, making it unsafe or impractical for the dog to be in the house.
- You may have a house party again making it unsafe and perhaps stressful for the dog to be in the house
- The dogs are in fresh air which is considered healthier than a stuffy, centrally heated house.

2.) Necessary Supplies and Equipment

A number of the following items are mentioned in the chapter 'What to know before you buy'. However, we will now go into more detail. There are extra items, not listed here, that will be useful to help with training which will be covered in the training section, such as training dummies, whistles etc. For now however, the following are the basic items you should ideally have, to help care for him on a daily basis.

IMPORTANT: Make sure you have all the equipment and accessories needed BEFORE the puppy arrives. Do not leave everything up until the last minute, adding unnecessary stress to your life.

a) Checklist for initial supplies and equipment

- Food and water bowl
- Puppy food and treats
- Suitable size dog bed with bedding
- Puppy size collar or harness and lead
- Basic grooming equipment
- Assortment of soft toys and chew toys
- Flea treatment and wormer if the puppy has not recently received these. (Again these are covered in more detail in the grooming section and the section on parasites) Also ask your vet to recommend flea and worm treatments. Although these may seem more expensive than pet store brands, they are usually more effective. They can also advise you on a plan of treatment, which usually depends on the size and weight of the dog and dosage per kilogram etc
- First aid kit
- Poop bags
- Sprays and deodorizers
- Stair/doorway baby gate
- Pet insurance
- Canine toothbrush and toothpaste (not immediately essential, but good to have on hand to use within the first 2 weeks or so. This is covered in more detail in the grooming section. However, your local pet supply will no doubt be able to advise you on suitable products to buy to get you started)
- Crate (optional)
- Play pen (optional). Start by looking at items available at your local pet supply.

b) Initial supplies

You will undoubtedly be busy spending as much time as possible with your new puppy when he first comes home, so make sure you have prepared all the items he will need for his arrival

Essential shopping list

You will be looking at one off items such as a crate and ongoing expenses such as food and pet insurance. The following will offer details from the previous list of essentials to get you going. Most towns and cities have a good pet store where you should be able to get most if not all items needed. I personally would get your initial supply, certainly food, from the local pet store before you look at buying perhaps the same items cheaper online.

Bowls for food and water

Avoid plastic as these can easily scratch and harbour bacteria. Tough wearing stainless steel are considered the best choice as it is easy to clean and again does not harbour bacteria. However, even though ceramic has the risk of breakages they are a far healthier option to plastic. The weight of ceramic also makes it more difficult to overturn. It is possible to get nonslip stainless steel dishes, which seem like a good idea. Cheaper versions do seem to have a removable rubber ring, that although may not be as risky as plastic, still has the potential to harbour bacteria if not regularly cleaned. I personally prefer the dishes that have their own stand, elevated versions are easier for the dog to eat and drink. They are often recommended for dogs such as Whippets and Greyhounds who are at risk of gastric torsion.

Food

You should have been given a diet sheet or at least the information from the breeder with the type of food the puppy has been living on. Stick to that diet initially as changing the diet is likely to cause stomach upsets with the puppy.

Treats

Treats will be an important addition as it is advisable to use these for any positive reinforcement training, including early toilet training. Again the breeder may have been offering treats, but if not I suggest asking the advice of you local store as to a good quality food treat that they supply. Certainly do not be tempted with the cheapest you can find. However, my own preference is to make them yourself. It is easy to buy a block or cheese or corned beef for example. Cut them into small cubes of no more than 1 cm square, spread them on a tray and freeze. Once frozen you can then put them in a freezer bag and take out a handful or so for a training session. You could also search the internet or Youtube for [homemade dog treats] to get more ideas. Again, treats are advisable as a training aid, so it is likely you will be using a lot initially. Try to ensure that as well as being nutritious, the treats help to exercise gums and clean the teeth.

Suitable size dog bed with bedding

A soft donut type bed is a good idea, for him to snuggle into. Many breeders and dog owners also recommend a 'vetbed' type product for possible accidents. You don't have to buy the most expensive or luxurious, but make sure it is a reasonably good quality that will withstand regular washes. Washing the bedding can be done once a month or sooner depending on the extent that the puppy is bringing dirt in on its coat. Again go with recommendations from pet stores but it is advisable to not get a dog bed much larger than half their eventual size. You

will then need to purchase another suitable for their adult size in several months time

Again, there are many more choices from hard plastic bucket types to all soft padded base and sides. It is probably more important the choice of bedding, whether you use an old blanket or duvet or again, buy sheets of 'Vetbed', or similar product. When you are house-training your puppy it is certainly best to use an old blanket or a towel, just in case your puppy has an accident. Once your puppy is fully trained, however, you can upgrade to a plush dog bed or a thicker blanket that will be more comfortable. Many people choose to use a temporary box whether cardboard or otherwise and then a proper bed when they are nearing their full grown size in a few months time. The other consideration with a choice of bed is the issue of the puppy chewing anything and everything. In this respect beanbags, foam and wicker baskets can potentially be destroyed in no time. If you opt for a crate, to make it more comfortable, you should line it with a soft blanket or a plush dog bed. You may also wish to purchase a specific crate mat, many of which are water and chew proof.

In addition, having a relatively thick double coat, do not be surprised if he decides to sleep or rest on a cold hard floor. It may look uncomfortable to you, but this will be particularly desirable for him when he wishes to cool off during warm weather or when the heating in your accommodation becomes too much.

Lead and collar

A specific puppy lead and collar is recommended initially. But these do not have to be of a high quality or expensive. A young puppy is hardly likely to have the strength to break the cheapest collar or leash. But remember that as they grow you will have to replace them for their adult size. Flat collars are obviously better than traditional choke chains which can cause damage to the neck and throat whilst an over exuberant puppy is first getting used to them. Flat collars can be either leather or nylon webbing and preferably the wider the better again to alleviate any potential force to the throat area. Traditional Whippet collars are often recommended for young puppies as they are much wider and more comfortable than standard flat collars.

Depending on the law for your area, ID tags with your name and address may be a legal requirement, whereby this should be clearly displayed and attached to the collar if the dog is taken into a public place.

Grooming

The grooming requirements for a young puppy are likely to be different to that of an adult dog. All puppies have relatively soft coats and so a soft brush or similar will be sufficient initially. Nail clipping is also something that many dogs do not like, so getting them used to this as early as possible is highly recommended. This again will be covered in the chapter on grooming. However, as a rule, only the very tip of the nail should be taken off, if necessary. It is important that you know how to do this, as it is easy to cut the 'quick' of the nail and make it bleed.

Grooming Supplies

You will find more specific, detailed information in the chapter on grooming. However, for now the following will give you some indication as to what you will need. Grooming a Labrador is simply a matter of a quick brush once or twice per week. The grooming tools you are likely to need to brush and bathe your Labrador at home include:

- Bristle brush
- Pin brush
- Slicker brush
- Medium toothed comb
- Shampoo and conditioner
- Tooth brush and toothpaste
- Nail clippers
- Ear drops
- Cotton wool
- Dry towel
- Hair drier
- Optional flea comb
- Optional grooming table

Some people also like to use make use of the following:

- rubber curry comb
- Hound glove
- Rubber mitt

- Trigger spray bottle

Toys

These include toys that you interact with your dog, such as for retrieving, tug toys etc, Kong type toys to stuff with food for added interest, general chew toys and puzzle toys offering mental stimulation.

Chew toys

Chewing is an important and natural activity for dogs at any age and serves a number of very useful purposes. For the young puppy, chewing can relieve the discomfort of teething. At any age the act of chewing releases endorphins, which in turn has a calming effect. Dogs will also chew to cope with boredom or frustration, as well as symptoms associated with separation anxiety. With a wide variety of chew toys it is a very important alternative to floss teeth and exercise gums in the absence of raw meaty bones. They also hopefully provide a distraction and an alternative if you accidentally leave shoes lying around that you would prefer to keep intact. More seriously they provide an alternative to chewing electrical cables which can obviously be dangerous, potentially causing a fire risk, and fatal to the dog if the cables are live. Different dogs, like different toys, so your best bet is to buy several different kinds and let your dog choose which ones he likes best.

First aid kit

It is advisable to familiarise yourself with general first aid awareness and in some cases this may be necessary to save your dogs life. First aid kits are obviously useful for anything that does not require veterinary attention. You can of course make up a first aid kit yourself. I would however, recommend buying one from your local pet supply initially.

Poop bags

Consideration for pedestrians and other dog owners means that any faeces needs to be picked up and properly disposed of. Many local authorities insist on this and non-compliance can lead to a sizeable fine. You can buy disposable poop bags, but do consider cheaper options such as disposable nappy bags for babies or other bags, which are biodegradable.

Sprays and deodourizers

Accidents can and will happen but make sure that the product you use is safe for a dog to be exposed to. A good natural alternative spray cleaner/deodourizer is vinegar. Although obviously not a cleaning agent, an anti chew spray can be effective in keeping a puppy away from items that they may find attractive to chew, but are difficult or impractical to remove from a room, such as part of a wooden chair or other furniture.

Stair/doorway baby gate

Simply restricting your puppy access to a room or part of the house is far easier than trying to train him to keep out. The foot of a stairway is an obvious area that could be hazardous for a puppy to climb. Baby gates are also useful if you need to keep the puppy temporarily confined to one room. They also enable the puppy to see what is going on, rather than having the door shut. This will not make the puppy feel so isolated.

Pet insurance

If you are debating whether it is worth taking out insurance I would at least seriously consider it whilst the puppy is relatively young. There is no easy option with pet insurance and it really is a question of researching what cover your dog gets for the price you pay. Local insurance companies are a good place to start as are internet comparison sites, as well as recommendations from friends or your vet. Again, insurance is also covered in the chapter 'What to know before you buy'.

Crate

A crate basically offers a dog a den for them to rest in, safe confinement when travelling by car and a safe place for them to reside when you cannot supervise them. If you use it correctly your dog will not view time spent in the crate as punishment and there is no reason to believe that keeping your dog in a crate for short periods of time is cruel. If you use the crate properly while training your Labrador he will come to view it as a place to call his own. He will soon see it as place where he can

go to take a nap or to get some time to himself if he wants it. This of course assumes that you leave the door open or remove it. Covering the crate is also a good idea as it makes it more dark and secluded, which many dogs like.

When selecting a crate for your Labrador, size is very important. For the purpose of house training, you want to make sure that the crate is not too big. It should be just large enough for your puppy to stand, sit, lie down, and turn around comfortably. Dogs have a natural aversion to soiling their dens. If your puppy's crate is only large enough for him to sleep in, it will be more effective as a house-training tool. When your puppy grows up you can upgrade to a larger crate. As crates can be expensive, you may wish to choose one that will be suitable for the size they will be as an adult.

Puppy pen

Once again a puppy pen is a great idea to give them freedom to romp but to also stay out of harm's way. These can be set up indoors or outside in the garden/yard. Your local pet supply should have examples to give you an idea of the size and price.

CHAPTER TEN:

PREPARING FOR THE ARRIVAL

This chapter includes details to help you make your house and garden safe for your puppy or adult dogs arrival. It also provides advice about setting up a crate and establishing house rules. In the following pages, you will find some important steps to take in dog proofing your home:

1.) DOG–PROOFING YOUR HOME

Please note, the following will make a number of references to 'puppy proofing', but is intended to indicate both adults and puppies.

Your Labrador will want to explore every nook and cranny of his new home. Part of that process involves his teeth. Keep all items that are valuable or dangerous away from him. This particularly includes electrical cables that may be live and therefore risking an electric shock and at worse a fatality. Puppies will not see the value or the danger, so please be aware that it is not your Labrador's fault if something gets chewed. Never use harsh corrections. Instead use a firm "No" to indicate your disapproval. However, this needs to take place the moment it happens, otherwise your dog will be left confused as to what you are unhappy about. Then simply replace the item with a chew-able dog toy.

Anywhere within your home that your Labrador is allowed to wander needs to be proofed. This is similar to baby proofing your home, and requires you to go down on hands and knees and see what dangers lurk at adult or puppy eye level.

The whole point of this is to get you to think about any potential hazards for your Labrador. Remember, they are relying on you as their guardian, in much the same way as a child.

A) PREPARING THE HOUSE

Again, it is very important to keep a young puppy safe from potential dangers. Your dog or puppy will be naturally curious about their new surroundings and will want to explore. You literally need to put yourself in your dogs shoes, getting down on your hands and knees and go through every room to see potential hazards from their vantage point. Plan for restricted areas including staircases, and consider baby gates as it is easy to forget to close doors.

The following presents you with a checklist of possible hazards in and around the house:

- Prevent your Labrador from jumping up on any unstable objects such as bookcases.
- Do not allow your Labrador access to high decks or ledges, balconies, open windows, or staircases. Instead use baby gates, baby plastic fencing and therefore prevent accidents from happening.
- Keep your doors securely shut and again prevent a potential accident.
- Never slam doors with a Labrador puppy in the house. Use doorstops to make sure that the wind does not slam a door in your Labrador's face.
- Clear glass doors also pose a danger since your Labrador may not see them and run right into one. Use a screen door.
- Make sure any live 'chewable' electrical cables are safely out of reach, either tied up high enough or by cordoning off risky areas
- Fit child locks on any ground level cupboards containing harmful chemicals
- Check that any 'chewable' items shoes etc are out of reach
- If you have an open fire make sure you again restrict access and/or have a fire screen in place
- Be aware of any furniture or furnishing that contains anything toxic, paint or otherwise that a puppy can easily chew and ingest.
- Check for toxic plants, medicines, sharp objects etc.

Potential hazards will include the following:

Electrical cables

A dog and young puppy in particular should not have access to any electrical cables that can be easily chewed. This can obviously lead to a fatality if the cable is live. It can also create a potential fire hazard if a cable is not live, but is chewed through sufficiently to leave internal wiring exposed. If possible keep all cables out of reach, if not, enclose cables with a cable tidy or cable cover. In the case of areas where many cables are gathered, simply prevent access by cordoning off the area. I would not personally want to risk merely using anti chew sprays, which can be used as a general deterrent to a certain extent.

Ornaments

You will obviously not wish to have valuable vases broken, but fragments can retain sharp edges and if mouthed by a puppy could easily cut their mouth or small pieces swallowed. Ornaments should therefore be placed out of reach.

Cupboards

The main hazards here are cupboards at floor level containing chemicals or medications, or glass bottles that can fall out and break if a puppy decides to climb in and explore. But care should also be exercised with similar cupboards higher up which could also contain medications or harmful chemicals that could easily fall out. Your safest option is to fit childproof locks and the instruction to other family members that everyone who needs to access a cupboard, locks it afterwards.

Rubbish/garbage bins

There is no point in attempting to teach a dog to stay out of rubbish bins. If they can find a way in they will do. It is far safer and more practical, if bins are at ground level, to use bins that are either lockable, or fitted with mechanisms, which make the lid difficult if not impossible for the dog to open.

Dog Toilet

This refers to a toileting area that your dog has to use inside your accommodation. In particular, this may be necessary if you live in an apartment where normal house/toilet training is not practical. There is a large choice of commercial dog toilets which you may wish to consider by doing a simple Google search such as [toilet for dogs]. Alternatively, have a dedicated corner preferably on a tiled floor that can easily be cleaned. As with any house-training, a puppy or dog will need to be taught that this is a permissible area to relieve themselves. Hopefully, this will be for emergencies only and they will do all of their toilet business when you take them for a walk, which is another good reason to regularly take them for walks, or employ someone to do this.

House toilet

It is probably best to restrict access here and simply keep the door closed at all times. The main hazard is again the possibility that your dog will get access to cleaning chemicals and may even attempt to drink out of the toilet bowl. At the very least if they accidentally gain access, then get into the habit of keeping the toilet seat down and any chemicals out of reach, preferably locked in a suitable cupboard.

Natural fuel/Gas or electrical fires

Regardless of the type of fire used, make use of a suitable fire-guard and particularly with electric fires ensure that there are no cables exposed. Some dogs will want to get as close as possible to a fire and in the case of a log fire, can easily become a burns victim if a log should fall out.

Dog bed

You may have a dedicated dog bed spot, but will still find that your dog likes to lay elsewhere in a room or part of your home. In this respect you may wish to set up beds or bedding in favourite spots. Wherever these sleeping areas are, try to ensure that they are draught free and that they will not be disturbed if people are walking past or opening doors onto them.

Water and food bowls

Most people will locate these in the kitchen, but please make sure the dog has a regular supply of clean fresh water. Also, be aware that in winter when you have the heating on and in hot weather, they will drink much more. This is also likely to affect the regularity of them needing to relieve themselves.

Doors and gaps

These are more considerations when you initially assess your home for hazards. You may need to restrict access to certain rooms and should therefore be vigilant that the doors to those rooms are kept closed. There may also be parts of the room where they do have access, which you also wish to prevent access. This could be gaps in between or behind items of furniture or appliances, which should be blocked off to avoid the dog becoming trapped, or them finding things to chew.

Full-length glass doors and windows

The main hazard in this case is that your dog runs straight into it. Other than boarding the lower part up the only other thing you can do is put stickers on the glass or attach strips of coloured tape across.

Letter box

Chewing is again the issue here if post or newspapers drop through the letter box onto the mat for your dog to find. Simply fit a specific wire basket to catch anything coming through the door.

Stair gate

This effectively restricts their access to dangerous areas or any rooms they need to be restricted from entering. Obviously the top of a stair case is relatively high. As you can imagine, a young puppy climbing up such a stair case, could easily fall down and have a serious accident. A locked stair gate would hopefully prevent this.

Houseplants

Houseplants could be a tempting plaything for any dog who wishes to dig in the soil or attempt to chew a poisonous plant. They can be easily knocked over on the floor and you may be tempted to sit these on a decorative plinth out of reach. Again, they may be out of reach but could be easily knocked to an extent that the pot falls and potentially injures the dog. You may therefore wish to consider keeping these in a restricted access area.

B) A SAFE YARD/GARDEN

The same consideration you give for preparing your home should be given to potential hazards in the garden.

Fences need to be high enough, around 6ft, more so as the puppy gets older, when they may be tempted and able to jump over. There should be no gaps in fences or hedges which a small puppy can easily crawl through. Make sure the gap between a gate and ground level isn't large enough for a puppy to escape.

Ponds should have a surround to keep the puppy out and or covered with wire meshing.

Make sure no garden chemicals, sharp tools etc, are accessible and keep these locked away in your shed.

Ensure your garden does not contain any plants poisonous to dogs.

The garden gate

Most importantly, this needs to be secure and kept locked so a puppy or adult dog cannot simply walk out, potentially onto a busy road. As a matter of routine, check that the gate is locked before you let your dog out. Again, check that there are no gaps where a puppy can squeeze through or wriggle under. As well as the fence, this also needs to be high enough, therefore preventing an older puppy or adult dog from jumping over.

Electrical cables

Similarly to inside your house, these should again be enclosed or kept out of reach to avoid any chewing and potential fatalities.

Ponds and/or swimming pools

Ideally access should be prevented using some form of boundary or sturdy wire mesh covering the pond. If you do not wish to do this, then always supervise especially a young puppy. Older dogs may not be as much of a risk as they will find it easier to climb out of a pond if they fall in, but may not be able to do so with some swimming pools.

Dog toilet area

If say for example you have a bitch and a lawn, you may wish to train her to urinate in a specific area, therefore keeping her off the lawn. Bitches generally leave bleach like patches all over a lawn in places they have urinated. You could therefore encourage the use of a purpose made dog toilet similar to those used for apartments/flats.

Plants

Plants that are poisonous to dogs should be removed. Most if not all dogs like to eat grass and some dogs instinctively know what they can and can't eat. Others will not discriminate and will eat anything. "Plants Potentially Poisonous to Pets."

Is also listed in the resources section at the end of the book. The link is as follows:

http://www.humanesociety.org/assets/ pdfs/pets/poisonous_plants.pdf

Sheds or storage areas

Storage areas have the same function as cupboards and should be used to keep hazardous chemicals and sharp tools and garden implements out of reach. Sheds and storage areas should therefore be locked. Also get into the habit of closing doors before you leave sheds or storage areas. Any power tools should not be operated with the dog running loose in the garden. Keep your dog inside the house until you have finished cutting the grass or trimming the hedge for example.

Children's play area

It is advisable to keep access restricted here as there may be children's toys lying around that you do not wish destroying. Many people use bark chipping's for play areas, and these will be a temptation for a puppy to chew and ingest, some contain harmful chemicals. There is also the risk that your dog may start using the area as a toilet and consequently your children would be in contact with urine or faeces.

Garden mulch

Always be mindful of what you are using as a mulch, as again if it is possible, your dog will find it. Always use untreated bark chipping's and avoid mulches such as cocoa shells, which may still contain residues of cocoa, which could result in a fatality if ingested. Large pebbles are often recommended to prevent dogs from attempting to walk on flowerbeds, as they find it uncomfortable to walk on. They also provide a very useful mulch.

Chemicals

You should carefully read the instructions for chemical sprays for plants, lawn treatments, pest killers such as slug/snail pellets etc, in relation to exposing your dog.

Fence or other boundary

It is highly advisable to ensure the garden is properly secured with a suitable fence or wall that is high enough (6 feet as a minimum but higher for more determined dogs) to discourage them from jumping over. Even if the garden has a natural hedge, dogs can easily find their way through. If there is any possibility of the dog digging under the fence it may be necessary to dig a trench and sink plastic coated wire fencing at least a foot deep to prevent them digging under. A possible alternative is to lay a concrete path or paving slabs around the edge.

Digging area

Digging is usually a symptom of boredom and can be problematic if a dog chooses to excavate your prized flower beds or even sections of lawn. Digging can also result if a dog wishes to burying something. Sandboxes or a dedicated digging area can be created using a timber board box approximate dimensions of 2ft x 3ft x 6 inches deep or larger if your garden will take it. Once you create a box frame, simply dig a pit 6 to 12 inches deep and fill with either sand or compacted soil.

Shaded area

You may already have a garden table and chairs with an umbrella which a dog will undoubtedly make use of in hot weather when they need to cool off. Trees or large shrubs also offer useful shaded spots. Either way, try and make sure that there are several options available even if you have to create a roofed canopy especially for that purpose. Also be aware that some dogs will lay in the sun longer than is healthy for them which could lead to sun or heat stroke. If there is a risk of this, encourage them to use the shaded areas or as a last resort take them back into the house, particularly when the day is at its hottest. It is often far cooler inside a double glazed house on a hot day, particularly if you can leave windows open at either end to create a draft. You may also wish to make use of a 'magnetic screen' that allows you to leave the back door ajar, but keeps flies and other insects out.

Faeces and urine

Once you start toilet training your dog, you may wish to teach your dog to defecate in a specific area. But most people do not mind as long as it is outside of the house. Either way, as a matter of routine, each day you should check your garden, particularly pathways and other areas regularly used and pick up any faeces. As well as being a nuisance to have to clean it off your shoes if you tread in any, it can also be a health risk. You will also find that you have to disinfect pathways, otherwise you will soon notice a strong stale urine smell. If there is a possibility that your dog will lick any concrete areas, you may be safer spraying vinegar. Otherwise, spraying a diluted disinfectant will kill the smell and keep the area healthy. Most local authorities accept dog faeces as part of their regular bin collections, if not consider the following:

Unless your water authority forbids it, flushing faeces down your own toilet is an option

You may wish to compost it separately if you are not keen on mixing it with other compost you may have. Over time provided it is fully aerated it naturally decomposes and loses its smell.

Specific containers 'dog loo' can be buried in the garden and the faeces added along with an activator which breaks the faeces down.

There are worms that feed specifically on animal waste including Tiger Worms Eisenia fetida also known as "Manure Worms". If you are interested in creating a wormery for the purpose of composting dog faeces, check with a local wormery supplier for suitability and advice.

Plant containers

Provided the plants are non-toxic to dogs, be aware that plastic tubs may be subjected to chewing. Some dogs may not bother the tub or the contents. But if chewing does become an issue, consider stone, terracotta or metal. If male dogs are likely to urinate on any potted plants it may be a good idea to buy tall pots or keep these on a raised plinth that will not be easily knocked over if bumped.

2) TOXINS TO BE AWARE OF IN YOUR HOME

Again, you'll need to watch your Labrador puppy very carefully for the first few months to make sure that he does not get into harm's way. If the kitchen is made into the puppy's sleeping area,

make sure that all cleaning supplies are removed, locked away or placed elsewhere. Labrador pups are curious, and it can take as little as a few minutes for your puppy to get into a poisonous cleaning product.

Possible toxins to be aware of may include the following:

Insecticides; Human medications; Household cleaning products; Foods that we consume that have a toxic effect on dogs such as grapes and chocolates; Rodenticides; Plants; Garden and pool products; Glass, razors, bathroom products; Coins, small batteries and other small objects that may easily be ingested

A) CHECKING FOR TOXINS IN PUPPY TOYS

Before purchasing toys for your Labrador to play with, you'll need to check that they are lead free and cadmium free.

Dog toys that contain DEHP- bis (2-ethylhexl) phthalate have been found to have a huge effect on the reproductive system of rats, even at very low doses.

3) ESTABLISHING RULES BEFORE YOU PUPPIES ARRIVAL

If you have no intention of applying strict or specific house rules, then the following will not concern you too much. If you are particular where your dog will be allowed to venture, or if you are not sure either way, hopefully you this will give you a few things to think about.

One of the biggest, if not the biggest problem with 'behaviour issues' around the house is a lack of consistent 'house rules'. As with any training the puppy needs to be taught what they can and cannot do and where they can and cannot go. It is therefore advisable to draw up a list of do's and don'ts and make sure that all members of the family stick to this. Dogs are like people in that they like to know where they stand and if things keep changing it is bound to confuse them and leave them frustrated. It is not fair on him when you allow him on the sofa one day but not the next, or let him jump up at you, but shout at him when he does the same to a visitor.

Draw up a list of house rules and make sure everyone sticks to it

The list should include who will be responsible for the dogs care including: feeding, exercise, playtime, house-training, obedience training. Importantly, never let him be without fresh clean water, so everyone needs to check their bowl regularly. Try and be consistent with times that you feed, exercise, play games, train, sleep time etc.

Some people are OK with the dog using the sofa, others are not. It's not the end of the world but again you all have to agree to an all or nothing situation. Couches and other furniture are often the focus of problems where a dog is initially allowed to lie on the couch. He may then object or become hostile when there are attempts to move him. If you have no objection to him lying on the couch with you, it may still be worth training him to only expect this when invited. This will ensure that if problems arise you can soon ask him to leave the couch.

Toilet training is particularly important anyway, but again all family members need to know and follow the routine. Toilet training and crate training will be covered in detail in the chapters that follow.

Be consistent with restricted areas and where they can access (usually this is where ever you spend most time such as the kitchen or lounge). Of course the puppies safety is the most important in terms of keeping him away from potential hazards. In this respect, think about any rooms that you do not wish your dog to enter. House training is often made easier if he is restricted to a limited number of rooms that he could potentially do his toilet business in.

As part of toilet training, and restricted access, many people like to utilise puppy pens. This also allows you to keep the puppy safe when you are not available to supervise them.

Decide whether you wish to crate train the puppy. It will be much fairer on the puppy to start sooner rather than later when the puppy will have perhaps become used to more freedom.

Feeding food at the table encourages begging, and although it is hard to ignore his sad pleadings it is often better to ignore begging. But again, there has to be consistency from all family members.

Similarly, cooking or preparing food can illicit the same problem, so some people prefer to train their dogs to accept it when you are preparing food in the kitchen, they are not permitted in and the door will be closed.

This should go without saying, but reward based, positive reinforcement training involves no shouting or harsh physical punishments. This should not be confined to training sessions but should occur all the time.

Once you have puppy proofed the house, leaving nothing dangerous, poisonous or valuable for the puppy or adult dog to have contact with, everyone should ensure that this is maintained. Therefore nothing should be left around for the puppy to chew or eat.

4) WHERE WILL YOUR DOG SLEEP?

Deciding where your puppy will sleep is important. Many people choose to allow their dog on the bed, which is fine. However, it's important to understand separation anxiety if you sleep with your dog, and are allowing him to be with you at all times. Separation anxiety is caused by over-attachment, and sleeping in your bed can be part of the reason for that.

Again this is a decision that you need to decide on and stick to. Many people opt to 'eventually' keep the dog in the kitchen or another room over night. Many also opt to crate train their puppies from day one. Please again remember that this is not punishment and most dogs like their own space. What you may have to do however, is to allow the puppy to be in their crate in or near where you sleep. You should then aim to gradually move the crate closer to where you eventually intend them to sleep. The kitchen is also generally used because most are tiled and therefore easier to clean if any 'toilet accidents' occur over night. The kitchen is also usually the immediate door out into the garden, where you should be encouraging him to do his toilet business during their toilet training and thereafter.

A) THE FIRST NIGHT

On the first night when you bring your puppy home, I suggest that you don't leave him alone.

Imagine how he would feel after being in the warmth of his nesting area with his mother and siblings to be then completely alone. So make a conscious decision to stay in the room where your puppy will be sleeping for a couple of nights. You can also invest in a very specific puppy comforter meant for the first few nights in a new home, they can be warmed in the microwave and some even have heartbeats.

If you have decided that your puppy is going to be eventually sleeping alone, then it's not a good idea to allow him to sleep on you. It would be much better to lie on the couch and have him on the ground beside you. That way you can offer a comforting hand when needed but he will be learning to leave behind the warmth of bodies at bedtime. You can introduce the crate right at the beginning if you prefer, or wait until that first couple of nights are over. Eventually you will be able to leave a happily secure puppy in his sleeping place with ease.

An older dog that will be sleeping in another room in the beginning will probably howl and bark for the first few nights. Do not panic though because this is often due to unsettled feelings rather than severe separation anxiety. It usually wears off when the dog begins to feel secure.

5) Setting Up Your Labrador's Crate

Again we will talk more about crate training in a later chapter. For now we are looking to establish a place to keep the crate located on a permanent basis.

Once again, the important thing about introducing your dog, whatever his age, to the crate is to make it a nice place that he finds welcoming. Put a cozy bed, toys and maybe even a stuffed Kong or other activity toy in the crate and allow your dog to sit in there with the door open to begin with.

If you need to have the crate close to you, in order to make your puppy feel secure, then this is fine too. But remember to then gradually move it away later. What some trainers suggest, is that for the first few days when your puppy arrives home, you have the puppy in the puppy crate with you in your bedroom. This will hopefully allow you to hear if the puppy stirs and needs the toilet. What

you then do is to gradually move the crate just outside the bedroom door. As the days progress, you can edge the crate further away until it is in your downstairs kitchen or wherever you wish to keep the crate over night. By doing this, the puppy will hardly notice he is no longer sleeping right beside you.

The overall objective is to show your puppy that his crate is a most comfortable bedroom to the point that he chooses it as his resting place, all on his own.

When you do start to close the door of the crate, only do it for a short time. The idea is that your dog never thinks that he is going to be trapped against his will. Never just push the dog in and close the door as this can easily cause a phobia.

CHAPTER ELEVEN:

Bringing your Labrador puppy / adult dog home

This chapter will deal with preparations for bringing your dog home. It will also offer reminders and checklists to make sure everything is in place. You will also be presented with information about introducing your dog to the rest of the family. Although much of the text states bringing a puppy home, it is also intended to refer to an adult dog.

1) Bringing your dog home

The day will arrive when you finally bring your puppy home to live with you. You will now need to arrange a suitable time with the breeder to collect your puppy.

You should also check the following a day or two before:

- Have you thoroughly puppy proofed the house and yard/garden?

- Do you have all of the accessories you will need most, importantly food?
- Have you arranged a place for the puppy to sleep including bed, bedding, puppy pen and crate if you intend to use them?
- Have you chosen, registered with a vet, arranged an appointment date for any necessary vaccinations?

2) ARRANGING TO BRING HOME YOUR PUPPY FROM THE BREEDER

When you finally pick your puppy up from the breeder they are bound to provide some sort of a puppy pack. This should include at the very least all of the relevant paper work, including the pedigree, health certificate and perhaps your new Kennel Club documents. Always remember to ensure you also receive the following:

The puppy will need to continue with the diet the breeder will have been feeding. Hopefully they will give you a few days or a week's supply, unless you have previously purchased from a local pet supplier. Make sure you get precise details (diet sheet) for feeding times as well as any other recommendations from the breeder.

Please continue to feed according to this plan, as any sudden changes will affect his digestive system with a possible upset stomach and diarrhoea). Do not worry too much if your puppy does not seem to be eating the recommended amount as he may have lost some of his appetite with the anxiety and upheaval of leaving his mother and siblings. However, if this continues for more than 24 hours, consult your vet.

Once he has settled in after a few days he should start to finish his meals. If he is finishing his meals every time then by all means give him more, and again if he leaves some, then cut back slightly.

Please also remember that each breeder will have different ideas about how they feed their puppy. Again, do not worry if it is different to what you may have read or been told. The important thing is that he is fed a high quality nutritious diet and at the set times he has been used to for the past few weeks.

We will talk more about feed and feeding later, but just to give you a rough idea of a typical feeding schedule, it may include 4 or 5 separate meals spread out over the day from 7 or 8am to 10 or 11pm. The food the puppy may have been fed could well consist of a quality commercial diet consisting of tinned puppy food with puppy mixer. It could also include cooked fish, scrambled egg, milk and rusk, cooked chicken, vegetables, rice, puppy milk, minced beef/lamb/pork etc. In this day and age of BARF diets, do not be too alarmed to find that the breeder has started feeding the puppy a predominantly raw diet of some sort. Whatever the diet, stick to it and if you have a particular diet you would prefer to give him, give this gradually while substituting odd meals until the diet has been changed to your preferred one.

Remember to check his worm and flea/tick treatment schedule; that is, when he was last wormed/flea treated, when he is next due and which worming medication was used.

3) THE FIRST DAY HOME

If at all possible do not bring home your puppy during the holidays when your home is likely to be busy with guests and unusual noises.

Plan to take a few days off from work when you bring your Labrador puppy home. Ideally a couple of weeks would ensure that you get fully used to the demands ahead and your puppy is not left alone at this crucial time. The next few days will be time consuming, and will need direct supervision from you. This will involve using management tools such as baby gates, possibly his crate, exercise pen and puppy pads.

Bringing a new dog home is an exciting and sometimes even a terribly scary time. If you follow the right stages of introduction for the dog though, both into your home and your family, everything should go smoothly.

During this area of the book I will explain how the puppy may be feeling; how you can communicate properly with your new dog and how to make life easy for all of you within this crucial settling in period. One of the most tempting things to do when you bring a new dog home is celebrate their arrival. Everyone comes to meet the new family member and everyone wants to stroke, pick him up, cuddle him etc, particularly if the new arrival is a gorgeous Labrador puppy.

When you bring a new puppy home it is important to remember that he will be confused and learning all of the time. That said, if the young dog has a lot of positive, gentle interaction even from day one, it will build his confidence. For this reason the new and young puppy may benefit from some careful visitors. A new adult Labrador is a different matter. An older dog will need a quiet time in the home for the first few days. The adult dog will not welcome a stream of visitors on day one. The new dog will likely be scared and nervous. Remember that he will have little understanding about what is happening in his life and the best way you can approach this is keep quiet and allow him to get used to the new environment in his own time.

Similarly the adult dog should be left well alone by family members whilst he is settling in. He can get some positive attention and fuss if he asks for it, but should certainly not be cornered or forced to accept attention. Many canine rescuers have to take dogs back into their care because a problem has occurred on day one or two that could easily have been avoided if the dog was given space and respect to settle into the new home before excited new owners forced their attentions on him.

A dog learns how to react to things, in his life, based upon past experiences. In addition, canine communication is very different to the communication that occurs between people. In actual fact the average new dog owner trying to make friends with a scared Labrador by trying to touch him is having the exact opposite effect on their recently arrived dog.

I always ignore a new dog into the home. I barely look at them but offer attention if they ask for it, if they approach you. A very scared dog is allowed to hide where he is happy until he is ready to come out and learn to join in with everyday life in his own time. A crate would be a likely place the dog would wish to retire to. It would also be very helpful to cover the crate with a sheet for even more privacy.

There is something that very few people tell you when they present you with a new dog, whatever age he may be. You may think that you have made a mistake. This is an absolutely normal reaction to such a big change in your life. Whether you have brought home a scared teenage dog, a confident adult Labrador or a needy puppy, you may panic before things settle down. With a puppy, you will worry about why he is crying, whether you are feeding him properly, and how you can be sure that he stays happy and healthy. When you bring home an adult dog, he may show separation anxiety, he may bark in the night for a few days and either be very clingy or completely aloof. An adult dog may be so worried that he shows his teeth in the beginning. It's important not to crowd a new dog and everything will settle down quickly. The dog that is left to settle on his own will have no reason to feel threatened.

So all I can say to you is expect accidents, expect upheaval and expect things to change for a short time; then if the dog settles perfectly, far better than you expected, at least you were prepared

4) CHECKLIST FOR THE ARRIVAL OF YOUR PUPPY

As soon as you arrive home with your dog, take him to his designated toilet area and allow him to empty his bowels if needed. Allow him some time to do this, as he may wish to explore.

- Next, try him with some of the food provided by the breeder, and also provide a drink of water. Having had a drink of water, he may need to toilet again, so take him to the toilet area once again.
- At whatever time you arrive home, plan the next meal as if it was a normal day and he was receiving four meals and the next one was e.g. his third of the day. Again do not worry unduly if he doesn't eat. He will not starve and things will soon settle down.
- You will next probably introduce him to your home. As long as you supervise him you may wish to let him wander around exploring the rooms.
- Make sure everywhere is puppy proofed and you have decided on house rules such as which rooms he can go in, and either keep out of bounds doors shut or put baby gates across doorways.

Certainly have a stair gate in place preventing him from climbing the stairs and potentially falling down.

- If you have to leave him unsupervised, hopefully not for too long, either have a designated room to enclose him, or have a play pen available. This will allow him the freedom to wander and to view what is going on, but also keep him safe.
- Once again, some people also introduce the crate training at this point.

You will also find a useful checklist in chapter 22 of things to do each week. For more detailed information regarding toilet/crate training etc, see the chapters that follow.

Please do not encourage your dog to bark, whine, whimper etc (in fact these should be discouraged by any dog). It is endearing to have your little puppy to speak like this, but please do not be tempted to encourage this by getting him to speak or ask for food etc. If you encourage this, it will reinforce a desire to bark when he wants something. For the average pet owner, barking and whining can be a real problem that can be difficult to correct. As with most problem behaviours that you wish to avoid, the worse thing you can do is acknowledge and encourage it, with words or physical contact. The best thing to do is ignore it, turn your back, and walk away. As long as you do not encourage the puppy to think that the behaviour is acceptable. Of course this does not mean that you want to discourage your dog from vocalising and remaining mute. If he barks to go outside to toilet, this is great and should be encouraged. But the point is, he should only be encouraged to bark for specific reasons, not all of the time. Always be aware that you should talk to him and encourage him, when he is doing something desirable. But never encourage barking, whining etc for the sake of it, unless you suspect he is ill. If you fuss him as you should, then fine, but if he starts to get vocal, then stop and ignore the behaviour. He will soon learn that he doesn't get rewarded for whining or barking.

Retrieving and carrying things should be encouraged from day one. By all means talk to him with 'good boy/girl' and make a fuss when he is carrying objects, as long as the items are not valuable

or dangerous. Swapping should be encouraged for anything you do not wish him to have. This is effectively taking another item, perhaps one of his toys, and offering that to him in exchange. So once you offer the other toy, he will probably drop the one he has and take the one you are offering. Remember to not get into a tug of war match, (he needs to retain a 'soft mouth' in other words holding gently and not gripping tightly or ripping), but gently take hold and say for example, 'leave' or 'give', and gently take it.

We will go into more depth and detail later, but retrieve training is something that should be approached correctly and systematically. Please do not attempt any kind of retrieve/fetch games until you know exactly how to do this. It may seem odd as people have been throwing balls and sticks for dogs to retrieve for years without any noticeable problem. We will discuss this in the advanced training chapter.

Recall training is also an area that should not be taken for granted, and from day one. For example, it is not advised to call the puppy unless he is already coming back to you. So in the early stages please refrain from calling him randomly, unless again he is looking or coming back to you.

In these preliminary stages, give him all the fuss and attention he needs, but please make sure you follow these basic rules.

5) First Introductions

If you are bringing home a young puppy this will be easier because the puppy, when carefully handled, will generally be accepting of anyone and everyone. In the case of bringing a puppy home, the other animals in the family must be considered. Some older dogs that you may already have, are completely overwhelmed by the new squeaking, face licking, and generally overly keen puppy.

In the beginning they may not want to be anywhere near the baby dog. If you live with an older dog, ensure that a puppy does not get walked on and harassed in those early days, particularly if he is worried. Similarly take extra care with the cat and any other pets you may have.

If you are bringing home an older dog, to a home with an existing dog, it is important to take all resources away that may cause friction. So pick up toys, treats and anything that either dog may guard. In particular, I have witnessed more dog fights than anything, where food is concerned. Remember that a new dog may feel insecure, therefore guard things for that reason alone.

It's a good idea to let two older dogs meet on neutral ground. This is obviously to avoid any territorial issues that may arise. This can be the park or somewhere similar, rather than just bring the new dog directly home. Walking them together first will allow them to get used to the scent of each other and do the 'meet and greet' and make initial friends, without the tension of perceived territory.

6) DOGS AND CHILDREN

A) DOGS AND PLAY

Children are naturally inclined to want to play and will probably view a dog as just another plaything.

Dogs also love to play, but will not tolerate being subjected to physical abuse such as having their tail or ears pulled, chasing and teasing them, or being hit.

Please also remember that children can significantly encourage excitement and chaos with a Sporting/Gundog. This can be exacerbated if two children or a group are involved. The puppy will be only too willing to join in with a child who wants to run, play chase games and generally interact with a fun loving Sporting/Gundog. In their excitement however, the puppy, if large enough, could easily knock a young child over, or playfully nip them.

In this case, both need to act in a self controlled manner, as the last thing you want is for the puppy to become over excited and nip a child.

Also be aware that dogs can easily view two young children play fighting as the other child attacking your child and step into a territorial defence mode. Be equally mindful of the fact that other children may also not have been taught correct etiquette around a dog.

B) TEACHING RESPECT FOR DOGS

Please be aware of the following, which needs to be conveyed to children who are exposed to your new canine family member:

- Dogs are not toys or playthings and can potentially bite if sufficiently provoked
- The child should never shout, scream, hit, kick, otherwise abuse, or intimidate the dog
- Dogs should be treat with respect and consideration. The dog is not a toy; a young puppy is very fragile.
- The dog should never be teased or chased until the child learns how to safely play games with the dog. Do not allow your child to follow a dog that has tried to move away from the attentions. This is a recipe for disaster because the dog can feel cornered and think he has to resort to aggression simply to be left alone.
- Children should be taught by you demonstrating how to stroke or pet a dog carefully and gently, perhaps demonstrating this with a toy before supervising the child with the dog. Patting a dogs head is often seen as acceptable, but should be discouraged as many dogs do not like it and to the dog it can easily feel like they are being struck. Dogs should be stroked gently on the back, neck and chest and occasionally the head. Children should be taught to not stroke or disturb a dog if they are sleeping or eating.
- The dog should not be encouraged to jump up at the child or anyone for that matter
- Just as you do between two dogs, watch out for resource guarding between dogs and children. Children should not be encouraged to give and take toys or engage in tug of war games with dogs, as this can easily lead to a dog bite. Children tend to grab at toys and food bowls, particularly the little ones. A dog could easily see this behaviour as a threat and snap in return. If a dog takes one of your children's toys, the child should be instructed to ask you to get it back, and not attempt this themselves.

- It may be tempting for the child to pick a puppy up, but again there is a risk that the child may drop and injure them, squeeze them too tightly or choke them.
- Always ensure that before eating, the child should be taught to wash their hands if they have been handling a dog.
- Children should not be permitted to take a dog for a walk unsupervised, unless an older child can show that they can safely control a dog that may suddenly take off after a rabbit or squirrel

Children should also be taught respect for other dogs. It is easy for a child having been brought up around a dog to become confident with them and assume all dogs are the same. They should always ask the owner, who will be able to advise if it is safe, before petting their dog. A child should never attempt to approach a strange dog that is not accompanied by an adult, no matter how friendly they seem.

c) Allowing a child to help with caring for the dog

It is important that children should be encouraged to become involved in caring for your dog. However, please do not expect the child to take full responsibility and always check that things have been done if you should give them regular tasks.

Tasks should include all care aspects such as feeding, watering, grooming, going on walks and if old enough holding the lead, acceptable playing, helping with training, letting the dog out to do his toilet business etc.

A rota is a good idea as this will encourage everyone to get involved in all aspects and not get bored with doing the same things all of the time. This also ensures that everyone bonds with the dog and no one becomes the dogs favourite or centre of attention.

d) Keeping children safe

The media is regularly reporting the occurrence of dog bites and this isn't always the so called volatile dangerous breeds such as Pit Bulls and Rottweilers. Dog bites can happen to anyone, but many reported cases have been towards toddlers. Most of these dog attacks also occur in the home.

A young child is unlikely to recognise subtle warning signals until it is too late and some dogs attack without growling. Even when a child has been taught how to correctly interact with a dog they can become complacent or push their luck being excessively rough.

More dog bites occur as a result of a dog being wrestled and roughed about, by a child who has not 'read the rulebook' on canine body language, and the consequent warning signals that dogs give other dogs before they bite. A child may not be aware that a growling dog means, 'go away or I will bite you'.

A mother dog will usually correct or snap at a puppy that play bites a little too hard or becomes otherwise annoying. In a similar way some dogs will growl and then snap at a child or adult that has over stepped the line of this dogs comfort zone.

Therefore, for a dog to safely interact, supervised by an adult, a child should ideally be at a reasonable level of maturity, at least 8 years old, well mannered and having been taught to respect and care for a dog. Once a child has been taught how to correctly interact with a dog they should always be respectful of a dogs potential unpredictability. You should never become complacent and always be mindful that even the most placid, patient, easy going dog should not be left entirely unsupervised with a child of any age.

7) Introducing Your Puppy to Children

Again, Labradors are a very social and people-oriented breed and as previously mentioned, they tend to get along well with children. This doesn't mean, however, that you can just put your puppy in a room with your kids and expect everything to be fine. Just as you need to ensure that your puppy is safe in your home, you also need to teach your children how to properly handle the puppy for their own safety.

If you manage your family well and teach an all-round respect, you will be able to integrate the new dog in perfectly. Before you know it, everyone will be great friends.

Follow the tips below to safely introduce your puppy to children:

- Before you bring the puppy home, explain to your children how to properly handle the puppy. Tell them that the puppy is fragile and should be handled with care.
- Tell your children to avoid over-stimulating the puppy. They need to be calm and quiet when handling him so he does not become frightened.
- When it is time to make introductions, have your children sit on the floor in your home and bring the puppy to them.
- Place the puppy on the floor near your children and let the puppy wander up to them when he is ready. Do not let your children grab the puppy.
- Allow your children to calmly pet the puppy on his head and back when he approaches them. You may even give them a few small treats to offer the puppy.
- Let your children pick up the puppy if they are old enough to handle him properly. If the puppy becomes fearful, have them put him carefully back down.

If at any point during your introductions the puppy becomes afraid, you should take him out of the situation and place him in his crate, play pen or sleeping area where he can feel safe. Do not let your children scream or act too excitedly around the puppy until he gets used to them. It will take time for both your children and your puppy to get used to each other and you should supervise all interactions.

Please do remember, that where children are concerned or you already have a few pets, be extra careful of where your attentions go. After all, you want all of your pets to get along with each other, as well as your children. So do not create jealousy by fussing over your new Labrador puppy and ignoring your other pets. Share your attention equally between all your pets, so that the relationship starts off well. Much of the future relationship between all of your pets, will depend on what happens during the first few days.

CHAPTER TWELVE:

LABRADOR TOILET TRAINING

Do you remember the old saying 'rub his nose in it'? For many years this was traditionally how house-training was carried out. Poor dogs! Toilet training a human baby is no easy process and yet unfortunately many puppies are expected to toilet train in next to no time. Toilet training is a relatively easy process provided you are patient, follow a few simple rules and keep to a regular routine.

Once again, if the text refers to a puppy, it is intended to also mean an adult dog. Unless of course the adult dog has already been toilet trained.

Housebreaking a Labrador puppy need not be a difficult task. It is simply a case of teaching your dog, as soon as you can, that outside of the house is where he does his toilet business.

Toilet training for success is a matter of putting everything that you can into those first few days. The more times your puppy gets it right in the beginning the quicker he will learn what you want from him. Labradors are generally known to be very clean, so hopefully you will have few if any accidents, and toilet training should take no time at all.

1) NECESSARY TOILET TRAINING SUPPLIES

For perfect Labrador toilet training you won't really need a great deal. Some puppy pads or sheets of newspaper, an odour neutraliser (non ammonia based) and a sharp eye along with a swift movement if you notice your puppy needing to suddenly go.

I say an 'odour neutraliser' because a generic cleaning product is not enough. General cleaning fluids do not necessarily rid the environment of the urine smell, and the dog will always return to a smell when looking for a toilet area. Incidentally, a good natural cleaner/neutraliser is vinegar. It is obviously free from harmful chemicals and can be used as a safe cleaning fluid to generally clean tiled floors, cupboard sides or anywhere else the puppy may come into contact.

2) GOOD TOILET TRAINING PRACTICE

Get into your mind, the idea that for the next few days, you will be a puppy taxi. This basically involves picking your puppy up and taking him outside at least every half hour to one hour.

It is important to realise that until you can gauge your puppies toilet habits reasonably reliably it is advisable to start at every half an hour. If you are confident, you can extend this to every hour or so.

Similarly it is a good idea to expect to use puppy pads or sheets of newspaper in the beginning. Ultimately once the puppy is toilet trained he will go outside to toilet every time. However, in the initial stages, expect to have to lay down puppy pads or sheets of newspaper, in case of accidents. These can be gradually phased out, and will be explained later. But do remember that your puppy has a tiny bladder at the moment, and he will not be able to hold it for long. In time, you may only need to put puppy pads down overnight until your dog's bladder and bowel matures.

Please remember that during any training, rewarding correct behaviour will ensure the behaviour is repeated once the connection is made.

3) TOILET TRAINING ROUTINE

Hopefully the breeder will have started toilet training the puppy. Whether this is the case or not, start toilet training from day one when the puppy arrives at your house. We have already noted this in the 'bringing your dog home' chapter. However, you are presented here with a step by step procedure. Again, the very first thing you should do the first day you bring your puppy home is to take the puppy to the garden or yard and set the puppy down.

- It doesn't really matter exactly where in the garden or yard this is as long as the puppy urinates or defecates outside of the house.
- The puppy should be permitted to wander about and hopefully do his toilet business.
- As soon as the puppy does either toilet business, offer lots of praise and a treat.
- Once this has occurred take the puppy back into the house.
- From this moment forward you need to follow a routine and try and stick with it.

It is really your choice, but the most practical place in the house to start toilet training from is the kitchen. This is often the preferred place as most kitchens are adjacent to the yard/garden and they generally have a tiled or at least waterproof floor that is easy to clean.

Choose a convenient spot in the kitchen in close proximity to the door. Lay down the puppy pads or newspaper in an area of approximately 1 meter square. This will act as a focus point for the puppy to always go to if he needs to do any toilet business. As the puppy gets used to the toilet training routine you can then gradually decrease the area to a small square.

The following will give you some idea of a typical routine to follow:

1. Approximately every 1/2 hour, presuming your puppy is somewhere in the house > open the kitchen door and call him > as he gets into the kitchen, step outside so that he follows you.

2. As well as every 1/2 hour or so; follow this routine and take him out after he has eaten, slept, played and had a drink because these are the times he will most likely need to go.

3. As soon as he is outside > close the door behind you and say the word 'toilets' or 'wee wee'. You may have to repeat

this a number of times. The idea is that he associates the act of doing his toilet business with those words. These words should most importantly be used the moment he starts to do his toilet business.

4. It is also very important to 'mark' (acknowledge desirable behaviour with 'good/clever boy' or whatever) the moment he pees > I also prefer to again repeat the word or words 'toilets' or 'wee wee' whilst he is actually peeing. Again it is all a question of associating the act with the words. Always remember in the initial stages of toilet training to reward with lots of praise and a food treat, every time he goes. A reinforced/rewarded behaviour will always be repeated.

5. You will need to be with the puppy even if it means standing over him. Therefore be prepared to wait with the puppy for up to 10 minutes or so until he obliges.

6. You do not have to do this all the time, but just until he is successfully going outside to his toilet area to eliminate.

7. If you find the puppy does not do any toilet business after 10 minutes > take the puppy back inside > but be prepared to repeat this routine from this point, every 10 minutes until he urinates and/or defecates.

8. If he does his toilet business the first time, assume he should be OK for another 1/2 hour from that point (but also note the 'Toilet Training Timings' section that follows)

9. Again 1/2 an hour later repeat the process.

This might sound like a lot of vigilant watching and waiting, but the puppy will soon get the hang of it. Eventually the puppy will associate him doing his toilet business with going outside to do it and he should wait at the door and bark/ask to go out. He may also excitedly wander to the door indicating that he would like to go out.

Please remember that until your puppy has learned this new behaviour/habit, you will need to supervise him at all times. This will only last a short time but will pay off. You should therefore commit yourself to keeping an eye on your puppy around the house, for signs that he may need to go at any moment.

You may see signs such as the following: he may lick his lips, yawn or glance at you. Or if you notice him wandering about, sniffing or circling, anticipate he may need to do his toilet business.

Toilet training; Timings.

A puppy will be around 30 weeks of age before he has matured sufficiently and consequently gained full control of his bladder, generally able to hold it for 8 to 10 hours.

Once again, a young puppy will generally need to urinate approximately every half hour to 1 hour whilst he is awake. This is why you are strongly advised to take him out every half hour to make sure you do not risk him having a toilet accident before the hour.

It is a good idea to time when he first toilets and then time every half hour from that point. You may also find however, that when you do take him out 30 minutes later, that he just doesn't want to toilet. But if you can, wait 5 or 10 minutes before coming back in just in case.

However, if after another 10 minutes (40 minutes total), he still hasn't gone, don't wait another half hour as he may be ready to toilet 10 minutes or so later. In this case bring him back in, but carry him back out to his toilet area 10 minutes or so later.

You really just need to be aware of your puppies approximate timings as sometimes he will hold it for an hour another time half an hour.

Or he may even go and leave you thinking it is safe for another half hour, and need to go again after 10 minutes.

What to do to avoid accidental peeing

*   Again it is important to keep an eye on your puppy for accidents, or any signs that he may need to toilet.
*   If you notice him about to go, don't shout, but in a raised urgent voice, say something like 'outside for toilets', or 'outside for a wee wee' > at the same time quickly move towards the kitchen to encourage him out.

- If you are close enough, scoop him up and take him outside or to the nearest puppy pad.
- Even if your dog has begun to go in the wrong place quickly and quietly pick him up and take him outside. He should stop, the moment you raise your voice.
- Do not make a fuss or get angry with him whilst you do this. As soon as you are outside > put him down and wait as before > periodically repeat, 'toilets' or 'wee wee' > Even if he does a tiny bit, reward him and offer lots of fuss and praise.
- At any time when you are unable to be in the same room, simply leave the puppy in the yard or garden, provided it is safe and secure. This assumes that it is a fine day and you are still at home. It would be very inadvisable to leave the house with your puppy stuck outside alone.
- If you have to leave the house, or during sleep times, a segregated part of the kitchen such as a play pen is also advisable. In such cases make sure that you have his bed, toys, water bowl etc in the area.

The puppy is unlikely to soil his bed, but place paper down to absorb any accidental soiling. Dogs along with other animals have a natural inclination to keep their nest or den clean and will therefore choose to eliminate in designated spots away from their sleeping area.

4) TOILET TRAINING PROCEDURE INDOORS

If the previous toilet training exercises are done at frequent intervals throughout the day. The puppy will quickly realise that they are not expected to hold their bladder for long. You will therefore find by sheer repetition that the puppy will quickly learn what is expected and will only ever eliminate outside.

However, when in the house it is probably a good idea to make sure the puppy is with you wherever you are so that you can keep an eye on him and prevent any accidents elsewhere.

It is also advisable to keep any doors closed to avoid him wandering into another room. Alternatively have a training lead (for example 3 to 5 meters long) attached to him and yourself to keep him within a certain radius.

Once you are confident that your puppy knows that he has got to toilet outside, you can start to introduce him to other rooms. Eventually you will have the whole house open to him and not have to worry about shutting any doors.

Remember that if your puppy is finding toilet training difficult you should restrict his access to one room, usually the kitchen, particularly if left alone for an extended period of time.

Clearing soiled puppy pads/newspaper.

You will need to clear away any soiled paper/ pads on a daily basis. It will then be necessary to use your vinegar or neutraliser in the general area. You will then want to replenish the area with fresh pads or paper.

An important tip to use in the early stages of toilet training is to leave a piece of the soiled, damp paper. This is particularly important for any initial indoor training. The obvious reason for this relates to scent marking. The dog will naturally return to the area they can smell as scent marked. If you clear the soiled paper and put fresh unscented paper in its place, the pup may not remember where he last went to toilet, or not be able to smell the odour. If you leave a piece of the soiled scented paper, he should instantly recognise this as the place to go. It is important that this only takes place in the very initial stages when you are trying to get the puppy to target the puppy pad. Again, once he is successful at this, the next stage is to move the whole thing outside. But again the scented piece will be useful at that stage. Once he knows were he should toilet, leaving the soiled paper will be unnecessary.

5) NIGHT TIME ROUTINE

As you have no doubt now gathered, a puppy does not have a large enough bladder to cope with long periods without having the opportunity to relieve themselves.

For night time toilet training it is therefore necessary to follow additional procedures:

1. Take the puppy out 5 or 10 minutes before you go to bed. Hopefully he will be ready to do his toilet business. Once he is used to this routine he should be ready to pee at this time.

2. It will be necessary to confine the puppy inside the playpen if you have one > or the kitchen with his bed, accessories and puppy pads/newspaper spread out 1 meter square approx. You cannot realistically expect accidents to not happen initially, so be prepared.

3. Some people prefer to sleep down stairs and move the play pen to where they are so that they can be woken if the puppy starts to whine or restlessly moves about.

4. If you sleep in your normal bed however > it will be necessary to set an alarm 4 to 5 hours after you retire. This assumes that you have left your puppy in the kitchen area.

5. The first day, try 4 hours and hopefully the puppy will not have eliminated and therefore be ready to go when you take him outside. It may seem contradictory that he will need to go every 1/2 hour to an hour during the day, but now you are told 4 hours. The point is that provided the puppy is able to sleep they will probably hold their bladder for longer.

6. If you are successful after a week or so at this time, try 5 hours. However, if at any point you are woken in the early hours, with his short, "asking to go out", bark, he may need letting outside. Again please don't ignore this, and if it is possible, please do attend to the dog as it will be uncomfortable for him to be expected to hold this until the morning.

7. If after 5 hours he has soiled the play pen or kitchen > move back to 4 hours for a while.

Ultimately you want him to avoid habitually soiling inside the house. So setting the alarm and getting up mid way through a normal sleep pattern will be a small sacrifice for a month or so. Having said all of that, and I hasten to add I am not necessarily recommending this, but some dog owners simply restrict their dog to the kitchen and leave the dog to it. They simply put paper down, fully expecting the dog to do the toilet business on the paper each night. They then clear this away and disinfect each morning. The choice really is yours as to what you prefer to do.

6) CHECK LIST AND SIGNS THAT YOUR PUPPY WILL NEED TO TOILET

When is a puppy more likely to do their toilet business?

- Mornings and early evening.
- When they first wake up after quite a few hours sleeping, whatever the time of day.
- After drinking and eating.
- When you release him from his crate if and when you get around to crate training.
- When active, chewing a toy, physical exertion, whilst playing a game with another dog or family member can have a similar effect to eating.

If an accident happens, then in future be aware of how long the puppy was playing before they relieved themselves, and take him out for a toilet break, before this time.

- If he starts sniffing or circling, and obviously as soon as 'he' raises his hind leg or 'she' squats.
- He suddenly becomes distracted or preoccupied for no obvious reason, or he wanders from an area he has been playing in for some time.
- If he is inside and he looks towards the door to his toilet area.

As you are now forewarned please accept any toilet accident as an accident that you were not aware of.

There is no point in getting upset or angry with the puppy as they will have no idea why you are shouting, hitting, locking him in his crate or outside or any other punishment. Again, as with all training, a dog will only recognise the very last thing he did as the reason he is being punished or rewarded, not something he did 5 minutes or even 30 seconds ago. If you do not correct him the very moment he does something wrong, he will not get the connection.

You simply need to clean up the mess and try harder next time to pre-empt any future accidents.

Please remember that this is part of his training and he is only doing what comes natural to him until you show him that he should not toilet in the house.

In an 'emergency', if you notice your puppy suddenly squat, or cock his leg, and you are too far away, startle and interrupt him with a loud noise. Hopefully he will not be tempted to carry on with his toilet business. Try to avoid some physical gesture you use for any other command such as clapping your hands or slapping your thigh for a recall command.

You then need to get to him a.s.a.p, scoop him up and take him outside to his toilet area, put him down and wait quietly until he toilets.

If you have made the noise, shouted 'No' or whatever, and he continues peeing, don't be tempted to go into a rant telling him how bad he is. Simply clean up the mess without making a fuss and certainly do not speak or acknowledge this.

The whole point of not getting angry is that you need to avoid the puppy associating urinating or defecating as a bad thing for him to do. It is likely that he will seek somewhere to toilet where and when you aren't present.

7) CRATE TRAINING INTRODUCTION

Please note: Crate training is something that I would not recommend using in conjunction with toilet training for a young puppy. Many people for various reasons, lock their dogs in a crate overnight. For an adult dog, this may be a practical and feasible option as they can generally hold their bladder overnight. But as you now know, it is not fair to expect a puppy to hold their bladder in the same way.

Although it is necessary to bond with the puppy, it is not desirable for the puppy as well as for the handler to be with each other all of the time. In this respect, interaction and solitude should be

carried out in regular short episodes throughout the day.

In order to ensure that the puppy does not become dependent and reliant on you every minute of the day, the puppy therefore needs to become accustomed to spending time alone. It can seem cruel to not include the new puppy in family activities at all times. It can certainly be cruel for the puppy to have all of this attention, and then suddenly be left alone for hours. There is no wonder that conditions such as separation anxiety consequently develop.

If he has not been conditioned to sit or lie quietly and patiently, then he is bound to bark or whine in frustration, for your attention. You should therefore ensure that he gets used to spending time alone, and the best tool for this purpose is his crate.

Again, the crate should not be viewed as a cage that he is locked up in. It should be seen as a den or sanctuary, where the puppy can feel safe and secure. Many dogs feel the need for solitude and to have the option for their own space. You will therefore find that many dogs like to hide away either under items of furniture or behind sofas etc.

As with any training, you should build crate training up gradually and repetitively over time. But commence once he has settled in and is happy and confident in his new home.

Start with a couple of minutes of alone time, so he barely realises you are not there, and is confident you will return. Then increase to 5 minutes, then 10 and 15 and so on. Once again, never extend this for longer than 1 hour for toilet training reasons mentioned previously.

By exposing him to alone time in this way, he will develop greater independence and self reliance.

A) INITIAL CRATE TRAINING

Initial crate training should ideally take place in a room where there will be people present.

Prepare the crate with his bed, bedding and toys and leave the door to the crate open. VETBED is often used for whelping and many pups will have been brought up with this. It is very useful as a bed/crate liner as it is very durable and machine washable. Water proof foam, 'chew proof' mattresses specifically for crates, are also a good idea.

1. Put a few food treats at the back of the crate to encourage him to go in > You should let him wander in and out of the crate even if he picks the food up and goes back out again > If he stays there to eat the food then all well and good > Sooner or later he will associate going into the crate as a rewarding experience. As with any training > when he successfully goes into the crate to get the food > offer lots of praise.

2. As soon as you start this routine also add the words 'on your bed' or 'in your crate', or simply 'bed' or 'crate'. Say these in an enthusiastic , encouraging tone of voice. These words will then become the 'command' words for when you need him to go into the crate at bed time or any other reason.

3. Once he has become accustomed to spending time in the crate with the door open, start closing the door behind him for very short periods. So the routine would be (i) have the door open and drop a few food treats to the back (ii) at the same time, call him in with the command word you have chosen (iii) as soon as he goes into the crate to get the food, praise him and quietly close the door behind him (iv) Once he has eaten the food and comes back to the door of the crate > pause a few seconds, providing he remains quiet and doesn't whine or start barking > open the door again. Please remember to only let him out if he is quiet. If he whines, wait until he stops before again opening the door. He will soon realise that by not whining, he is let out of the crate (v) as soon as he comes out of the crate, offer lots of praise.

Please also be aware that if he does start to whine he may persist and this could be 10 minutes or so. If this is the case you will need to choose a moment, when he is quiet and quickly open the crate. It is very important that you do not give in and let him out while he is whining. You need to time it so that he isn't whining when you open the door otherwise he will think he just needs to whine to be let out. It may seem very cruel to ignore him like this, but as long as you stay in the room with him, he should soon stop, at which point you open the door and give him lots of praise.

Do not view crate training as a traumatic experience that you should avoid doing just because he is whining or crying. He will resist most things that he does not like and will very quickly get used to the idea. It is no different to him pawing and rolling about on the floor to get his collar off. If you give in to his crying, he will cry every time.

B) EXTENDING CRATE TIME DURING THE DAY.

On a night for example, your puppy will settle down for a lot longer period than during the day. It is also obviously dark, quiet and no one around to give him attention. But do not expect him to be happy to stay locked in a crate when he is wanting interaction during the day.

- When you start extending his crate training, close the door as before. Now as soon as he is waiting to be let out, wait for 2 seconds or a slow count of 'one and two and', then open the door as long as he has remained quiet.
- During the first day aim to do this about 10 to 15 times.
- Now repeat this procedure, increasing the time by 1 second each time.
- So when you have repeated this at 2 seconds up-to 15 times, increase to 3 seconds for another 10 to 15 times, and so on.
- You can also extend his time in the crate with the door closed by feeding him his meals in the crate. As you can imagine, he will at least be preoccupied for as long as it takes him to eat the meal. Again, place his food bowl in the back of the crate so he has to go all the way in to eat. At first leave the door open. However, once your puppy is comfortable eating his meals in the crate, you can start to close the door while he is in it. Open the door again as soon as he is finished eating. As before, each time

you feed your puppy in the crate, leave the door closed a few minutes longer after he has finished eating, until your puppy remains in the crate for 10 minutes after eating.

- After extending his time in the crate with you present, start to leave him in the crate whilst you leave the room. So once he has finished his meal and is waiting at the door, leave the room for a few seconds, then return and let him out. Each time you do this extend by a couple of seconds until you get to 1 minute, then 2 minutes, 3, 4, and so on. Again, If he starts whining or crying, you may have increased the duration of your absence too quickly.

This kind of repetition will very gradually condition the puppy to accepting the crate and he will soon settle without any problem. There is no real time limit as to how long this will take, as again you should only increase the time when he is not whining and asking to come out.

One additional point to note when you take him out of the crate each time, is to get into the habit of taking him or calling him to his toilet area.

This is important as you do not want him to get into the habit at some point of coming straight out of the crate and doing his toilet business within the house.

Please also remember to never leave your puppy alone in the crate for extended periods during the day.

Once again, refrain from extending crate training beyond an hour until he is at least 6 months of age. By this time you may have successfully managed to condition him to accepting being in the crate for a few hours. You could now attempt extending this over night.

c) CRATE TRAINING DURING THE NIGHT

It is assumed that at this stage he will be accustomed to being locked in the crate for an extended period of time. Again, this should have been carried out in the previous initial crate training.

The important thing is that with correct crate training your puppy will soon get used to the fact that night time is for sleeping. All the attention and

activity of the day comes to a halt for everyone not just him. The first time is likely to be as hard as it gets for him and he may well start whining, crying or howling for attention. Again please remember to only let him out once he has stopped whining.

There are a number of items you can use to make this a lot easier and more bearable for him. Draping a blanket over the crate is a good idea as this can make it more of a cozy den for him. A lot of dog trainers swear by comforters such as a ticking clock, radio or TV left on low volume. A heat source, heat pad, hot water bottle and lots of cuddly toys are other good comforters as these are thought to replicate his litter mates. However, if a heat source is used this should not make him too warm. Also be careful that whatever you use is safe for him, ensuring that he can neither bite through an object nor burn himself.

Most young puppies will not last 6 hrs without needing to toilet.

As before for his initial toilet training, there is no easy way around this. You are again strongly recommended to make the sacrifice of getting up early for a few weeks, to let the puppy do his toilet business.

This will ideally mean setting your alarm for 4 or 5 hours time after you go to bed, then getting up to let him out to toilet.

This should be approached differently to his initial toilet training. You can expect the odd toilet accident initially, but it is not fair to leave him locked in a crate, having to hold it for any length of time. You are taking a big risk that the puppy will have to toilet overnight and if not allowed to empty their bowels, are likely to mess up their crate and get into the habit of doing so again.

If when you come down he has messed up his crate then you will need to set the alarm 30 minutes to an hour earlier.

It will make it a lot easier if you realise that as the weeks and months pass, this need will get less and less until they can go a full eight or nine hours without having to toilet.

d) THE PROCEDURE WHEN YOUR ALARM GOES OFF:

Take him out of the crate and call him to his normal toilet area, where he should relieve himself as soon as he gets outside > Give him lots of praise if he does > but wait with him if he doesn't, before he hopefully eventually relieves himself.

Once he has done his toilet business > bring him straight back in and put him in his crate and then leave him again while you go back to bed.

E) CRATE TRAINING ACCIDENTS

Once again, most breeds or individual dogs are unlikely to mess or do their toilet business where they sleep, unless they are locked in a crate for hours without the opportunity to relieve themselves.

An obvious reason for eliminating away from the den is to lessen the chances of spreading disease through harmful bacteria, parasites, organisms etc.

So please do not blame your dog for any accident in the crate as it is most probably because he has been in the crate too long and he simply couldn't hold it.

Do not keep him in the crate for any longer than you know he can comfortably manage. Always give him the opportunity to toilet outside before putting him in the crate.

Be aware that he may have had a big drink of water before going in the crate. You may therefore need to prevent access to water an hour or so before you retire to bed. For obvious reasons, if he has water available all of the time, he is more likely to drink and therefore need to go. If it is particularly warm over night, then allow a reasonable amount of water in the crate.

Talk to your vet if you suspect urinating is happening more frequently than normal as he may have some sort of infection or disease.

If you are starting to feel frustrated that it is taking too long please just be patient. At any point, please do not be tempted to keep the puppy outside in a garage or kennel, even for a double coated breed who are traditionally able to withstand reasonably cold temperatures. It will be too much for a young puppy if there is a drop in temperature. Not to mention the fact that the puppy will be frightened, anxious etc and is likely to whine and cry.

8) ADULT AND RESCUE DOGS

Older dogs can have housebreaking problems based on a few different things. If a dog has never lived indoors or never been house-trained, then he may assume it is natural to do his toilet business anywhere, including indoors. This is not his fault as he hasn't been toilet trained, nor taught the social etiquettes that we live by. You should therefore apply the steps above in the same way to show the dog what you want. It may take longer, but you should get there eventually, so be patient.

When you bring a rescued Labrador home, it's important to expect at least a couple of accidents, regardless of whether he has been toilet trained or not, simply because he or she will be confused and nervous.

A) SCENT MARKING

- Male dogs may scent mark in the new home if they are un-neutered or particularly nervous.
- Scent marking is the dog's way of showing other dogs that he is there, and can be a nervous reaction or a hormonal response.
- Castration can help with the male dog that scent marks, but is not a definite solution as it can cause further insecurity in some worried dogs. It is worth speaking to your vet if you are having a problem like this.

B) ELDERLY DOGS

Dogs can lose control of their bladder with old age. This is a sad situation and one which we have to adapt to because we love our dogs. The vet can prescribe specific treatments for leaking and may need to check out your dog's overall health, if this is an issue.

Many older dogs fail to make it through the night in the last months/years without needing to go out. Again, the best solution is to put down plenty of newspaper for him to go on. Cleaning this up in the morning is a small sacrifice to pay, as you need to make things as easy and comfortable for them as possible.

CHAPTER THIRTEEN:

LABRADOR SOCIALISATION

1) WHY SOCIALISE

Please note: socialisation should continue as soon as the puppy comes to you at 8 weeks old. However, it is considered that the 'critical period' for socialisation is from 3 to 4 weeks of age to approximately 12 to 16 weeks old. What this means is that if you leave socialisation later than this, he will start to develop a wariness and at worse fear, towards certain things and people. Before this 12 to 16 week period, he will be happy to accept most things presented to him. The puppy that has been thoroughly socialised from a few weeks to 12-16 weeks will be confident, sociable and friendly and will remain that way.

There are so many dogs in rescue shelters and homes that simply do not know how to react in social situations. This is because they have never learned what to do in the company of other dogs, children and crowded areas or around other animals.

However, stop for a moment and think of street dogs in Europe and similar places. You never see them fighting do you? They manage to get on with no tension and certainly no aggression. They never bark at cars or people.

The street dogs never seem to worry too much about their surroundings. Which points to the fact that there must be a specific reason for the behaviour. You guessed it, the reason for poorly socialised dogs is us humans, more specifically the restrictions we impose on them.

We leash them up, stop them interacting, panic when another dog comes towards them and often keep them well away from social situations altogether. Then when a puppy gets to a few months old we complain about their social behaviour.

It is possible to grasp back some social skills with an older dog, after the 'critical period' has elapsed. Yet the dog that isn't positively socialised as a puppy, will never really be completely relaxed in new circumstances.

Positive socialisation should incorporate everything that you possibly can into a dog's everyday life as early as possible. Not only that though, every experience should be positive.

Incidentally, if you intended to use your dog as a working Sporting/Gundog, it would be vital that in addition to socialisation around the house and in outside social situations, the dog would also need to be exposed to their future working environments. This would include areas you are likely to frequent whether for shooting, training or general leisure.

This should include experiencing the terrain, scents and any wildlife they come across. As well as de-sensitising and developing no fear, they will also begin to develop an instinct for hunting.

A good socialisation schedule will include positive experiences of and with;

As many dogs as possible; Buses; Cars; Children; Domestic animals; Farmed animals; People of all ages; Push chairs; Sounds such as recorded thunder and fireworks; The groomer (if you are to use a professional); Trains or trams; Unusual looking people (those wearing hats and unusual clothing); The veterinary surgery; Wildlife

Socialisation locations include:

Car rides or bus rides if you take the bus; Visits to local parks; Country walks; Trips to the seaside

As you are likely to walk your dog, he will get regular daily exposure to traffic, other dogs and people etc. But try and go at different times and change routes so that you are not seeing the same things.

2) THE 'CRITICAL PERIOD' AND SOCIALISATION

A) PUPPY DEVELOPMENT AND EARLY SOCIALISATION

So what exactly is the 'critical period' and why is this important?

During a puppies early weeks, they are very much aware of sounds for example, which is why it is so important that they are exposed to all household sounds, and therefore become desensitised and unafraid. Any new sound as well as sight when this becomes applicable, is likely to frighten the puppy at first, until they realise there is nothing to fear.

It is also very important that the puppy receives adequate socialisation with the mother and litter mates during weeks 4 to 8 of its life, otherwise there is a risk of them being dog aggressive, fearful and generally anti social.

The brain of a puppy is growing right up to about 5 months. However, the importance of social interaction continues up to 12 months of age. Again this is why it is very important to continue his socialisation when he comes to live with you.

As previously mentioned, what is known as the 'critical period' occurs in a puppies development roughly between 3 to 16 weeks of age. During this period, the puppy is at its most impressionable and easily influenced.

Famous studies carried out by Scott and Fuller and documented in their book (Genetics And The Social Behavior Of The Dog; 1965) highlighted the 'critical period' and established a number of very important findings:

Among their many experiments they discovered that puppies that had no human contact up to 7 weeks of age, were then exposed to humans and took 2 days before they attempted to make contact.

In a different experiment, puppies were deprived of human contact for 14 weeks. After this period contact with humans began and resulted in the dogs showing extreme fear of humans. The puppies consequently behaved like wild animals.

Although the experiments were conducted with limited individual cases, the results were a startling indication of how important socialising was and is during those early stages.

If you therefore assume that the critical period of 3 weeks to 16 weeks has to be adhered to, then we have to hope that the breeder has started the socialisation from 3 weeks, which is why you should always question them about this. It then gives the new owner another 4 to 6

weeks to continue this vital socialisation.

Again, many behaviour problems are cited as a direct result of failure to provide adequate early socialisation during the critical period. The consequence of this is that thousands of dogs are euthanised every year globally.

3) SOCIALISATION, AND WHO YOUR DOG SHOULD INTERACT WITH

Socialisation isn't something you teach a puppy as such, as they effectively teach themselves. But we need to facilitate this by exposing them to a wide variety of experiences and environmental stimuli.

Although socialisation is a vital component of a puppies development, you should guard against flooding the puppy too soon with stimuli likely to frighten him. In the initial stages, large groups either at a park or obedience class are likely to overwhelm and become a stressful, fearful experience for him. In such situations, you may notice him display signs of obvious unease such as a fearful look, or calming signals such as yawning or licking his lips. So gradually expose him to stimuli and desensitise him gradually, rather than throwing him in at the deep end. For example a trip to the park should be at a time when you know there will only be a few people about rather than crowds of people and dog walkers.

At first, aim to socialise him a few times per week and if he reacts in any kind of adverse fearful way, take him out of the situation. However if possible, allow the pup time to investigate and go toward the stimuli in their own time.

You certainly want to avoid any kind of negative impact on the puppy as this could easily have a lasting effect and be difficult to cure. Some early experiences known as imprinting become fixed and in some cases this is irreversible and remains with the dog for life.

As the puppy gets older and his confidence grows, he will be less intimidated. You should then increase his exposure to different dog types, sizes, ages, temperaments and larger groups etc.

Also, please do not make the mistake of thinking that your dog only needs to be exposed to experiences in your immediate environment. Take him to different locations and expose him to different people, animals, vehicles etc.

It really is important that he experiences as many unusual places, people etc as possible, to ensure he is comfortable and unaffected by any eventuality. In fact whenever you go anywhere at all, if it is practical and safe to do so, take your puppy with you.

A) SOCIALISING WITH OTHER DOGS

Your dog ultimately will need to learn canine manners from other dogs. In turn this teaches him good behaviour, social skills and etiquette. Early exposure to lots of different dogs, ages, sexes, breeds etc is vital, in particular for the Sporting/ Gundog. However, he will need to learn that although he may well be the happy go lucky breed that he is, who wants to play, not every dog or breed will share his point of view. Gundogs do need to be exposed to some dogs that are unfriendly or show hostility. It is a mistake to only allow your puppy to interact with dogs they know, and you know to be friendly. This only gives a false sense of security as the friendly, familiar dogs will no

doubt tolerate his exuberant behaviour, which may not be tolerated by dogs that wish to be left alone. Being exposed to relatively unfriendly, aloof dogs will also teach and hopefully prevent him from bounding up to strange, potentially hostile dogs in the future. Such occasions could possibly initiate a dog fight or attack. However, do make sure that the owner of any strange dog that you introduce your dog to, has theirs on a lead and can control and prevent their dog from attacking your puppy, should they attempt this. Ultimately, the under socialised puppy who hasn't experienced lots of different dogs, will possibly fail to read the signals to back off, and again an unintentional fight or attack could occur.

B) PLAY AND INTERACTION WITH OTHER DOGS

For the Sporting/Gundog, play is where they hone their skills to eventually hunt. These early 'hunting' or survival skills include: chasing, stalking/ pointing, eyeing, nipping, grabbing, retrieving etc.

Most adult dogs in general have a desire to play and interact with other adult dogs. Although adult dogs do play, the type of play is not the typical rough and tumble, chasing etc that puppies engage in, but more subtle forms of engagement.

As adults and puppies play differently, an over exuberant puppy can get into trouble with a less tolerant adult who is no doubt easily annoyed at such immature behaviour.

An adult however, will be more forgiving with a puppy than with another adult, and will teach the puppy appropriate social skills.

For a puppy, play is also vital regardless of the breed as they learn important social boundaries such as bite inhibition and respect for other dogs etc. In the litter for example, puppies will let other puppies know if they are not happy with certain rough play.

But again, quite often puppies will be far more boisterous than adults and under socialised puppies can grow up thinking this type of behaviour is perfectly acceptable. It is therefore important that well socialised and experienced adult dogs are available to correct inappropriate behaviour from a puppy.

Also be aware that the temperament and age of other dogs can have an effect on a young puppy. An older, larger juvenile puppy is likely to be too strong and rough for a young puppy.

This can lead to your puppy developing a defensive and perhaps aggressive approach to other dogs. It is therefore advisable in the initial stages at least, to try and allow interaction with other puppies of similar ages and temperaments.

The problem with adult Sporting/Gundogs however, is that many of them behave like puppies and juveniles even once they mature, and again get into trouble with less understanding, tolerant non Sporting/Gundog adults.

Terriers and other breeds for example, who were bred to be independent and solitary in their working and interacting generally have a reduced desire to play and interact beyond puppyhood. They can therefore be intolerant and hostile of breeds such as the Sporting/Gundog who still wants to play and interact as if they are still puppies.

C) PROBLEMS THAT CAN OCCUR DURING PLAY

Do be aware that if your dog is associating with, or being made to associate with incompatible, domineering breeds, perhaps in a class situation or dog park, they may have a negative experience and possibly pick up unacceptable social behaviour.

Many Sporting/Gundog breeds, again because of their friendly playful natures can also become victims and can easily learn to fear certain bullying dogs.

Dogs being pack animals tend to create a pack association when they get together with other dogs. It isn't about any kind of 'alpha dynamic', but a general status, 'pecking order', or hierarchy is established, which isn't necessarily fixed and can therefore change from moment to moment.

Unfortunately what can happen if a group of unknown dogs get together, rather than give and take play occurring, a pack can be formed and bullying or chasing a weaker perceived dog can take place. It therefore becomes more like the prey/hunt instinct taking over which is not pleasant, desirable, social behaviour.

Be aware of such dogs, and in such cases your puppy may be better off spending quality time with you alone exercising, playing fetch or training,

without having to endure such dogs. Again, if any such interactions ever become hostile, simply pick your puppy up and take him away from the situation.

D) SOCIALISING WITH PEOPLE

Dogs generally being social animals, like to interact with each other as well as receiving social interaction, attention, love and affection from us, their human guardians.

Interaction with people typically teaches them their place amongst humans, and how to behave around the house.

Kennel bred, puppy mill dogs rarely get to see anyone other than the person who handles or feeds them. As well as limited human interactions, they are also largely isolated from interacting with too many other dogs.

Such dangerous neglect can result in a puppy that grows into adulthood either timid, fearful, hostile, aggressive and potentially dangerous toward other dogs and humans.

When greeting people, perhaps other dog walkers, always ask them if your dog can greet their dog. It is probably best to ask any strangers if they could keep their distance at first and then gradually introduce each other. Also asking them to perhaps crouch down and encourage the puppy or offer tasty treats. This will all help to positively reinforce the experience.

Children that are unfamiliar to the puppy can also pose a similar problem as they can be more unpredictable making sudden spontaneous movements likely to make a puppy frightened or wary.

Always pre-empt if an adult or child appears overbearing, perhaps if they attempt to pick the puppy up, which may shock the puppy. But don't make a fuss yourself if you have to intervene. The puppy can easily associate your reaction as confirmation that this is something to be feared.

4) VACCINATIONS AND SOCIALISATION

Veterinarians have for many years advised puppy owners to restrict a puppies access to other dogs and areas frequented by dogs until approximately 16 weeks of age when they should have completed their immunisation programme. The main reason for this is the serious risk to the puppy of contracting one of the deadly diseases such as Distemper or Parvo Virus, which the inoculations are supposed to protect them against.

Canine behaviourists conversely assert that if a puppy does not obtain sufficient socialisation during the 'critical socialisation period', then you risk behaviour and temperament problems developing which can be difficult to correct.

They also argue that there are far fewer puppies catching one of the deadly diseases, as opposed to the many that develop serious behavioural issues, resulting in needless annual euthanisations. Consequently owners either embark on behaviour management courses or give the dog up to a rescue organisation where the dog again potentially faces being euthanised.

It has furthermore been asserted that the death rate of puppies contracting the aforementioned diseases is considered to be significantly low, even when the puppies are socialised in areas of potential risk during the inoculation period.

As you can see, it is an obvious dilemma that on the one hand the puppy needs to meet as many different people as possible during their 'critical socialisation period' but on the other, certain opinions assert they should not leave the house to do so.

So what is the answer to this obvious dilemma?

Once again it is fair to state that there will always be a certain risk of a puppy contracting a disease. Obviously the risk factor is greatly lessened if the puppy remains indoors, but again their socialisation will suffer.

A) MINIMISING THE RISKS:

In general you are strongly advised to not take risks at this critical period and if possible only allow dog to dog contact with animals that you know have been fully vaccinated or are at the same stage of vaccination as your puppy (at least one, preferably two vaccination jabs).

If you know other vaccinated dog owners that will allow you to visit them and allow your puppy time to play and interact with their dog, then so much the better.

As meeting many different people is vital it may be necessary to rely on as many people as

possible visiting your home. For a busy household, this will probably not pose a problem. But if visitors are infrequent, you will probably have to be a little bit more proactive, by inviting people round for that purpose.

You can also consider organised puppy classes with owners in a similar position to yourself. Dedicated puppy groups do exist and give puppies the chance to socialise with other puppies who are between the 8 and 16 week critical period and also going through their immunisation programme.

You would be well advised to check your area for such a puppy group to ensure your puppy is at least mingling with other puppies and owners.

B) TAKING THE PUPPY OUTDOORS:

It is also recommended that whilst a puppy is going through his vaccinations, during his 'critical' socialisation stage, should you decide to take him outdoors, that you carry him, particularly in areas where other dogs are known to frequent. Ideally you should avoid areas where other dogs are known to urinate or defecate, as again this could pose a potential disease risk.

- You are certainly strongly advised not to allow him to wander about on public ground where other dogs have frequented, even if there are no other dogs present.
- He will of course be unable to sniff or scent mark himself but at least he will be exposed to traffic noises and sites that will ensure he does not develop abnormal phobias.
- If you do meet other dog walkers, do not allow the puppy to come into direct contact with their dog.

Please see the chapter on 'Keeping Your Labrador Healthy' for details on vaccination schedules.

CHAPTER FOURTEEN:

FEEDING YOUR LABRADOR

In addition to providing your Labrador with a safe habitat, you also need to give him a healthy diet. The food you choose for your Labrador will have a direct impact on his health and wellbeing, so do not skimp! It may be tempting to save money by purchasing an inexpensive 'budget' food but you will be robbing your dog of vital nutrients. Skimping on cheap dog food might save you money in the present but it could lead to health problems down the line that might be expensive to treat. In this chapter you will learn the basics about dog nutrition and receive tips for feeding your dog.

Please be aware that this section on feeding and nutrition is broad ranging and goes into quite a bit of detail. Please do not be tempted to skim read or skip this part. Of all the chapters covered I would say that this is on a level with only buying health tested puppies. It is also probably the most important and sadly over looked aspect of caring for your dog.

1) NUTRITIONAL REQUIREMENTS FOR DOGS

Just like all living things, dogs require a balance of nutrients in their diet to remain in good health. These nutrients include protein, carbohydrate, fats, vitamins, minerals, and water. Dogs are a carnivorous species by nature so meat plays an important role in their diet, but they do require some carbohydrates as well. Later you will read about the BARF diet. Part of that diet recommends that you feed carbohydrates such as raw fruit and vegetables. This is best served finely chopped, using a food processor or similar. You may also find that dehydrating this allows you portion it up and freeze it. It is quite easy to prepare and simply involved spreading a food processed mixture onto large baking trays and slowly baking it at the lowest heat setting in your oven. You will also need to leave the oven door ajar to allow moisture to escape. Use a wooden spatula or similar to turn the mixture over every hour or half hour. The mixture is generally ready when the particles are all relatively dry. However, you should be aware that it can take 8 or 9 hours, so only attempt this on a day when you or someone else can supervise the cooking all day. To make this more appetising for the dog, mix the dehydrated veg with food processed cooked egg. You can also mix the whole thing with one of the recommended oils such as rapeseed.

You may also be interested in checking out a commercial supplier. One such UK supplier for example can be found at the following link: **https://purepetfood.co.uk/**

Below you will find an overview of the nutritional needs for dogs in regard to each of the main nutrients. Keep these nutritional requirements in mind when selecting a dog food formula for your Labrador.

Protein – This nutrient is composed of amino acids and it is essential as a source of energy as well as the growth and development of tissues, cells, organs, and enzymes in your dog's body. It is particularly important for puppy growth, but when the dog reaches maturity, protein is only necessary for maintenance. When the bitch is pregnant and whilst she is feeding pups, she will also need extra protein. Protein can be obtained from both animal and plant-based sources, but animal-based proteins are the most biologically valuable for your dog. There are two categories of amino acids; essential and non-essential. Non-essential amino acids are those that your dog's body is capable of producing. Essential amino acids are those that cannot be produced by the dogs body and therefore he must get this from his diet. The most important essential amino acids for a dog include lysine, arginine, phenylalanine, histidine, methionine, valine, tryptophan, leucine, threonine, and isoleucine.

The quality of the protein can therefore be determined by what extent it contains these essential amino acids. The quality can also be indicated by how well the dog digests the protein. Commercially processed dog foods that contain high levels of cereals are generally considered to contain poor quality protein. The problem is that these products can indicate relatively high levels of protein, but the type of protein contains low if non-existent sources of essential amino acids. Good quality protein would be found in dairy produce such as milk and cheese also eggs and obviously meat.

Protein deficiency would cause all sorts of problems and generally have a serious debilitating effect on the body. Examples of diseases would include, immune deficiency, poor bone growth and muscle development etc. Adult dogs would be greatly affected, but imagine the devastating effects to growing pups. Again, this is a common problem with poor commercially processed or homemade diets that are either badly designed or contain poor quality cereals.

In the same way that a protein deficiency will cause problems so will an over consumption. The main problems with over feeding protein involve kidney disease. Growing pups and lactating mothers require almost twice as much as an adult dog. The actual percentage of good quality protein needed for an adult dog would be approximately 8 to 10%, and a lactating bitch and growing pups about 18 to 20%.

Carbohydrate – The main role of carbohydrates in your dog's diet is to provide energy and dietary fibre. Dogs do not have a minimum carbohydrate requirement but they do need a certain amount of glucose to fuel essential organs like the brain. Carbohydrates are derived from plant sources and are either soluble or insoluble. Soluble consist of simple sugars mostly found in fruit, as well as sugar cane etc. Insoluble carbohydrates, complex or starches as they are otherwise known, originate from vegetables and grains for example leafy veg, potatoes, corn, pumpkin, beans, peas etc. Vegetables as carbohydrates that we feed to our dogs should be raw and fresh. Or as previously noted, carefully dehydrated, therefore not damaging nutrients and enzymes to any great extent. I hasten to add 'vegetables' and not produce such as corn, rice, wheat etc, or products such as pasta. The vegetables should also be processed, finely chopped or crushed, for greater digestion and therefore absorption. Carbohydrates have featured as a significant ingredient in processed dog food. But in a natural sense, carbohydrates are not as important to dogs as it is for humans as a source of energy. Dogs should not be given large amounts of carbohydrate over a prolonged period. Their internal workings are not designed to handle significant amounts of this type of food source.

Fibre - Fibre is also an important component of carbohydrates, which isn't ingested but aids greatly with the internal workings. Fibre is also either soluble or insoluble. Soluble basically means that it absorbs water; swells and bulks up to a gelatinous matter. Examples include; oatmeal, apples, beans etc. Insoluble fibres do not absorb water, but act as a bulking agent. Although stating the obvious, insoluble fibre is pretty much parts of vegetable matter that do not absorb water, such as the skins. They act to slow down digestion, aid greater absorption and make the stools easier to pass.

A dog's body is only capable of digesting certain kinds of carbohydrate and too much fibre in the diet is not good for them. It is usually recommended that a mixture of fast and slow fermenting fibres are best. The reason being that too much slow fermenting fibre such as cellulose is likely to cause a sluggish digestion. Bran is considered a good source of fast fermenting fibre but too much could cause diarrhoea. Somewhere in the middle is a moderately fermentable fibre such as beet pulp which is a common ingredient in dog foods.

(Values for 100g of beef, chicken and pork fat)

Beef Fat	Chicken Fat	Pork Fat
100 g	100 g	100 g
Saturated 42 g	Saturated 30 g	Saturated 32g
Monounsaturated 50 g	Monounsaturated 21 g	Monounsaturated 21 g
Polyunsaturated 4 g	Polyunsaturated 45 g	Polyunsaturated 11 g

Fats – This is the most highly concentrated form of energy so it is an important part of your dog's diet. Fats provide your dog with twice the energy of protein and carbohydrates. Fats are also important for providing structure for cells and for producing certain types of hormones. They are also necessary to ensure that your dog's body can absorb fat-soluble vitamins. Your dog needs a balance of omega-3 and omega-6 fatty acids in his body and it is best if these fats come from animal-based sources instead of plant-based sources.

Again fat is the best energy food source, but the consumption of fat depends on the lifestyle of the dog. All dogs need some fat. But a sedentary, house dog will obviously need far less than a working dog or feral dog or wolf, who are dependent on food for survival and use up large amounts of energy in the process. Too much fat, in the case of a relatively inactive house dog, would lead to obesity, high cholesterol and other diseases, possibly leading to death.

On a more positive note, fat is essential for providing insulation for the body as well as protecting the nerves. It facilitates absorption of vitamins A, K, D and E. In essence, fat is a vital component of every cell in the dogs body. It is important to note that like other food elements, fat has to be provided in the diet.

Essential fatty acids are especially vital for the correct functioning of the dogs body. Without this, the dog will develop a whole host of diseases. It is also important to note that not all fats are recommended. There is a big difference between 'Essential fatty acids' and 'Non-essential fatty acids'.

There is a hormone called 'prostaglandins', which plays an essential role in regulating all bodily functions. Prostaglandins are formulated using essential fatty acids. If essential fatty acids are absent, then non essential fatty acids are utilised, and this results in an imbalance, malfunction and disease.

Essential fatty acids are the types of healthy fats we are told to eat such as omega rich 3, 6 and 9 fish oils. Chicken and pork fat, or lard, are surprisingly excellent sources of essential fatty acid, that may not be healthy for human consumption, but are excellent for dogs.

Non essential acids consist of fats such as beef or mutton suet.

Again, chicken and pork fat are considered excellent sources of 'essential fatty acids'. Animal fat is generally saturated fat that is considered bad for human consumption. The table above indicates that beef, chicken and pork fat have similar levels of saturated fat. But look at the monounsaturated amount for beef. Chicken and Pork are the same and relatively low, but beef is over twice as much. Also notice the very low polyunsaturated amount for beef at only 4 g. Pork fat is almost 3 times as much and chicken fat is over 11 times as much.

Fats that are considered very healthy for human consumption include Olive oil and Canola or rapeseed oil. However, these are very rich in Monounsaturated fats, which if fed to dogs to any great extent would cause an essential fatty acid deficiency. Other oils high in monounsaturated fats include: Peanut oil, sunflower oil, hydrogenated soybean oil, palm oil etc. Polyunsaturated fats are therefore considered to be of greater value to dogs than monounsaturated.

Other than pork and chicken fat, other excellent sources of 'essential fatty acids' include polyunsaturated rich oils such as corn oil, flaxseed/

linseed oil, soybean oil (however, be careful that the soybean oil is not hydrogenated. Hydrogenation is a process that effectively changes soybean and other oils from polyunsaturated to monounsaturated.)

Safflower oil is also recommended as an excellent source of polyunsaturated fatty acid. However, be careful with Safflower oil, as there are two types, one is high in monounsaturated fatty acid and low in polyunsaturated, this is known as (oleic acid). The other high in polyunsaturated fatty acid and low in monounsaturated, known as (linoleic acid).

So to summarise, excellent sources of essential fatty acids include chicken and pork fat, and polyunsaturated rich vegetable oils. Fats to avoid include beef fat (tallow), mutton fat etc , and vegetable oils rich in monounsaturated fatty acids.

Omega 6 Fatty Acid

These are essential fatty acids that are found in pig and poultry fat, as well as many sources of vegetable oil. Many of the commercially processed dog foods as well as home cooked foods based on beef and cooked grain, are likely to be lacking in these fatty acids. As you know, a lack of these essential fatty acids results in a number of diseases for our dogs such as skin disease, reproduction and growth problems. High levels of Omega 6 fatty acid are found in the following list in descending order of potency; corn oil, cotton seed oil, un-hydrogenated soybean oil, linoleic sunflower oil, peanut oil. Also present, but to a lesser level of Omega 6 are flaxseed oil, olive oil, palm oil, rapeseed (canola) oil.

Omega 3

These important fatty acids are mainly found in fish oils and fish. They largely benefit the brain and nerve functions, so can affect vision, brain activity and fertility in males etc. Flaxseed/linseed oil, is particularly high in Omega 3 and to a significant but lesser extent, canola (rapeseed) oil and soybean. All other oils have omega 3, but to a smaller degree. As linseed/flaxseed is particularly potent, it will be tempting to use this. However, be very careful to only use linseed/flaxseed intended for animal or human consumption.

The type available from DIY stores, intended to treat timber and make putty soft etc, is poisonous to dogs and should never be given to them. Also be very careful about giving your dogs fish oils as there is a risk of over dosing their supply of vitamins A and D. If in doubt avoid feeding fish oils.

Have a look at the following source link which gives a vast array of sources, flaxseed and fish oils being the highest:

http://nutritiondata.self.com/ foods-0001400000000000000000.html

Rich mammalian sources of omega 3 include; eyes and brains etc. Most meats are quite low, but rabbit and lambs liver are considered the best sources.

If supplementing your dogs diet with omega 3 and 6 fatty acids, always ensure to supplement with vitamin E also. Without the presence of vitamin E, these essential fatty acids have a tendency to go off and become rancid in the dogs body.

If you were looking for an oil with a good balance, corn oil and soybean oil are generally considered the best to combine both omega 6 and 3.

Vitamins – Your dog's body is incapable of producing most vitamins, so it is essential that he get them through his diet. Some of the most important vitamins for dogs include vitamin A, vitamin D, vitamin E and vitamin C.

The Importance of Vitamins:

Sufficient dietary minerals can be obtained from natural sources such as raw meaty bones and the veg, eggs, dairy products mentioned previously. There does seem to be a problem in this regard with processed foods, in that dogs can potentially receive far more minerals than they need. However, vitamins do have a tendency to be lacking in certain cheap processed formulas. Vitamins are vital for the correct functioning of the body and its many organs. A lack of certain vitamins will lead to diseases.

We typically know vitamins by their letters of the alphabet, A, B, C, D etc. If certain vitamins are absent, then deficiency diseases are bound to manifest. If the dog is getting just enough vitamins, then they will not necessarily show signs of obvious disease, but they are not really at an optimum healthy level. When vitamins are in abundance, then they not only prevent deficiency diseases, but act as a defence against disease. So an abundance promotes health, resists disease, greatly aids reproduction and basically allows the dog to have long term fitness and stamina against stress. In essence, an abundance of vitamins helps all the bodily functions to work efficiently to their optimum level. However, this does not mean that vitamins should be administered at higher unlimited levels. It is possible for an overdose or toxic level to be reached with certain vitamins such as A or D. For severe illness such as with cancer, quite often high doses of vitamin C are administered to combat the disease. Vitamin C and B for example are relatively safe to administer in this way, although I would not recommend this without consulting a vet or nutritional specialist.

Commercially produced dog food is at risk of lacking essential vitamins for a variety of reasons. Dog food is often made up of cheap fillers such as grain and animal by-products and then cooked at high temperatures. What little vitamin value that was present in its raw state is likely to be destroyed or greatly diminished during the cooking process. Vitamins can also be destroyed when mixed with minerals. We will talk more about this later. Also, vitamins that are exposed to air have a limited shelf life. So if dry dog food is not kept in an air tight container it will quickly deteriorate.

The exact same problem can occur if you home cook food for your dog. With the best will in the world, you can use a variety of top quality ingredients but during the cooking process many vitamins can be destroyed. This would be more significant during old age, puppy growth or stages of reproduction or lactation.

What are vitamins?

Vitamins comprise of water soluble and fat soluble. Examples of water soluble are vitamin C and B complex. Vitamins A, D, E and K are classified as fat soluble.

To a certain extent, water soluble vitamins are stored by the body, despite a contrary opinion that they must be supplied on a daily basis. As mentioned previously they can also be given at much higher doses than are recommended. However, there would be little point in giving high doses that

are likely to be excreted, but a dose similar to a human dose would probably be adequate. Again, any that is not immediately used or stored is simply urinated out of the body. It is perfectly safe for the dog and no harm is done.

B Complex

They are extremely important for processing fats, proteins and carbohydrates and turning them into energy. This energy is vital for all bodily functions, for the general purpose of daily activity and for growth. A dog given sufficient Vitamin B would be full of life, bright and energetic, generally be and look fit and healthy. The dog deficient would be totally the opposite, so lacking energy, dull, and overweight. They also play a vital role with the nervous system. Again a deficiency would indicate a nervous dog, whereas sufficient levels would indicate a calm, happy dog.

Similar to humans, a lack of the B complex vitamins can seriously affect the nervous system. It can also have a serious effect on the body during stressful periods. It can also have a significant effect on the energy levels of the dog. The B vitamins are usually administered all together as a complex rather than given separately, unless there is an obvious singular B Vitamin deficiency.

Other problems include:

Under development; Deficient immune system; Production of antibodies is diminished; Lack of antioxidants; Thymus gland problems; Lack of anti ageing; Tissue degeneration; Free radicals are not eliminated from the body; More prone to stress; Problems with blood production, reproduction, tissue repair, growth.; Skin and fur problems occur.

In essence they are vital for all bodily functions. They are vital for the health and wellbeing of our dogs at all stages of life.

Rich food sources of B complex include:

The best sources of B complex as a whole are liver and brewers yeast. Brewers yeast is often recommended as an excellent source of B complex vitamins. It is also a good source of protein. But other B vitamins, not the full B complex, are present in foods such as brown rice, wholemeal bread, meat, eggs, offal, dairy produce, green leafy veg etc.

Vitamin C

The same rules apply to vitamin C as the above information on the B complex. They are stored by the body to an extent. Can be administered safely at high doses, albeit any not taken up by the body or immediately used, would be eliminated through the urine. Dogs do produce their own vitamin C to an extent, which leads some people to assert they do not need any additional. However, although opinions differ, it is best to give extra in order to ensure your dog is at optimum health. Dogs in the wild would still be eating a lot of vitamin C rich food, and probably to a greater extent than a lot of domestically fed dogs, who are generally reliant on receiving all their nutrients from commercial food.

Unlike humans who cannot make or store Vitamin C, dogs actually produce this in their liver. However, during times of stress or ill health they would require probably more than the body can naturally produce. Apart from stress and perhaps over work, problems can occur relative to reproduction or for the growth of pups.

Vitamin C promotes the following:

Helps eliminate toxins; Fights infection and generally boosts the immune system; Heavily involved in the healing of wounds etc; Greatly alleviates the stresses of reproduction, lactation, weaning; Essential for collagen production and other growth factors; Generally boosts the body in relation to wear and tear associated with exercise and body rejuvenation. Also greatly helps with the ageing process

Again, as with the B complex, this vitamin is not necessarily dangerous in high doses. However, excess vitamin C, can cause diarrhoea. This is not dangerous and a reduction in dosage clears the problem.

Under normal healthy conditions it will not matter a great deal what type of vitamin C your dog receives. Vitamin C is known as ascorbic acid, but be aware that there are different forms such as calcium ascorbate, ester C and sodium ascorbate. It is important to know this because if for example your dog suffers with hip dysplasia calcium ascorbate should not be given, because of the extra calcium. A dog with heart disease should not be given sodium ascorbate, due to the sodium.

Fat soluble vitamins

Vitamins A, E and K have anti ageing/antioxidant properties. Vitamin D and A, in particular should never be given at high doses as they are extremely toxic at high levels. The other problem is that unlike B and C vitamins, these are stored to a greater extent in the body. The effect of topping up, again can potentially build up to toxic levels. Having said that, despite the dangers of toxic overload, all of these vitamins should never be allowed to become non-existent as diseases will arise as a result of the deficiency.

Vitamin A, is vital for most if not all of the bodily processes. It is particularly important for sight, immune system functioning, mucous membranes, skin, adrenal glands, reproduction, growth etc.

Vitamin A Deficiency – Vitamin A as you know, is a type of fat-soluble vitamin that comes from liver, dairy, and certain yellow vegetables. This vitamin is essential for the healthy formation of bones and teeth. It also plays a role in healthy skin, coat, and eyesight. A deficiency in Vitamin A, may cause poor growth and development, skin problems, poor coat quality, eye problems, and immune problems. These deficiencies would be more problematic with dry food as opposed to canned.

Vitamin E

Vitamin E is a fat-soluble vitamin that plays a role in metabolising fats and supporting healthy cell function. Sources of vitamin E include liver, vegetable oil, wheat germ, and leafy green vegetables. A deficiency of vitamin E can lead to reproductive disorders as well as disorders of the liver, heart, muscle, nerves, and eyes. It can also have a negative impact on your dog's bowels.

Free radicals that are present throughout your dogs body, pose a real problem in terms of cancer, premature ageing, arthritis, strokes etc. Free radicals are actually formed in the dogs fat tissues, and if left to sit there can go rancid. Vitamin E, otherwise known as an antioxidant, is the best antidote for these free radicals.

Vitamin E combats so many problems that can affect your dog. Examples of this are; arresting premature ageing. Helping to prevent heart disease, blood clots that cause strokes. It typically acts as a barrier to disease and toxic heavy metals. Greatly aiding reproduction and energy production as well as producing vitamin C. Vitamin E is also necessary to help fight infection.

As mentioned previously, Vitamin E is also greatly needed if oils such as linseed oil, corn oil, sunflower oil, cod liver oil among others, are a significant part of your dogs diet. The major reason revolves around vitamin E preventing fat rancidity. When dogs ingest these types of polyunsaturated oils there is a risk they will go rancid, and vitamin E is the answer to make sure this doesn't happen. It is important to know that whilst vitamin E combats the effects of fat rancidity, the process of combating actually kills the vitamin E. So although it does the job your dog needs, it obviously needs replenishing. So feeding lots of polyunsaturated oil, without sufficient vitamin E in the system, will eventually lead to a deficiency and resulting disease.

Sources of vitamin E

High levels of vitamin E are found in dark leafy greens. They are also found in the polyunsaturated fats mentioned as causing a problem with rancidity. These are wheatgerm oil, cottonseed, safflower, soybean etc. It may sound paradoxical, but although they have reasonably high levels of vitamin E, it only becomes a problem when the fat starts to go rancid. When this happens, as previously mentioned the vitamin E, counteracts this but in the process, dies off and so causing a deficiency.

Liver, eggs, certain grains as well as dairy produce are other good sources

Toxic side effects

Immediate large doses can cause temporary high blood pressure, but vitamin E is not known to cause any significant problems or side effects. Of course this does not mean you should administer large doses for the sake of it. As with any form of supplementation, do not attempt this without the advice and direction of vet or nutritional specialist.

Vitamin D

You probably already know this as the sunshine vitamin. Sunbathing or just spending short periods of time in direct sunlight, provides our bodies with vitamin D. However, if it is a cloudy day or the area is affected with airborne pollutants, mist, smoke etc, then the effects are greatly diminished and supplementation may be needed. The same goes for our dogs. It is thought that 10 to 15 minutes of 'direct' sunlight would provide our dogs with their 'recommended' daily dose.

Vitamin D plays an important function by aiding absorption of phosphorus and calcium. It also regulates the depositing and if need be, the withdrawing of calcium and phosphorus from the bones.

The main issue as to whether the dog is receiving enough vitamin D revolves around how much direct sunlight they are exposed to per day. If the dog is fed a meaty bones, BARF diet, and is exposed to even a small amount of sun per day, they should not need any supplementation. If that isn't the case, then they will probably need some form of supplementing.

Cod liver oil has always been seen as one of, if not the best source for vitamin D, but all the fish liver oils contain good amounts of vitamin D to varying degrees. Fish such as herring, catfish, salmon, trout, mackerel, sardine etc are also great sources.

Toxic effects

Vitamin D is similar to vitamin A in that much care is needed to ensure your dog does not receive too much. One of the main problems involves calcium and the possibility that too much calcium is deposited in the body. This in turn can cause abnormal bodily functioning.

Recommended ammounts

Vitamin D is particularly important for growing puppies as a deficiency can result in bone diseases such as rickets. If you notice a poor appetite and therefore poor growth and weight loss, then a deficiency of vitamin D could be the problem. Bone problems will be evident such as fractures, malformed or misshaped bones, enlarged joints etc.

Deficiencies of vitamin D may well arise in dogs on a bad diet of poor quality commercially processed food, dogs predominantly fed meat, older dogs that have difficulty manufacturing vitamin D or even lack of sunlight.

Vitamin K

Vitamin K has a variety of health promoting uses. It is particularly important as a blood clotting agent, as well as growth, reproduction, healthy skin, anti ageing properties and as an antioxidant. There is an interesting connection with vitamin K and faeces, as vitamin K is produced in the large intestine, by bacteria which is then passed into the faeces of most animals. So if you see your dog eating another animals faeces, it could well be an indication of a vitamin K deficiency. It may not be, but at least you know that they are actually getting nutritional benefits such as an intake of vitamin K. Incidentally faeces can provide high levels of protein, fatty acids, vitamins including B, K, antioxidants, minerals and fibre. So in fact, dogs that eat faeces could be indicating a lack of a number of vitamins and nutrients in their diet, not just vitamin K. But again, please do not automatically assume this is the case. I have known two dogs that were fed exactly the same diet and were both in excellent condition and yet one would regularly eat horse faeces whilst out on walks. This was never a significant amount. The dog in question would also stop at every puddle she passed and drink out of water containers left for horses. She could well be getting some mineral benefit but rightly or wrongly it was assumed she was one of those dogs that likes to pick at and taste anything.

Other sources of vitamin K are dark green leafy vegetables such as kale, chard, spinach etc and other vegetables such as salad veg, brassica veg etc. Liver and fish are also good sources.

Vitamin K Toxicity

Natural vitamin K is actually non toxic, and it is unlikely your dog will eat enough natural foods in a day to cause an over load. However synthetically manufactured vitamin K can be toxic in high doses. Very high doses of over 100 times the recommended daily dose are likely to have a toxic effect.

Once again, provided your dog is receiving a BARF type diet with plenty of raw meaty bones, vegetables and other food sources, any kind of supplementation is unlikely to be necessary.

Minerals – Minerals are a type of inorganic compound that cannot by synthesised and thus must come from your dog's diet. The most important minerals for dogs include calcium, phosphorus, Magnesium, Selenium, potassium, sodium, copper, zinc, and iron. Minerals are particularly important for developing and maintaining strong bones and teeth.

The two most important minerals for a dogs health, particularly the growing pup, and generally breeding and reproduction, are phosphorus and calcium. The main natural source of these in terms of a dogs diet are found in raw (not cooked) bones. As well as calcium and phosphorus, bones are also likely to store copper, chromium, iodine, iron, magnesium, manganese, potassium, selenium, strontium, zinc etc.

Dr. Ian Billinghurst, states in Give Your Dog a Bone

"Do realise your dog will not, cannot, suffer mineral deficiencies, imbalances or excesses, when raw meaty bones make up the bulk of its diet. This applies to dogs of all ages, including puppies. And I don't just mean puppies of the smaller breeds: I mean all breeds of puppies, including most definitely the giant breeds".

An imbalance of any essential vitamin, mineral or other element can obviously have major health consequences. But a major problem associated with mineral imbalance isn't necessarily a deficiency, but an over dose. Too much calcium can result in the calcium combining with other essential minerals such as zinc, iron, copper etc, and preventing the absorption of the zinc, iron, copper etc. This in turn would set up a deficiency of the zinc, iron, copper etc.

Too much sodium or salt can result in cardiovascular disease and hypertension. An excess of phosphorus can lead to diseases such as kidney failure. All of these problems can be the result of feeding dogs either poor quality commercial dog food, or over supplementation.

Problems with Supplementation

Once again, be very careful about any kind of supplementation without first of all taking the advice of a vet or nutritional specialist. Certainly be cautious about supplementing in isolation. Again, calcium seems to be a big culprit of diseases and disorders for both growing pups as well as adult dogs. But because it is well known that calcium can negate other minerals, there is a temptation to supplement these other minerals such as zinc, copper and iron. All manner of skin, skeletal growth and arthritic conditions associated with this kind of mineral imbalance can occur. In fact any mineral that is supplemented in isolation can cause an overdose, resulting disorder or disease.

Problems with blood tests to establish deficiencies

Establishing a nutritional deficiency via a blood test should not be relied on as conclusive. The following link to an article highlighting this, indicates that certain blood tests have revealed no deficiency in particular diets. But after further investigation a serious deficiency has been diagnosed and successfully treated:

http://www.petmd.com/blogs/thedaily-vet/ktudor/2013/nov/why-blood-tests-are-not-good-for-testing-nutritional-status-in-pets-31029

Of course blood tests and other testing can in certain cases, be the most efficient way of diagnosing a problem. But again, where diet is concerned it is usually a question of elimination of symptoms and possible causes.

Water – Water is undoubtedly the most important nutrient for all animals. Your dog would be able to survive for a while without food if he had to, but he would only last a few days without water. Water accounts for as much as 70% of your dog's body-weight and even a 10% decrease in your dog's body water levels can be very dangerous. Provide your Labrador with plenty of fresh water at all times!

It is common knowledge that tap water is processed using a number of chemicals and there is much debate as to possible links to cancer. Obviously the reasons for this chemical processing are to kill bacteria present in its raw state at sewage plants. Many people are now filtering tap water

as a way to purify this tap water as much as possible. This is also a good idea for dogs. As you will regularly see dogs drinking out of puddles, another good idea is to try and recycle rain water. Admittedly in areas of pollution, there is a risk of acid rain etc, but there is a good chance that rain water will contain fewer potentially harmful chemicals than tap water.

2) THE IMPORTANCE OF DIET – NUTRITIONAL DEFICIENCIES

Although we cover diet in the feeding section, it is included here from a health, disease and deficiency point of view. As well as vitamin deficiencies mentioned above we will touch on mineral deficiencies here.

As you will no doubt now be aware, if you do not provide your dog with a healthy diet, his body will not be able to function as it should, and he may be more likely to develop illnesses and infections. In addition to providing your dog with high-quality dog food, you also need to make sure that his diet provides certain nutrients. Dogs are prone to developing certain nutritional deficiencies which can produce some very real and dangerous symptoms.

Some of the nutritional deficiencies to which your Labrador is most likely to be prone may include:

General Malnutrition – Malnutrition is defined as the imbalanced, excessive, or insufficient consumption of nutrients. Some of the signs of malnutrition include an emaciated appearance, poor skin and coat quality, bad breath, swollen gums, abnormal stools, growth problems, poor immunity, lack of energy, and behavioural problems.

Magnesium Deficiency – Magnesium and potassium are the most abundant substances in cells, so a magnesium deficiency can be very serious. Magnesium is required for most metabolic functions and in the development of healthy bones and tissue. Symptoms of magnesium deficiency include weakness, trembling, depression, behavioural changes, and loss of coordination. Careful treatment for this deficiency is essential because too much magnesium can be fatal for your dog.

Iron Deficiency "Anaemia" – Iron is required to produce and develop red blood cells and those blood cells help to carry oxygen throughout your dog's body. A deficiency of iron can lead to anaemia, a condition in which your dog doesn't have enough healthy red blood cells to carry oxygen to organs and muscles. Symptoms of iron deficiency anaemia include loss of appetite, decreased growth, lethargy/weakness, depression, rapid breathing, and dark-coloured stools.

Calcium Deficiency – We have already touched on calcium, but additional information is included here. As previously noted, your dog requires a delicate balance of calcium and phosphorus to maintain healthy bones and teeth. Calcium is also important for nerve, heart and muscle function as well as blood clotting. A calcium deficiency can lead to spasms, lameness, heart palpitations, anxiety, bone fractures, arthritis, high blood pressure, and more. This type of deficiency is often caused by a high-meat diet because meat is very high in phosphorus. This can lead to an imbalance of phosphorus and calcium.

Additional Problems with calcium excess

Dried food has been more of a problem of calcium excess, with some cases showing up to a dozen times the amount actually needed. Obviously from a growth point of view calcium is a vital nutrient. However, in excess the calcium not absorbed by the body is eventually excreted in the faeces. The problem, as you have already learned, is that calcium combines with other essential minerals such as zinc and results in the zinc not being absorbed by the body. However, as well as zinc, copper and iron are affected in the same way which can result in anaemia. Where zinc deficiency occurs, the aforementioned problems associated with skin diseases, stunted growth in pups, reproductive and immunity problems are likely to manifest. In addition wounds take longer to heal, the nervous system is affected, bone abnormalities occur, testicular growth is affected, the thyroid gland doesn't function properly, the body loses protein, etc. To say the least, the results of a zinc deficiency are pretty grim.

An excess of calcium is also known to be a contributory factor in dogs suffering with bloat. When the body detects a calcium excess it produces 'gastrin', which is a hormone that thickens the ends of the stomach and makes the expulsion of gases difficult to pass.

So again, in addition to deficiencies in certain vitamins or minerals, dogs can also suffer from an excess of certain nutrients. For example, too much vitamin A can cause your Labrador's bones to become brittle and his skin to become dry. An excess of vitamin D could cause your dog's bones to become too dense and for his tissue and joints to calcify. Too much vitamin C can lead to kidney stones, excess calcium can lead to phosphorus imbalances, and too much polyunsaturated fat (such as from fish oil) may lead to a vitamin E imbalance.

3) CALORIE REQUIREMENTS FOR DOGS

Your dog requires a certain number of calories each day in order for his body to maintain proper function. Calorie needs for dogs vary from one breed to another and they also depend on the dog's age, size, sex, and activity level.

On the next page you will find a chart outlining the basic calorie needs for dogs at different ages:

The calorie information in that chart

is a basic guideline. Your dog's individual needs may be different. The best way to determine how many calories your Labrador actually needs is to calculate his Resting Energy Requirement (RER), and to then modify it according to his age and activity level. The formula for calculating your dog's RER is as follows:

RER = 30 x (weight in kg) + 70

For example, if your dog weighed 45 pounds, you would use the following formula: RER = 30 x (45/2.205) +70. So (45/2.205) = 20.40816327, then multiply that by 30 = 612.244898, then add 70 = 682 rounded down to the nearest whole number. You will note that in order to determine your dog's weight in kilograms you need to divide it by 2.205 first. So using our formula and the example given as shown above, a 45-pound dog has an estimated RER of about 682 calories. To determine your dog's daily energy requirements you will need to multiply his RER by a factor that varies by age and activity level. Use the chart also on the next page to determine what number to multiply your dog's RER by:

So following on, if we use another example, in this case our 20 lb dog in the chart; to get to 684

Calorie Needs For Dogs (Per Day)

Type of Dog	10 Lbs	15 Lbs	20 Lbs
Puppy (Under 4 Months)	618 Calories	-	-
Puppy (Over 4 Months)	412 Calories	-	-
Normal Adult Dog	329 Calories	438 Calories	547 Calories
Active Adult Dog	412 Calories	548 Calories	684 Calories
Pregnant Female	618 Calories	822 Calories	1,026 Calories
Lactating Female	824+ Calories	1,096+ Calories	1,368+ Calories

higher in both protein and consequently, calories than adult dog foods. This accounts for the needs of growing puppies. In pregnant females you typically do not need to start increasing rations until the last three weeks of gestation. Once the dog gives birth, her calorie needs will increase again so that she can produce enough milk for her puppies, and to compensate for any body mass she may have lost. The more puppies in the litter, the higher her calorie needs will be.

we calculate as follows:

20 divided by 2.205 = 9.070295.

9.070295 x 30 = 272.1088.

272.1088 + 70 = 342.1088

Now taking into consideration the activity level of the dog as light so multiply the RER by 2; we multiply 342.1088 by 2 = 684 rounded to the nearest whole number

Based on the information in the chart below, you can see that puppies and pregnant dogs, perhaps unsurprisingly have much higher calorie needs than adult dogs. When your Labrador puppy is growing he will need to eat a lot more than he will when he is fully grown. Puppy foods are typically

When your dog gets older, his calorie needs will drop. Senior dogs typically require 20% fewer calories than younger dogs because their metabolisms slow down and they become less active. Many dogs become overweight as they age because their owners do not reduce their feeding portions to account for changes in metabolism and energy. Once a dog becomes obese it can be difficult for him to lose weight, so be especially careful with your dog's diet once he reaches "senior" level around 7 years of age.

It is important to realise that these are guidelines only

Resting Energy Requirements (RER)

Type of Dog	Daily Calorie needs
Weight Loss	1.0 x RER
Normal Adult (Neutered)	1.6 x RER
Normal Adult (Intact)	1.8 x RER
Lightly Active Adult	2.0 x RER
Moderately Active Adult	3.0 x RER
Pregnant (First 42 Days)	1.8 x RER
Pregnant (Last 21 Days)	3.0 x RER
Lactating Female	4.8 x RER
Puppy (2 to 4 Months)	3.0 x RER
Puppy (4 to 12 Months)	2.0 x RER

and should not be taken as exact figures to use:

If you do a Google search for [basic calorie calculator for dogs]

You will find the following websites illustrate the same formula used here.

http://veterinaryteam.dvm360.com/calculate-calories-pets-need

http://www.peteducation.com/article.cfm?c=2+1659&aid=2612

If however, you check out the following Pet MD link you will notice a different formula used:

http://www.petmd.com/blogs/nutrition-nuggets/jcoates/2013/aug/how-many-calories-does-dog-need-30849

This formula is (RER) = 70 (body weight in kg)^0.75. The '^' is supposed to represent an exponent or to the power of. So for example $(2)^3$ means 2 x 2 x 2 which = 8. If you are not familiar with using exponents then you will find the formula I have used more user friendly.

So using this new formula to compare the original, lets take the initial example of a dog weighing 20.40816327kg or 20.4kg for simplicity. For illustration purposes we will not use the activity level multiplier. Now multiply this by the power 0.75. So (20.4)to the power 0.75 or $(20.4)^{0.75}$ or 3/4 if you wish = 9.598925601 rounded to 9.6.

If we then multiply this by 70; so 70 x 9.6 = 672. Using our original formula the result was 682. So as you can see the two results are very close.

There are also other sites using this alternative formula such as the following:

https://vet.osu.edu/vmc/companion/our-services/nutrition-support-service/basic-calorie-calculator

Again they are a good rough guide of what you can expect to feed. You will obviously also find that a specific brand of commercial dog food will give their guidelines usually based on the weight of your dog. But always use comparatives such as the ideal typical body weight, activity level, whether the dog looks too fat or thin etc.

So what is a good diet choice for your Labrador dog? Well, you have many options and some dog owners like to mix and match, to keep things interesting for your dog.

4) HOW TO CHOOSE A HEALTHY DOG FOOD

Now that you have an understanding of your dog's nutritional needs you are ready to learn how to choose a healthy dog food. If you walk down the aisles at your local pet store you could easily be overwhelmed by the sheer number of options you have. Not only are there many different brands to choose from but most brands offer several different flavours or formulas. In this section you will learn the basics about how to determine whether a commercial dog food is healthy or not.

Commercial Dog Food

The history of commercial dog food goes back to the 1850s when it was first manufactured in England. This product largely consisted of processed bone meal and cereals. Some 30 odd years later, U.S. mill owners realised the huge profit potential of taking their by-products and turning it into dog food. In 1922 the first type of canned dog food was produced using horse meat. This basic idea is still used today with a few modifications. In an age where millions are spent on advertising, it is no surprise that commercially produced dog food is the most well known and unfortunately, popular method of feeding our pets.

If you should opt for a commercial food don't look at the promises on the packaging, but turn it around and look at the ingredients on the back, this will tell you so much more.

If there is anything that you don't recognise don't buy the food until you have found out what the ingredient is. If the main ingredient is some kind of meat followed by the words 'meal' or 'derivatives' don't buy the food.

In our fast paced world, where fast food chains flourish and ready meals fill supermarket shelves, it is unsurprising that dogs are fed in the same way. It has to be said, opening a tin of dog food or feeding a few scoops of kibble takes a few minutes of our time. Tinned stuff can be stored anywhere for years and an opened bag of kibble will remain relatively fresh for a month or so. All we need are the food manufacturers to feed us with words such as 'healthy', 'nutritious', 'premium', 'complete', 'balanced diet' and we are sold. I personally have mixed feelings about commercial foods. Again some brands are better than others and if you are pushed for time initially then it can offer an OK temporary alternative. I would not however, recommend this in the long term. I would at the very least incorporate raw natural foods, preferably a permanent BARF diet.

Get Cooking

Your second option is to cook your dog's food at home.

This is actually quite easy and there is no reason why you can't alternate between home prepared dog food and a good quality commercial food.

A careful mix of sweet potatoes, green leafy veg, beans and legumes with added white fish or other protein source is a perfect home-made dog's dinner. Adding some type of oil is also good for the coat and the joints. Again, please refer again to the section on essential fatty acids and the various suitable oils.

If you make a big pot of food at a time you can of course portion this into suitable containers and freeze, if you have the space. As long as you vary the types of carbohydrate and protein, then you should easily meet all of your dog's vitamin and mineral needs over a few weeks recurring.

However, be careful with home cooked food and realise that even though you know what has gone into this food, it may be deficient in certain nutrients. What some people tend to do to be extra sure that they are meeting their dog's nutritional needs is usually along the following lines. They alternate between commercial food and home-made then add a digestive enzyme with a vitamin supplement prepared for your dog. Surely the fact that they are having to add a digestive enzyme and vitamin and mineral supplement indicates that the food is deficient in some way.

Why food is cooked

Wild feral dogs and wolves will eat rotten 'contaminated', flesh and bones, other animal faeces, animal guts etc. In other words, food that we would consider infected, laden with germs likely to make us ill. But for the dog or wolf, these are a rich source of nutrients the dog needs such as enzymes, vitamins, proteins, antioxidants, fatty acids etc. The digestive system of the feral dog is actually no different to the domesticated dog.

We humans, view cooking as necessary as it breaks food down, making it more digestible. Again the digestion of dogs is somewhat different to us, and the digestive system of domestic dogs is actually not dissimilar to its ancestor the wolf.

Many dog owners will assert that they feed their dogs cooked food and the dogs thrive and show no obvious immediate signs of ill health. The point is, the dogs are unlikely to die immediately, but there is a likelihood for them to gradually show signs of ill health and premature ageing, resulting in an early death.

The main reason commercially produced dog food is cooked is to kill germs and parasites. Cooking also destroys much of the vitamin content and food therefore loses much of its nutritious value. Furthermore, cooking destroys antioxidants which again combat the effects of ageing. Lysine and methionine, two essential amino acids are also thought to be destroyed by the cooking process. Without them, the dogs health in general and resistance to disease is affected. Problems associated with general growth, skin, bones as well as problems associated with pregnancy can also manifest.

The cooking process actually changes the molecular structure of food and affects the digestibility of proteins for dogs. This change results in the food potentially becoming foreign to the body which can cause allergic reactions, indigestion and at worse, be carcinogenic.

Unfortunately, cooking additionally destroys enzymes. Living enzymes naturally break food down until it decays. As cooking kills the enzymes it therefore slows this process down, which means the food can be stored for longer. This is great news for the commercial dog food industry and us the buyer to an extent, but a lot less so for the dogs.

Enzymes present in raw food are proteins which not only aid the digestive system, but actually slow down the ageing process. As well as aiding digestion, food enzymes are known to have major health benefits for dogs. These include: as well as anti ageing, pancreas functioning, alleviating joint disease and arthritis. Lack of enzymes also contributes to a process known as 'cross linking'. Cross linking is a devastating ageing process that contributes to inelastic wrinkled skin, hardened arteries, damaged genes resulting in reproductive problems, birth defects and at worst cancer. Other diseases associated with premature ageing include heart disease, kidney disease and arthritis.

It is generally the pancreas which naturally produces enzymes. If sufficient enzymes are present in food, then the pancreas does not have to produce any extra. If the required enzymes are not present, then the pancreas has to work to produce them. If the pancreas is overworked, then certain conditions and diseases can appear such as Pancreatitis and diabetes.

Other problems with home cooked food

- Lack of essential fatty acids
- A soft mush and therefore nothing to chew on to promote dental health
- Generally contains rice, pasta or other grain or cereal based ingredients and therefore not dissimilar to commercially processed foods
- Problems associated with cooking i.e. killing of enzymes, vitamin and mineral degeneration, lack of antioxidants. Again because of the combined stew/cooking, the same problems associated with mineral combination will occur, such as zinc and calcium.

Problems feeding table scraps

In all probability, table scraps are unlikely to represent a complete diet. They are bound to be lacking in essential nutrients such as protein, calcium and other essential vitamins and minerals. They are also likely to be high in meat trimming such as fat or from gravy, and carbohydrates such as vegetables. Of course this sort of diet is likely to be very palatable for the dog, but particularly if high fat sources were given, would quickly lead to obesity. Many vets advocate that whilst perfectly acceptable in moderation and on occasion, table scraps should certainly not represent the bulk of a dogs diet.

Raw Feeding

Over the last few years raw feeding has become increasingly popular and most that try it never go back to cooked food for their pets. Raw feeding is so popular that manufacturers are preparing raw food in the same way as they have been preparing cooked food for years.

The idea behind this feeding type is that the dog's diet is as natural as possible. It is based upon the diet a wild carnivore would eat. Some meat and offal, some bones and green vegetables; all raw are fed to the dog in order to mirror the wild diet. The wild diet would usually have been small prey animals, grass, greens and bones.

Advocates of this feeding type usually state that it is the best decision that they have ever made on behalf of their dog whilst there are very few that turn away from raw feeding after trial-ing it.

There are some precautions to be aware of if you are considering raw feeding though. There have been some links between infection of arthritic joints and raw meat. Similarly too many raw bones can cause digestive blockages. However, most cases associating bones and digestive problems relate to cooked bones. Some experts also believe that our dogs were more scavengers as they developed and ate less meat than we think.

I suggest that if this feeding type is something you may consider, then do a lot of supplier research first. The commercial raw foods are varying in quality much like the commercial cooked dog foods. If you are putting your dog's diet together at home then it's vital to consider varied and balanced nutrition.

If you are changing your dog's food at all then remember to wean gradually from one to the other as a quick change can easily be the cause of stomach upsets.

Barf Diet

The BARF diet (Biologically Appropriate Raw Food Diet) was first developed by veterinarian, Dr. Ian Billinghurst. The BARF diet contains thoroughly ground raw and meaty bones, raw vegetables, raw offal and supplements. You can find these in patty form, which you can break up into bits when feeding your adult Labrador. Although Dr.

Billinghurst suggests it is safe to feed raw meaty bones to growing puppies, some breeders and vets are against the idea, for reasons such as upset stomachs and the need to build them up to such a diet. He does however say in his book 'Give Your Dog A Bone' that he has successfully reared puppies on such a diet. He goes on to say that he would start them on minced chicken wings, bone and all, then soon after give them the whole chicken wing and so on.

If this interests you, please do refer to one of the following excellent books:

'Raw Meaty Bones' and 'Work Wonders' both by Dr Tom Lonsdale. 'Raw and Natural Nutrition for Dog, by Lew Olson PhD. Also 'Natural Nutrition for Dogs and Cats' by Kymythy R. Shultze.
Also please refer to the following website links:
For Tom Lonsdale
http://www.rawmeatybones.com/

For Ian Billinghurst
http://www.barfworld.com/html/dr_billinghurst/meet.shtml

https://www.drianbillinghurst.com/
By the way, I am in no way affiliated or connected to the authors, they are books that many forum contributors recommend and that I have personally read and found useful and inspiring.
Many veterinarians have claimed that this diet helps dogs with skin disorders, which are allergic to grain, preservatives, and other added ingredients found in commercial brands.
There has also been some negative feedback about this diet, such as the threat of Salmonella and Listeria monocytogenes strains. This has been predominantly asserted by the FDA.
I have to say that I am a great believer in feeding 'raw meaty bones' and there have been some excellent studies and books written. As mentioned, Ian Billinghurst an Australian Vet and Nutritionist originally proposed the idea that dogs have become ill and are dying prematurely because they have been deprived of their natural inheritance, 'raw meat and bones', (a raw diet). His books are still available but quite expensive, but his best seller 'Give Your Dog A Bone', is available reasonably cheaply as a Kindle download. The book is excellent and is well worth a read. I have only predominantly fed raw meaty bones and other raw ingredients to adult dogs, but I cannot comment on his assertion that it is perfectly acceptable to feed pups a BARF diet. In my experience, my dogs have not only looked much brighter, fitter and healthier, but their stools are more solid and their breath has been relatively odourless.
I think if I have to sum up the message for BARF, raw meaty bones feeding, it is that you need to ask questions of the whole commercial food industry and that feeding a more natural primitive diet will provide your dog with greater health and longevity. Probably on a par with only buying puppies that come from reputable breeders who health test the parents, I would say nutrition is the other most important consideration regarding the health and happiness of your dog. Of course obedience training and knowledge of your dogs behaviour are important aspects for successfully keeping a happy relationship with your new friend. But I believe too much emphasis is placed on 'Dog Whisperers' and their training being the be all and end all. If your dog is not healthy, it will not be happy. Ask yourself the following questions: Would you rather spend a small fortune on regular visits to the vet over the duration of your dogs life? Or would you rather your dog is happy and healthy and destined to live a longer life, with far fewer visits to the vet? Please do consider the BARF diet at whatever stage of life your dog is.

Points to bear in mind with feeding a raw diet.

Chewing raw meat and bones exercises and massages the teeth and gums, above all keeping them clean. If the teeth and gums become diseased and infected, they create toxins and bacteria which will be ingested and contribute to ill health.
It is important that you keep any raw food separate from your own, for obvious reasons of cross contamination. This includes thoroughly cleaning surfaces and utensils with hot soapy water and anti-bacterial sprays suitable for food surfaces. I store raw meat in lidded containers within the fridge with all other fresh perishable foods. But

I would urge you to keep raw meat frozen and take out as much as you need for no more than 3 days. You will then need to thoroughly wash the containers before replenishing with frozen meat.

Again fresh meat and bones will need refrigerating, but there is nothing to stop you buying in bulk and freezing portions. Any refrigerated food can be kept in seal-able food storage containers.

To a certain extent frozen food loses some nutritional value, but is far more beneficial than cooked/processed food.

Summarised list of raw barf diet foods

- Raw meaty bones and muscle meat from: chicken, pork, beef, rabbit and lamb
- Offal/organ meats: liver, kidney, heart etc
- Eggs
- Dairy produce: milk, butter, cheese, yoghurt.
- Seafood: All oily fish
- Vegetables: Dark green leaves, brassicas (cauliflower, cabbage, broccoli etc), root veg, salad veg, sweet potato etc.
- Fruits: Most fruits including apples (however, be careful to remove the pips as these are considered to be poisonous), bananas. Definitely not grapes and the dried varieties such as raisins, sultanas etc
- In addition brewers yeast as an excellent source of the B complex vitamins.
- The polyunsaturated oils mentioned.

Food separation and combination

Food combination and separation relates to the idea that food should be neither cooked nor combined in one complete diet. The premise of the commercially processed food is that the 'complete balanced' diet is cooked and contains a combination of food groups that the dog receives at each and every meal.

Ian Billinghurst suggests that wild dogs, feral dogs, wolves etc, will never eat a balanced meal (in other words, all of the food groups represented in one meal) and that a balanced diet is reached over time. So he suggests that one meal is likely to consist of entirely vegetarian in the form of the stomach contents or guts of a herbivore killed (This is usually the first thing a carnivore will eat, particularly if it is starving and needs to be nourished quickly). Another meal will be offal; liver, kidney, heart etc. Another will be muscle. Another, predominantly fat. Yet another will be entirely bones, hair and hide, which may well be one of the final parts of the animal eaten as all the rest is picked and stripped over a number of days.

So if the dog took this approach, day one would consist of all of the vitamins, minerals, carbohydrates and fibre mentioned as part of the vegetation food group. Day two is likely to be partly protein, but also the vitamins and other elements associated with liver and the other offal meats. Day three would be mostly protein. Day four would be mostly essential fatty acids via the fat. Day five would be mostly the minerals of the bones. So in this hypothetical scenario over a 5 day cycle the dog has received protein on mainly one day, vegetation on mainly one day, essential fatty acid on only one day. To be fair, vitamins, minerals and other elements will be present on each day, but not in the concentrations assumed for protein or carbohydrates or essential fatty acids.

Food combining is particularly problematic where calcium is concerned. As previously noted, calcium causes all sorts of problems with the absorption of essential minerals such as zinc, copper and iron. So it would be best to feed a product that has very little calcium but a good source of zinc, copper, iron and other minerals, separately from a relatively high calcium intake. Feeding offal, such as liver, kidneys, heart etc, allows your dog to feed in this way, similar to the way it would feed on a wild kill. It generally would have its daily feed of offal, and as offal is digested relatively quickly this should mean that any bone/calcium absorption should not interfere with the mineral absorption.

The advantage with a food separation diet is that certain raw foods that may seem high in certain elements are really not being given on a constant every day basis. One of the big problems with processed foods are that a lot of the same elements such as calcium and phosphorus, protein and salt, are given daily. The result of that is an overload of those nutrients and all of the consequential problems on various organs of the body, such as overworked kidneys, liver etc.

A lot of the food separation practice involves keeping proteins and starch foods separate and therefore promoting greater health.

Raw meaty bones should be fed separately from other elements such as the vegetables. The key to a healthy balanced diet is not the way dogs are fed on a commercially processed diet. In this case, they receive every element, i.e. protein, carbohydrate, fats, vitamins, minerals etc all in one go, and on each day. This causes a lot of problems in the natural functioning of the dogs body. The correct, natural way should be to make each meal different and separate the different elements to ensure no overload takes place and no mixing of certain elements likely to conflict with each other.

Balanced diet in this sense is your dogs natural eating habits taking place, and not the artificially forced balance of commercially processed foods. In a sense, we are bound to eat different meals each day, but they are bound to be a combination of protein, carbohydrate and fat, with the associated vitamins and minerals of those foods. Again, dogs are not designed to eat that way.

Feeding your dog bones

There seems to be a common misconception that feeding bones to dogs is dangerous. There are obviously many horror stories of bones splintering and causing internal bleeding, bones having to be surgically removed, impacted bones in the gut, dogs having bones hanging out of their rear end as they try to pass them, etc. Most of these problems however, happen with cooked bones. Bones that are cooked effectively dry out and lose their relative elasticity and become hard, brittle and splinter prone.

Raw bones

Raw bones, despite their hard, solid form are still living tissue full of nutrients. As well as marrow, essential fat, anti oxidant properties and enzymes, they also contain calcium and phosphorus in a perfect balance, necessary for a dogs needs. As previously noted the raw meaty bone/BARF diet is also suitable for growing puppies as well as older dogs. In fact many owners and breeders insists this is their preferred way of raising puppies.

This is particularly the case when we consider that puppies require sufficient phosphorus and calcium whilst growing and raw meaty bones take away the guess work of how much calcium and phosphorus you would otherwise have to feed if feeding processed food. Again, Ian Billinghurst states that bones actually contain the exact proportions of calcium and phosphorus needed. As previously noted, this has been a problem where some breeders over supplement calcium, when feeding a commercial diet.

Raw meaty bones also provide all of the essential amino acids your dog needs.

As you already know, from the point of view of essential fatty acids, pork and chicken fat and consequently their bones, are a richer source than beef and lamb, which have relatively low amounts. However, that isn't to say that you should not feed beef and lamb bones also. They do have the same mineral and protein value, but again, lack the same high level of essential fatty acids that pork and chicken have.

Raw bones are also excellent sources of the fat soluble vitamins A, D and E. When bones are cooked, those vitamins are lost, which is another important reason why you should never feed dogs cooked bones. Cooking bones also destroys much of the nutrients of the bone marrow. Similarly to the A, D and E vitamins, the marrow is an excellent source of nutrients vital for a strong immune system. This not only fights infection and generally keeps our dogs in peak health, but also promotes longevity.

As well as the meat component, the bone in combination is said to provide the dog with its entire protein requirements. However, caution must be exercised where a dog has become obese. Please bear in mind that feeding raw meaty bones is an important addition for any dog. But because of the highly nutritious energy giving properties of raw meaty bones, giving too many will only add to the obesity. But again, please do consider including a moderate amount regularly as part of their diet.

It is also suggested by advocates of raw meaty bone feeding, that they will in themselves provide just about every nutrient your dog will need. The benefits include:

All of the important minerals; Essential fatty acids; Vitamins A, D and E (as previously noted, the K vitamin is manufactured in the bowel of the dog); Enzymes; Antioxidants; Optimum protein needs; Most of the B vitamins (as well as vitamin C to an extent, dogs produce their own B complex vitamins); Blood forming and immunity benefits of marrow

A raw meaty bone diet is suitable for every dog whether Rottweiler or Pug. It is also suitable for every age group. In essence it is suitable for lactating female dogs, working dogs, growing pups, senior dogs, as long as their teeth are sound.

Buried bones

Raw buried bones will gradually decompose with their own natural enzymes, and should be perfectly healthy for dogs to eat. Buried cooked bones will still decompose, the bacteria however, can produce toxins that could make your dog seriously ill. Incidentally, the likely reason your dog is burying bones is over feeding. So their natural survival instinct takes over, and any left over is saved for later.

Teeth cleaning

If dogs are not given the opportunity to chew, rip and crush bones, such as when they are fed soft processed food, their teeth and gums will suffer. The very action of chewing on meat and bones generally cleans the teeth, scrapes away tarter, massages the gums and teeth. The obvious advantages of this are a lack of gum disease, tooth decay, abscesses and a decreased chance of the body being poisoned via an infected mouth. Once again, the breath of bone chewing dogs rarely smells.

Problems feeding mostly organ meat

Constant feeding of heart, kidney, steak, tongue, liver etc, have been known in the long term to produce an imbalance and consequent disease. One such case involved the dog developing hepatitis which manifested in lethargy, arthritis, skin disease as well as high cholesterol. This type of diet produced an overload of protein, phosphorus, Vitamin A and a deficiency of calcium.

Problems feeding mostly fish

Certain raw fish contains an enzyme that destroys B1 vitamins. Oily fish fats affect Vitamin E. This is usually more significant if fillets of fish are given and not whole fish. The dog would benefit from eating the bones, head, internal organs that are all likely to contain the necessary B and E vitamins. Once again, feeding fish occasionally is perfectly acceptable, but as a main dietary source will cause all manner of complications.

Problems feeding mostly meat

A dogs diet consisting of mostly meat and in particular cooked meat, can result in diseases associated with skin diseases such as eczema, heart and kidney disease, arthritis and at worse cancer.

Similarly, as above with an all offal diet, a meat only diet, is significantly lacking in calcium to the extent that they would only be receiving about 5% of their actual requirements. As you may well expect, the main problem with all meat is the concentration of protein. In addition, phosphorus levels are excessive. There would also be notable deficiencies of Vitamins A, D and E together with copper and iodine. The lack of calcium as well as the other vitamins and minerals deficiencies, in particular would also be extremely detrimental to a growing puppy. Even if these were supplemented in some way, it is never advisable and there are much better, safer ways of feeding them. But again, as with the other specific food only diets, in moderation meat is an essential component of a balanced diet.

5) TYPES OF COMMERCIAL DOG FOOD

There are three main types of commercial dog food; wet, dry, and semi-moist. Dry dog foods are the most commonly used and they are also referred to as "kibble". This type of food is typically packed in a bag and they are usually extruded in the form of pellets or small biscuits/cookies. Dry dog foods come in a wide variety of flavours and formulas and they have a fairly low moisture content. For this reason your dog is likely to need a greater amount of water than usual. Wet dog food obviously has a higher moisture content. Wet foods are typically cooked at very high temperatures to sterilise them and then packaged in pressure-sealed containers. Semi-moist dog foods come in the form of soft, chewy pellets typically packaged in pouches or sachets.

In addition to these types of commercial dog food there are a few other options. Dehydrated dog food is becoming popular among pet owners who want to feed their dog's fresh or raw food but who want a product with a longer shelf life. Fresh dog food comes in refrigerated or frozen varieties and it is one of the most expensive options when it comes to commercial dog food. Fresh dog food can also be freeze-dried to remove most of the moisture content (thereby increasing the shelf life) without resulting in a loss of nutrients by cooking.

The type of dog food you choose for your Labrador is largely a matter of preference. Most dog owners choose dry food because it is the most, convenient, cost-effective option and because it lasts the longest. If your dog has food allergies or special dietary restrictions, a fresh or frozen dog food may be a better option because these foods are often made with limited ingredients. Senior dogs, who have trouble chewing dry food may prefer moist or semi-moist foods. You can also just soak dry food in water or broth to soften it.

Problems with dry food

Many kibble products have improved greatly over the years, and are of a good quality. The following however, is associated with the cheapest or worst cases and is intended to highlight why you should not opt for a cheap product.

Processed food, particularly dried 'kibble' has in some cases been found to contain an insufficient amount of zinc. It is generally made up of ground cooked bone and offal with cereal. It can contain a low nutritional value and can be hard to digest. It can contain excess calcium and starch. There can be low levels of vitamins, minerals, protein, essential fatty acids. It also promotes tarter build up and consequent gum disease.

Some dry feed can contain insufficient amounts of essential fatty acids. This to a large extent is a major contributory factor to severe skin conditions. Incidentally the conventional drugs and medical treatments used to treat these conditions, generate massive revenues to the veterinary medical industry year in year out. Money wasted by you the consumer not to mention the discomfort and suffering to the dog.

Fats and vitamins that are present, quickly deteriorate resulting in an even lower nutritional value after only a few weeks. It can be low in energy value and high in insoluble fibre. It can cause bladder infections and stones which can result in difficulty passing urine and may require surgery or special diets to remove the obstruction.

Problems with semi moist food

This is considered to be marginally better than dry dog food. The energy levels are higher due to an increased carbohydrate content derived from ingredients such as corn syrup. They generally contain a low water content, about 30% and certain additives/preservatives to give them a greater shelf life. As they have a similar composition to dry food, they are also associated with much the same diseases and other health issues.

Problems with canned food

There is a very high water content present in canned food, approximately 80%. So in other words, what nutritional value that remains makes up only 20% of what you are buying. The cost of buying tinned dog food in comparison to dry food is usually at least double. Again the ingredients are similar to the other processed foods, but in general the percentage of cereal can be less and animal derivatives, more. They are also in general more palatable to dogs than the others probably due to the moist meaty texture. As with all canned products, their two main advantages are a greater shelf life and are extremely convenient. Other than that, they carry the same health problems as the other types of processed foods.

Problems with tarter build up

Where dogs are given the opportunity to rip, tear and crunch raw meaty bones their teeth are cleaned and gums massaged. With processed foods this function is lost. Even dry food where it is thought that the dry composition has an abrasive, cleaning effect. The result of chewing raw meaty bones, is that their mouth generally remains healthy and odour free. Contrast this with dogs fed on processed food and we take it for granted that the rancid 'dogs breath' is normal.

The high levels of carbohydrate and calcium present in some processed foods are thought to be a major contributing factor to tarter build up that attacks the teeth and gums. Eventually this leads to serious gum disease and tooth decay. Tartar harbours bacteria, which in turn feeds off and thrives on the carbohydrates present in processed food. These bacteria attack and infect the mouth in general and specifically the teeth and gums causing painful gum infections and tooth decay, resulting in rancid breath and ultimately tooth loss.

In 1993 it was reported that 90% of dogs in the U.S.A ate processed dog food. In addition, veterinary dental treatment was said to represent over one third of vets income. In 2014 according to some surveys, processed dog food consumption was thought to be around 85%. Obviously not a great deal has changed.

Not only does this mouth bacteria cause serious localised problems, but the bacteria has a general toxic effect on the whole body, causing general ill health. The bacteria enters the blood stream and seriously affects the major organs of the body causing diseases of the lungs, heart, kidneys and reproductive organs etc.

As the legal obligation of manufacturers has generally been that their 'complete formulas', contain a minimum level of certain nutrients, it is fair to assume that there isn't necessarily a specified amount. Some scientific analysis carried out in Australia showed certain foods contained less vitamins than the legal requirement. In some cases there was an excess. Obviously if your dog requires a certain level of nutrients for optimum health, if this is lacking they will develop diseases associated with a deficiency. In a similar way, an overload of certain vitamins or minerals can cause diseases and health problems. Excess protein for example can cause kidney disease. Excess sodium is associated with heart disease. As you know excess calcium causes zinc deficiency as well as growth problems and bloat. Over time, this can result in the devastating effect of major organ failure.

Why the complete/balanced diet, that the commercial package promotes, such a problem

The idea of having a complete balanced diet in one convenient package sounds like a great idea. The problem is, as we have already discovered, if certain elements such as calcium are allowed to interact with other essential minerals such as zinc and copper, they result in indigestibility of those minerals. The complete diet which effectively combines a whole host of nutrients means that if it is the only source of zinc or copper etc, then the body will likely not be absorbing those elements which results in a deficiency. The same problem occurs when B complex vitamins go through the heat process of cooking and also interact with other certain elements. They too can become immobilised and not ingested.

So the problem arises when we attempt to feed the dog all of the elements combined. Once again, by combining certain elements, they interact and interfere with their individual effectiveness. As previously noted, in its wild primitive state, the dog would be unlikely to ever get a chance to have all of those elements together in one meal.

There are similar problems when mixing protein and starch. Early scientific research into digestion feed trials for dogs, largely involved the separate feeding of starch rich foods and protein. Significant results were noted that dramatically altered the health of patients.

Additional problems associated with commercial dog food

As you now know, the quality of commercially prepared dog food is a hot topic. The dog food industry is a high earning one and often owned by huge corporations that often put profit before the health of our dogs. Many dog food ingredients are not fit for human consumption and although vitamins are added to dog foods we cannot be certain whether they are of good enough quality to have an effect on the health of our dogs. Unless an ingredients list on a bag or tin of dog food is completely transparent the meat within dog food is usually rendered and described as 'meal' or 'derivatives'.

But what do these hazy terms actually mean?

Rendering is a process which involves putting bones, carcasses, beaks, hooves and tails into a huge tub and heating it so high that any virus cells, bacteria or antibiotic content dies. The fat content rises to the top and is scooped away. The remnants are ground up into a hot pink sludge of body parts. And this substance is what will eventually become commercial dog food. Rendered foods are permanently deemed unfit for human consumption for health reasons. Yet we unknowingly feed it to our dogs. After the food becomes kibble it is coloured to look nice and then sprayed with fat, in order to tempt dogs to eat it. Tinned foods have a lot of salt added, as do the little pouches meant for small dogs, which is no good for the dog's heart.

Thankfully and due to many different investigations inclusive of the dog food project by Sabine Contreras many smaller business are developing better food, made from whole food ingredients that are much better for our dogs. www.dogfoodproject.com describes the entire investigation and is well worth a read.

Admittedly the following article relates to 2007, but it still makes scary reading as to how the so called safe dog food diets can infiltrate the food chain with contaminated supplies.
https://en.wikipedia.org/wiki/2007_pet_food_recalls
Again, negative feedback about BARF diets, such as the threat of Salmonella and Listeria monocytogenes strains, has been predominantly asserted by the FDA. As part of a study between 2010 and 2012, by the FDA Center for Veterinary Medicine, 196 samples of raw dog food were analysed. This was in the form of frozen ground meat. 15 proved positive for Salmonella and 32 for Listeria monocytogenes. Again it is not fair to comment whether or not this sample represents a fair overall reflection of contamination threat in all cases. Or whether those figures would be the same with a different set of samples.

Once again, the dog owners who favour raw feeding and oppose processed foods, believe the contamination risks suggested by FDA are relatively negligible when you consider the obvious benefits gained to the dogs health. Although the FDA do not recommend raw diets they do acknowledge that there are pet owners who prefer to feed this way and furthermore suggest ways to deal with these possible contaminants

You can read the full article here:
http://www.fda.gov/AnimalVeterinary/ResourcesforYou/AnimalHealthLiteracy/ucm373757.htm

For additional information on processed dog food, please read the following:

http://www.dailymail.co.uk/news/article-2546512/How-pet-food-killing-dog-feeding-parsnips-yoghurt.html

6) READING THE INGREDIENTS LIST

Again, legal requirements state that food contains minimum recommended amounts of certain nutrients. Labelling does not necessarily have to state that the food will be the best option in terms of your dogs health, longevity, reproduction, growth. There will certainly be no mention that the food may lead to a premature death and a number of associated health issues.

Some of the reasons manufacturers process dog food the way they do include: greater shelf life and the ability to take questionable ingredients and make a product more appealing to the consumer, namely us the public.

As previously mentioned, in order to create this greater shelf life, most of the nutrients or everything that would otherwise benefit the dog, such as enzymes and micro organisms, have to be removed. The most efficient way of doing this is by cooking. Preservatives such as salt and sugar will be added which in addition to promoting a greater shelf life, also make them more appetising to the dog.

Having said that, as previously noted, commercially produced dog food seems to be the most popular option for dog owners. Like many other dog owners, you have the choice to feed your dog this way if you wish. As with most products, some are better than others. If you do opt for processed dog foods, whether as a temporary measure or otherwise, please do take the time to evaluate different brands and formulas. The best way to do this is by looking at the label and the ingredients list. For customers in the U.S.A, when you evaluate a bag of dog food for instance, the first thing you should look for is a statement of nutritional adequacy from the American Association of Feed Control Officials (AAFCO). The statement should look something like this:

"[Product Name] is formulated to meet the nutritional levels established by the AAFCO Dog Food nutrient profiles for [Life Stage]."

The American Association of Feed Control Officials is responsible for monitoring and regulating what goes into animal feed including pet foods. This organisation has set standards that pet foods must meet in order to be considered nutritionally adequate for dogs in certain life stages; puppy, adult, and senior. If the dog food label does not carry an AAFCO statement of nutritional adequacy, you should move on to another option. On the other hand, just because a product carries the AAFCO statement doesn't necessarily mean that it is good for your dog.

In the United Kingdom, the Pet Food Manufacturer's Association (PFMA) exists to provide pet owners with guidance for selecting pet foods. This organisation is the principal trade body for the U.K. pet food industry with more than 70 member companies, representing about 90% of the U.K. pet food market. The PFMA does not put a statement on pet food labels in the same way as AAFCO; but they do strive to raise pet food industry standards and to promote pet food products deemed as safe and nutritious.

Incidentally, there is also a new fact sheet on labelling with regards to the pet food ingredients list. As a Labrador dog owner you should always be checking and improving your dogs health, wellbeing, weight and shape. PFMA has a downloadable Dog Size-O-Meter that you can keep on hand. For more information, visit:

pfma.org.uk/dog-pet-size-o-meter/

Everything that we eat contributes to our health. The same will apply to your Labrador. He is entirely dependent on what you feed him. Keep in mind that although you may be thinking that your Labrador looks healthy enough, it takes

years for a not so healthy dog food to take its toll on your Labrador's health.

For more information about pet food labelling standards in the U.K., visit the PFMA website here: **http://www.pfma.org.uk/labelling**

The European Pet Food Industry Federation

This federation was formed in 1970 and represents the pet food industry in 26 countries. This representation is carried out via their network of 18 national or regional pet food industry associations. The main goal of this federation is to promote the views and interests of around 650 European pet food producing companies. Its goal is to make sure that all pet food manufactured is safe, nutritious and palatable. For more information, visit: **http://www.fediaf.org/who-we-are/**

The U.S. Food and Drug Administration (FDA)

The FDA releases press releases regarding pet food recalls from the firms involved. The FDA is an organisation that consists of the Office of the Commissioner and four directorates overseeing core functions of the agency. To learn more, visit: **http://www.fda.gov also http://www.foodsafety.gov/**

The best way therefore, to truly evaluate the nutritional value of a pet food is to examine the ingredients list. Dog food labels include a complete list of ingredients that is organised in descending order by volume. This means that the ingredients present in the highest quantity/volume appear at the beginning of the list. This makes it easy for you to get a quick sense of a product's nutritional value. If the first few ingredients are healthy ingredients, the product is probably a good choice. If however, the first few ingredients are low-quality fillers, you should move on.

When evaluating the ingredients list for a commercial dog food, you want to see a high-quality source of protein listed first. Fresh meats like chicken, turkey, beef, and fish are good options but do not be turned off if you see something like chicken meal. Fresh meats contain about 80% water so, once the dog food is cooked, their weight is much less than the original. Meat meals have already been cooked down to a moisture content around 10% so they contain up to 300% more protein than fresh meats. A high-quality commercial dog food might list a fresh meat first followed by a meat meal second.

In addition to high-quality protein sources, you should also look for digestible carbohydrates and animal-based fats in the ingredients list. Carbohydrates that are easily digestible for dogs include things like cooked brown rice, oats, and barley. Be wary of wheat and corn-based products however, because these ingredients often trigger food allergies in dogs and they are low in nutritional value. The number of carbohydrate sources on the ingredients list is also important to consider. Dogs do not require a great deal of carbohydrate. Only about 15% of your dog's diet should come from carbohydrates. Low-quality dog foods contain as much as 30% to 70% of this nutrient.

If you see an ingredient such as chicken fat or poultry fat on the label for a commercial pet food, do not be turned off as it is a good thing! As you learned previously, fats are a highly concentrated form of energy and they play an important role in your dog's diet. Fats from animal-based sources are particularly beneficial so you should look for things like chicken fat and fish oil in your dog's food. Plant-based fats like flaxseed oil and canola oil can also be beneficial but animal-based fats are more biologically valuable to your dog.

In addition to the main ingredients on a dog food label you also need to pay attention to the things near the end of the list. This is where pet food manufacturers like to sneak in things like artificial flavours, colorants, and preservatives. Avoid ingredients with the word "by-product" attached, as well as chemical preservatives like BHA and BHT. Be aware that these ingredients might be spelt out instead of abbreviated. You should also avoid things like corn syrup, MSG, food dyes, and again low-quality filler ingredients like corn and wheat gluten.

So when you next look at a dog food label, as well as the ingredients, consider the following:

Does a food label or advertising assert that the food has been tested on dogs over a long term,

and therefore state that the product supports long term health, a long life, effective for reproduction and growth? If not then you need to question why not? If they could state these long term health benefits then they would certainly be advertising the facts.

So in short:

Will the food keep the dog healthy?; Will the food fulfil the needs of growing puppies?; Will the food aid dental health, produce healthy litters of puppies, ensure adult dogs remain healthy and live to a ripe old age?

In essence, is there proof via scientific data, that the food has been proven to promote health, longevity, dental health, delayed ageing and absence of degenerative diseases. Obviously in order to prove that, clinical trials will need to have been carried out over a dogs lifetime. In other words, the claims made by manufacturers is not based on speculative assumptions. It would also need to be proved that the dog is in excellent health and this is due to being fed on this particular diet. The type of proof needs to demonstrate that trials were carried out by an unbiased independent laboratory. You would also need to see the actual food analysis found.

7) QUALITY COMMERCIAL FOODS FOR LABRADORS

Again, I cannot say that any processed feeding regardless of so called quality would be a first choice or preference for me. However, my intention is not to dictate my opinion, but to give an overall picture of what is available. You are then free to make your own mind up and choose. My preference is to feed as natural and healthy as possible, a good quality BARF diet will provide this. Perhaps feeding occasional table scraps or commercial feed when you are pushed for time. To quote Ian Billinghurst again, he asserts that he cannot recommend any processed product. This is mainly due to the cooking process involved, the combining and the aforementioned complications that can result from this.

But again if you wish to pursue a quality commercial product always use the preceding guidelines when reading the label and at least ensure that the following applies:

The product is made with high-quality sources of animal-based protein; This formula is rich in antioxidants, dietary fibre, amino acids etc; It provides a balance of essential fatty acids, omega-3 and omega-6 fatty acids; Any whole grains present are brown rice, oatmeal or similar; Antioxidants are present to support your dog's immune system; The product is free from corn, wheat, and soy as well as artificial flavours, preservatives, and colours; A correct balance of vitamins and minerals at recommended adequate doses is also present.

8) How Much to Feed Your Labrador

Apart from keeping our dogs fit and healthy by feeding their body vital vitamins, minerals and other nutrients, the main thing that food provides is energy. This energy is obtained from all the main food groups including carbohydrates, protein and fats. Again, these need to be given in the correct amounts for the dogs needs. Not enough of those elements would result in malnutrition, too many would naturally lead to obesity. It is all about when a dog most needs these food elements. This will be most needed for purposes of reproduction and puppy growth. Times of stress and extreme activity levels such as may be expected from working dogs. Cold weather will also see a need for extra food resources. Strangely enough the opposite is not the case. Whilst we live on light meals such as salad during hot spells, dogs use a considerable amount of energy in order to cool down, by panting.

Where a dogs diet needs to account for these extreme uses of energy, it is necessary to bear in mind the energy values of the three major food groups. Weight for weight, fat is by far the richest of the three in terms of energy value, in fact this is actually double either carbohydrate or protein. If the dog needs an energy rich diet because it is a working dog, for example, then a fat rich diet would be appropriate. This type of feeding for a dog that is not burning the fat off, would result in an obese dog destined for health problems. In general, you should be very careful not to over feed your dog. Obviously the opposite of this is also true, you do not want to underfeed your dog,

because being under weight is also unhealthy for your dog. It is not an easy remedy to keep your dog at an optimum weight. You can usually see if the dog is over or under weight. A more accurate way is to weigh the dog on a regular basis and feed accordingly. Again, I would personally take the ideal weight for your type of dog as a guideline and then as accurately as you possibly can, provide meals that will keep your dog at an ideal weight. And once again, routinely weigh the dog to see where any fluctuations occur. You will soon get an idea of whether your dog is getting enough food. Also remember to take into account periods of extra activity as mentioned previously.

Feeding your puppy

As you have already learned, your Labrador's calorie needs will vary according to his age and activity level. Feeding a puppy however, is a little different from feeding an adult dog. You have to remember that the growth of the puppy happens in a comparatively short space of time. You may hear recommendations along the lines of allowing your puppy to eat as much as he likes. You need to be very cautious taking this approach. The assumption is that increased calories will result in quicker, abnormal growth rates or spurts. In any case, feeding a dog more than he needs at any age is likely to lead to obesity. Studies have also found that dogs from the same litter fed a certain diet lived less than certain litter mates consuming up to 25% less of the same diet. In other words, feeding less than the dog would eat, 'ad-lib' feeding, results in a dog likely to live longer than if they were permitted to eat as much as they want.

It is however, fair to say that many dogs are good about eating when they are hungry and stopping when they are full. In this respect, if you were to feed so many meals per day, you may find that your puppy or adult dog will not eat certain meals. If your puppy isn't obviously ill, it is likely to be that he doesn't feel the need for the extra food. So do not worry too much about serving him a precise amount each time. If he leaves some it is probably fair to assume he is eating all the calories he needs to fuel his growth and development at that meal.

However, please be aware that the majority of gundogs, including Labradors, can be quite gluttonous where food is concerned. This includes both adults and puppies, so whereas a lot of breeds will only eat as much as they need, your Labrador is likely to gorge himself given the chance, or start burying or hiding food. Depending on what you are feeding them, you are advised to feed the recommendations on the product label. In the case of raw feeding they an adult dog may require about 5% and 10% of their body weight in raw meat and bones, depending on their activity level. Again, the best way to gauge not over feeding, is to monitor whether you think they are putting on too much weight. You should at least be able to feel a couple of their ribs, if not you are probably overfeeding and should cut back the amount per meal.

Generally, you will typically be told that from 8 weeks to 12 weeks their daily food ration should be split into 4 meals.

From 12 weeks to 26 weeks this should be reduced to 3 meals per day. However, the amounts may need to increase in accordance with his increased body weight, and perhaps increased activity level.

26 weeks to 52 weeks, this is further reduced to 2 meals per day. Although some people feed one meal only, but perhaps the same amount split into two is preferable. This can be split equally or a larger amount given in the evening, for example, one third in the morning and the rest in the evening. The amount given should be increased by approximately half as much again on top of their normal daily allowance if they are working or you feel their normal activity level has increased.

At one year and after, most dog owners will be feeding either one or two meal per day. I prefer to feed twice per day. Around 10 am I provide almost all of their daily requirement. On some days they eat everything and then perhaps the next day only half. If they eat everything, I do not give any extra now, but feed a second meal around 3pm. This is about half that of the first meal. They get nothing else, no treats etc, until around 10 am the next day. If however they have left some from 10 am, I refrigerate that and they get that along with some extra, perhaps about half as much again. They get fresh clean water all of the time which is changed at least once per day. Again, this is for two adult dogs. You could feed your puppy in the same way, but again with the extra meals included.

The important thing to realise is that you use a good quality puppy food. As to how much you give per meal, if you are splitting the meals, depends on the weight of your pup and the recommended amount stated on your brand of food. Again, a lot depends on the quality and therefore nutritional value of the product, which is why it is important to not skimp on price especially for puppy food.

But whichever plan you follow, once your puppy reaches maturity you should start rationing his meals. You can choose how many meals to give your Labrador each day, but again most dog owners recommend dividing your dog's daily portion into two meals. To also help you determine how much to feed your dog, follow the feeding suggestions on the dog food package in relation to the previous calorie needs mentioned. Keep in mind that feeding suggestions are just that, suggestions, so you may need to make adjustments. Start off with the recommended amount for a few weeks. If your dog gains weight you'll need to cut back a bit. If he loses weight, you should increase his rations a bit. You can always ask your veterinarian for suggestions if you aren't sure whether your dog is at a healthy weight.

Keep in mind that during the puppy stage you'll need to:

- Ensure that your Labrador puppy is gaining weight steadily by frequent veterinary check ups during the puppy stage. You may also wish to buy a scale and weigh him every week.
- Watch out for obesity
- Feed the correct puppy diet appropriate to instructions given by your vet or the dietary guidelines on the back of the food package you buy your Labrador. Be aware however, that the guide that manufacturers state is just a guide and again will vary depending on the dog and workload.
- Avoid feeding only a one-sided diet of meat only. Mix with other natural food stuff.
- Avoid feeding your puppy poor quality commercial dog food, any junk food or

table scraps that contain empty calories
- Keep your Labrador away from dangerous foods like chocolate, grapes, candy and gum that can be deadly to dogs

Another factor you need to consider in regard to feeding your Labrador is how many treats you give him. When you are training your puppy, you should use very small treats. You should also limit the number of treats you give him if it is likely to exceed his daily calorie needs.

Be aware that wheat gluten is a particular problem for certain dogs including gundogs. If your dog shows signs of loose faeces or other allergy symptoms a gluten free product may be necessary. So for Labradors with ingredient intolerances or food sensitivities, choose a brand with a single-source of animal protein and real deboned meat as the first ingredient and a healthy, simple list of additional grain-free, gluten-free ingredients. Many health problems in Labradors can be avoided by feeding a high quality grain-free diet. Yet one needs to pay attention to the ingredient list even though it's labeled as grain-free.

9) Toxic Foods Affecting Labrador Dogs

In addition to making sure that you provide your Labrador with a healthy diet, you also need to be careful NOT to feed him certain foods. It can be tempting to give your dog a few scraps from your plate but certain "people foods" can actually be toxic for your dog.

Below you will find a list of foods that can be harmful to your Labrador:

Alcohol; Apple seeds; Avocado; Cherry pits; Chocolate; Cocoa mulch fertilizer; Coffee; Garlic; Grapes/raisins; Gum (can cause blockages and sugar free gums may contain the toxic sweetener Xylitol); Hops; Macadamia nuts; Mold; Mushrooms; Mustard seeds; Nuts; Onions and onion powder/leeks; Peach pits; Potato leaves/stems; Rhubarb leaves; Tea; Tomato leaves/stems; Walnuts; Xylitol; Yeast dough

If your Labrador consumes a food that he shouldn't have, you should call the Pet Poison Control Hotline, just to be on the safe side. The specialist on the other end of the line will be able to tell you if the amount your dog ingested is potentially toxic. If it is, they will walk you through the steps to induce vomiting to purge the item from your dog's stomach, or recommend that you take your dog to an emergency vet. You may also be able to speak to a licensed veterinarian on the phone for a fee around $65 (£50 exchange rate May 2017).

10) Toxic Plants Affecting Labrador Dogs

Not only do you need to be careful about which foods you keep out of your Labrador's reach, there are also plants that can be toxic to all dogs. If you have any of the houseplants listed below in your house, make sure you keep them well out of your dog's reach. For toxic outdoor plants, remove them from your property or fence them off for your dog's safety.

A list of toxic plants harmful to dogs can be found below:

Azalea; Baneberry; Bird-of-paradise; Black locust; Buckeye; Buttercup; Caladium; Castor bean; Chock-cherries; Christmas rose; Common privet; Cowslip; Daffodil; Day lily; Delphinium; Easter lily; Elderberry; Elephant's ear; English Ivy; Foxglove; Holly; Horse-chestnut; Hyacinth; Iris; Jack-in-the-pulpit; Jimsonweed; Laurels; Lily of the valley; Lupines; May-apple; Mistletoe; Morning glory; Mustards; Narcissus; Nightshade; Oaks; Oleander; Philodendron; Poinsettia; Poison hemlock; Potato; Rhododendron; Rhubarb; Sago palm; Sorghum; Wild black cherry; Wild radish; Wisteria; Yew

Additional information can be found at the following web link:
http://www.humanesociety.org/assets/pdfs/pets/poisonous_plants.pdf

CHAPTER FIFTEEN:

INITIAL LABRADOR OBEDIENCE TRAINING

In this next chapter we will cover specific step by step obedience training methods for your Labrador.

The intention here is to offer basic obedience such as 'sit', 'stay', 'down' etc. The next chapter will deal with more advanced training. This advanced training typically represents the type of training a working gundog would go through. If you are only interested in basic obedience then this current chapter will be all you need. The advance training will cover aspects of gundog training including: basic and advanced retrieve; exposure to gunshot; introduction to water; quartering; hunting in the field etc.

All of this may hold no interest for you and you can easily skip the advanced chapter without any detriment to you or your dog. If you are more interested in advanced activities such as agility or dog sports there are many excellent books out there. I would suggest you do an Amazon search using search terms such as [dog games]; [canine games]; [dog agility]; [dog sports] etc. Books by Claire Arrowsmith, Kyra Sundance, Mary Ray, Laurie Leach etc are always popular choices.

However, I would strongly advise you to consider teaching your dog the 'stop' command. It is similar to the 'down' command which we will cover here, but goes into much more depth and detail. For many gundog trainers, the 'stop' command is THE most important command you can teach your dog. When properly taught it should reliably stop your dog instantly, wherever he is or whatever he is doing, and this may be in an emergency. It does however involve using a relatively inexpensive whistle, which is very simple to use. Details of which will be given in the Advanced chapter, section on whistles. Recall training is also very important, and although basic training involves some sort of recall or 'come' command, it will be covered here. It will however be included with instructions again including the whistle; but you can follow the exercise without using the whistle quite easily by simply omitting the whistle part.

Please note that the text throughout the chapter will also be interspersed with information for working Gundogs. Don't be put off by this if you are only interested in a well behaved, well mannered house dog. It it is merely intended to put into context the traditional, and in some cases, current purpose of the breed.

In addition to receiving step-by-step instructions for training your Labrador dog, you will also learn the basics about different training methods and canine learning theory.

IMPORTANT: Please read through this chapter to familiarise yourself with certain training procedures that should be initiated when your puppy comes to live with you. These include preliminary 'recall' and 'heel' etc.

1) How your Labrador may react during training

The Labrador is a very intelligent breed that typically responds well to training but he can sometimes be easily distracted. Some Labradors also have a bit of an independent streak. This can result in him being stubborn when he does not want to do something. This wilful attitude has been noted in working dogs whilst hunting when they can suddenly decide to do their own thing (hunt for themselves)and ignore you. However, their single mindedness can prove to be a major advantage when they are in pursuit of certain bird scents, which other dogs would miss, relentlessly pursuing it. Please remember that it is important that you are patient, firm and consistent during training sessions. For the best success, you should plan to keep your training sessions short and fun so that your Labrador gets something out of them each time.

2) Popular Training Methods

When it comes to training your Labrador, other than traditional gundog training, you may come across a variety of different training methods. Traditional punishment-based methods are unfortunately still used by some trainers, gundog or otherwise. Thankfully this has been superseded to a large extent by modern positive reinforcement methods which can also include clicker training. In this section you will receive an overview of popular training methods in use today.

A.) Positive-Reinforcement Training

One of the most popular training methods used by trainers today is positive reinforcement. This type of training involves 'operant conditioning' (we will cover this shortly), in which the dog learns to associate an action with a consequence. In this case, the term consequence does not refer to something bad, it is just something that happens as a result of something else. In other words cause and effect. The goal of positive reinforcement training is to encourage your dog to WANT to do what YOU want him to do.

The basics of positive reinforcement training are simple; you teach the dog that if he follows your commands he will be rewarded. For example, you teach your dog to respond to the word "Sit" by creating an association for him with the word 'sit', and the action of him sitting down. In order to teach him to associate the command with the action, you reward him with a treat each time he sits on command. It generally only takes a few repetitions for dogs to learn to respond to commands because food rewards are highly motivational for most dogs. It's a simple concept, but it can go wrong very easily. Don't worry too much for now as the procedure will be explained as we go. Timing is very important in order to get the dog to associate a cue word with what you want him to do.

Once again, the key to successful positive reinforcement-based training sessions is to keep them short and fun. If the dog enjoys the training, he will be more likely to retain what he has learned. It is also important that you make the connection between the command and the desired response very clear to your dog. If he doesn't understand what you want him to do, he will become confused. It is also important to pair the reward immediately with the desired response. This helps your dog to make the connection more quickly and it motivates him to repeat the desired behaviour.

B) Positive-Reinforcement Training; The Gundog Training Perspective.

There seems to be much confusion about when is the best age to begin gundog training. The traditionalists have always believed this as being between 6 and 10 months of age. In some cases the opinion is that the dog should be older than this. This begs the question, what is the reason behind leaving it this late. The usual reasons revolve around building and developing confidence as well as a strong hunting/retrieving drive, and that early training would hinder the development of those qualities.

Adherents of positive reinforcement training, argue that the hunting drive will not be hindered providing the puppy has ample exposure and freedom to hunt and explore for themselves. It is furthermore argued that merely teaching the puppy basic obedience such as sit, stay and heel work is unlikely to eradicate the puppies natural inbuilt desire to hunt.

It is fair to agree to a certain extent the view of traditional trainers that not all dogs are the same and a particularly sensitive individual could significantly lose the desire or instinct to hunt or retrieve if 'too much' repetitive gundog training such as retrieving is given too early. Again the traditional view makes a valid point where the natural instinct to hunt may be hampered, at worse lost as the dog will be always watching the handler or afraid to make a mistake.

The view is that the dog should be allowed to hunt, but to take directions or guided, if needed or should the dog go wrong. The overall objective is that the trained dog will be confident and keen to work and hunt, but be disciplined and equally keen to please the handler.

But again, if we look at the way traditional gundog training has in the past, and still is being administered, we can see additionally why the puppy was left to their own devises until the 6 to 9 month mark, when 'serious' training started. Confidence is the big issue here, as the puppy had to become spirited bordering on troublesome. The so called 'breaking' would then begin. Traditionally, breaking would involve punishment tactics such as hitting, slapping, scruff shaking etc. These are not even considered appropriate methods by many traditional trainers now, but 'snapping' the choke chain back, is still common practice. A young, impressionable, vulnerable puppy can be severely affected rendering them intimidated, frightened and wary with such training. The older dog is considered tougher mentally and physically, and able to accept this without it affecting them too much.

Traditional trainers quite rightly assert that their training is completed much quicker. However, if a fundamental reason for delaying traditional training is because of the corrections and aversive methods, then positive reinforcement which doesn't involve aversive methods, can and should logically be started much earlier. It is also fair to state that non aversive methods take longer in comparison, because of the 'proofing'(this is basically the dog carrying out an action in a variety of different 'distracting' locations and under different circumstances), necessary to get the dogs doing

what we need them to do. It is also worth pointing out that much of the hunting training will only commence after the puppy has spent a considerable amount of time mastering basic obedience 'sit', 'stay' etc.

Another important thing to note here is that a lot of the traditional training view point focuses on dogs that were not meant to be kept in the house but in kennels. If you live a busy family life, then the puppy will need to contend with behaving and keeping out of mischief or even danger. A traditional dog kept in kennels will be relatively safe and not have much more than their play time and daily exercise, which is all bound to occur away from the house. If you live in an urban area, then there is a strong likelihood that lead walking will be necessary. The flip side is, if you live in the country side, where apart from keeping a dog on the lead if they exercise where livestock are present, lead work will probably be only necessary on shoots or field trials. In other words much of the obedience training needed to keep the house dog well behaved is deemed unnecessary for a dog living in kennels.

For the family dog, things are so much more complicated. We have to keep a balance between, on the one hand allowing the puppy to happily grow and develop. On the other hand, we have to maintain order in the house, where everyone lives safely and harmoniously. In other words it is necessary that the puppy fits in with our lifestyle, and behaves.

For the traditional gundog trainer they can easily leave obedience training such as heelwork much later in the dogs education. But for a family who needs a dog to have manners and to behave in the house as well as on the lead out walking in public places, obedience training has to start at an early age.

However, they are not mind readers and therefore need to be shown what to do to achieve this.

In order to make the positive reinforcement approach work, you ideally expose and encourage the dog to freely hunt and explore by themselves in the initial puppy stages. You also start the basic obedience training at the same time. The key however, is to keep these obedience sessions entirely separate from their 'free time' explorations.

You therefore ensure that there are no negative associations whilst they are pleasing themselves exploring and hunting. However, it is important to state here that where any free running is allowed, this should take place in a safe relatively enclosed area, or a long training leash should be attached.

Please remember to not rush the initial puppy training. Always keep the sessions short as their initial attention span is quite short. In other words they will be easily distracted and it will be a mistake to force them into doing disciplined training when they would rather be playing. The whole point of any training is that the puppy keeps a high confidence level by being given the opportunity to succeed at every step, and never set up to fail.

c) Punishment–Based Training

Punishment-based training is not as harsh as the word suggests. It is not exactly the opposite of positive reinforcement training, but it is very different. While positive reinforcement training is about encouraging your dog to repeat a desired behaviour, punishment-based training is about discouraging your dog from performing an unwanted behaviour. The goal of punishment-based training is to teach your dog that a certain action results in a negative consequence and thus the dog will choose not to perform that behaviour in the future. Traditionally, punishment would unfortunately be in the form of physical acts likely to cause pain to the dog. Fortunately things have evolved to the extent that punishment now involves ignoring the behaviour or withholding a treat or praise.

The limitation with punishment-based training methods is that they are generally only effective in teaching your dog to stop doing something rather than teaching him to respond to a certain command. It is also important to note that punishment-based training can have a negative impact on your relationship with your dog. Even though your dog may stop performing the unwanted behaviour, it may not be because you taught him that the behaviour is undesirable. He will likely only associate the behaviour with him having done something wrong, when he ideally wants to please you.

Again, a typical example of this 'punishment' approach is that you simply ignore an undesirable behaviour. With normal positive reinforcement you reward good behaviour that you have asked for. If the dog then jumps up or starts barking at you, you simply ignore the behaviour by not acknowledging it by not speaking, touching or turning away from the dog.

Traditional punishment-based training approaches in the past would involve aversive techniques that would result in the dog learning not to perform the undesirable behaviour. The dog would also learn to be fearful of you and in some cases aggressive. If you know anything about dog behaviour, you may already know that in most cases, aggression is born of fear. Even the most even-tempered dog can become aggressive if he is afraid. If you use traditional punishment-based training methods you not only risk teaching your dog to fear you, but there is also the possibility that he will become aggressive with you, or someone else, at some point in the future.

Note: I would like to point out here, that you should NEVER, under any circumstances hit your dog. It is not only cruel, but an unnecessary action on your part. If you are ever having recurring behavioural issues with your dog, you should either seek an alternative approach or in extreme cases, seek the help of a professional dog trainer/ behaviourist.

d.) Clicker Training

Clicker training is a type of positive reinforcement training. With this type of training you use a small clicker device to help your dog form an association with a command and the desired behaviour. Because this is the most difficult part of positive reinforcement training, clicker training is often a very quick and effective training method. To use this method you follow the same procedures as you would for positive reinforcement training but you click the clicker as soon as your dog performs the desired behaviour and then give him the reward. Once your dog identifies the desired behaviour you then stop using the clicker so he does not become dependent on it.

A quick idea of how this works is to firstly get your dog associating the clicker with getting a reward, usually food. So for example you throw down a piece of food. As soon as the dog picks it up, you click with the clicker. You repeat this a number of times. Very quickly the dog starts to associate whatever he does with hearing a click and getting a food reward. So once he hears a click he knows food will follow. You proceed with this by next using a command word such as 'sit'. As dogs naturally sit anyway you can quickly capture the action of sitting with a click. Timing is essential here, so as soon as the action of sitting is performed you click. Once you have repeated this a number of times you add in the cue word 'sit'. Say the word 'sit' just before he sits. As he starts to sit, click, then give him the food reward. There is more to it than that, but that is basically how this works and how you proceed with other commands.

If you want to get a visual idea of how clicker training works, there are some excellent videos on Youtube, you may wish to check out. Just type clicker training and take your pick. If you are interested in much more detailed information about clicker training, books by Karen Pryor are usually recommended, although I am sure others are useful also.

Fortunately clicker training has become popular for gundog training. There are a couple of useful books that use a clicker training approach. If you are interested, search Amazon books using the search term [gundog clicker training]

E) Training Recommendations

As you have probably gathered by now the only method I can recommend is some form of positive reinforcement training. Whether you opt for the method taught in this chapter or choose a clicker training approach, is entirely your choice. As the Labrador is considered to be a sensitive gentle personality, you are certainly not recommended to use any harsh treatments. Labradors are a very intelligent breed so they typically pick things up fairly quickly. Using a clicker may help you to speed up your training sessions once you learn how to use the clicker effectively.

3) How dogs learn

The problem for the Sporting/Gundog is that aspects of their natural instinctive behaviour can get them into trouble with our civilised, ordered lifestyles. How they naturally act is then deemed as being a 'problem behaviour' which we are expected to train out of them, or at least to suppress to an extent. The answer is not to attempt to mould them into humans, but to work with their natural instincts and tendencies and teach them acceptable behaviour that will make them well behaved members of the family.

For a start, although for centuries dogs have successfully adapted to living side by side with humans, they are still dogs who think and act very differently. They do not perceive things the same way, cannot reason, solve problems, learn or communicate in quite the same way as humans. We therefore need to understand how they do learn and then teach them how to be well behaved, to keep them safe and us happy.

A) How dogs learn: 'learning theory'

Before we get into the actual training, it is important to point out the learning theory behind how dogs learn. Modern dog training and how puppies learn are governed by two main types of learning. These scientific theories are operant conditioning and classical conditioning.

Classical conditioning; most famously relates to Russian scientist Ivan Pavlov's experiments which became commonly known as 'Pavlov's dogs'. The experiments basically studied how dogs salivated when hearing the sound of a bell ringing. This would indicate to the dog that food was about to be given. It worked to the extent that the very act of the bell ringing would initiate the dogs to start drooling in anticipation that food would soon follow.

In modern dog training, words or sounds are used to gain the same effect. Clicker training that uses food as a reward has exactly the same effect. The sound of a click indicates to the dog that they are about to receive a food reward. The idea is to use something that the dog finds highly valuable, such as food, and use this to motivate and train them, consequently getting the dog to do what we want.

Operant conditioning; involves 'punishment' and 'reinforcement' to make changes in behaviour.

Punishment; is not, or certainly should be nothing to do with pain, violence or any harsh treatment. Punishment in this sense is something unpleasant to the dog that ensures that a certain behaviour is not repeated. Examples include sudden loud noises, smells, bright lights, being ignored or isolated. As previously noted, ignoring a behaviour is usually recommended as this simply and clearly indicates to the dog that they do not get rewarded if they repeat a particular behaviour.

The difficulty is finding the trigger that works for the individual puppy. A firework may terrify one dog, but have absolutely no effect on another. Obviously many Gundogs are un-phased by gunfire or at least conditioned to be that way.

A young impressionable puppy who is reliant on you for his safety and welfare, should never be exposed to any form of punishment. If in an emergency you have to scoop the puppy up away from danger, then fine. This is likely to shock and frighten the puppy, but you have to potentially save the puppies life, so such a drastic act is necessary. Under normal circumstances, any kind of harsh treatment, even an angry voice or tap on the nose can have a long term detrimental effect on your relationship and bonding with the puppy. The last thing you need is for the puppy to be wary or at worse, fearful of you. Modern dog training usually avoids, and finds most aspects of punishment unnecessary.

Reinforcement; or 'positive reinforcement', is the opposite to punishment and therefore the most acceptable method in use. The idea is that the puppy initiates a desirable act and is rewarded, or the act is reinforced to ensure the puppy repeats it. Reinforcers or rewards include; toys, food, games, attention, kind words of encouragement etc.

There are grey areas whereby puppies are rewarded unintentionally by us. Usually this occurs with attention we give them for undesirable behaviour. For example, the dog jumps up and we handle the dog to push it down. We may think that this rebuke is showing the dog our dissatisfaction, but to the dog he may still view this as attention that he craves and therefore is rewarded. In this case it would have been better to ignore the dog (a subtle form of punishment), best executed by physically turning away from him as he jumps, and importantly not speaking either. In essence the puppy will soon learn the difference between when we are happy with them, they are rewarded, and when we are not, the behaviour is ignored and they are not rewarded.

There is a very subtle example that relates specifically to the Gundog, which is a successful retrieve. gundog puppies will naturally wish to pick things up and bring them to you. You will naturally be delighted by this and will offer lots of praise and encouragement. A subtle problem could occur if the puppy drops the object. You could easily do one of two detrimental things. You either inadvertently praise them as they are coming back to you and at the same time they drop the object. The puppy can easily view the dropping of the object as praise worthy. A working gundog should never be trained to drop an object as they are coming back to you. This is particularly important as they may drop an injured bird, that would otherwise die a slow and painful death. The other problem is that you could get angry and make the puppy feel the act of retrieving is a bad thing. Again the best course of action is to ignore the act and never reward it.

Four learning stages

Learning basically takes place in four stages as follows: Acquisition; Practice; Proofing; Repetition.

- New knowledge acquisition (you teach sit a number of times so that when he hears the word sit he automatically sits)
- Practicing the knowledge to become better (you repeat this to solidify the new behaviour)
- Apply this to other situations (proofing/generalising). (You increase the level of difficulty by practicing in different locations with added distractions). This is important as he learns to listen to you and carry out an action wherever you are and who ever is present. Please see the section on proofing/generalising at the end of the chapter
- Repetitively practicing this new behaviour all the time, not just in class or during training sessions.

B) POINTS TO BEAR IN MIND FOR SUCCESSFUL LEARNING:

The puppy is always rewarded for desirable behaviour, and never rewarded for undesirable behaviour.

Avoid acts of 'self rewarding', such as wilfully chasing, taking food from the table or out of bins. In other words, second guess the puppy and keep them away from any such temptations.

Again, please be aware that positive reinforcement should be practiced all the time and not just on the training field. Many potential problem behaviours could develop without you realising this.

4) OTHER TRAINING CONSIDERATIONS

A) THE INDEPENDENCE PHASE

As your puppy grows in confidence, he will naturally become more independent and start to explore for himself. There is no definitive age that this will happen as some develop this after several months whereas others take over a year. Being a Gundog, you will notice his instinctive hunting behaviour start to develop. He will focus on following scent trails, which will mean he is not clinging to your heals. But you will need to ensure he doesn't get carried away and goes too far. So recall will be important at this stage and he should be encouraged to return to you when you call. If he seems to ignore you, it is likely to be him getting lost in the moment. Provided you are in a safe area away from danger such as a busy road, then there is probably no need to panic or worry unduly. If you are concerned about giving too much freedom in this way, please do attach a long 10 meter or so training lead, or a retractable leash. What is important is that he learns to enjoy his independence from you. This freedom is what the traditional gundog trainers deem as being necessary for their effectiveness as a working hunting dog. However, it is also necessary to strike a balance between them doing their own thing, but you being in control when the need arises.

5) INSTINCTS: THE PACK/PREY DRIVE AND TRAINING

Before we get started on training your Labrador; the following will give you a brief insight into what drives him as well as the need to work with their instinctive drives to successfully train him.

How Sporting/Gundogs or any dog behaves instinctively may not be acceptable to the family needing a well behaved dog.

Because Sporting/Gundogs are hardwired to react to game or prey, a first time encounter may elicit a host of behaviour such as becoming excitable by barking, quivering, lunging at the leash etc. Depending on the breed, they may even instinctively react by pointing or stalking. This is merely dogs being dogs and nothing at all abnormal. However, in order for the dog to behave and not take off chasing the bird or whatever, we need to train self control.

We are not looking to extinguish this instinct or suppress their interest, but to teach them to change their normal instinctive reaction. It is therefore far better to understand their natural reactions and work with that rather than making the dog do something they do not have an instinctive desire or inclination to do.

This does not mean that we should allow them to react as they normally would without our guidance. We are not wanting to make them unhappy or spoil their fun, but to keep them safe from danger.

So, although Sporting/Gundogs have a very sociable people oriented side to them, otherwise known as a 'pack drive', you also need to be aware that they additionally have a very strong 'prey drive'.

The prey drive or any other drive is triggered by what the dog instinctively feels the need to do at any given moment. He can be happily walking by your side in 'pack drive' perhaps nudging you for attention one moment. The next moment he sees a rabbit or a bird and switches into 'prey drive' and all attention on you vanishes as he is compelled to chase after the rabbit.

Drives

Triggering the pack drive is needed to reliably control the prey drive which causes problems such as chasing and generally ignoring commands.

We develop pack drive by generally engaging him with training, play, bonding, interacting, touching, praising him etc.

The difficulty with drives however is that with most dogs, but not all, the pack drive is much harder for us to trigger than their prey drive. The prey drive is certainly harder to over-ride once triggered. Fortunately for us, Gundogs have a relatively strong 'pack drive'. But again this needs to be encouraged to maintain a reliable self control. Play can be used very effectively in working between pack and prey drive. Games involving us, the dog and a chase element offer a good example.

Incidentally food is part of their prey drive. This is primarily why in primitive terms wolves, feral dogs or similar hunt or scavenge. It is therefore unsurprising that food can be such a powerful motivating factor when teaching or wishing to control a dog.

In order to effectively prevent the dog from reacting to anything likely to trigger the prey drive, this self control has to be taught. You only have to see how a well trained gundog has to behave on a shooting field to see how effective gundog training is and has to be. However, this training takes time and does not happen over night. So be patient with the following training steps.

6) COLLAR/HARNESS & LEASH TRAINING

A) A WORD ON THE HAZARDS OF USING COLLARS IN THE FIELD

It is extremely important that when out in a field environment where there is cover such as hedges, collars of any type should never be worn by your Gundog, puppy or adult. A dog can very easily pass through hedges and get snagged quite severely and sometimes with fatal consequences. Chord choke type leads are always recommended for this purpose. The choke lead, being all in one, simply passes on and off the dog as required.

B) WALKING EQUIPMENT (COLLAR OR HARNESS AND LEASH)

Dog walking equipment should be introduced carefully, particularly to a puppy, and only the kindest collars or harness types should be used.

A harness is generally better than a collar, as it redistributes the weight of his body and naturally, immediately stops him pulling on the leash.

Dogs are far easier to control on walks when wearing a harness and there is no nasty pulling and coughing, as often happens on a standard collar and leash.

If you intend to use a collar however, initially use a small leather or man-made collar suitable for a puppy.

When you put his puppy collar on, do make sure that it is not too tight. You should quite easily be able to slip two fingers under the collar. It is up to you whether or not you allow him to wear the collar around the house on a daily basis. Please however remember that he will be growing day by day so it is important to check that you can still slip two fingers under the collar, every other day.

Most puppies do not like having to wear a collar, but this is something you should apply within a few days of his arrival.

In the early stages he will do everything to get the collar off. So simply accept that this is not cruel and wait for the scratching and head shaking etc to stop once he gets used to it.

Basically when you first introduce a Labrador puppy, or older dog, to a collar or harness make it a nice and positive event. Pop it onto the dog and play for a while, then remove it again whilst the dog is still happy. After doing this a few times, add the leash and allow the dog to trail it behind in the house or garden.

Putting the collar or harness on

As with any new training you can always sweeten the experience with a treat.

- Some people simply put the collar on and leave the puppy to get used to wearing it for an hour or so.
- Or if you prefer, you can do this in 5 or 10 minute stages by first putting the collar on > offering a treat > leave him five or ten minutes > take it off and repeat several times.
- Remember to give him lots of praise whilst he is accepting the collar, but ignore any protestations

- You can then take it off and leave him a few minutes so that he knows the collar is no longer on.
- You then put the collar back on, once again offer a treat, but this time leave him with the collar on for an hour or so.
- You next attach the leash to the collar and allow him to wander around with the lead trailing.
- Again leaving this on for 30 minutes to an hour, so that he gets used to it.
- All of this should be done supervised as it could be dangerous for the pup if the lead in particular gets caught and potentially cause a choking.
- Once your puppy seems happy wearing the collar and leash, he should be ready to go for a walk.

c) INITIAL WALK

Obviously we are not training the puppy to walk, but introducing him to the restriction imposed by applying the collar or harness and leash.

The following training steps are to help you prevent pulling on the leash. They are simply to make your Labrador walking experiences happy and relaxed forever.

The steps may take longer if the dog has learned to grab the leash in his mouth or fight against the tension, but if you persevere they will still work.

You will have more success with this if you start the training with few if any distractions. It is therefore best to utilise your yard, garden or a large room.

Training Steps;

1. With your dog on his leash, walk a couple of steps and if the leash stays slack say 'good boy/girl' > offer lots of praise and a treat. Please note that a slack leash is what we want and it is only that which should be rewarded.
2. If the leash becomes tight at any point, do not acknowledge this by speaking or offering any kind of reward. He needs to realise and associate that when he pulls on the leash he does not receive

a reward.
3. If the leash goes tight you may need to change direction a few times to initiate a slack leash. If your puppy does not follow immediately you may have to stop and call him by saying 'this way' or using his name, perhaps slapping your thigh as you do. I also find that by simply stopping, thus breaking the sequence of him pulling, is often enough to make him realise he shouldn't pull. Try and avoid suddenly stopping without him realising and yanking him to a stop. Give him chance to stop, by calling him.
4. As soon as any tension vanishes from the leash, again say 'good boy/girl' > offer lots of praise and a treat. In other words we are 'marking' the desired behaviour with praise and a treat.

Be patient with this and please don't get into the habit that some 'impatient people' seem to do, and pull the poor dog back with enough force to pull him over. The dog is keen and excited to be out walking and sniffing about. Given the chance he wants to go off and do his own thing. So again, please be patient and considerate.

Repeat and practice this several times, rewarding a slack leash each time. You should soon notice he gets into the habit of not pulling, but instead walking nicely.

Teaching a Labrador to walk easily on a leash will probably take 3 to 6 training sessions in a quiet area. It will then need practice (proofing) in various areas, gradually increasing distractions, to become flawless behaviour. This will eventually require exposure to roads and busy traffic. You will need to get to a point of teaching him to sit and wait at the road side until it is safe to cross.

7) OBEDIENCE TRAINING – TEACHING BASIC COMMANDS

Whilst your puppy may not be able to comprehend complex commands right away, you should be able to start basic obedience training at a fairly young age. Although we will cover other aspects of training here, however, there are five main commands which form the basics of obedience training;

Sit, Down, Come, Stay and Heel. In this section you will receive step-by-step instructions for teaching your Labrador these five basic commands.

However, before we get started with those basic training commands I want to firstly remind/introduce you to a couple of useful preliminary aspects of his training. In the initial stages of training, please make the training sessions relatively short. Ten or Fifteen minutes of good concentrated practice should be fine initially. When you feel he is keen to carry on, extend these lessons. Or practice these commands frequently at odd times around the house, rather than appoint one session for a designated time. The idea is that you can use the training at a moments notice when required anyway.

Just to recap, to be successful with this training, you need to clearly communicate to your dog when he has successfully completed an action.

Again we will illustrate this by using a previous example of clicker training. Clicker training as you know is based on issuing a click at the precise moment the dog performs desired behaviour. If the dog has been clicker trained, they will know that when they hear a click they have (a) performed acceptable behaviour that we want and (b) they are about to be rewarded for it.

The principal works the same without the clicker when we say 'good' or 'good boy/girl'. When the dog hears that word or words again he knows he has performed behaviour that we are happy with and he is about to be rewarded.

What we are effectively doing is 'marking' the behaviour with a click or a praise word 'good'.

A) SIT

For the dog that sits naturally, it is simple to capture or mark the behaviour with a click (or "good boy/girl"). It is also possible to easily lure the act, so that the dog is in the sit position.

This is a position that comes so naturally to a dog that most Labrador dogs, as they are so naturally intelligent, will pop into the sit position if you show them something that they want.

All you now have to do is teach him to sit on command.

Please note that 'sit' is also taught in the advanced gundog chapter utilising additional steps to

take. If you only wish to teach your dog the basic sit presented here, it will not affect your dog also learning the advance sit work later. The basics of sit presented here will be needed for that anyway.

However, the sit exercise in the next chapter is taught in conjunction with a whistle command and hand signal. What you will find is that teaching your dog using a whistle command, gives you more control and flexibility. The sit taught here uses a verbal sit command which can be limiting if you need to stop your dog at a distance. For this reason I would strongly urge you to read the section on 'sit' in the next chapter and consider incorporating that from the beginning of your dogs training.

To teach your dog to sit on command, follow these steps:

Please note that the following assumes that the dog is already standing. If not, then it may be necessary to lure him into a stand. You can do this by using the treat to draw him into a stand by moving it away from him, then acting quickly with the following steps:

1. Kneel in front of your Labrador and hold a small treat in your dominant hand > Pinch the treat between your thumb and

forefinger so your puppy can see it, but can't take it.

2. Hold the treat directly in front of your Labrador's nose and give him a second to smell it.

3. Immediately move the treat slightly away from your puppies nose, towards you and upwards > then move it away from you > towards the back of your dog's head. This again is a technique known as leading or luring, in that you lead your dog to perform the required action.

4. Your dog should lift his nose to follow the treat and, in doing so, his bottom should lower to the floor

5. The moment that he starts to sit > say the cue word 'sit'. You are affectively marking his action of sitting with the cue word 'sit'.

6. As soon as your dog's bottom hits the ground, praise him excitedly with 'good boy/girl' to let him know he has performed desirable behaviour > finally give him the treat as his reward.

7. Repeat this sequence (1) to (6) several times until your puppy gets the hang of it.

8. Now when you get to step (5) say the cue word 'sit' as soon as he starts to sit, but for step (6) start delaying when you praise him and give him the treat. In this way he will retain focus for longer.

9. Now instead of repeating the sequence (1) to (6) > walk away from your dog and hopefully he will follow > before he gets chance to sit, say the cue word 'sit' , leaving out the luring part.

10. Hopefully he will sit down > if he sits praise him and give him the treat.

11. Now practice (9) & (10) a number of times.

By proceeding this way you are getting him to sit simply by using the cue word 'sit' . This is ideally what you want to achieve. So you now should not have to lure with the food anymore, but simply say 'sit' and he should sit.

Teaching a Labrador to sit in this way will probably take 1 to 3 training sessions in a quiet area then it will need practice in various areas.

Gradually increase distractions, to become a flawless command. Again Please see the section on proofing/generalising at the end of the chapter for examples of increasing distractions.

Another useful way of practicing the sit command is as follows:

Early 'Sit' conditioning

A useful method to ease in the idea of the sit command for your puppy is as follows:

1. During feeding, you take the food bowl with food and whilst the pup is excitedly moving and bouncing about waiting for you to place the bowl down, simply hold the bowl until he becomes calm and stops.

2. At this point there is a strong likelihood that he will sit > As soon as he starts to sit > say the cue word 'sit'.

3. As his bottom touches the floor > mark him actually sitting with a verbal 'good boy/girl'.

4. Wait a couple of seconds and place the bowl down, the food being his reward.

It would be useful to attempt this every feeding time from day one, as soon as he comes to live with you.

B) DOWN

Once you have taught your Labrador to sit, teaching him to lie down is the next logical step.

The down command is not a requirement for a traditionally trained Gundog. However, the down command has similar benefits to the sit command in terms of controlling your dog. It can have a number of benefits including, stopping him in his tracks, telling him to drop at distance in an emergency, if for example he is approaching a road with busy traffic. It can also settle him down when visitors come to the home, if he is getting over excited or is about to jump up on someone.

The easiest way to teach a dog the down position initially is to lure the position. After a few successful attempts, he will be offering to get into the position very quickly if he thinks you have something he may want.

For this exercise it doesn't matter if he is standing or sitting to start, as long as he is not already lying down.

To teach your dog to lie down on command, follow these steps:

1. Kneel in front of your Labrador and hold a small treat in your dominant hand > Pinch the treat between your thumb and forefinger so your puppy can see it.
2. Hold the treat directly in front of your Labrador's nose and give him a second to smell it.
3. Give your puppy the "Sit" command and wait for him to comply. Unless of course he is already seated, or again standing.
4. Once your puppy sits > immediately move the treat quickly down to the floor in between your puppy's front paws > Make sure that you keep hold of the treat for the time being. Do not let him take the treat. He may be tempted to raise up to a sit or stand position, or even do a grab and run.
5. Again it is best to place the treat on the floor within his reach in between his front legs. If you place the treat in the right position, you generally find that he will crouch down into a beg position as he follows the treat.
6. As soon as he starts to assume the down position say the cue word "Down", or "Lie Down" > Again it is important to say the word as he is carrying out the act > He will then begin to associate the cue word 'down' with the action of lying down.
7. Your puppy should now hopefully be assuming the lying down position as he

attempts to take the treat > The instant he is actually lying down > again mark this with a click if you are using a clicker > or praise him excitedly with 'good boy/girl' and let him take the treat. It is important that he remains in the down position before you offer praise and allow him to take the treat. The other problem you may find is if his rear end remains raised. You will find steps to take for this following these steps. If your puppy stands up instead of lying down, calmly return to the beginning and repeat the sequence (1) to (7). The important thing is to not acknowledge this with praise or giving him the treat. Again, you do not want him thinking that the down is him assuming a beg position.

8. If he carries out the correct action, repeat this sequence (1) to (7) several times until your puppy gets the hang of it and is successfully carrying out the 'down' action each time.
9. Now instead of repeating the sequence (1) to (7) > walk away from your dog and hopefully he will follow > before he gets chance to do anything, say the cue word 'down'. This will obviously skip the 'sit' command. Hopefully he will start to assume the lying down position. If he does and as soon as he is lying down, offer lots of praise and give him the treat.
10. Now practice step (9) a number of times.

When Things Go Wrong

There are some extra options for the dog that is simply not getting the idea. You can sit on a chair and lure your Labrador under your outstretched leg.

1. Sit on a chair that is high enough so that you can sit comfortably and stretch your leg out, placing your heel to the floor, your outstretched leg at an angle to the floor.
2. Depending on which side your dog is on > hold a treat with which ever hand will be comfortable to tempt him through the triangular gap

3. He should hopefully be 'lured' and start to crawl under your leg > Again as soon as he starts to assume the down position say the cue word 'down'.

4. Hold the treat to the floor > As soon as he is in the down position offer lots of praise and let him take the treat.

5. Practice steps (1) to (4) until he is successfully repeating this.

6. Now as before, stand up and walk away from your dog and hopefully he will follow > before he gets chance to do anything, say the cue word 'down' . Hopefully he will start to assume the lying down position on his own. If he does and as soon as he is lying down offer lots of praise and give him the treat.

7. Be patient here, and be prepared to repeat steps (1) to (6) a number of times. But if after countless attempts, nothing seems to be working then try the following: As you go through the sequence above, if his back end is sticking up in a beg position, gently apply some pressure to his hips. As you gently push down say the words, 'down' or 'lie down'. Again, as soon as he does it, and doesn't immediately get up, click or praise to mark the behaviour and reward.

Teaching a Labrador to lie down will usually take 3 to 6 short training sessions in a quiet area. You will then need to practice in various areas, gradually increasing distractions, to become a flawless command. Please see the section on proofing/generalising at the end of the chapter for advice on distractions.

c) COME/ RECALL

For basic obedience, teaching your dog to come to you when called is incredibly important. Say, for instance, that you open the front door of your house one day and your Labrador rushes out before you can stop him. Your dog does not understand the danger of a busy street but if you have taught him to come to you when called, you can save him from that danger. In an emergency situation, your 'down', 'stop' or the 'stay' command can be vital. Using either one of those will hope-

fully stop him in his tracks. You can then call him back and away from any danger.

The Labrador needs to be taught to come back when called as soon as possible and in careful stages.

Most dogs can either be very responsive to recall or happy to leave you standing all day, calling his name in vain, whilst he chases rabbits or squirrels around the park.

Recall training can be broken down into easy steps. The exact same approach is taken when teaching recall as when teaching anything else to the dog. You always set the dog up to succeed; never allow room for failure; therefore building his confidence high.

With recall you need to make certain that your dog sees you as the most interesting and attractive prospect in the area. If you are red faced and shouting his name with frustration he is less likely to want to come back. He will naturally think you are angry with him.

There are some very specific habits that you can procure when teaching recall;

Please do remember that Labradors do have a reputation to take off after rabbits, and some without adequate recall training, can run away. Always be on your guard to potentially hazardous areas (busy roads etc) and therefore avoid accidents. I once had a situation with an Irish Setter that took off across a field, after she had picked up the scent of something. I literally shouted my head off and fortunately she came to her senses and came running back. Dogs can easily give chase to rabbits and if you are near a road there is a chance the rabbit may cross, along with your dog. Please pre-empt and avoid this from happening. If in doubt, keep your dog on a long 5 or 10 meter training type lead.

If you get a situation as described above, never punish your dog when he gets to you. Always be welcoming and friendly, no matter how frustrated you are, or he may not come back at all next time.

Early recall training

Recall training, or what many trainers refer to as 'come', is simply getting your puppy to come to you when called.

In the early stages of puppy recall however, a puppy is not always keen to obey in this way. As your puppy grows in confidence he will go from being under your feet all day, to wanting to wander off, explore and generally do his own thing.

What you therefore need to do, is to condition or encourage the puppy to come back to you at random times around the house or garden.

This is only early stages training and works by getting the puppies attention, coaxing him to come to you, and as he is running back, use the recall word, (and for gundog training purposes, the whistle and hand signal also).

It cannot be stressed enough how beneficial it will be to start using the recall cue word, whistle command and hand signal, at this early stage. He will therefore get used to associating these commands with coming back to you, in the very early stages, and make further training so much easier.

Before we start, please be aware of a few useful pointers as follows:

- Unless in an emergency, try and avoid running after your puppy. This can often lead to a chase game which all puppies love, and he is likely to carry on running away anyway.
- The exception to this is if he is running towards an open gate or open field onto a road. Once again you need to pre-empt this and take measures to train him in an enclosed or a secure area.
- Also be aware that he may try and engage you in a chase game, by coming up to you and then darting away.
- If you continue with advanced gundog training, when you get into retrieving dummies, if this behaviour where not ignored, he may do the same with the object, which again should not be encouraged.

Early recall exercise

Once again in the initial stages, this is best started in your yard, garden or other safe enclosed space with limited to no distractions

Again you will be using the cue word, whistle command and hand signal as follows:

As a reminder there is a small section in the Advanced training section giving advice about purchasing a whistle. Again it is highly recommended to make use of one. They are also cheap to buy and use.

- The whistle command should be several short pips/toots (pip, pip, pip, pip) = come back/recall
- The cue word should be something like 'come' or 'here'
- The recall hand signal to use is to throw your arms wide (ideally this is holding your arms straight out, at around a 90 degree angle to your body (approximately parallel to the ground); palms facing towards the dog)

1. Lets assume your puppy is wandering around your garden, sniffing and exploring > Allow the puppy to wander and explore for a few minutes.

2. Whilst he is busy sniffing and investigating, in other words not paying any attention to you > make a funny noise, high pitched or whatever, or call his name to get his attention

3. As soon as he looks towards you, suddenly move or jog in the opposite direction > The puppy should soon notice you disappearing and start chasing you > If not then pat your thigh or use a hand clap to encourage this > If you are using a whistle command, it is best to put the whistle in your mouth at this stage before the next steps. The whistle should be on a lanyard around your neck, as you will need to drop this from your mouth to give the verbal cue.

4. Keep checking back unless you decide to jog backwards > As soon as he starts moving towards you, blow several short pips/toots (pip, pip, pip, pip) on the whistle > almost simultaneous to this, throw your hands wide for the hand signal > drop the whistle from your mouth > issue the command word 'come', 'here' or whichever cue word you have chosen to mark the behaviour of him being recalled. As with the other

training exercises, you have waited until he starts the action. You then 'mark' the behaviour with the verbal, whistle and hand signals.

5. Always try and let your puppy catch you, so either slow down and stop or fall to the floor, which the puppy will love as he tries to lick your face.

6. It is important that you only use the cue word; whistle signal and hand gesture, IF he is already coming back to you. That way he immediately associates the command with the action of coming to you.

7. When he gets back to you, reward him by giving him lots of praise and perhaps a piece of food.

8. Repeat steps (1) to (6)several more times.

9. Practice this procedure for two or three weeks, each day.

10. After you have practiced this for a few weeks, test his response to one of either the recall command 'here', the whistle command or hand signal > Practice each one on its own a number of times > then alternate each one randomly. It should only take him a week or so to get the hang of this, but practice every day until he is coming back to you as soon as you issue the command word 'here'.

11. Only when the recall command is solid and reliable, use the whistle or vocal cue, when he is not looking at you.

12. Around the house at random moments, call him or blow the whistle > This is a big step forward as this is effectively formal recall training > In other words, you are wanting him to come back to you as soon as you give the whistle, recall word, or hand signal if he is looking at you > If this does not happen then proceed as follows.

13. If at any point the puppy starts to blatantly ignore you use the correction word 'No' or 'Ah ah', to get his attention > Be careful with your tone of voice here, as you do not want to frighten the puppy

14. Once you have the puppies attention, repeat either or all of the recall commands > As he will not have heard this correction up until now, you may have to coax him by kneeling down and offering lots of encouragement.

15. Again, if he successfully comes back to you offer lots of praise.

16. Keep practicing this every day, and again don't just practice on the training field. Practice recalling and praising him around the house and garden.

Rapid recall

This exercise gets the puppy used to responding immediately and with speed. It should therefore condition a quicker response.

He simply responds to the whistle, verbal cue or hand signal > returns at speed > is immediately sent off > you then repeat.

The easiest way of approaching this exercise is to use pieces of food that you throw away in order to send him away, then recall him.

1. Recall your puppy to you (whistle, verbal cue or hand signal) > as soon as he gets close to you > throw a piece of food as far as you can in any direction which the dog should race after

2. Once he has picked up the food and as soon as he looks at you > issue the recall command, (whistle, verbal cue or hand signal) > It is important to time the recall command, as soon as he has picked up the food and is about to return. In other words you will see that his intention is to pick the food up and return to you.

3. Again as soon as he gets close to you > throw a piece of food as far as you can throw it, but this time in the opposite direction > repeat this several times.

4. Once he has the hang of this > throw the food shorter distances for a more rapid recall.

5. Now repeat the exercise in different areas/locations and with gradually added distractions

It is important to use the food as a strong incentive and physical object to chase. You could use a dummy or favourite toy, but until he is practiced retrieving a dummy you may not be as successful with a rapid recall.

A few pointers to bear in mind

In the initial stages, only use the recall command when he is either looking at you, or actually coming back to you. Once he has learned to associate the recall command with the action of coming back to you, you will of course be able to simply blow the whistle, or use the cue word. This is ultimately the whole point and objective, in order for you to use it in emergencies or when he is preoccupied doing something else such as chasing a scent or rabbit. Using the hand signal will obviously only work if he is actually looking at you.

Don't make this a chore, but get into the habit of repeating the recall a number of times each day. Soon it will become a really ingrained habit and you will have taught the puppy recall as part of a game and not regimented formal training.

If he runs away and then comes running back, always offer lots of praise for him coming back and never punish the act of him running away. Even though you know he initially went wrong by running away, an act that you do not want, the last thing he did was to come back to you, which is what you want.

Remember that it is necessary to teach a young dog an effective recall in as many different environments and with as many varying distractions as possible, in order to make it reliable.

Failure on the dogs part to respond to a recall can include the following:

- The stimulus of sighted or scented prey outweighs the desire to come back to you.
- The dog has not been exposed to sufficient environmental experiences and has therefore not been sufficiently desensitised to the stimuli.
- Incorrect or insufficient reinforcement/reward (it is important to always reward correct behaviour and that you get the timings correct)

- Teaching the recall has only occurred initially and has not been maintained regularly.

Once again the 'recall' is particularly important for breeds with a strong prey drive such as Gundogs.

It is hard for dogs who are highly driven to hunt, to suddenly be expected to stop hunting and return to you. The recall therefore needs to be seen by the dog as part of him hunting. This is the reason many gundog trainers start recall 'conditioning' in the very early stages. In other words he should ideally associate it as part of a fun hunting game. Not some boring discipline that takes him away from doing what he would rather be doing.

If you do advance into high stimulation situations (live game; pheasants, rabbits etc) it is important to use the long line for the dogs safety.

Please note that the reliable recall can take many weeks or months to achieve.

D) EARLY RETRIEVE

The following is intended to give the puppy a basic introduction to retrieving an object. He will later on be introduced to formal retrieving, which is best practiced once he has learned other commands such as stop, sit, recall etc.

Please first of all be aware that although many gundog breeds instinctively pick up and retrieve items, they do not always realise that you want them to return the object to your hand. It is therefore advisable to start at relatively short distances and then build up. This will ensure that he gets into the habit of retrieving to hand at all times. If left untrained the dog may run off with the object or drop it before he gets back to you.

Early retrieve exercise

This exercise can be practiced along with the early 'recall' in your house or garden. However, please be aware that in the initial stages, giving the puppy too much space can encourage him to wander off. It is therefore advisable to initially practice in a narrow area such as a hallway or any long narrow lane, even if you have to construct something yourself.

The first dummy you use should be lighter than the 1Lb dummies you will be using as you move further into dummy work with advance training. A simple dummy can be made very easily using an old sock stuffed with rags, tied off at the open end.

1. Have your puppy on a training lead or retractible so that he gets used to this and you can control him should he wish to attempt to run off with the dummy.
2. Firstly encourage your puppy to come to you and let him inspect the dummy > Once he shows sufficient interest, toss the dummy a few feet > say something like, 'go fetch' > he will hopefully run and pick the dummy up > the moment he picks it up > excitedly offer praise and encourage him to bring it back, by calling his name.
3. If he doesn't want to bring the dummy back to you > encourage him by saying the words 'here' or 'come', and move away from him > hopefully he will follow.
4. When he gets back to you, hopefully with the dummy > praise him and gently take the dummy > use the command word 'give' or 'leave' at the same time.
5. If he refuses to leave > you may have to hold the dummy with one hand and gently prise open his jaws with the other > all the while saying 'leave'.
6. Do not be tempted to engage in a tug of war as he will hold on tighter and this may encourage him to rip the dummy.
7. Repeat the exercise 5 or 6 more times. Aim to practice each day and gradually increase the distance by 1 foot or so each time.

However, as with all early training, do not over do this, as it can soon lose its fun factor for the puppy and become a chore that he gets bored of and resents doing.

Progress can be made with the dummy by throwing longer distances, then hiding the dummy for him to find or throwing into long grass etc.

As the puppy gets older, the dummy should be made appropriately larger until he reaches adulthood, and the dummy resembles in weight and size a large bird such as a pheasant or goose.

Tennis balls are also an excellent training tool that are easy to throw and of the right size for most dogs to pick up easily.

If he has successfully picked up the dummy, brought it back when called, and handed this over to you, you will have taken a big step in his training.

It is important however, that he doesn't get into the habit of dropping the dummy. He therefore needs to be taught that he must hold onto it until you take it. Again it is not imperative that you insist on this if you have no interest in gundog competitions etc, but it is still good practice and discipline.

A working gundog that got into the habit of dropping the dummy in practice is likely to do this in the field. The whole point of field work is that the dog retrieves a bird that is shot. It is equally important that they also retrieve an injured bird that would otherwise suffer and possibly have a slow death.

It is also important for these training exercises, that the dummy is not seen as his plaything that he can wander off and start chewing.

The action of the retrieve therefore needs to be made very clear. When you instruct him to retrieve, in this case a dummy, he needs to go to fetch it, pick it up and bring it back to you.

We will go into more advanced retrieves in the next chapter 'Advanced gundog Training'

E) STAY

After you have taught your dog to come to you on command, the next logical step is to teach him to stay or wait until you call him.

When teaching the stay command it is not important what his starting position is. The important thing is that he stays where he is until you recall him back to you. But for the purposes of this exercise we will use the 'sit' command, but again he could be standing or lying down.

To teach your dog to stay on command, follow these steps:

1. Kneel in front of your Labrador and hold a small treat in your dominant hand > pinch the treat between your thumb and forefinger so your puppy can see it.
2. Hold the treat directly in front of your Labrador's nose and give him a second to smell it.
3. Give your puppy the "Sit" command and wait for him to comply.
4. Now say "Stay" in a firm, even tone and hold your palm up towards the dog (similar to the stop signal a traffic policeman would give) > now take a step or two backward away from your puppy. You have issued the 'stay' command, but this assumes he has remained seated, or his 'action' is to stay whilst you issue the verbal 'stay'.
5. Pause for a second then walk back up to your puppy > provided he stays, click or praise to mark the fact that he has stayed put > reward him with a treat.

6. Repeat steps (1) to (5) several times, rewarding your puppy each time he stays.
7. Each time you practice this, aim to increase the distance between you and your dog. You can measure this in paces if you like, so two steps to four, then eight and so on. So start him in the sit position as before and say 'stay', holding your hand up to him > I usually keep repeating the 'stay' cue word as I walk backward > Once you have walked back quite a few paces > stop and pause as long as you feel he is concentrating > Then walk back > praise and give him the treat as before.

Once he is successfully remaining in a stay position you can increase the level of difficulty with the following exercises:

The stay is a very important behaviour that not only teaches steadiness and control, but also allows you to increase the 'stay' command at a distance; add distractions that may prompt him to move from the 'stay'; increase the duration in terms of how long he stays for; he stays regardless of where the handler moves to.

Those four aspects should be taught in order to increase a reliable stay, so do not merely add distance and duration, but also distractions and where you move to.

Duration and distance relate to one another because as you increase the distance, i.e. walking away, you are taking time so adding duration.

But you can add duration being close to the dog by pausing.

'Stay' in relation to orientation

1. Start the exercise with your dog in a sit position with you standing in front of your dog.
2. Say 'stay' and hold your palm up towards the dog (again similar to the stop signal a traffic policeman would give)
3. Take one step back with either foot but keep the other foot rooted to that spot. In other words you are pivoting on the one foot and not moving away as such > Return to the start position > Mark the behaviour with a verbal 'good' or click

> Offer a treat and as soon as he takes it > hold your palm up in the stay signal > Say 'stay'

4. Now take one step to your right > again pivoting and not actually moving away > Return to the start position > Mark the behaviour with a verbal 'good' or click > Offer a treat and again as soon as he takes it > hold your palm up in the stay signal > Say 'stay'

5. Take one step to your left > again pivoting and not actually moving away > Return to the start position > Mark the behaviour with a verbal 'good' or click > Offer a treat > Say 'stay'

6. Take one step back, but this time slowly walk all the way around the dog returning to the start position > Mark the behaviour with a verbal 'good' or click > Offer a treat

7. Repeat steps (1) to (5) but increase to 2 steps then 3 and so on.

8. If the dog moves at any point as you increase the steps, take a step back until you can increase the distance again. Make sure the dog can successfully repeat each step at least twice before moving on.

This will be a lot for your dog to do in one go so have a break in between sessions or concentrate on moving backwards facing your dog before adding the orientations of going all the way around.

Some dogs are very sensitive to the slightest body language movement. Therefore be aware of how you are moving if you are having problems with a dog that moves as soon as you do. In this case, move much slower.

Walking around the dog

Once you are successful moving left, right and back at a distance, then attempt to walk around the dog at distance. For this you will need to get your dog to stay as you walk away. Then start walking around him

Start moving around from the left then the right. At this stage you may have moved away ten steps or more.

However, if the dog moves when you walk around, again you may have to go back to the beginning making one step movements and increase the steps again.

You may even have to hold your palm close to the dogs nose and as you move around keep your hand there prompting the dog to stay.

Further 'Stay'

You simply advance here with both generalising (I.e. proofing, as described at the end of the chapter) in different locations and adding distance.

Once the stay is accomplished at a set distance test this with the distraction of walking around him in a circle.

1. Start in front of the dog at a certain distance.

2. Give the stay command and walk in a circle over to the dogs right side.

3. Now walk back and over to the dogs left side.

4. Next again walk over to the dogs right but continue walking all the way around.

5. Once you are back in front walk over to the dogs left side all the way around and back to face the dog.

6. Now increase the distance several feet more and repeat (1) to (5).

Add levels of distraction by not facing front but having your back to the dog or side on. Walk faster > break into a slight jog > jump up and down on the spot > do star jumps etc.

Practice a stay as you do some chore or activity around the house. The idea here is that you give the stay command but do not pay the dog any attention.

Also remember to practice the above exercises with him standing or lying down.

You will next need to be in a location where wildlife likely to trigger the prey instinct will be present. For this you will need to work with a long training lead or retractable, attached for his safety in case he decides to give chase. You should then build up the distance gradually.

Practice any or all of the stay exercises so far covered.

Distraction

Distractions should be anything that the dog has an impulse to move towards. Initially distractions can be anything in the immediate surroundings.

However, a good item to start with would be a favourite toy. You simply get your dog to stay > you walk a few steps away > place the toy on the ground > walk back to the dog > provided they have stayed in place > give lots of praise and fuss.

Additional Examples similar to those highlighted in the proofing section, should be used until you can reliably get him to stay when other dogs or wildlife are likely to appear, prompting his instinctive desire to chase.

Please remember that any time he moves or attempts to give chase, you should firmly say 'stay'. If he ignores you and goes anyway, start the exercise again. Do not offer a treat or praise. Don't shout at him, get angry or attempt to go after him (he will only be able to go as far as the training leash any way).

F) Heel

Teaching a Labrador to heel is easy. Or it should be if you have been using this initially when you started his general walk training earlier.

The ultimate objective of 'heeling' is to train the puppy to walk at your side, under control, without the use of a lead. For the average pet owner

who walks their dog on the pavement, perhaps near a busy road, you would need the peace of mind, that your dog is safe from danger. Obviously a collar would need to be worn and lead attached. In certain countries such as the UK, it is a legal requirement that when walking on a public highway a dog must be attached to a leash at all times.

A lot of trainers teach walking to heel with him on a leash first, then off leash in a safe area. The traditionally trained gundog in particular needs a level of heel control whereby they effectively heel, but without a collar and lead. As previously noted, Gundogs on a shooting field should never be allowed to run loose or hunt, wearing any kind of collar. Again, this is purely for the safety of the dog as he could easily get caught when flushing in thick undergrowth. This could cause a serious injury to the dog, at worse the dog could become snagged and possibly choke. Once again, all in one slip leads are generally used, which can be easily removed. These are also a very good piece of walking equipment, even for the average dog walker.

Initial 'heel' conditioning

From the day your puppy arrives, you are strongly advised to encourage him to walk beside you around the house or in the yard or garden.

1. Pat your leg, encouraging him to you with words such as 'here [his name]', or 'come on' etc, which should have him coming to your left or right side.
2. When he comes to you and stays to 'heel' at your side > say the cue word 'heel' > remember to give him lots of praise and perhaps the occasional treat.
3. After a number of repetitions like this, just use the cue word 'heel', when you want him to come to your side.

Incidentally, for gundog purposes, which side you walk your dog at heel has usually been dependent on whether you shoot right or left handed. So if you were to shoot a gun with your right hand for safety and practical reasons you would heel your dog on your left, and vice versa.

Having said that quite a number of gundog people prefer to train their dogs to walk on either side. This obviously gives you flexibility to choose depending on your circumstances. Perhaps walking near a main road and wishing to keep your dog safe to the inner side of the path. It is also useful if you walk two dogs either side of you.

So bearing this in mind, do not feel restricted to which side he should walk to heel. Certain competition rules insist that a dog must heel on one side or another. It is for this reason that I prefer to teach a dog to heel on both sides which leaves you with the freedom to choose.

'Heel' training:

It is important that you have the loop of the lead through whichever is your preferred lead hand, so it hangs on your wrist. Unless you intend to practice with both sides in which case you will use both hands anyway. Your puppy should then be on the opposite side to that. So if you hold the loop of the lead in your right hand, have the dog walk at your left side and vice versa. This is more for control and safety of your puppy in these initial stages. With the other hand, in this case your left, grip the lead, so that it is relatively close to your dog, again giving you greater control. This will also act as a guide or restraint to let your puppy know where you want him, should your puppy surge forward or hang back.

When you are teaching a dog to walk to heel it is important that you focus on the position of the dog and not on the leash.

It is also advisable to use a short lead in the initial stages of heeling to prevent the dog from surging ahead or lagging behind, which can obviously happen with a long training lead. Once he is reliably heeling at your side you can slacken the lead but be prepared to verbally keep him in check.

To keep pulling or jerking the dog back from a tense leash, to a slack one, whilst stating the command to heel is not really what we want to be doing. This can turn into a form of harsh training, which we want to avoid.

You should proceed with official 'heel' training as follows:

You can do the exercise with or without a lead, but only do this without a lead if you are in an enclosed yard or field away from a busy road or other distractions.

1. Call him to you and get him to sit directly in front of you. Attach his leash if you are leading him, if not then carry on to step (3).

2. Hold a treat to his nose, as before so that he can sniff or lick, but not take it.

3. Now lure him around the back of your legs to your left or right side > So whilst holding the treat in front of him, draw this to your left or right side which he should follow > The moment he is beside your leg, say the cue word 'heel' > Once he is beside your leg, hold him there with the treat to his nose, but do not allow him to take it. This might seem long winded. But the idea is to get him to associate the cue word 'heel' with the action of coming to, or being at your side.

4. Or for simplicity you may prefer to start the puppy in a sit position > get him to stay > then move to either the right or left hand side of the dog.

5. Now that you are in this position, with your puppy beside your right or left leg > Please make sure that you hold the treat near your leg and not out in front.

6. With the treat held to his nose start to walk forward > as soon as you move, he should follow the treat and remain at your side > again the moment he starts to walk at your side say the cue word 'heel'.

7. Keep repeating 'heel' periodically as you walk, as long as he is actually 'heeling' at your side.

8. When you have walked a few paces > give him the treat and offer lots of praise.

9. Repeat steps from (6) to (8) with another treat and gradually increase the level of difficulty by walking further and withholding the treat for longer each time. But remember in these initial stages to have the treat in your hand, held to his nose, whilst you walk.

In the initial stages you will find that you have to crouch down to reach your puppies nose. But eventually do this standing up. So again show him the treat and move forward > but this time stand up > quickly draw the treat away > and walk a few paces > all the while saying 'heel' > when he has successfully walked with you several paces > bend down and give him the treat, offering lots of praise.

Again repeat step (9) but keep increasing the distance you walk before giving him the treat and praising him.

Corrections

If at any point he tries to jump up to grab at the treat, you probably have the treat too high.

You will need to bend just enough to keep it at his nose and just remember this will only be for a short while until he gets used to the 'heel'. You should then be able to stand upright as you walk.

You will also reach the point where you can stop the treats, or just give the treat when you finish. Or you may prefer to not use treats at all, but simply use your hand to lure/lead him as you walk. The food however, usually gives him more of an incentive to follow you.

If once you are no longer luring him with the treat, he gets distracted and starts moving away or in front, do an about turn and walk in the opposite direction. You may have to pat your leg and again say 'heel' or 'this way'.

Once again, if your puppy continues to pull at the leash, you may need to stop and stand still until your pup understands that he's not going anywhere until he listens. Once your puppy understands that he only receives praise when he begins to respond appropriately, it will only take a few days before he's walking right next to you without pulling on the lead.

Once he is successfully carrying out the 'heel' in a straight line, I would suggest walking in zig zags, 90 and 180 degree turns. This is more or less what happens in agility training and dog shows. The dog follows precise paths at your side. This will also help if you find your puppy gradually starts walking ahead and eventually pulling at the lead.

Also try altering the speed at which you walk, walking normally then exaggeratedly faster or slower than normal.

This is usually the method recommended for a dog that pulls, as the walk becomes unpredictable for a dog that would otherwise surge straight ahead.

Whilst on a leash, if he moves ahead or lags behind, once he reaches the end of the short leash,

it will stop him going further.

Eventually however, you should get to a point where he can heel like this without the lead. But be prepared for him to move ahead or behind once you remove the leash. In this case if he fails to respond to your heel command and wanders off, an effective remedy is to blow the stop whistle. But obviously this will only work if he has practiced the stop command before hand. Again, the 'stop' will be covered later. Once you have issued the stop command, which hopefully stops him instantly > praise him for stopping > walk to where he is, stand next to him and wait for 20 or 30 seconds > then continue with the heel.

Pausing before continuing, will ensure that the dog doesn't associate you stopping him as punishment > commence heeling with the leash applied.

Teaching a Labrador to walk nicely at heel will probably take 4 to 6 training sessions in a quiet area.

Further 'heeling'

Once the basic 'heel' command is being successfully carried out, it is just a question of proofing or generalising the heeling with added distractions and in different locations. Also remember that once your dog learns to heel he will get plenty of practice during normal lead walking exercise. In this respect you should not have to keep repeating the 'heel' cue, but only if he moves away from you.

With most of the advanced work it is important to start testing distractions that will trigger their prey instinct such as rabbits or birds.

In other words it is important to take him to locations where such wildlife will be present.

At this point you will need to begin with your dog on a leash but work up to being off leash.

But as usual attach a loose safety line.

G) 'STAND'

The 'stand' command is beneficial when you need your dog to stay where he is, but the sit or down would not be as suitable.

Situations where the stand will be particularly useful would be when you need him to stand and stay when grooming, visiting your vet, bathing or drying him.

In those cases you need to be able to get all around him.

What it means is that you can ask him to stand rather than have to physically lift him into that position.

To get him to stand, you will also need him to stay.

1. Start in either the sit or down position > but obviously not already standing.
2. Kneel in front of him with your treat as before and slowly move the treat away from his nose towards you > You may have to stand and move away.
3. Hopefully he will follow you by standing > the very moment he initiates the action of standing, say the word 'stand' > pause a moment and say 'stay' > again pause a moment and provided he has successfully stood still > praise him and give him the treat.
4. practice and repeat steps (1) to (3) a number of times.
5. If at any point he attempts to move out of position simply issue the 'stay' command. If he completely ignores you, repeat steps (1) to (3) again as many times as necessary.

Your objective is to be able to issue the 'stand' command and hopefully he will 'stand' and 'stay'

A good way to practice this is, once he is in the stand position is to start to massage or stroke him, all the while saying, 'stand'. Also start practicing this when you groom him. Praise him if he stands for a while. You can also hold him if he moves or raise his back end, or lure him forward, if he tries to sit. Again say stand when he stands, and praise as before. It is useful to imagine everything a groomer or vet may need to do. So lift his paws one at a time and stroke each leg etc.

8) Phasing Out Food Rewards

Food is a highly motivating reward for dogs. But you do not want your Labrador to become dependent on a food reward indefinitely to perform the desired behaviour. Once your puppy starts to respond consistently with the right behaviour, when you give him a command, you should start phasing out the treats. Start by only rewarding your puppy every second time. Then cut it back to every third time and so on. Even though you are phasing out the food rewards you still need to praise your puppy so he knows that you are pleased with him. You may even choose to substitute a food reward for a toy and give your puppy a brief play session with the toy as a reward instead of the treat. Do not feel guilty that your poor dog is looking sad, disappointed and bewildered by no longer receiving his treat. All dogs are only too happy to please their owner, and he will soon get used to no longer getting the treat every time. Of course you are free to treat your dog occasionally. But you are doing his long time health no favours by constantly giving him treats. Also please be aware that there are dog trainers who do not use treats at all and successfully train happy dogs.

9) Discipline Whilst Training

We have now talked a lot about positive reinforcement training as opposed to any punishment based methods. I always advocate a firm but fair approach and dislike the idea of 'disciplining' a dog. But it is worth clarifying your approach to training. Most dogs behave perfectly well and respect you as their carer. Some dogs however, can have a wilful personality and they will sometimes test you and misbehave. Again, I would never advocate hitting a dog nor would I advocate being a strict disciplinarian for the sake of it. But if your puppy does appear to be developing wilful disobedience, the following will be worth bearing in mind.

Remember a well behaved adult is the result of a correctly trained puppy, given firm basic training.

Your dog will respect you when you are firm but fair, and when you say 'No', they should know this by your tone of voice. You obviously do not want to become a sergeant major, barking commands. But if say for example, you tell your dog to stay or wait and he starts to move before you have given the word, then tell him in a slightly disapproving voice, 'No'. Some trainers like to use a short, sharp 'Ah Ah'.

Do not feel bad, or feel that you are being cruel and do not forget that this training could potentially save your dogs life in an emergency situation. In this respect, I would not advise shouting at your dog whilst generally training your puppy. However, if you are in an emergency situation shouting may be the only way to shock or frighten your puppy into realising something is seriously wrong. If you shout all the time, he will probably see this as normal, and be unable or unlikely to differentiate when something is seriously wrong.

Sometimes he will need to know that he is doing wrong with a firm 'No' or 'Ah ah'. It will be even more satisfying to him, when you shower him with praise. Also remember some personalities need and respect someone who they take as a strong leader. Again, without wishing to get into a debate about 'alpha dog' training, dogs generally respect you when you are firm but fair.

10) PROOFING/GENERALISING BEHAVIOURS

Initial learning should take place in a single distraction free room or area such as your back yard or garden

Advantages of a yard or garden include:

- Limited distractions and plant cover, which could harbour wildlife even in your garden.
- Limited wild animals as they are likely to stay away whilst you are present

Once behaviours are learned in a distraction free area it is necessary to generalise different locations including the following if these have not already been used:

Kitchen; Other rooms in the house; Driveway; Front yard or garden; The previously mentioned locations with other people present; Whilst out walking (again go at different times, so they get used to it when things are quiet and busy with lots of other dog walkers.); With you taking up different positions sitting down, standing in different areas, lying on the floor; Standing in front of the dog; Standing at the side of the dog; Standing with your back to the dog

When moving on and adding levels of difficulty to exercises it is important to increase or improve on the following if they are appropriate:

Increase the distance; Increase the duration; Add and increase distractions; Change directions

In all cases take note of how fast the dog complies as an indication to whether he is ready to move on or whether you have moved on too fast

Public areas:

Once behaviours are learned and proofed in familiar places, it is necessary to practice and 'generalise' the behaviours in unfamiliar surroundings, for example

A recreation area; Public fenced park; Sports field; A field or park where some wild animals and other dog walkers may be present

It is very important to always apply a long training leash until your dog is demonstrating a reliable 'stop' and 'recall'

Exposure to different locations and countryside

After you have trained and proofed in the previous areas it will be time to expose him to terrain and countryside where game and other wildlife are present.

Exposing the dog to a variety of terrain obviously depends on where you live and whether you are able or willing to travel to a variety of locations.

Such locations should ideally include the following:

Flat land fields; Hilly ground; Crop fields if you have permission; Wooded/Forest areas; Marshland; Hedgerows; Walls; Fences; Dykes; Ditches; Ponds; Lakes; Streams; Rivers etc etc

Please note; initially dogs should only be exposed to water with a gradual slope such as a shallow pond rather than a shear drop.

With experience you can graduate to seaside beaches, lakes etc.

However, check that there are no potential hazards and consider the dogs safety by fitting a life-jacket.

CHAPTER SIXTEEN:

ADVANCED LABRADOR GUNDOG TRAINING

This chapter will follow on from the previous chapter. Most of this section contains new exercises specific to gundog training. However, there is an extended section which relates to the 'sit' command previously taught, if you wish to expand on this. Once again, most of this will only interest you if you wish to expand your training or are interested in gundog training. But as mentioned in the previous chapter, if you have no interest in anything else in the chapter, the one exercise I would seriously consider here is the 'stop' command.

However, many of the exercises presented here will give you far greater control of your dog than basic training can offer. It is for this reason that I would urge you to consider continuing and practicing the exercises in this chapter.

1) RECOMMENDED ACCESSORIES

The following is a list of every accessory you are likely to need if you are serious about Advanced gundog training. However, you do not need to rush out and buy every single item. This section is intended to give you some guidance of recommended accessories you may need at some point. However, please read the chapter which will highlight items you are likely to need now such as the whistle, a selection of dummies, slip lead, training leads etc. Other items such as dummy launchers are useful but not vital items.

Quality release clip collar: Flat buckle collars are also recommended for training as opposed to traditional choke chains etc. These are more for pavement walking and not if you take your dog out into the country side.

Slip lead: Equipment needed for training a gundog is not dissimilar to any other dog with the exception of the slip lead/collar. These effectively act as an all in one lead and collar and are essential when hunting where hedges and thick undergrowth is present. For obvious reasons a dog can easily become entangled and choke, so the slip collar allows you to quickly remove the collar for off lead hunting and quickly apply it again when the dog returns.

Normal 5 or 6ft lead for general leash walking.

A 30 foot approx (10 meter approx) minimum check cord and/or a similar length retractable leash. Although a 15 foot approx (5 meter approx) can be used initially: These are an invaluable training aid as it allows full control, easy correction and greatly lessens the chances of things going wrong.

If you have to use the check cord to stop your dog in an emergency be aware that grabbing the cord may cause friction burns on your hand/hands.

For obvious reasons therefore you are advised to wear gloves or at least a glove on the hand you will be grabbing the rope with.

http://www.Gundogsupply.com/

Standard harness to be used with long check cord leash. This will be safer for the puppy, in case he takes off running and you have to suddenly stop him.

Whistle: One of the Acme 210 to 212 whistle range are recommended and choose one only rather several different pitches. Acme 210½ or 211½ gundog whistles are quite popular

It is also not recommended to buy a hand crafted bone type which are difficult to replace with the exact same tone that a plastic one will have.

Waterproofs: For wet weather, dark brown, green or black waterproofs are recommended as are rubber boots or wellingtons.

A suitable **dummy for a puppy:** A light dummy for a puppy (some people will use an old sock stuffed with cloth rags)

Larger **one pound canvas dummy**

Optional **3lb and 6lb** canvas dummies

A floating **rubber dummy** to retrieve from water

The colour of the dummies should ideally be white, black or some variation of, although green are common.

The fluorescent orange type you would think would be the most visible but are actually more difficult for dogs to see, particularly against green or brown

Tennis balls of different sizes if possible

Toys with different squeaks

Soft toys resembling ducks, pheasants or other animals, preferably with floppy parts

Chew toys, plastic gnarl bones (never give your dog cooked bones, as they are known to splinter, causing internal problems), other soft toys etc. These act as additional reward/reinforce/motivators.

A **clicker** unless you use a verbal marker and suitable reward treats.

Water bottle and water dish for a drink when on a remote location.

First aid kit for you and your dog.

A compass and map for navigating unfamiliar terrain.

A shoulder bag to carry dummies, toys, leads etc (some people prefer traditional game bags for this)

Other accessories can be used which are not vital in the early training stages, but may come in use later:

Tracking collars which provide GPS and indicate when your dog is moving and when they are on point.

Bird calls including duck, quail, pheasant etc.

Rabbit fur covered dummy.

Marker poles for blind retrieves.

Dead Fowl Trainer or **Dokken** used for retrieving, which resemble ducks, pheasants etc, usually with a hinged head to replicate the weight and movement of the real thing.

Dried game bird wings.

Optional **dummy launcher** for longer distances: A dummy launcher is not vital, but will be something well worth considering for advanced gundog training. They are recommended for advanced retrieves over long distances both over land and into and across water. These have the dual purpose of simulating gun fire, the blank cartridge to launch the dummy, and also the capability to propel a dummy a lot further than you could throw it).

Starter pistol to expose the dog to gunfire if you intend to shoot.

A variety of **bird scents** to apply to dummies. Bird scent for the dummies are a very useful training aid.

2) WHISTLE AND HAND SIGNALS

Traditionally gundog hunting/shooting has involved the use of signals or cues to be given by whistle, hand or body language. This has been of particular benefit when a dog is working at distance. Obviously for training and when in close proximity to the dog, some verbal cues will be necessary.

In addition, game are able to hear anything above a whisper, even at long distances, so talking and verbal cues have typically been discouraged.

Whistle commands

Whistle commands are generally limited to three basic cues as follows:

- A single whistle blast for a second or two duration (this varies between trainers; some use a single, short, sharp toot; others use one long whistle blast of several seconds duration) = stop/sit, look at me, Pay attention, wait for the next command. This is particularly applied to any Gundog, but for HPR training where a dog has to work at distance it is beneficial when you wish the dog to slow down to a stop and also to remain steady when on point.

- Several short pips/toots (pip, pip, pip, pip) = come back/recall.
- Two short pips (pip, pip) = to change direction, for example getting the dog to turn in left or right when quartering.

Practice these before you use them and remember that consistency is vital, otherwise the dog will be confused about what he is being asked to do.

As the previous chapter has noted, whistle commands are advised from the early stages of training. Take any opportunity to use the whistle, for example if during early training the puppy suddenly comes running back to you, blow the recall whistle.

Eventually you can discontinue with the vocal command once he recognises what is required and simply use whistle commands.

3) INTRODUCING GUNSHOT

Please note: The exercise is introduced early in this chapter, as it is generally considered beneficial to introduce a puppy at an early age.

For the gundog owner with no interest in shooting, field trials etc, then this exercise will not really be necessary. However, if you are likely to compete in field trials or some other capacity, then the following will give you a basic overview.

The objective of familiarising a gundog puppy to gunshot is to effectively desensitise them. In other words the puppy needs to be unaffected by the sound of a gun going off. For obvious reasons if the dog is frightened by gun fire, which is possible as a lot of dogs fear fireworks etc, then it will not be suitable in the shooting field.

Exposure to gunshot:

This can be started when the puppy is around 8 weeks old but the same routine can be carried out with an older puppy or adult.

1. With a starter pistol or a dummy launcher, have a friend go to one end of a field with a starter pistol.
2. Whilst you preoccupy the puppy with a game or allowing the puppy to play with other dogs and generally becoming comfortable sniffing or playing, signal to your friend to fire a shot.
3. The puppy will probably look up but hopefully not recoil with fear.
4. Get your friend to come ¾ of the way in, again taking a shot whilst you play with the puppy.
5. Get them to come half way, then ¼ way.
6. At first it will be advisable to attach the 30 foot check cord or retractable leash for safety purposes in case the puppy takes off running.

You do not have to repeat this until later in his training.

If at any stage the dog or puppy shows fear then do not proceed coming closer until they are again comfortable at remote distances.

Another advantage of exposing your dog to gun shot, which again will only be of interest for anyone intending to pursue game shooting or field trials, is that the dog needs to be trained to 'drop to shot'.

Dropping to shot simply means that the dog stops and sits upon hearing gunshot. It is therefore necessary for him to first of all fully learn stopping to the whistle (the 'stop' command). You then proceed as follows:

1. Get a friend to help you with this as they will need to fire a shot some distance away. This can be either a starter pistol, dummy launcher or shot gun.
2. Go through the exercise for stopping to whistle, a single short whistle blast = stop/sit.
3. As soon as you have blown the whistle > simultaneously signal to your friend who should then immediately fire a shot.
4. Provided the dog has previously been exposed to gunshot they should not be fazed and by proceeding like this, will quickly associate gunshot with stopping or dropping.
5. Repeat this several more times, then try firing the shot only, whistle the stop whistle, which hopefully they will stop and sit to.

Practice this as many times as necessary until you are only firing the shot to indicate they have to stop and sit.

However, please be aware that if you intend to enter your dog for field trials teaching the dog to 'drop to shot' will cause problems when retrieving. For the purposes of field trials a dog is expected to complete a retrieve when gunshot is fired.

4) ADVANCED 'SIT' COMMAND FOR GUNDOGS

The following is intended to extend the basic obedience training 'sit' previously covered

Basic 'sit'

Please note: the basic 'sit' command covered in the previous chapter, is often best combined with the 'sit to one side' command, but not vital if you add this later on. It is however, considered easier to combine the two at the same time. The implications of this are that the dogs becomes conditioned to only sitting in front facing you, and becomes confused if expected to now sit at one side. However, it should only take a little bit longer to add sitting to the side as well.

For gundog purposes, the 'sit' is often used in conjunction with the 'recall' and the 'stop', but is used to good effect as a general control command.

Again, sitting down is natural for any dog, but is a key immobilizer along with the 'stop' command for the Sporting/Gundog. This often needs to be carried out at an instant regardless of distractions, such as birds flying by or rabbits bolting from nearby undergrowth. So as well as being an important obedience command, the sit is a very useful control mechanism.

You will have occasions when you need to stop him in his tracks, such as he is about to go rushing off somewhere, or he is jumping up at you or other people or anything you do not want him to do. You can second guess an impulse that he is about to do something and stop him. You can therefore arrest him in his tracks, simply by getting him to sit wherever he is. It is for such reasons that it is taught as part of the 'stop command'

It can also be used to anchor the dog when putting a collar and lead on, examining him, to politely greet someone etc. As previously noted, for the initial training, use a room in your house or the back yard/garden without any distractions.

Quite often it is necessary to seemingly go back to basics, even though he may have progressed in training to an advance level. A new exercise or version, will need to be taught, practiced and proofed, as if it is the very first thing you have taught him.

Incidentally, the traditional gundog terminology for the 'sit' command, has always been 'hup'. If you suspect you may wish to advance your gundog training, or are contemplating shooting at some point, then 'hup' may be preferable to 'sit'. But its not the end of the world if you have trained with the word sit, and you continue using that.

Sitting to a whistle and hand signal

As you have seen in the previous chapter, many general dog trainers teach the sit command simply by luring the dog into a sit > issuing a verbal 'sit' cue > marking the behaviour with a click or verbal 'good' > and finally a reward to reinforce the behaviour. gundog trainers generally follow that procedure also, but add a whistle and hand signal. The significance of this is that done correctly, you can get your dog to stop, sit and stay at a distance without having to shout 'sit'.

I would therefore strongly suggest incorporating using the whistle and hand signal from the beginning. This will therefore condition the dog to associate the whistle, hand and verbal signal with the 'sit'.

Incidentally, the hand signal for the sit command will be carried out in two different ways, depending on how close you are to your dog. When you wish to signal to him at a distance, hold the palm facing away from you vertical, but at an approximate 45° angle to the ground in a similar way to a policeman stopping traffic. You will obviously notice that this is slightly different but similar to the 'stay' hand signal previously taught. You will also no doubt note that the important objective of the 'stay' and 'sit' is to get the dog to stop. So if he thinks you are asking him to stay, then in fact we are. So there is no need to worry about whether this will confuse him.

When in close proximity, for example when he is next to you, hold your palm parallel to the ground, about chest height, as if signalling a down command, or pressing the palm towards the ground.

You are also likely to use variations of the two hand signals together. Firstly using the traffic police hand signal to stop or stay the dog and a variation from that where you tilt your hand from vertical to parallel, to get him to sit.

Remember, the whistle is simply a single whistle blast for a second or two duration. So the sequence would be as follows:

Please read through the following, and fully familiarise yourself with the procedure before you begin. It may look complicated at first, but it is quite an easy procedure once you know what to do. It is important to break it down like this so that you can see the mechanics of it and how the dog will best learn the command

Getting A Dog To Sit In Front Of You

Among other reasons, the front sit is necessary if you want him to deliver an object that they have retrieved. The objective is therefore to get the dog to sit in front of you from the recall.

Please note: You will recognise similar steps for the 'sit' from the previous chapter. However, as previously mentioned, additional elements of the whistle and hand signal are included.

For this exercise you will need a clicker if you use one; a few pieces of food and your whistle.

1. Prepare yourself with a piece of food in your dominant hand > your whistle should be around your neck for easy access > Pinch the treat between your thumb and forefinger so your puppy will be able to see it.

2. Recall your dog with which ever cue word you have chosen ('come', 'here' etc) > and as he gets towards you place your whistle in your mouth > hold out your food hand to your dogs nose, making sure he cannot take it > give him a second to smell it > if necessary Kneel in front of him

3. Pull your hand towards you and up to a level six inches or so above the dogs nose so that he is forced to look up > The dog should start to sit at this point.

4. Please note that if the dog lunges forward or upwards in an attempt to grab the food, you have probably lured the

dog too far in either direction > You will soon know where you can place your hands in relation to your dog so that the dog simply looks up and sits.

5. If he doesn't sit at this point it may be necessary to 'lure' him as we did in the previous chapter > again holding the treat a few inches away from his nose so that he doesn't grab it > simply move the treat away from you, over and towards the back of your dog's head > as he looks up and follows the food he should naturally sit.

6. The moment the dog starts to sit, either at step (3) or (5) > blow the whistle (single short blast) > drop the whistle out your mouth > use the hand signal previously described (palm facing down towards the ground) > say the cue word 'sit' > [those three steps need to happen all at the same time, or as near as without pausing] > again it is important to only say the cue word as the dog is actually carrying out the action of sitting > It is also important to say the word once to mark him actually sitting > Not before when he is standing or coming to you, or after when he is taking the food > Otherwise he may associate the word sit with coming to you or taking the food.

7. The very moment the dogs rear hits the ground, click with your clicker or praise him excitedly with good boy/girl; this effectively marks the 'sit' behaviour > and finally reward/reinforce with the food.

So to summarise the 'sit' procedure up to this point:

» As he starts to sit > blow the whistle > use the hand signal > say the cue word 'sit'; all almost simultaneously.

» Once he has actually sat down > mark the 'sit' > give the food reward/reinforcer.

Repeat steps (1) to (7) as many times as necessary until the response is conditioned/habitual.

Remember to start from the beginning at any stage if either you or the dog goes wrong.

It is doubtful, but again, if after all this, you find that he doesn't seem to be getting the idea you can apply gentle pressure to the top of his hips

» again, as he starts to sit > blow the whistle > use the hand signal > say the cue word 'sit' > and once again, the very moment his rear hits the ground > click with your clicker or praise him excitedly with good boy/girl; effectively marking the 'sit' behaviour > and finally reward/ reinforce with the food.

It is important to note that you can delay giving him the food reward by several seconds or so. However, it is very important that you only blow the whistle; use the hand signal; and issue the command, as he is going through the motions of actually sitting. Additionally it is equally important that you correctly time 'marking' the sit the very moment he is actually seated, not before or after.

So the full sequence should be as follows:

- You lure him with food, your hand close to the dogs nose pulling your hand far enough up and away from him to induce a sit.
- As he starts to sit you a) blow the whistle b) use the hand signal c) say the cue word 'sit', as close together as possible.
- As soon as he is actually seated, mark the sit with a click or "good boy/girl". The verbal cue word or click to marks the action.
- You then give him the food reward to let him know that the act of sitting and the associated cue word 'sit', has resulted in the reward. The food acting as a stimulus/reward/reinforcement.
- After a number of repetitions you shouldn't need the luring, but simply issue the whistle, hand and verbal signal. Eventually you should be able to get to the point where only the whistle is needed.

Corrections if things go wrong

He may start to walk backwards as you raise the treat in front of him and over his head. This usually happens if you move it too fast and he assumes you are moving forwards and he needs to catch up. If this happens, simply move the treat at a slower pace, so that he watches it rather than feels the need to move.

He may also try to jump up and grab the treat which usually happens if you are offering the treat out of his immediate reach, in other words, too high. In this case make sure the treat is close enough, not too close and not too far away. You will soon know once you practice a few times.

Sitting At One Side

This is an alternative to him sitting in front and will be used when he is walking to heel and you need him to stop and sit at your side. It is also generally used in obedience trial competitions.

Please see the explanation previously at the beginning of the sit instruction.

This is usually carried out with the dog on the left hand side and the food given with the right hand, but there is nothing stopping you reversing this. I would strongly advise practising both left and right for reasons of flexibility.

1. Start this with your dog in a standing position, as taught in the previous chapter (eventually you will practise this walking to heel) > move over to the dogs right, so that you are both facing forward with the dog at your left leg.
2. If your dog attempts to sit in anticipation, simply lure him to a stand with your hand with the food held to his nose and walk him forward into a stand.
3. You should now have your hand with the food in front of the dogs nose with him standing > Now raise your hand up 6 inches or so above the dogs head usually at the tip of his nose, not too far back or forward.
4. Hopefully the dog will start to sit > if not as for the sit alternative > draw the hand back over the dogs head so that he follows it with his eyes and drops into a sit.

5. Now follow the previous 'front sit' steps (6) and (7) and any of the recommended adjustments if necessary.

6. Repeat steps (1) to (5) as many times as necessary.

Ideally, alternate this with the normal 'sit' in front, above so that the dog does not get stuck with one command only and remains flexible.

Eventually you will notice that your dog doesn't need a verbal cue but simply reads your hand signal and or whistle. He will even start to drop into a sit as soon as you stop moving and simply stand there. Obedience trials have sometimes carried rules whereby the use of hand signals and cue words are not permitted and the dog sits accordingly when you stop.

Moving on

Once you have practiced the above steps:
[luring him > blowing the whistle > hand signal > verbally saying 'sit' as he starts to sit > then marking the 'sit' with a click or 'good';]

try the steps without luring, but simply saying 'sit', or just the hand signal or the whistle. In other words, adding the cue word 'sit' before the dog actually sits. Do the same using only the hand signal or the whistle.

It is at this point that you should phase out giving a food treat every time, but give him lots of praise for a successful sit.

Also be careful not to reward a sit unless you have asked for a sit, blown the whistle or used the hand signal. Otherwise the dog will start to sit when they feel like it, not when you need them to.

It is good practice to test the sit at speed. For this you will need to ask for a sit, blow the whistle or hand signal > marker word 'good' > treat > repeat > ask for the sit/whistle/hand signal and so on.

See how many you can get through in a minute.

Further 'Sit'

The sit at this point has been carried out when the dog has been in close proximity, either in front or one side of you. You ideally need your dog to sit regardless of where you are and where he is. In other words when you issue the sit command the dog needs to stop and sit where ever they are.

If you do not teach them and practice this, what happens is that they associate the sit command with coming back to you, then sitting.

So as above, ask your puppy to stay where they are, walk a few paces and then call him to you > Alternate using either the verbal cue, hand signal or whistle > gradually increase the distance each time

Experiment using either the verbal cue, hand signal or whistle, but issue these before the puppy gets back to you. You will practice more of this in the 'stop'. But it is important to note that he should not get used to only sitting at your feet every time, but wherever you decide to stop him.

You also need to further develop the 'sit' by generalising and proofing which should occur for example when: heeling, again whilst you move away or around, sitting down, laying on the floor etc. So you give the cue word 'sit' once you are lying or sitting down. The locations should also change and gradually introduce more distractions such as more people or dogs etc. However, be prepared for your dog to come back to you to sit. Which is why it usually works better in conjunction with the 'stop' command.

It is obviously advisable to not reinforce/acknowledge, if he does come back to you to sit. Simply ignore it and offer lots of praise and a treat when he does sit and stay at distance. Make sure that this is solid, well practiced and that the dog is successfully completing each sit most of the time before moving on.

You next need to add distance and distractions. As before it is simply a matter of starting at the reliable distance you were at for the further sit and gradually increase the distance by a few feet.

If the dog breaks the position then go back a few steps and build up again.

5) THE 'STOP' COMMAND

The 'stop' is probably THE most important command you can teach ANY dog. However, it is a vital component in successfully controlling the Gundog.

Please note: The 'sit', 'stay' and 'heel' commands should already have been taught before you can successfully apply the 'stop' command.

The 'stop' command is technically applied as part of a recall for training purposes. But instead of the dog returning to you, you get him to stop immediately at a mid point or any where else on their way back to you. Ultimately the stop should be taught not only as part of a recall but also if he is going away or to either side.

When properly trained, the stop command will ensure your dog will instantly stop wherever he is and wait for the next instruction. The 'stop' is an extension to him coming back and sitting at your feet. In this case he should stop and sit where he is the moment you blow the stop whistle, usually at a distance.

However, whilst out walking your dog, in an emergency situation it is useful to apply this to stop them in their tracks. They could be heading off away from you, perhaps towards a dangerous busy road.

It is also sometimes used to redirect the dog that is heading the wrong way on a 'directed retrieve' or 'send back'. It is therefore easier to stop them, then send them a different way. Redirecting is often applied as part of a hunt/quartering.

Initial 'stop command' training

The stop command actually means 'stop', 'sit' and 'stay' but should be used as an isolated command. It is useful to begin to teach this as part of the 'heel' command as follows:

For this exercise use your normal walking leash attached to his collar:

1. Give the 'heel' command and start walk your puppy to heel > suddenly stop > issue a verbal command 'stop sit' > at the same time give one single whistle blast/toot on the whistle as well as a hand signal as follows: palm held flat, thumb to the chest, palm facing down and parallel to the ground. You will notice this is similar to the 'sit' command hand signal. Obviously you want him to sit, and it is your action (body language) of suddenly stopping which hopefully conveys that yes you want him to sit, but also stop.

2. Hopefully whilst heeling, your puppy will keep to your side and stop when

you stop suddenly. If he stops and sits then offer lots of praise. If he stops but doesn't sit keep still but give the verbal, hand and whistle signals > if necessary, repeat the verbal, hand and whistle cues, as many times as needed until he sits. However, don't be tempted to say 'sit'. You ideally need him to associate this as a new command which again is 'stop/sit'. This may seem contradictory, as he has been taught the same signals for the previous sit. However, the difference now is that you are in motion and he should get used to travelling any distance and needs to get used to stopping and sitting on cue.

3. Again move forward > giving the 'heel' command > then suddenly stop > issuing the commands as above > and lots of praise if he is successful

4. Repeat this several times for this session at different distances along the walk.

Over the next few days repeat this training then after a few days like this, try without the verbal command and just issue the whistle and hand gesture. If this doesn't work at this point, issue the verbal command as well but keep trying with just a hand gesture and whistle.

Try to get to a point where you are just issuing the whistle and he will hopefully stop and sit as soon as you give one short whistle toot/blast.

Once he stops and sits to these commands > the next time he stops and sits, don't speak but carry on walking to test if he stays seated > If not, do not worry as the next step is the 'stop/stay'

'Stop/stay command'

This follows on from the initial stopping whilst heeling. It involves getting him to stop and then stay as you walk away about 10 feet or so, then get him to come to you with several short pips of the whistle.

For this exercise you will need to use your long training leash or retractable leash attached to his collar

1. Walk your puppy at heel as before > suddenly stop > issue a verbal command 'stop/sit' > at the same time give

one single short whistle blast/toot on the whistle as well as the hand signal, palm held flat, thumb to the chest, palm facing down and parallel to the ground.

2. This time, with the puppy hopefully sitting at your side > step in front of him > issue the 'stay' command > and then step back about 10 feet (3 meters approx) or so. (Repeat the stay command, if he makes a move; if necessary move back a shorter distance)

3. Stop a moment > give the 'recall' (verbal = 'come' or 'here'; whistle = several short toots; hand signal = hands thrown wide) command > when he gets back to you offer lots of praise

4. Repeat steps (1) to (3) several times for this session > gradually increase the distance between you and your dog.

Again, over the next few days repeat this training then after a few days like this try without the verbal command and just issue the whistle and hand gesture. If this doesn't work at this point, issue the verbal command 'stop/sit/stay' as well but keep trying with just a hand gesture and whistle.

Try to get to a point where you are just issuing the whistle and he will hopefully stop, sit and stay as soon as you give one single short whistle blast/toot on the whistle.

Also aim to get to a point where you are just issuing the cue word 'stop', rather than stop/ sit/ stay and the single short whistle blast/toot.

Then practice everything so far with just the single short whistle blast/toot

If at any point he is not responding with just the single short whistle blast/toot, include the verbal cues and hand signals if necessary. But always be aiming to phase out everything except the the single short whistle blast/toot

Please be patient here as it may take quite a few sessions for him to get the idea.

The Full 'Stop' Command: using the whistle and hand signal:

For this exercise you will again need to use your long training leash or retractable leash attached to his collar:

1. Walk your puppy at heel as before > suddenly stop > issue a verbal command 'stop/sit' > at the same time give one single short whistle blast/toot on the whistle as well as the hand signal, palm held flat, thumb to the chest, palm facing down and parallel to the ground.

2. Again, with the puppy hopefully now sitting at your side > step in front of him > issue the 'stay' command > and then step back about 10 feet (3 meters approx) or so. (Repeat the stay command, if he makes a move)

3. Give the 'recall' command, but about halfway give the 'stop' command. Hopefully by this stage, this should simply be the single short whistle blast/toot. But again, if necessary use the verbal cue and hand signal if needed.

4. If he stops straight away then immediately walk up to him and give him lots of praise. This will be a big successful step.

5. However, if he does not get this and comes straight back to you, it is recommended that you take him back to the very spot you issued the stop command and again get him to sit and repeat from (1). Do not make a fuss, or say anything, just simply give the 'heel' command and walk him back > ask him to sit and stay, while you again walk back to your start position.

6. Proceed from (3) to (5). If again he doesn't immediately stop and sit, but seems determined to come right back, try saying 'No' or 'Ah ah', and hold up your palm 'stay' hand signal, which will hopefully stop him in his tracks.

7. You will need to repeat from (1) as many times as necessary until he stops immediately you give the whistle command, mid way through the recall.

As before, increase the distance and vary at what point you stop him. Eventually you will be at the end of the training lead. Hopefully at this point he will be well practiced, and you can attempt this by releasing the leash.

Again, do not get frustrated or angry with him, if he ignores the command to stop and comes back to you without stopping. Simply start the procedure again and do not be tempted to either offer praise and certainly do not shout at him.

Once he gets it right, excitedly offer praise so he knows at that point he has succeeded.

Once again, the 'stop' command is a very important aspect of the whole training process and you are therefore advised to continue with this until he is reliably carrying this out every time.

However, be aware that some dogs will be well behaved when they know they are attached to a leash but ignore all commands and run riot when you release them. In this case In the initial stages of the stop command you are strongly advised to keep your dog on a long training leash. If once you release him, he is misbehaving and ignoring you, try the following:

1. Attach your long training lead and your shorter walking leash.
2. Release the shorter one so that he knows you have released him but keep the longer one attached.
3. Continue as usual with the stop command and if he ignores you and races off, he will come to an abrupt stop when he reaches the end of the training leash.
4. Hopefully this will be sufficient to let him know that you are giving him freedom but he cannot run off and ignore you.

It is also very important to practice being unpredictable with commands. Always vary when you issue the stop signal and for how long you stop him, before sending him to continue with the retrieve. If you always stop him at the same point he will easily anticipate stopping at a particular point rather than waiting and listening for your command. If you are not careful he could start to make his own mind up about when to stop and you suddenly have disobedience.

6) OFF LEAD RUNS

Once he has learned a reliable 'stop', 'sit', 'heel' and 'recall', you can introduce off lead runs whether in the countryside or a large field.

The idea here is to allow him to freely wander for short distances exploring, but to also keep him in check by calling him back to heel and getting him to stop and sit periodically. You are therefore utilising and testing everything that he has learned up to this point. This will effectively train him to realise that although he runs free and hunts, he also has to respond to commands from you when necessary.

Failure to do this would probably see him pleasing himself, possibly running riot or worse still give chase and risk a road accident or other accident rushing into rough cover.

Off lead running

Some trainers recommend allowing their dog off lead running, scenting, hunting in a separate location to where you train them. The idea is that they associate the two locations for specific purposes rather than allowing them a free run on the same field and then expect them to concentrate and focus on training. The same would apply for shooting terrain where they would be expected to focus on your direction rather than pleasing themselves.

Regardless of his behavior outdoors though, this breed really needs a free run every day in order to be truly healthy.

Even the very best behaved pet that is happy to settle in the home, whether he has been for a run or not, will suffer if he isn't given the opportunity to stretch his muscles. A bored Labrador dog can easily become depressed, destructive or even aggressive.

Owners give many reasons for not giving a Labrador the free run that he needs, most of the reasons are fear in one way or another. The main concern is that the dog owner is scared of their pet running away and never coming back.

However, always be mindful of where you let them free run. It is always important that where there is livestock grazing pastures, you keep your dog on a leash. In some cases this is a legal requirement. Land or livestock owners also sometimes have the legal right to shoot a dog they suspect is attacking their animals. In this respect, you should always ask permission from the land owner.

7) THE RETRIEVE (SEND BACK)

The basic retrieve (also known as 'the send back')

This retrieve work moves on from the initial retrieve exercise covered in the previous chapter 'Initial Obedience Training'.

This is the basic marked retrieve that involves you throwing a dummy and ensuring that your puppy does not go and 'fetch', until instructed to do so.

You will need a 1lb training dummy, or something similar, to hand for this next exercise.

If you are using a retractable training lead for this make sure that the lock is on. Or if you have a normal long training lead, make sure that you hold on to enough of the lead so that your puppy cannot leave your side. The reason for this is as soon as you throw the dummy the puppy will possibly try and run to retrieve it.

Again, we only want the puppy to fetch this when instructed to do so. Start this exercise as follows:

1. Walk with your puppy at heel, to a part of a field in a safe area that is relatively close to a fence or hedge > blow the stop/sit whistle and use the hand signal for sit. Your puppy should now be seated next to you, both facing the same way.

2. With your puppy at your side, again make sure that he cannot run off by either having the retractable on a lock or holding a normal training lead close to you.

3. Throw the dummy a couple of meters, no more than three meters (10ft approx) away from you.

4. If he tries to move, the leash will stop him running off > but again blow the stop/sit whistle and use the hand signal for sit > You may have to repeat this a few times until he settles.

5. Once settled, make sure you release the lock on the retractable or let go of the normal training lead, but keep the loop around your wrist.

6. Provided your puppy is at your side > sweep your hand towards the dummy, pointing forward, bending at the knee if necessary > give the verbal command 'go back', or 'back' (some trainers use phrases such as 'get on' here, but I prefer to use the get on when sending left or right, and 'go back' when sending him back). > Be prepared to repeat the 'go back' command if he is not sure what to do and again encourage him with the pointing forward. Make sure you are allowing him slack from the leash > Hopefully at this point he will run up to the dummy > pick it up > and bring it back to you. He cannot run away with the dummy as you have him attached to the lead.

7. If he doesn't immediately bring it back use the recall command. So immediately follow the verbal command 'here' > with several short pips/toots of the whistle > and throw your hands wide for the hand signal > Repeat this as many times as needed until he brings it back to you.

8. As soon as he returns with the dummy make a big fuss of him > and if he offers you the dummy > take it. If he holds onto it whilst you fuss him > then that is fine at this stage. Let him hold the dummy > then gently take hold of the dummy and say 'leave'.

9. Again, avoid encouraging him in a tug of war game > As soon as he lets you, gently take the dummy from him > again give him lots of fuss and praise > But if he drops the dummy at this stage > do not acknowledge this with any verbal rebuke such as a 'No' > But certainly do not praise him, as he may think this is

acceptable to drop the dummy and get into the habit of doing this every time.

Moving on

Eventually you need to get to the stage where you are doing the heel, the recall, the sit/stay and the retrieve all without the use of a collar and lead. However, for the time being it will be safer to increase the training lead length to 5 meters then 10 then 15 and so on. At which point after a while your dog will have had sufficient practice that he can be trusted and relied upon to respond 100% to these commands.

When you do eventually remove the lead do this gradually.

1. So for example mid way through your session > walk him to heel > as you walk try and unclip him without him noticing and carry on the heel work.
2. After a few minutes > clip the lead back on > and carry on the session with the lead.
3. Then each day increase the time off the lead until you have been doing this for a week or so.

If in any doubt, when you do the training without a leash, always work in an enclosed paddock or field well away from traffic.

Please bear in mind the following pointers for all of the following retrieves:

When starting with the retrieve it is important to get the puppies focus before you send them for a retrieve. In other words we need him to be looking at us before we send him off. This may require waiting until he gives us eye contract.

Any time he deviates from the exercise, command him to stop/sit, before moving on.

If at any point in the training things seem to be getting out of hand, stop the retrieve training for 5 or 10 minutes, and practice some other exercises. Then start again with the retrieve work.

He may not understand what is expected of him the very first time you throw the dummy to retrieve. If this happens, simply walk up to the dummy, call your puppy to you and get him to sit. Now throw the dummy, but this time throw it half the distance previously, and go through the retrieve routine again. If the puppy picks up the dummy but refuses to come back with it, blow the stop whistle.

As long as he is still holding the dummy, call him to you with the recall, 'here' command, again hopefully he will come back. As usual, if he successfully brings the dummy back to you, give him lots of praise.

8) TWO DUMMY SEND BACK

Once he is successfully retrieving the dummy for the previous exercise it is time to move on to sending him out for two dummies.

It is important that the 2 dummies are at least approximately 30 feet (9 meters approx) apart. If they are too close there is a temptation for him to go to one then the other, rather than just concentrating on bringing you one at a time, before you send him off again.

To start with, you can throw these an approximate distance of 5 meters from yourself. But for longer distances you will either have to place these at some distance either walking the dog at heel to a spot, getting him to stay while you walk to a suitable spot to drop the dummy, then do the same for the other. Use a dummy launcher if you have one, or get a friend to place them while you wait with your dog seated at your side.

Choose an open field in a safe area that does not have too much grass growth.

Once again, use the training leash for this, (it is best to use a training leash of at least 10 meters, preferably 15 meters, to allow plenty of slack) and allow plenty of slack. Bear in mind that he will be going out approximately 5 meters to each dummy, so allow him slack of at least 7 or 8 meters. As a reminder it is often more practical to carry the training leash separately and walk him to heel with a slip lead

1. Again, walk with your puppy at heel, to a part of a field in a safe area that is relatively close to a fence or hedge > blow the stop/sit whistle, with hand signal > he should be seated by your side, both of you facing towards the direction you will be throwing the dummies
2. Issue the 'stay' command > take his slip lead off and attached the training leash > making sure that you unravel enough

slack of about 7 meters > throw one dummy diagonally to your left about 15 feet (4.5 meters approx). The dummy should therefore not be to your immediate left, but forward and towards your left, ahead of you at an approximate 45 degree angle > pause a few seconds > throw a second to your right, again 15 feet (4.5 meters approx) diagonally > so that the two dummies are approximately 30 feet (9 meters approx) apart.

3. Again with your dog at your side > sweep your hand pointing towards the last dummy that you threw > your arm should be parallel to the ground > bending at the knee if necessary > give the verbal command 'go back', or 'back'

4. He should run out and retrieve the first dummy > as soon as he gets back to you, take the dummy > give him a treat/offer lots of praise

5. Again, if he doesn't return immediately follow the previous basic retrieve instructions (8) to recall him

6. Get him to sit at your side > Now sweep your hand as for (3) pointing towards the second dummy > bending at the knee if necessary > give the verbal command 'go back', or 'back'.

7. He should run out and retrieve the second dummy > again as soon as he gets back to you, take the dummy > give him a treat/offer lots of praise

8. Repeat steps (1) to (7) throwing the dummies further each time, until as above you have to place, launch, or have a friend place them. By the time you reach the full extent of the training leash with you holding it, it will be necessary to trust him by not holding it. However, keep it attached but allow him to drag it. If he does take off, it should be possible for you to run and catch up with the leash if not the dog. At this point make sure it is safe to do so, and there are no distractions present that will tempt him to take off.

Repetition of the send out command and pointing to the dummies is a very important aspect of gundog work. This gets him relying on you indicating/pointing to on object which he cannot himself see, in other words the 'blind retrieve', which will follow.

9) TWO DUMMY RETRIEVE WITH LEFT, RIGHT AND AWAY HAND SIGNALS)

The following exercises will require the use of left/right hand signals. This is a similar exercise to the two dummy send back. However, this time you are positioned at a distance in front of the dog. The dummies are also placed to the dogs immediate left and right. The idea is that the dog runs out immediately to his left and returns the dummy to you. You then walk him back to his start position and send him for the second dummy.

The following will briefly describe the hand signals and how to apply them:

Verbal cue

For either the left or right, issue the verbal command 'get on'. Again some trainers use 'seek on' particularly when sending left or right whilst the dog is 'quartering'.

Whistle cue

Again the whistle cue to send him left or right is two short pips/toots on the whistle 'pip, pip'. It is important to introduce it here as this will be his cue for when he eventually 'quarters'.

Hand signals

Hand signals used for directional cues should be clear and direct.

To send the dog to his left, your right arm needs to go out parallel to the ground, to your immediate right. Your body should slightly lean that way also so it will be necessary to bend at the knee. To send him to his right, your left arm should be thrust out similarly horizontally to your left, again leaning your body the same way.

Hopefully you will be at a stage in his training where he has practiced retrieves quite a number of times. He is therefore less likely to run off with the dummy, and so a training leash should be unnecessary.

However, if you do experience problems, it is advisable to attach a long training lead; 10 meters will be OK initially, but 15 and 20 meters will be needed as you progress. Again use the point previously mentioned about keeping the leash attached but without you holding it. Again, letting him drag this so that you can more easily catch it if necessary.

This exercise is best practiced with your dog close to a fence or hedge. The advantage of this is that he will have an obvious line to run parallel to, rather than a wide open space where he may be tempted go off course.

1. Again, walk your dog to a part of a field in a safe area that is relatively close to a fence or hedge > heel him around so that you both have your backs to the fence/hedge > blow the stop/sit whistle > ask him to stay > he should stay seated whilst you carry on walking forward, away from the hedge > walk about 10ft (3 meters approx) away > stop and turn to face him > (if he carries on walking with you, you should immediately stop > blow the single short whistle blast > and walk him back to the start position > again getting him to sit and asking him to stay).

2. Once you are facing him 10ft (3 meters approx) away > throw the first dummy about 20ft or so (6 meters approx) to your right or left, roughly in line with his immediate right or left > now pause several seconds before throwing the second in the opposite direction roughly the same distance.

3. Please bear in mind that most dogs will naturally wish to retrieve the last dummy you threw out: At this point it is advisable to put your whistle in your mouth ready to give the 2 toot/pip cue > Pause again before giving a left or right hand signal for the last dummy you threw (again use the previous description for hand signals) > at the same time give two short pips/toots on the whistle 'pip, pip' and the 'get on' command [again all three should

be done simultaneously] > sending him in the direction pointed, to pick up and retrieve the dummy back to you. Again, if he does not respond to you pointing left or right with the 'get on' verbal cue, repeat this. As a last resort you may have to walk over to the dummy, which should prompt him to follow. Then walk back to your starting position, recalling him with the dummy if necessary.

4. Offer lots of praise if he successfully follows your direction and returns the dummy (if he seems uncertain what to do > issue the hand signal, verbal cue and whistle signal again > If he goes in the wrong direction blow the stop whistle and if necessary walk him back to the starting spot and repeat the command).

5. Once he successfully returns the dummy, walk him back to his original start position and repeat steps (2) to (4) to retrieve the second dummy.

Repeat this several times during this session and for as many sessions as it takes until he is reliably executing the exercise. Also vary the order you send him and the distances you throw each time. Sometimes send him several times in the same direction by throwing the retrieved dummy out to the same side.

10) The 'go back'

The 'go back' is used if you have already issued the 'send back' (retrieve), but he hasn't gone far enough out/away. So you need to send him further out to search for the dummy. This situation is how you may have to direct him, if for example you were hunting and had shot a bird and you were now directing him to where you know the bird has fallen.

The procedure is simply to 'stop' him where he is > then issue a 'go back' command.

Please note it will be necessary to use a slip lead to quickly release him after you have walked him at heel.

Again choose an open field in a safe area that is relatively flat and does not have too much grass growth.

1. Begin by walking your dog to a part of a field, in a safe area, that is relatively close to a fence or hedge > heel him around so that you both have your backs to the fence/hedge > blow the stop/sit whistle > ask him to stay.

2. With your dog seated at your side > throw a dummy in front of you both about 3ft (1 meter approx) away. Make sure he remains seated throughout and doesn't suddenly chase after the dummy. If he makes a move for the dummy, again blow the stop whistle.

3. Now walk him at heel, passed the dummy, about 10ft (3 meters approx) or so away from the dummy so that you both have your backs to it.

4. Stop and again get him to 'sit' and 'stay' > release his leash or take the slip lead off while you walk on a further 10ft (3 meters approx) or so away your dog > turn around facing him. He should now be facing you with his back to the dummy. Again if he tries to follow you, as soon as you become aware of this, blow the stop whistle. If necessary, walk him back to the start position and issue the 'stay' command. Then walk to your last position 3 meters away from the dog.

5. After a short pause issue the 'go back' command > For this you sweep your arm from its resting position, in an arc in front of you, into the air, pointing to the sky, palm facing forward. Now slightly motioning towards the dummy > give the verbal command 'go back' or 'back'.

6. Hopefully he will understand that he should turn around > run towards the dummy and retrieve this back to you.

7. Again offer lots of praise when he does.

Repeat this as often as necessary until he is successfully completing the 'go back'. Eventually increase the distance by walking further away once he is successful at a short distance. Also practice in different terrain with more dense cover.

If he fails to understand, it may be necessary to walk/lure him towards the dummy. Again repeat the verbal command and hand signal as you do.

Once he runs towards it, go back to your position so that he can return it to you.

11) THREE DUMMY RETRIEVE

As the name suggests, the three dummy retrieve will involve a left, right and go back dummy retrieve, all previously learned.

Please note that the exercise will be described here, but because each separate element has been detailed previously, you are asked to refer back to those, which are:

» The two dummy send back or Two dummy retrieve with Left, right and away hand signals, with the two toot whistle cue

» The 'go back'

1. For simplicity I would proceed as for the 'go back' steps (1) to (4). Get to step (4) of the go back and issue the 'stop', 'sit' and 'stay'. Now before you carry on walking for another 10ft (3 meters approx), throw one dummy to your left and one to your right. All the while ensuring your dog does not move. Now walk away from your dog for another 10ft (3 meters approx) > turn around and face him.

2. So now you should be facing him. There should be a dummy behind him, one to his right and another to his left.

3. You are then advised to send him in the direction of the last placed dummy, either left or right. Remember to use your left or right hand signal, two short pips/toots on the whistle 'pip, pip', and the verbal cue 'get on'.

4. Once he retrieves this dummy back to you > walk him back to his start position > then walk back to where you were stood > send him for the second dummy again remembering to use the same 3 cues or signals > then repeat for the third behind him > again, remember to use the hand signal for the 'send back' and the verbal cue 'go back' or 'back'.

5. Again repeat this several times during this session and for as many sessions as it takes until he is reliably executing the exercise. Also vary the order you send him and the distances you throw each time. Sometimes send him several times in the same direction by throwing the retrieved dummy out to the same side.

Once you need to increase the distances of each dummy beyond throwing distance either use a dummy launcher or walk so far and throw the dummy to increase the distance.

12) THE INITIAL BLIND RETRIEVE

As the name indicates, this is a retrieve that the dog should have no idea where the dummy is. This will closely resemble a typical scenario if he is having to search for a shot bird in the field. As previously mentioned he is therefore reliant on you giving him directions. For this reason dummies have to be placed without the dog seeing them. However, for the purposes of this preliminary exercise he will see where the object is thrown. The field that you choose should have grass that is cut relatively short. Ideally the dog should be able to see the dummy, or at least it should not take much searching to find. The idea is that he gets used to the mechanics of the exercise rather than whether it is an actual blind retrieve or not.

Initially it is best to send him on this 'blind retrieve', but in approximately the same spot as he picked the first up. If you have been sending him to the same area with previous retrieves he will expect to see a dummy and shouldn't therefore have to search very far.

You are advised to use a friend to help with this as he can stand at some distance away from you.

1. Ask your friend to stand relatively close to a fence or hedge, at a distance around 50ft (15 meters approx) away from you and your dog.

2. So wherever you are in relation to your friend, walk with your dog at heel to a central part of a field in a safe area, again around 50ft away from your friend, both of you facing him > blow the stop/sit whistle > ask your dog to stay.

3. Your friend should then throw a dummy either to the left or right. Again your dog will be able to see where the dummy has dropped > pause a few seconds then issue the 'send back' command; sweeping your hand pointing towards the dummy, bending at the knee if necessary, give the verbal command 'get on'. You are not using the two toot whistle command here as you are not strictly speaking sending him left or right, but sending him in a straight line.

4. The dog should run out towards the dummy > pick the dummy up > retrieve this back to you > as he is on his way back, your friend should throw another dummy in approximately the same place as the first. This time the dog will not see the dummy being thrown (this therefore provides a 'blind retrieve' to a certain degree).

5. Again as soon as he gets back to you, take the dummy > give him a treat/offer lots of praise.

6. Now get him seated by your side again > blow the stop/sit whistle > ask him to stay > pause a few seconds then issue the 'send back' command; sweeping your hand pointing in the same direction towards the second dummy > bending at the knee if necessary > give the verbal command 'get on'.

7. Again as soon as he gets back to you, take the dummy > give him a treat/offer lots of praise

8. Repeat this several times > once he is successful and reliable at this distance start to increase the distance in 10ft increments.

If at any point he struggles with finding the dummy, picking up or retrieving, simply shorten the distance. Always assume that you have moved on too fast and never blame or punish the dog.

13) ACTUAL BLIND RETRIEVES

All of the previous lessons learned so far will be needed for the 'actual blind retrieve'.

A few preliminaries will be necessary before you start:

The choice of terrain is important as it does not want to be too over grown nor cut like a golf course putting green. It will also be a good idea to plant or have someone plant several dummies before you introduce the dog to the area. You shouldn't bury them or make them difficult to find, but just out of obvious sight. Make sure these are sufficiently placed far enough apart, perhaps around 50ft (15 meters approx).

Also be aware of the direction of the wind when sending your dog out. Young dogs in general do better 'hunting' to a back wind (the wind blowing behind them) than running into a head wind. So adjust your positions according to you sending him away from a head wind. Quartering allows a dog to find scents, whereby a head wind will generally favour an experienced dog more, but a puppy may find scents difficult to pick up.

So again for the initial purposes of the blind retrieve it is easier to send him off down wind. As he gets more experienced picking up wind scents, introduce him to head winds on a calm day. Gradually increase the level of difficulty with greater wind strengths.

Important note:

Your dog will be introduced to a new command at this point, known as the 'Hi Lost'. 'Hi Lost' is the verbal command to let your dog know that he is close to the dummy. So if the dog is close to where the dummy is, you say 'Hi lost' to indicate to him that he needs to hunt/search in that area.

Some trainers also like to use a whistle command. There is no set command to use, but as long as it is different from any other, you can of course make your own up. For example, this could be one long drawn out blow of several seconds duration. As long as it is distinguishable from the short sharp stop pip, the several short pips to recall and the two short directional pips when quartering. At first he may not be able to make the connection that you saying 'Hi Lost' means that if he searches where he is, he will quickly find the dummy. However,

he will soon catch on once he starts finding the dummies soon after you say 'Hi lost'.

When you eventually send your dog to search, do not be tempted to control or direct the dog too much. Instead allow him to hunt freely, but intervene with stops, left/right hand signals etc if he gets totally lost.

1. Assuming that several dummies have been planted > Lead him to the approximate area where the first dummy has been placed about 20ft (6 meters approx) away from the dummy.

2. Make sure that he will be downwind of the dummy before you send him off.

3. Blow the stop/sit whistle, with hand signal > ask him to stay > he should stay seated by your side both of you facing towards the approximate direction of the dummy.

4. Now Send him off > sweep your hand pointing towards but not directly at the dummy > bending at the knee if necessary > give the verbal command 'go back', or 'back'.

5. He should run out, and hopefully not run straight up to the dummy, but begin to search back and forth > Give no other direction and allow him to hunt for himself.

6. If he veers off out of the area > issue the stop command, which hopefully he will stop and sit, looking towards you >

This is were you start to have fun with the exercise. Bearing in mind you know where the dummy is, you now need to give your dog directions to help him find it.

You are now therefore using everything you have previously learned as follows:

- The stop whistle
- The left and right directions, using the verbal cue word 'get on'
- The whistle signal, two short pips/toots on the whistle 'pip, pip'. To send him left or right.
- The go back command; verbal cue words 'go back' with hand signal (sweeping your arm in the air, pointing to the sky, palm facing forward > slightly motioning towards the dummy).

- The 'hi lost' verbal cue to indicate that he should hunt in that area.
- The 'recall'; four short peeps of the whistle.

By way of an example, the following will illustrate a possible scenario:

1. You send your dog off issuing the commands for a normal 'send back' retrieve.
2. He starts hunting around for 20 or 30 seconds but seems to be getting lost.
3. You know the dummy is further away than he is currently searching so > blow the stop whistle and he should stop and look to you for directions > issue the 'go back' or 'back' command.
4. As soon as he has gone far enough > blow the stop whistle > use the cue word 'hi lost', to get him hunting in that area again.
5. He searches but starts moving away to your right of the dummy > blow the stop whistle again > as soon as he stops and looks at you > thrust your left arm, parallel to the ground, blow two short pips/toots on the whistle, use the verbal cue 'get on', to send him to his right.
6. He then goes too far over to your left > blow the stop whistle > as soon as he stops and looks to you > thrust your right arm, parallel to the ground, two toots, verbal 'get on', to send him to his left.
7. As he goes left he catches a scent and wanders away from the dummy > you again blow the stop whistle > now blow the 'recall' whistle, to bring him back in towards you and the dummy > again blow the stop whistle once he is back in the general vicinity > give the 'hi lost' verbal cue > and continue in this way until he finds the dummy and returns it to you.

This will hopefully give you some idea of how you should proceed until he eventually finds the dummy and returns it back to you. Once he does, send him out to the approximate area of the second dummy and continue as per the example, once again depending on how you need to direct him.

14) STEADINESS

'Steadiness' is a very important aspect of a Gundogs training. It does not necessarily come naturally to them and so has to be trained.

The dog that hunts, flushes game and generally does its own thing, will be to say the least, untrained and therefore a nuisance on a shooting field. Furthermore, a dog that doesn't possess self control and steadiness will pretty quickly be disqualified from a field trial or working test. As you can imagine this will also pose problems for the family wishing to have a well behaved dog. In addition, the dog will be a danger to itself if it suddenly take off onto a busy road in pursuit of a rabbit or squirrel etc.

A major objective of all Gundogs is to indicate game (pointing, sitting etc) that they discover in undergrowth, but only 'flushing' on command. If the 'stop command' has been thoroughly learned by the dog then you should never experience him rushing off, flushing game and generally ignoring your commands for him to stop.

The following exercises will provide a good grounding in improving 'steadiness' already achieved with previous exercises.

Most of the exercises that involve him waiting until you ask him to move, are basically exercises in steadiness.

Practice steadiness as follows: You will preferably need 2 or 3 dummies for this exercise

1. Have your dog sit and stay and then walk back several meters.
2. Throw a dummy to the side of the dog about 2 meters away from him. If you notice him twitch as if he is about to go and pick the dummy up > immediately issue the 'stop command' a single short whistle blast. Repeat the 'stop command' as many times as it is necessary whilst he sits patiently. If necessary you may have to walk him back to the starting positions.
3. If he successfully leaves the dummy and stays where he is, walk over to him and give him lots of praise.
4. Now repeat steps (1) to (3), but this time, after you have thrown the first dummy,

throw another to the other side or over his head. Again, repeat the 'stop command' if necessary.

5. Wait a few seconds and then walk back to him again offering lots of praise.

It is important with this exercise that you do not let your dog retrieve the dummy. This is something that you should do as it shows the dog, that he does not always pick the dummy up, but only when instructed to do so.

You may also need to initially use the stay command, if he attempts to come to you. But the 'stop command' should be used when you want him to leave the object.

Steadying to a thrown dummy whilst out on walks

The idea here is to present distractions to the dog. Your objective is to attempt to control him reacting to the stimuli.

1. In the first instance have your dog on a leash and walk him to heel. Also have a dummy or two to hand.

2. At any random moment throw a dummy out in front of you and at the same time issue the stop command with whistle; again a single short whistle blast.

3. Ask your dog to stay whilst you walk over > pick the dummy up > and walk back to your dog > picking up the leash.

4. Provided he has stayed seated, give him lots of praise.

5. Repeat the exercise several more times each session

6. Steadying to a thrown dummy whilst hunting

7. Start by walking to heel with an extendable leash or long training leash then allow your dog to wander off in front sniffing for scents etc (technically he is hunting).

8. As he looks up throw a dummy again out in front as far as you can throw it > again issue the stop command.

9. Ask your dog to stay while you pick the dummy up as before and return to the dog.

10. Offer lots of praise if he has successfully stayed in place throughout.

11. Repeat several more times each time.

12. An extension to the above two exercises is if you can acquire a dead game bird, feathers intact or a rabbit etc.

13. Following the same procedure as the previous two exercises replace the dummy with the game.

To add a level of difficulty if you have a starter pistol or dummy launcher either shoot the pistol as you throw the dummy or fire a dummy from the launcher. (Please note that this assumes he has already been successfully exposed to gunshot)

Steadiness to live animals

Having access to a rabbit pen will be a big advantage to test his steadiness to live animals. It may be necessary to contact your local gundog club who should have details of trainers or individuals who may allow you access, even if you have to pay for its use.

In this case you should take the dog into a rabbit pen but keep him on a training lead, in case he should decide to give chase. You do not want him to catch or kill the animal but simply to control his prey instinct or impulse to chase.

Alternatively take him to an area where you know rabbits, squirrels, game birds etc are likely to be. Perhaps whilst out on a normal walk at a local park or a country walk.

1. Proceed as before with an extendable leash or normal training lead and allow him to freely hunt.

2. Watch for his reaction to having seen or scented a game animal > Anticipate him making a sudden movement at which point you should immediately issue the stop whistle and stay command.

3. Give him lots of praise if he does as you ask and does not give chase. Obviously ignore and do not acknowledge any impulse to chase.

4. Continue and repeat (1) to (3) during the session and repeat when ever you get the chance.

Once you are confident that he is reliable with a leash, attempt (1) to (3) without the leash. It is vital that this is only done in an area that is safe such as a fenced enclosed field or similar well away from traffic, in case his prey instinct takes over and he exits the field.

You may have to repeat this a number of times until he is reliably ignoring the impulse to give chase.

15) INTRODUCTION TO WATER

Most Gundogs are naturally drawn to water and introducing them to water should be part of a young puppies socialisation. However until they gain confidence swimming, they should be introduced gradually and always supervised. Any traumatic events can lead to him fearing water and refusing to enter.

At first, choose a stream, pond or lake with a gradual slope into the water. As to how far you should allow him to paddle, think in terms of how far you can wade out in a pair of rubber boots, or fishing waders if you have them. If in doubt buy and fit him with a doggy life-jacket for extra safety. Again for extra safety, attach a training lead to the life-jacket so that if he does swim out you can pull him back in before he gets into difficulty.

Incidentally, do beware of blue green algae commonly present in certain lakes, drains, streams, rivers or ponds, which is toxic and can cause death should the dog drink the water.

View the following links for further information:
https://www.gov.uk/government/publications/algal-blooms-advice-for-the-public-and-landowners

https://www.pets4homes.co.uk/pet-advice/blue-green-algae-and-its-risks-for-dogs.html

Alternatively, introduce him to a narrow, shallow stream that you can easily wade across with rubber boots. Certainly do not allow him access to fast flowing rivers or rivers with strong under currents. For the same reason, until your puppy gains strength and experience, avoid allowing him access to sea waters. Unless as before you supervise and the waters are calm and the beach is gradually sloping.

If he is reluctant to enter the water at first it is a good idea to entice him with toys, tennis balls or one of your dummies provided it is suitable for use in water.

Once he is confident entering water, you can try a short retrieve in the shallow end or across a shallow stream as follows:

1. Get him to sit and stay about 6ft (2 meters approx) near the edge of the pond, lake or stream.
2. Walk away from him towards the waters edge. You may have to issue the stay command to ensure he does not follow you.
3. Either cross the stream or wade into the pond/lake shallow end.
4. Now call him to you with the recall/come command; several short pips/toots.
5. When he gets to you offer lots of fuss and praise as usual.
6. If he has been entering the water previously he should have no hesitation. But if he does seem reluctant, encourage him by perhaps coming further towards him or use a food treat.
7. Now again get him to sit and stay about 6ft (2 meters approx) near the edge of the pond, lake or stream.
8. Again either cross the stream or wade into the pond/lake shallow end.
9. This time toss a dummy into the water again in the shallow end 6ft (2 meters approx) away from you near the waters edge.
10. Give the retrieve command. You will have to point towards the dummy and

give the verbal command 'go back', or 'back'. Hopefully, he will enter the water, grab the dummy and swim to you.

11. When he gets to you with the dummy offer lots of fuss and praise as usual

12. Again get him to sit and stay about 6ft (2 meters approx) near the edge of the pond, lake or stream, but this time you stand with him.

13. Toss a dummy into the water > issue the retrieve command > again, he should enter the water, grab the dummy, swim back to the bank, climb out and deliver the dummy to you. Make sure the bank is easy for him to climb out, otherwise you may have to lift him out. But eventually he will be able to do all of this himself.

14. When he gets to you with the dummy offer lots of fuss and praise as usual.

Once he gains confidence entering the water and as long as he is swimming confidently, increase the distances.

Again, please remember to fit a life-jacket to him when entering deeper waters.

16) HOW GUNDOGS HUNT: THE HUNTING CHAIN

The following is intended to give you an idea of how dogs naturally follow a 'hunting chain'. You can therefore see how aspects of training a gundog are supposed to fit in to this natural inherent skill.

Hunting is a natural instinctive behaviour for all dogs to varying degrees depending on the breed. It is a primitive set of behaviours that have been hard wired into them from thousands of years ago.

The actual act of hunting involves a set of behaviours with logical links that follow each other to a natural conclusion which in the wild would be to kill and to eat in order to survive. In the wild the chain of events would involve; scenting > searching > seeing > stalking > pausing > pouncing > chasing > grabbing > killing > eating or carrying > guarding etc.

In order to be useful to humans, specific training involves utilising and harnessing those instincts

but interrupting and controlling the chain of hunting, such as the kill and eat parts, to therefore help the hunter catch/shoot the prey.

A specific example involving a segment of the hunting chain involves the Pointing breeds. Selective breeding has ensured that their ability to stalk and pause has been exaggerated. In other words, hundreds of years of selective breeding has chosen to breed with only those dogs each time with the strongest natural inclination to 'point'. It is important to point out that pointing is a natural ability that the dog can either do or they can't. You can nurture and develop this trait, but you can't actually teach any dog to point.

The pointing dog would then typically be taught to 'drop' and then pounce or 'flush'.

Chasing and grabbing have been modified as part of the retrieve as the dog runs out and picks up shot prey, but obviously they are not expected to kill as the gun would carry out the kill.

So the trained gundog hunting chain becomes:

Scenting > searching > seeing > stalking > pointing (pausing) > dropping > flushing (pouncing) > game is shot > retrieve (chasing, grabbing, carrying).

The trained gundog hunting chain will not always, or be expected to follow through every single step to completion.

Usually at the point where the dog has located a bird or other game, and is 'pointing', we may interrupt them before they carry on. This could be to continue the hunting chain, recall or retrieve what is perhaps an injured previously shot bird.

From a control point of view, it is beneficial to us that we break the chain as it makes the hunt unpredictable to the dog. Otherwise they would anticipate what they do next, ignoring us, resulting in them hunting for themselves.

Dogs that are expected to flush such as Spaniels, follow a trained hunting chain that would proceed as follows:

You set them off; They quarter on the wind, picking up and following game scents as they go; They locate any game, usually in undergrowth; They flush the game when signalled to do so; The dog would simultaneously drop and wait whilst the hunter would shoot fleeing game.

If a bird or other game is shot the dog is sent out to retrieve using their sight, memory or direction from the handler of where they saw the bird drop. Utilising the wind to pick up scents. Or again looking to the handler for directions (as taught with the blind retrieve).

Finally retrieving the game by returning to the handler and delivering it to hand.

HPR's also flush but whereas the Spaniel works at close quarters to the handler, the HPR is expected to work at long distances out of gunshot range.

This is why they remain on 'point' (indicate the presence of game) so as to allow the hunter to get within shooting range.

They then flush in a similar way to the Spaniel.

You set them off; They quarter on the wind, picking up and following game scents as they go; They locate any game usually in undergrowth, freeze and point; They remain motionless/steady on point; They flush the game when signalled to do so; The dog would simultaneously drop and wait whilst the hunter would shoot fleeing game.

If a bird or other game is shot, the dog is sent out to retrieve using their sight and memory of where they saw the bird drop. Utilising the wind to pick up scents. Or looking to the handler for directions (blind retrieve).

Finally retrieving the game by returning to the handler and delivering it to hand.

Retrievers usually simply retrieve and their trained gundog hunting chain would proceed as follows:

You set them off; If a bird or other game is shot the dog is sent out to retrieve using their sight and memory of where they saw the bird drop. Utilizing the wind to pick up scents. Or looking to the handler for directions (blind retrieve).

Retrieving the game by returning to the handler and delivering it to hand.

You will notice that your dog gets more excited by certain aspects of the hunting chain, in other words they find these more rewarding and are therefore motivated to a greater extent. They may be equally motivated by all aspects, but take note if one or two stand out.

It is important to reinforce/reward these behaviours and mark them with a 'click' or verbal 'good'.

They may value all aspects of the hunt, but some dogs are not as keen on certain aspects as others. They may be highly motivated to hunt or search, but not so keen on retrieving.

This would be problematic if the dog was a retriever to start with and the reward for the other aspects of hunting is supposed to be the 'retrieve'.

Chasing may be more valuable to them than searching. Finding and following a scent may be what motivates them to start searching. Running or quartering may be highly motivating to them, more so than the flush.

It is therefore important to reward/reinforce what is most important to them and that they make the connection between this and the overall hunting chain. They will then hopefully be motivated by all aspects of the hunting chain.

Otherwise the dog may become bored and give up if they are constantly doing things they do not find particularly rewarding.

Some dogs lack the understanding, instinct or motivation to hunt and therefore need to be encouraged and taught certain aspects. They may not know that the scent that intrigues them is connected to the very game that gave off the scent. It could be that they have followed scents but never found live game at the end of it.

For this reason if you intend to hunt on the shooting field with live game, it is vital that the dog is exposed live game in the early learning stage. They need to actually find and flush live game, otherwise they will lack the motivation, not see the connection between hunting and finding the game and probably lose interest.

A) SCENTING OR TRACKING

Scenting or tracking is a skill that utilises the dog's incredible sense of smell. However, the dog needs to be exposed to ground and air scents in order for this sense to develop.

Dogs will pick up scents from the ground via soil and vegetation which have been transmitted from game as they have passed through the area or left faeces and urine markings. Ground scent indicates that something has been there and might still be in the area.

Air scent however, is a stronger indicator of where the game is at the present time which is likely to be close by. Air scent is emitted from the body which is then picked up carried and distributed by the wind.

All Gundogs should be exposed to both in order to develop and perfect this skill for the dog.

You will notice that different gundog breeds rely on or specialize in scenting a particular way.

B) HOW SPANIELS (FLUSHING DOGS) SCENT OR TRACK

Gundogs that are specialists at flushing such as Spaniels predominantly ground scent and occasionally take in air scent until they find ground scent. Once they have located ground scent they excitedly scan and run around the area, diving into undergrowth to flush game. They usually continue like this, flushing more game unless they are instructed to retrieve.

As they are expected to work at close quarters and as part of a team they have been specifically developed for this task.

They hunt by quartering (searching) across a downwind at close quarters, usually no more than 5 meters away, with their noses close to the ground. The close proximity is again to keep within gunshot range and to take into account a bird flying away, therefore increasing the distance from the gun.

C) HOW HPR (HUNT POINT RETRIEVE) SCENT AND TRACK

The HPR are expected to work at greater distances and therefore cover much more ground than the Flushing dog.

They typically utilise air scent much more, and home in on ground scent occasionally. When they have located something, they stand on 'point'.

As they move whilst quartering, they will raise and lower their heads accordingly 'fishing' for scents.

Again pointing has been used in order to indicate game and as this is likely to be out of gunshot range, give the hunter chance to get within gunshot range.

D) HOW RETRIEVERS SCENT AND TRACK

Retrievers are not usually expected to hunt the same way as the Flushing dogs or HPR's, but still need to use scent to locate fallen prey.

They will use air and ground scent to locate a bird killed at distance or an injured bird still moving at ground level.

17) HUNTING/QUARTERING

A) WHAT IS 'QUARTERING'?

Your dog will not need to be taught to hunt as such because he instinctively engages in this activity anyway. What needs to be taught is a controlled hunting, known as quartering, that benefits the handler. When their 'prey drive' takes over, an uncontrolled dog is oblivious to anything other than following the scent. It is therefore vital that he responds to your whistle commands and does not please himself. This is why it therefore has to be firmly ingrained from the early days of training.

Having said that quartering only controls the dog in the sense of keeping him within a manageable range. Once the dog has located a scent, you cannot expect him to follow the text book zig zag quartering pattern, as the scent can take him anywhere. The best that quartering can do is to maximise the dogs chances of catching a scent by efficiently covering the area.

Again Quartering is something you will see the dog doing when scent tracking; running back and forth to pick up scents. However, trained quartering involves controlling the dog by sending him to your left or right and bringing him back in again. The dog literally runs back and forth, in front, but working away from the handler in a narrow zig zag, S shape pattern parallel or at right angles, usually towards a head wind (with the wind). It is important to emphasise 'narrow' because if the dog takes a wide zig zag he will miss too much ground that may be scent marked. A narrow line will give him more of an opportunity to pick up valuable scents.

B) HOW THE DOG QUARTERS

An experienced dog will effectively quarter into a head wind, but usually at an angle to the wind. Moving towards a head wind allows the dog to pick up scents much easier as the scent is naturally carried toward them. When learning to hunt, once again a beginner dog is usually taught to quarter with the wind to their back for ease of picking up scents.

More experienced dogs able to distinguish scents better than a beginner dog will usually quarter at an approximate 45 degree angle to a head wind. At least one obvious advantage of this is that in a strong wind it is not as severe as a head on wind. This is known as quartering with a 'cheek wind'.

The hunter then follows within a short distance if a flushing dog is used, or a greater distance if pointers or HPR's are used.

Tail wind quartering

Despite the name, this still involves the dog quartering into a head wind.

If circumstances dictate that you cannot quarter as normal into a head wind, quartering with a tail wind is adopted.

- Here you start with you and the dog with your backs to the wind.
- You then send the dog out in a straight line ahead of you.
- The dog then begins to quarter back as normal into a head wind.
- You then move to the point the dog started quartering from and repeat the process.
- It basically involves the dog quartering toward you rather than away from you.
- Side wind quartering
- In this case you stand with the wind blowing across your left hand side.
- You send the dog to your right and the dog begins quartering towards the wind so that as he zig zags, he comes towards, then away from you.
- You and the dog then move forward and start the pattern again quartering the new section and so on.
- The above, are all options for quartering under different circumstances.

The important point to note, is that the experienced dog always quarters into the wind and therefore has a greater chance of picking up any scents. Quartering should therefore not merely involve following a zig zag pattern for the sake of it, but should always take into consideration the direction of the wind.

Problems can arise when organised shoots have a line of beaters who are instructed to beat a line regardless of the wind direction. This is fine if they happen to move into a wind and the dog can quarter as normal.

Quartering distances for Spaniels and HPR

The mechanics of quartering are more or less the same regardless of the type of Gundog. However, it is important to be aware of how the different gundog breeds hunt, and how this affects the way different breeds quarter. Basically Spaniels typically flush game within shooting range and therefore at close quarters to the handler. HPR and other pointing breeds however are expected to quarter at much farther distances. Spaniels basically quarter > find game at distances less than 40 meters > sit, which is similarly indicating it has found something > then flush on command. The HPR will quarter > find game, quite possibly at distances of around 100 meters or more > and point > wait for the handler > then flush when prompted by the handler.

Opinions differ as to the ideal quartering distance for normal hunting/shooting with a HPR. However, a distance of around 80 meters (260ft approx) either side, and around 40 meters (130ft approx) ahead is typical.

However, to give you some idea of how field trials and tests criteria can differ please view the following PDF link from the Kennel Club UK **https://www.thekennelclub.org.uk/media/609878/pointing_test_guidelines_2014.pdf**

Basically their criteria stipulates that a dog should quarter into a head wind side to side at 'beats' of at least 100 meters.

Spaniels on the other hand are expected to keep within a certain distance or radius, which for shooting purposes has to be within shooting range. Incidentally an optimum shooting range will differ depending on a number of variables. These variables can include; the type of bird, how fast they fly, whether they fly high or away, the type of gun used, the skill and experience of the person etc. Around 100ft (30 meters approx) is considered to be an average realistic shooting distance, although farther away can still be achieved. However, you need to bear in mind that the dog needs to be closer to you than this because once the bird is flushed, it does not give you much time to take a shot, before it is out of shooting range. So the dog should be quartering between 10 meters (around 33ft) approx and a maximum of 20 meters (around 66ft) approx. Hopefully this will give you some idea of how close you need to keep your dog in relation to where you are standing.

An obvious advantage that you have training a Spaniel to quarter as opposed to the HPR is that the Spaniel is easier to train, control and motivate. HPR's can easily go wrong the farther away from you they get. If they are not picking up scents, they can become easily bored quartering a pattern, or decide to flush and give chase rather than point and wait. Of course this is more likely to happen with young dogs still learning rather than trained adults.

c) Teaching Hunting/(Quartering)

To a certain extent the skills of quartering will already have been introduced when he is taught to retrieve. This will have included hand signals and sending him away.

Once again, it is good practice to be aware of the wind direction. Remember in the initial stages, always begin with the dog coming away from a head wind. As he becomes more experienced practice again moving towards a head wind. This ensures that he picks up oncoming scents that will trigger his desire to hunt.

1. Begin this exercise with a retractible or long training lead attached.

2. Stand facing a head wind and call your dog to you > blow the one toot stop sit whistle and use the hand signal hand parallel to the ground at chest height for sit > He should now be sat facing you, his back to the wind > attach the training leash > make sure that you have 3 meters approximately of slack > give him the 'stay' command

3. Now walk away from him about 8 feet (2.5 meters approx) away. Ensure again that you are facing a head wind and your dog has his back to it.

4. Now start walking across wind, left or right away from him > he should follow, but if not recall him by issuing the verbal command 'here' > immediately follow the verbal command with two short toots of the whistle (this isn't the actual recall as such, but moving him left or right, hence the two toots rather than several)> at the same time thrust your arm parallel to the ground in the direction you are heading.

5. He will hopefully follow your direction and should pass you heading the same way, but ahead of you.

6. Let him continue until he has nearly taken most of the slack of the training leash > blow the stop whistle > now repeat from (2) but in the opposite direction and continue like this, all the while moving in a forward direction.

7. He should ideally be following the typical zig zag quartering pattern.

8. If he picks up a scent, let him follow this for a short while > then blow the stop whistle > using your hand signal, direct him in the opposite direction, walking away from him as before.

9. Once he has got the hang of this > repeat the exercise extending the distance and the amount of slack on the training leash each time.

10. After a lot of repetitions, and if you are confident he has got the hang of it, and you can stop him and redirect with the whistle, repeat the exercise without a leash.

11. So at this point you should be able to set him off in one direction > blow the stop whistle > direct him left or right using the hand signal, 'get on' verbal cue and the two toot/pip whistle command > allow him to continue in that direction > blow the stop whistle > direct him left or right using the hand signal, 'get on' verbal cue and the two toot/pip whistle command >

12. Please note that it is important to keep the distances short initially for control purposes. He will obviously venture much further when 'quartering' but only once he is properly trained and under your control.

13. Repeat this routine for 5 to 10 minutes each day until he is reliably obeying the whistle, verbal and hand signals.

Alternative quartering exercise

If you have been using food in your training you may prefer to start with this exercise. You may also find that the he is struggling to grasp the previous exercise and wish to start with this one first, then move on without food

Begin this exercise in a room, your yard or garden where there are limited distractions.

1. As for previous exercises, prepare yourself with a piece of food in your dominant hand > your whistle should be around your neck for easy access > Pinch the treat between your thumb and forefinger.

2. Recall your dog, giving the recall whistle cue, several short pips (pip, pip, pip, pip)

3. Now about half way before he reaches you, throw the piece of food either left or right. As you throw the food, make this your left/right hand signal to send him left or right > at the same time blow the two toot whistle cue and give the verbal 'get on' command. He should chase the food.

4. As soon as he picks the food up that you have thrown and he has looked up and noticed you throw another piece of food in the opposite direction left or right. Again as you throw the food, make this your left/right hand signal to send him left or right > at the same time blow the two toot whistle cue and give the verbal 'get on' command. He should again chase after the food.

5. Repeat step (4) in the opposite direction and keep repeating this way for a few more minutes.

Once he seems to have got the hang of this, try continuing but without the food and just giving the right or left hand signal and issuing the verbal and whistle cues. Hopefully you can continue like this sending him back and forth in a quartering pattern.

As always, increase the distance gradually.

If you have problems with this at any point, take it a step back or back to small steps and build up again. Perhaps you will need to reintroduce food to maintain his interest and enthusiasm.

A few pointers to bear in mind.

Always build things up slowly, one step at a time before increasing the level of difficulty.

Gradually change the locations, distractions, distance, the direction you send him each time etc. This will keep things unpredictable and ensure the dog is paying attention and not simply going through the motions and anticipating.

Also bear in mind that when you are increasing the levels of difficulty, distractions, new location or introducing stimuli likely to trigger the prey drive, always use a long line for added safety and control in case they take off running.

Moving on

When first teaching a puppy to quarter we use their instinctive desire to want to be near us and follow us.

So we wander off, then move left, then right, then stopping and all the while the puppy is learning to follow a leader, a scent lead and ultimately to hunt.

If he picks up a scent and seems preoccupied, make a conscious effort to move purposely in the opposite direction in order to get him to follow. It is this type of movement/body language from you that will indicate to the dog that you have found a better area to 'hunt'. Ultimately we want him to trust us as part of the hunt. It is also advisable to direct him to areas where you know game resides as he will quickly trust your judgement and increase the likelihood of him following you.

Don't just purposely walk in the opposite direction, but change suddenly from left then to right and back on yourself again. Moving slowly towards (stalking) and stopping occasionally, (pointing), to observe areas also replicates the dogs natural behaviour and hunting style.

Be aware of how your body indicates movement to the dog however slight this may be. You can subtly lean forward, left or right to indicate moving in those directions or remain stationary and lean back to indicate stopping. The dog will begin to associate this type of body language cues with hunting behaviours.

Don't forget that although you want him to enjoy scenting/tracking and pleasing himself, to a certain extent, you also need to maintain control.

18) OBSTACLE TRAINING

Jumping obstacles

Please note, you are not advised to encourage your dog to jump obstacles until he has reached maturity in terms of muscle, ligament and bone growth. You should therefore not be in any rush to start any obstacle jumping until he is at least 9 months old preferably beyond a year old. Although he may be capable and willing much younger than this, he will be susceptible to muscle/ligament tears and potential bone breakages which can affect him for the rest of his life.

As part of his socialisation period he will probably have become accustomed to climbing steps and over a number of obstacles. This will build his confidence gradually. However these should always be supervised and never allow a young puppy to attempt jumping from high obstacles

If and when you do start training/jumping obstacles, as with all other training, start small and build up. In the real world once experienced he may be jumping 4ft high wire mesh fencing. Or perhaps dry stone walls or natural hedges. Please note, always be very careful to check fences for any barbed wire strands. Either avoid these or place a protective cover/sheet, perhaps your coat, over to protect your dog. You can buy special protectors for this purpose that are easy to carry.

Obstacles and training

You can make a suitable obstacle with a simple broom stick or other pole. You then use bricks, books, boxes or any stable containers that you can stack either end of the pole. Start the height at 6 inches or so and build up in 6 inch approx incre-

ments. Once you get to a certain height that he is tempted to crawl under, drape an old blanket or curtain over the pole to act as a barrier. Do not be tempted to increase the height before he is able and confidently jumping a particular height. It can take a few months or so before he is confidently jumping 3 or 4 feet in height. As always if he struggles to get over when you have increased to a certain height, go back a step.

As soon as he is jumping obstacles that you have set up at a similar height to those he will meet in the field, practice his jumping over field obstacles also. In other words actual wire fences, hedges, dry stone walls etc.

With wire mesh fencing it may be necessary to help him at first by placing his front feet onto the fence and lifting his back end as he climbs up and over. But some dogs use the wire holes to climb up and over without any help.

Once you have set up a suitable obstacle, proceed with training as follows:

1. Choose a cue word such as 'over' or 'get over' to use when you wish him to jump an obstacle.
2. Walk your dog about 6ft (approximately 2 meters) away from the obstacle > ask him to sit and stay.
3. Walk over to the obstacle > issue the recall command and as he approaches > issue the 'over' command, encouraging him to jump over.
4. If he walks around you may need to lure him over with your hand or jump over yourself which he should hopefully follow.
5. As usual if he successfully jumps give him lots of praise.
6. Repeat until he jumps the obstacle without you having to lead or lure him, but simply issue the 'over' command.
7. Next walk him about 6ft (approximately 2 meters) away from the obstacle > ask him to sit and stay, but you also stay by his side.
8. Throw a dummy over the obstacle and send him for a retrieve > If he seems reluctant to go you may have to wait by the obstacle and give the 'over' command

again so that he gets used to jumping over to pick the dummy up and jump the obstacle again to retrieve back to you > As he jumps over, walk away from the obstacle so that he is encouraged to retrieve back to you > If when returning he goes around the obstacle, either make this wider or stay at the obstacle to encourage him back over until he is reliably jumping over.

9. Gradually increase the distance and height of the object until he is clearing heights similar to those he will normally face in the countryside. However, only start to increase the height when he is successfully and reliably jumping the obstacle each time without being lead or lured.

Again, if he successfully jumps the obstacle and retrieves back to you give him lots of praise.

Gradually increase the distance between you and the obstacle. You may have to get your dog to sit and stay as you walk over to the obstacle > throwing the dummy over > returning to the dog > then issue the retrieve command. Alternatively use a dummy launcher for longer distances

19) Field Trials and Working Tests

The following is a very brief introduction to field trials and working tests. If this is something you may be interested in, please have a look at the links that follow.

Field trials are set up to artificially imitate as closely as possible an actual shoot. In this respect a line of guns and dogs will 'walk up game' until birds are flushed and shot. A notable difference between the two is that a judge will be present and among other things, decide which dogs retrieve birds that have been shot. The rules and procedures followed do differ between the UK and US trials. Field trials involve certain rules for example KC registration in the UK is a requirement as well as being a member of a gundog club.

Working tests on the other hand, again emulate a shoot, but these tests do not involve the shooting and killing of live game. In this case dogs follow exercises similar to retrieves used to train them. So dummies are used for retrieves and typically include blind, marked as well as retrieves with 2 and 3 dummies.

Hunt Test Programmes

The following links will provide more information on the subject.

AKC

http://www.akc.org/events/hunting-tests/pointing-breeds/articles/get-started/

http://www.akc.org/events/hunting-tests/retrievers/

UKC

http://www.ukcdogs.com

Kennel Club (UK)

http://www.thekennelclub.org.uk/activities/field-trials-working-Gundogs/new-to-field-trials-Gundog-working-tests/

Gundog Club UK

http://www.theGundogclub.co.uk/?page_id=926
http://www.theGundogclub.co.uk/Training/awardsscheme/tests/spaniel/1beginner.htm

http://www.theGundogclub.co.uk/Training/awardsscheme/tests/retriever/beginner.htm

NAHRA

http://www.nahra.org/

NAVHDA

https://www.navhda.org/

CHAPTER SEVENTEEN:

GROOMING YOUR LABRADOR

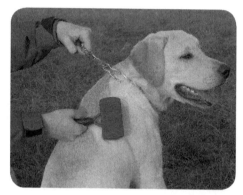

Grooming your Labrador is very important. Not only does grooming help to control shedding but it also helps to ensure that your dog's coat and skin remains healthy. In this chapter you will learn the basics about grooming your Labrador including tips for cleaning your dog's ears and trimming his nails.

Because the Labrador has a relatively short coat, it is reasonably easy to maintain. In fact only minimal grooming needs are necessary. All you should need to do in order to care for your Labrador's coat is to provide a quick, periodic brush with a bristle brush or slicker brush and a medium toothed comb, once or twice per week.

Unlike relatively long coated breeds, obviously having a short coat also means that no hair trimming or clipping is required.

Once again the Labrador is an average shedder throughout the year, with seasonal shedding (blowing of the coat), usually occuring in the spring and autumn/fall.

1) GROOMING AND PARASITES:

Before we get into the actual grooming and bathing, it is worth mentioning parasites that you may encounter whilst grooming. Parasites are mentioned in another chapter, but as you are most likely to notice fleas and tics etc, whilst grooming we will discuss dealing with those here. Fleas, tics and mites are the most likely culprits you will encounter. Fleas prefer to bury and hide themselves in a relatively thick coat, which being double coated will also include the Labrador.

The added problem with fleas, is that they can also set up home in the dogs bedding or the furnishings of your home. It is therefore necessary to not only treat the dog, but their bedding and your furnishings. If you ever get a particularly bad infestation, it may be necessary to call in professional pest controllers. I have never had to experience this, but have had experience with a minor infestation. I found that fumigating the house with a good smoke bomb did the trick. All I then had to do was to keep on top of any fleas invading either the dog or house with the occasional flea spray or powder on the bedding, and a number of remedies on the dog.

It is up to you what remedies you use on your dog. So called 'spot on' treatments are commonly recommended by vets. They do work, but a lot of dog owners, who are more organically inclined, are against the idea of applying these because of a potential toxic effect to the dog. It is not for me to comment about the long term effect of any such toxins to the future health of the dog. What you may also find from time to time is that popular products occasionally become ineffective. This happened with the market leader, Frontline whereby it wasn't as effective as it once was. I am not sure what its current status is. The vet that I currently use recommends a product called Stronghold as a much better alternative. I have to say that I have used this product and it does seem to work, with only the occasional flea showing up in what seems a dying state. My dogs appear perfectly healthy, vital and seemingly unaffected by this product. I hasten to add here, that I am in no way recommending nor endorsing any product, but am merely speaking about veterinary advice I have been given and personal experience. Other vets or individuals may well disagree with this information.

The following is intended as an overview of information relating to grooming Labrador:

2) LABRADOR GROOMING

Some dogs do not react well to grooming because they do not like being held still. Because grooming is so important however, you should get your puppy used to grooming from an early age. Brush your puppy for a few seconds at a time several times a day until he no longer seems bothered by it. Then you can cut back to one longer brushing session each day. You should also frequently touch your puppy's paws and ears so that once you start trimming his nails and cleaning his ears, he will be used to this kind of handling. When grooming, always be gentle and brush with slow careful strokes. The last thing you want is for your dog to start shaking and be left traumatised, or the very least, disliking the experience.

Labradors are generally a clean breed but they do need bathing occasionally, especially if they spend a lot of time outside. We will cover the procedure for bathing as we go. The labrador is one of the few breeds who actually love getting a bath. However, many professional groomers will state that a bath twice a year should be all that is necessary.

Grooming Tools

Opinions will differ as to necessary grooming tools but all you will really need are the following:
- Bristle brush
- Pin brush
- Slicker brush
- Medium toothed comb
- Shampoo and conditioner
- Tooth brush and toothpaste
- Nail clippers
- Ear drops
- Cotton wool
- Dry towel
- Hair drier
- Optional flea comb
- Optional grooming table

Some people also like to use make use of the following:
- Rubber curry comb
- Hound glove
- Rubber mitt
- Trigger spray bottle

Some people insist a bristle or pin brush is all you should really need to provide a good all over brush. Others prefer to use the slicker brush as they generally remove more hair. I would certainly suggest using the slicker during their seasonal 'moult', spring and fall/autumn. Otherwise the bristle or pin brush will adequately remove what little hair is shed the rest of the year.

General Grooming Guidelines

The regular use of a bristle brush or slicker brush is useful to promote a healthy coat and skin. Again, it is recommended that this is started at a young age to get the puppy used to this type of brush. It is simply a matter of brushing the entire coat with the lay of the coat. Again, be prepared to carry this out at least once or twice per week to keep shedding to a minimum.

As the Labrador is prone to certain skin conditions, it is not advisable to bath on a regular basis. Regular bathing strips the coat of natural oils and can promote dandruff and other scaling. Bathing should therefore only be carried out after several months or when the coat gets particularly dirty. In fact many owners suggest bathing should only be carried out every 3 months or so if necessary. Some working gundog owners even insist on no more than once every six months to a year.

Many people also make the mistake of assuming a 'doggy smell' is indication that they need a bath. This may be the case if it has been several months since the last one, or they have rolled in something whilst on an off leash run. But in actual fact the most frequent smell is sweat from the paw pads. Cleaning the paw pads with clean warm water on a regular basis, will go a long way to reduce this smell.

When you do bathe the dog, use a natural low pH shampoo and remember to rinse the coat well. It is also advisable to use an oil based conditioner after bathing. This can be sprayed on, and is non rinse-able and should be applied to the entire coat.

You should then dry the coat with a towel and brush the coat with a bristle or pin brush.

Like many drop eared breeds, problems with their ears can occur. Regular cleaning is therefore essential; we will go into more detail later.

Grooming procedure

It is up to you where you start but many people prefer to start from the head, working along the body and finishing with the legs.

1. Simply brush the entire coat, whilst dry using either the bristle brush or hound glove, for initial dead hair removal hair and any dried mud etc
2. At this stage it is often recommended by groomers to wet the hair, and once again using a rubber hound glove or mitt. The reason is that it removes even more hair than if you just brushed dry.
3. Next dampen the coat using a trigger spray bottle or after washing the coat over, (without shampoo) if he is particularly muddy after a field run.
4. Once wet use the hound glove relatively vigorously to further remove dead hairs.
5. Use a towel to dry
6. Blow dry the coat on a low heat in the direction of the lay of the coat.
7. Finish the coat off to a shine, with a bristle brush

Bathing your Labrador

IIMPORTANT: Please note that it is highly recommended that you remove any matted hair or tangles before bathing. An experienced groomer will tell you that it is almost impossible to remove matts and tangles once wet. Quite often, cutting wet tangles out is the only option. A professional groomer may have more success by spraying anti tangle/de-matting solution, if the dog is wet. But again this is all avoided if you take the time to properly brush and comb the coat, before you bathe.

Labradors are generally a clean breed when not exposed to wet muddy fields. However, they do need bathing occasionally, especially if they spend a lot of time outside. To bathe your Labrador at home follow the steps outlined below:

You can bathe your Labrador if he gets dirty, but you should avoid bathing him with shampoo when it is not necessary. Over-bathing a dog can dry out his skin and lead to skin problems. For bathing with shampoo, a good rule of thumb is between 2 and 3 times per year. In some cases you may be able to brush dry dirt and debris out of your Labrador's coat instead of bathing him.

As a matter of routine, I always use an old towel to dry my dogs legs and feet, on damp, wet muddy, outings. You will usually find that this sufficiently dries and cleans any soiled areas.

If you have to wash mud from their legs, feet or coat, please do this with warm water, but no shampoo. You can then either towel dry and or use a hair drier to ensure your dog does not get chilled. Again, avoid bathing your dog on a regular basis as this strips the skin and coat of natural healthy oils. However, when you do need to occasionally bathe, always use a quality shampoo recommended for use on dogs as human shampoos have a tendency to affect the skin more. Regular use of the wrong pH shampoo is likely to lead to scaling and skin irritation. There are numerous dog shampoos available for various canine skin problems. It is also advisable to use a good conditioner.

Don't forget that your dog relies on natural oils to keep the skin soft, healthy and free from drying out. The oil also has the benefit of protecting the coat and retaining its water resistance. It is tempting to consider how grubby and uncomfortable us humans feel when we don't bathe regularly. However, you cannot take that same viewpoint where your dog is concerned.

To bathe your Labrador at home follow the steps outlined below:

- Give your Labrador a good brushing, as previously mentioned, before you bathe him, to get rid of accumulated loose hair.
- Fill your bathtub with a few inches of lukewarm water. It is also recommended that you put down a bath mat so your dog doesn't slip in the tub.
- Place your Labrador in the tub and wet down his fur with a handheld hose or by pouring water over him. Because the Labrador's coat can be relatively

long, you may need to use your hands to work the water all the way down to his skin. Incidentally, please note that at any point once the coat gets wet, your dog will be naturally inclined to shake itself to remove excess water from its coat. There is not a great deal you can do, other than wear a different set of cloths to change out of when you get wet.

- Avoid getting your Labrador's ears overly wet when you bathe him. Wet ears are a breeding ground for bacteria that could cause an ear infection. In this respect you may wish to plug the ear canals with cotton wool or something similar. Make sure that this isn't small enough to enter the ear canal as you may end up with a bigger problem.
- Apply a small amount of mild dog-friendly shampoo to your Labrador's back and gently work it into a lather along his neck, back, chest and legs.
- Once thoroughly lathered all over, rinse the soap thoroughly out of your Labrador's coat and use a damp washcloth to clean his face.
- You may at this point wish to apply a conditioner
- Lift him out of the tub onto a dry towel. Use a large fluffy towel to towel-dry your Labrador, getting as much water out of his coat as possible.

A useful alternative if you do not want to use your bath tub to bathe him, is the following: You can buy relatively cheap garden hose connector sets, one of the attachments should screw onto the hose outlet to your shower. What I use is a 5 meter length of hose pipe with the snap connectors at each end. I then attach this to the shower unit via the attachment that you screw onto the shower outlet. For the shower end I use a multi spray attachment, again cheap versions are available for garden use. I then thread the 5 meter hose out of the bathroom window and shower/bathe my dogs near the sink outlet outside. Of course this is dependent on having a downstairs shower. You could also use a similar attachment if you have a mixer tap in your kitchen and again thread the hose through the kitchen window.

For any of the procedures mentioned up to now, if you would prefer to see these processes on video, please search the appropriate topic on YouTube.

Blow drying

When blow drying the coat, make sure you have it on a relatively low setting to lightly blow dry. Also ensure that you point the drier in the direction of hair growth in order to dry the coat flat.

You will no doubt have to blow dry the coat after you bath your dog unless it is a particularly warm day or you have the central heating on. If you use your own hair dryer, be careful that this is not at its highest hot setting. It is advisable to brush the coat as you blow dry and proceed as follows:

- You will probably only need to use the pin brush for this to slightly lift the hair as you dry. As you brush, go with the lay of the coat to loosen the hair. Concentrate on small sections and work systematically from the head to tail. You should continuously brush as you blow dry. Please be careful not to pull the coat as you brush. A professional groomer will have a hair dryer on a stand, therefore leaving both hands free. One hand will brush the coat, whilst the other will hold the coat taut in the opposite direction to brushing, and so avoid pulling the skin. Without the hairdryer on a stand, I have to say, the best alternative method is for you have an assistant help you.
- Now use the same technique on the legs

If you would prefer to see this whole process on video, please search [blow drying a Labrador] on YouTube. Please note that the whole blow drying process is likely to take anywhere between 15 and 30 minutes.

3) TRIMMING YOUR DOG'S NAILS

Trimming your Labrador's nails can be challenging and you need to be very careful. A dog's nail contains a quick; the vessel that brings blood to the nail. If you cut the nail too short you will cut the quick. This not only causes your dog pain, but it can bleed profusely as well. When you trim your Labrador's nails you should only cut the very tip to remove the point. Depending on what colour your dog's nails are, you may be able to see the quick and use it as a trimming guide.

It is generally recommended that you trim your Labrador's nails every two to four weeks. If you do it this often then you will only need to clip the slightest amount off the nail each time. This will reduce the risk of cutting the quick. Before you trim your Labrador's nails for the first time you should consider having a veterinarian or a professional groomer show you how. You also need to be sure you are using real dog nail clippers for the job. Please also be aware that you shouldn't attempt to clip your dog's nails routinely every two weeks or so, just for the sake of it, as he may not need it. You should notice that if your dog walks on pavements or your concrete yard, he will to a certain extent be filing them down anyway.

4) CLEANING YOUR DOG'S EARS

Because the Labrador's ears hang down over the sides of his head there is an increased risk for ear infections. Drop ears, as they are known, means that air and moisture get trapped under the flap of the ear, making it a breeding ground for bacteria. Again, your dog's risk for ear infection increases significantly if you get the ears wet, such as during a bath.

Cleaning your dog's ears is not difficult, but you do need the right supplies. Gear up with a bottle of dog-friendly ear cleaning solution and a few clean cotton balls. I would also advise you to speak to your vet about recommended ear solutions. Some solutions can be applied by using a syringe and approximately 1 or 2 ml of solution every week or so. If your dog is prone to ear mites as many dogs are, it also needs to effectively deal with those as well as generally cleaning the ear canal.

Gently lift your dog's ear and squeeze a few drops (or the recommended ml dosage) of the cleaning solution into the ear canal. Rub the base of your dog's ear with your fingers to spread the solution then use the cotton balls to wipe any excess away. Be careful not to attempt putting your fingers or the cotton ball into your dog's ear.

This could damage the ear canal or the ear drum if inserted far enough. Again the frequency with which you clean your Labrador's ears will vary, but you should aim for once every week or two.

5) BRUSHING YOUR LABRADOR'S TEETH

Please be aware that if you adopt the type of diet advocated by vets such as Ian Billinghurst, this next step is likely to be unnecessary. If however, you feed a commercial feed, particularly kibble, then this next section may be necessary. The idea of brushing your dog's teeth may sound strange but dental health is just as important for your dog as it is for you. In fact, periodontitis (gum disease) is five times more common in dogs than in humans. Gum disease is incredibly serious but it often goes unnoticed by pet parents, especially since many people think that dogs are supposed to have bad breath. Bad breath, or halitosis, is one of the most common signs of gum disease and could be indicative of a tooth abscess. Once again, please note that dogs regularly chewing on suitable raw meaty bones have relatively odourless breath. If you suspect an abscess, or anything un-toward, seek a veterinary examination as soon as possible. If you intend to brush your dogs teeth with a brush, you are advised to get him used to this as early as possible.

To brush your Labrador's teeth, follow the steps below:

Select a soft-bristle toothbrush to use. Most pet stores stock special toothbrushes for dogs.

Choose a toothpaste that is specifically made for dogs, never human tooth paste. They come in a variety of flavours, so select one your Labrador will like. He will probably like them all. Again, never use the tooth paste you use. These contain chemicals that can be harmful to dogs.

1. Get your dog used to having his teeth handled by gently placing your finger in his mouth against his teeth. Carefully manipulate his lips so he gets used to the feeling.

2. If you find he doesn't particularly like this, try dipping your finger in peanut butter or chicken broth so your dog learns to

like the treatment.

3. When you are ready to brush, place one hand over your dog's mouth and gently pull back his lips.

4. Apply a small amount of toothpaste to the brush and rub it gently over a few of his teeth.

5. After a few seconds, stop brushing and give your Labrador a treat for good behaviour.

6. Slowly increase the length of your brushing sessions over a few days until your dog lets you brush all of his teeth in one session.

In addition to brushing your Labrador's teeth at home you should also make sure he gets a dental check-up from the vet every 6 months.

CHAPTER EIGHTEEN:

HEALTH CHECKS AND FIRST AID

Before we get into the main health issues affecting the Labrador, this chapter will deal with important preventive care. There is also useful and sometimes vital advice on health checks and first aid.

1.) CHOOSING A VETERINARIAN

You may already know this but not all veterinarians are the same. They are only people after all. So to find a good vet that you get on well with, may take some time and effort.

It is vitally important that you are completely happy with the vet that you choose for your dog. This person may need to lead you through some very difficult times. So a veterinarian who is hazy when sharing information or blunt towards you, may be very stressful for your entire family if you have an ill dog.

You firstly need to locate the vets in your area. Simply contacting each one, even if you can only speak with the receptionist will give you a good idea of the type of practice this is. You could also conduct some community research, ask other dog walkers, go onto Facebook and find community pages of dog owners in your local area. Find out from other people what their experiences are of certain vets and learn from them. Having said all of that, you are not signing a contract that says you have to stay with a particular vet for life. You can try out the one you get a good feeling about, and if it doesn't work out, try another.

Choosing a vet in the USA

Veterinary medicine in the USA is popularly governed by either the American Holistic Veterinary Medical Association (AHVMA)

http://www.ahvma.org/

or the American Veterinary Medical Association (AVMA)

https://www.avma.org/

Some vets will belong to both organisations, but many are either one or the other with the majority attached to the (AVMA). What you will find is that their view points and practices do differ in terms of treatment, health and general care. Traditional western medical treatment whether animal or human is generally carried out to a specific body part either using medicine or surgery. The holistic practice effectively treats the whole body and is generally a gentler approach. Many advocates of the holistic approach promoted by the (AHVMA) see this as the best approach, unless major surgery or an emergency occurs in which case the (AVMA) approach is the sensible choice. The (AHVMA) vet will have no doubt been a (AVMA) graduate and therefore an (AVMA) practicing vet, before focusing on a more holistic approach. You are therefore getting the best of both worlds, in that they have access to all the drugs, vaccines, surgery etc, but choose to prioritise the healthier, holistic approach. The downside of the vet who isn't aware of a more holistic approach is their recommendations will be limited to their (AVMA) training, and they may not be aware of more holistic alternatives. So you are likely to be told you need to vaccinate your dog every year regardless, or told to only feed commercial foods and avoid raw feeding etc.

If you are located in other global regions it may be worth researching similar vets practicing holistic medicine as well as the traditional approach.

2) NATURAL THERAPY AND REMEDIES

Natural therapy is often passed over because conventional medicine has become such a big part of our lives. This is a pity in many ways as remedies, hands on therapy and a mixture of the two can have such amazing results.

Your veterinarian can diagnose, treat with drugs and give you advice. But it is up to you then to go away and explore all of the options available to you and your dog.

In the book Veterinary Secrets: Natural Health for Dogs and Cats, (2014) Dr Andrew Jones talks about veterinary medicine and how this relates to your dog. This book is a welcome addition to the care kit of any Labrador dog. Similarly the book The Veterinarians Guide to Natural Remedies for Dogs (2000) by Martin Zucker, is also a fantastic resource for any dog owner.

When to call the vet

You should call the vet if in any doubt whatsoever, but especially if you notice any of the following:

- Your dog has persistent sickness or diarrhoea for more than 24 hours.
- He appears weak, listless and not his usual bouncy, energetic self.
- Lack of appetite.

- If you suspect he has swallowed a harmful substance.
- If he has an accident that you suspect may have caused an injury or bone breakage.
- He cuts himself, risking infection.
- If he limps and doesn't have anything stuck in his paw pad.
- If you notice a discharge from his eyes, nose, ears, anus, mouth or anywhere else.

If you are in any doubt, you should not hesitate to call the vet.

3) DAILY HEALTH CHECK: ESSENTIAL HANDLING

You will get used to seeing your new friend on a daily basis and quickly get used to his quarks and how he generally behaves. It will therefore become very obvious to you if something is wrong health wise. If you suspect that your dog is ill, just remember that most serious illnesses occur simultaneously with a rise in body temperature. It therefore makes sense to take your dogs temperature, which if you haven't already got one, please do get a thermometer either rectal or ear. However, be aware of the ambient temperature, for example on a hot day you may notice a raised temperature, simply because it is hot. Incidentally rectal thermometers are usually cheaper and more accurate. If your dog is used to standing, you can probably do this yourself by holding his tail and with a small amount of vaseline or similar, insert the thermometer into his rectum. If he wont stand for you doing this, then you will need someone to help you hold him whilst you insert the thermometer.

A normal average temperature for a dog should be about 101.5 °F (38.6°C). If there is a rise of even a few degrees and this isn't the result of a sudden burst of exercise or hot weather, then assume there is a problem and consult with your vet a.s.a.p.

Preventative Care

From the very minute that you purchase your Labrador puppy, you will be responsible for his care. You'll need to take a few minutes each day to do simple health checks. Some of these can be done whilst grooming, such as feeling for bumps or loss of muscle. You will no doubt be able to see if your puppy or adult dog, looks ill, or seems weak and listless for no reason.

Daily examinations will include examinations for:

- Bleeding, swollen, or pale gums, loose or broken teeth, mouth ulcers, or bad breath
- Discharge from the eyes or nose
- Ears having a bad odour, redness or discharge
- The skin for parasites, hair loss, hot spots, crusts or lumps
- The feet for abrasions, foreign objects such as thorns, bleeding, broken nails or misaligned toes

What Will Early Handling Establish?

Handling your dog early on will teach him that being touched and health checked is a perfectly normal part of his life. This makes life so much easier at the vets along with making nail clipping and similar activities stress free.

Physical Manipulation

Handle your dog in whatever position is comfortable for him, whether standing, sitting or lying him down on his side, back, or front. The important thing is that you handle him. Also be initially wary of an older rescue dog until you know that they do not mind you handling them.

The Worried or Reactive Labrador

If you are bringing home an older Labrador then it is important not to push your luck in terms of handling. Remember that the dog will be confused and maybe even quite stressed.

A good way to carry out handling with a worried dog is to do it for a few minutes, or even seconds if necessary, at a time and reward with treats, then stop. The idea is to show the dog that handling and checking his ears, eyes and teeth etc, is a pleasant experience that brings nice food rewards.

Never force the worried dog beyond his limitations. Always stop whilst he is still relaxed and try

to understand that this may all be brand new to him.

Basic Massage and Muscle Care

Basic Massage can also be carried out when handling your dog of any age. By taking a few moments to first massage the dog's ears, where there are a lot of relaxing acupressure points, then moving your hands down his body and legs in even strokes, you will be able to check his muscle and skin for any abnormalities.

Any uneven muscle balance will show that there is a potential skeletal problem below the surface. This is something that can be carefully monitored and should really be checked by the vet.

Any heat or swelling in the muscle areas may show a deeper problem. Similarly if the dog licks his lips, yawns or tries to move when you touch a certain area of his body, then he could have some type of pain beneath the surface and is displaying calming signals as a response to your touch. It could also be nothing to worry about and the dog displays calming signals because they perhaps do not like being handled.

Once you have checked his overall body and legs you can look at specific parts as follows:

Feet

Firstly, take hold of each paw and look at the underside of the pads by squashing them open. This will help to check pads for cuts and foreign articles when you really need to. If you find any sharp object stuck in there, do your best to carefully pull this out preferably with tweezers. If this looks difficult, then you are probably best taking him to the vet, as soon as possible, to get them to extract it. Then check nails, and as previously mentioned, cut any that seem to have overgrown. Details for nail clipping are in the chapter on grooming.

Ears

Take a good look at the dog's ears and into the ear canal. They should be pink and clean with no thick or smelly discharge. Look out for signs of redness and swelling.

Again if you notice anything untoward, do not delay in taking him to the vet.

Eyes

Carefully examine your dog's eyes for swelling or redness. A small amount of sleep is normal. If you live with an adult or an older dog any blueness or blurring can be a sign of cataracts.

You can check your dog's vision by holding his face gently forward and dropping a balled up tissue or feather on the edge of his vision at each side of his head. If his vision is fine he will notice this straight away and respond, if not, he may have a problem. Again a trip to the vets will be best for further investigation.

http://www.vetstreet.com/care/the-ophthalmic-exam

Teeth and gums

Next check your dog's teeth and gums right to the back of his mouth. If you haven't already started, it is a good idea to start brushing your dog's teeth early. If you are doing this on a daily basis, you will soon notice any problems that will need checking at the vets.

http://www.animalwellnessmagazine.com/articles/alternative-dental-care/

Dental sticks are often used and are supposed to do a similar job to brushing. However, be careful as some contain sugar, and as well as being bad for the teeth and gums can add to your dog becoming overweight. Many people swear by fresh bones, but be careful not to give cooked bones as they can splinter easily and cause intestinal problems. Also it can be very painful for dogs to pass, in some cases it is necessary to operate to remove the blockage. If your dog ever suffers any problems associated with eating bones, then obviously avoid giving your dog bones. There is much debate about bone consumption for dogs. But weighing up the pros and cons, in most instances bones are probably healthier than manufactured dental sticks, if perhaps not as safe. Your dog will love them in any case, so the choice is yours.

Anus and Genitals

Now simply check the anus area and genitals for any abnormal discharge or swelling then finish by physically running your hands down the puppy's tail, again checking for any unusual lumps.

4) FIRST AID

As the owner of a Labrador dog it is a good idea to have at least a basic idea of canine first aid.

General first aid and its universal lesson is currently using the acronym Dr's ABC. By memorising this you have at least a basic idea of what to do if you ever find yourself in a first aid situation.

Danger

Remove the animal from any further danger, and be aware of danger to yourself in the situation.

Response

Check the response of the dog, is he conscious?

Summon help

Shout for help, ask someone to call the vet if possible.

Airway

Check the dog's airway, can he breathe Is there an obstruction?

Breathing

At this point there may be a need to re-trigger breathing for the animal. Holding the mouth closed you can gently breath air into your dog's nostrils. Try to visualise the size of his lungs and not over inflate them.

Cardiac compressions may be necessary at this point. The dog should be laid on his right side and the heart massaged in a similar way to CPR compressions for a human. It is usually recommended that a ratio of one breath to every five compressions (approximately every 3 seconds) is given. How many compressions are given per minute depends on the size of dog. For a dog over 14kg in weight 80 compressions per minute are generally recommended. A small dog less than 14kg is usually given approximately 100 per minute.

The heart is approximately located in the chest area above his front left leg. There is usually a stronger beat on the left but it can be felt on both sides.

Traditionally the basic sequence for CPR has been as follows:

1. Check for signs of breathing which should be noticeable around the chest or by placing your cheek to your dogs mouth.

2. Check for a pulse which if this is not noticeable around the heart area, can be felt via the femoral artery. This is located on either of the back legs, on the inside of the leg, near to the top of the leg. By feeling inside that area, if there was a pulse, you would feel it quite strongly at that point. It will be worth you detecting that now, so that you know where to look and how it should feel.

3. If neither breathing nor pulse are detected, start chest compressions. With the heel of your hand, press reasonably firmly, but not too firmly otherwise you risk cracking a rib. Count five compressions

4. Now move over to your dogs mouth/nose, holding the mouth shut, steadily blow into both nostrils and you should see the chest expand.

5. Again move over to the chest and compress five times again.

6. Keep repeating the sequence until he starts to breath.

Please read the following articles for additional information:

http://www.petmd.com/dog/emergency/common-emergencies/e_dg_cardiopulmonary_resuscitation
http://www.peteducation.com/article.cfm?c=2+1677&aid=1604

http://www.telegraph.co.uk/pets/news-features/dog-cpr-administer-first-aid-properly/

If you prefer a visual demonstration, please search Youtube using a search term such as [CPR on dogs]. The following link has a Youtube demonstration that you will probably find useful.

http://www.dailymail.co.uk/sciencetech/article-3433385/How-dog-CPR-Vet-reveals-best-way-check-pulse-restore-breathing-pet-collapses.html

However, you may also be interested in the following link regarding new findings on correct CPR. Although the link is for Vizslas, the information is relative for any dog.

http://www.vizslaforums.com/24-general-chit-chat/3728-new-cpr-method.html

Circulation

In an emergency, the dog's pulse and circulation will need to be checked. If bleeding is apparent then the wound will need to be put under pressure and elevated if possible in order to contain the bleeding.

After first aid has been carried out, the dog should always be taken to see the vet as a matter of urgency.

There are some particular conditions that can develop very quickly and can cause rapid health deterioration; which as a Labrador owner it is important to be aware of. One of these is heat stroke or heat exhaustion.

5) HEAT EXHAUSTION

Problems associated with hot weather.

Dogs are not as tolerant of heat as humans. Their ability to sweat is limited to sweat glands in their feet. If you didn't already know, panting is the main way that dogs keep cool. Heat is lost with increased airflow over the tongue, windpipe and throat causing a cooling effect as well as moisture evaporation. All breeds of dog are at risk of heatstroke in hot weather, but certain short nosed breeds, younger dogs and puppies as well as old and overweight dogs, are more susceptible.

In the warm summer months it is therefore vital to keep your dog away from hot sun. Heat exhaustion can potentially be a fatal condition.

Dogs should never be left in hot cars, in particular with no ventilation, full sun or hot areas from which they cannot escape.

The symptoms of heat exhaustion are as follows;

Excessive panting (however, as dogs do this naturally anyway, in most cases it is not indicative of a problem); Restlessness; Loss of focus in the eyes; Deterioration of consciousness; Staggering; Collapse

If you suspect that your Labrador dog is overheating, it is vital never to take the panicked action of immersing him in cold water, as this can cause shock or even heart failure. It is therefore necessary to do this gradually. Remove the dog from full sun and either drape damp towels over his body or dribble water over him to cool his overheated body gently. If the body has been exposed to overheating, then it is vital to get your dog checked by the vet for symptoms of long term damage.

A relatively new invention in the dog equipment world is the cooling vest. It can be placed in water then put onto the dog in hot weather. The water wicks the heat away from the dogs body as a process of evaporation. If you believe that your dog is particularly susceptible to hot weather, then a cooling vest is a really good investment.

If your dog is likely to spend time out in the sun, in your garden or yard, you should ensure that there is at least one shaded area for him to lay and keep cool.

6) ESSENTIAL EXERCISE

Dogs are generally considered to be similar to humans in their exercise requirements and can adapt to their circumstances. For example, the dog that is placed in quarantine will eventually leave, in a healthy condition, having spent several months in a pen with a run not much bigger than a small garden to exercise in. But their muscle tone will have deteriorated to a certain extent. Rescue dogs spending large parts of the day in kennels are in a similar position. A dog will nevertheless become healthier, fitter and with greater stamina levels, the more exercise it receives.

Having said that, dogs need daily active purposeful exercise, such as long walks, off lead runs, play activities and not just being turned out in a large yard or garden where they are likely to just wander about or lie down. Please do remember that although you will hear recommendations of certain breeds ideally needing a yard or garden,

it is not the same thing as a purposeful walk or off lead run. A yard or garden is great if you intend to play fetch games, in an obvious safe area etc. Throwing a ball or stick has long been a popular alternative to help tire your dog out. Setting up an agility course, if your garden is large enough, with tunnels, ramps, platforms, short ladders, weave sticks etc, is a great way for you to interact and to tire a dog, preventing boredom. Indoor games such as hide and seek, scenting, tracking food, short retrieves etc are useful on days when the weather prevents normal exercise.

The exercising of your dog obviously gives you the perfect opportunity to exercise yourself. As a daily routine with the obligation to exercise your dog you are unlikely to fall into the trap of not following an exercise routine or a trip to the gym because you cannot be bothered today. Research your local area for suitable locations to exercise your dog. As well as the pavements in your immediate neighbourhood these may also include; Local fields, wooded areas, dog parks, other local parks. Also check that it is permissible to exercise dogs in these areas.

Every Labrador dog needs daily walks, and will certainly not be happy at home all day. Remember that Gundogs were purposely bred for their stamina and ability to keep going all day if necessary. Unfortunately many pet owners fail to recognise the innate needs of such dogs to have a similar outlet, now that the average family home no longer requires them to flush and retrieve game birds.

The adult Labrador ideally needs a good long walk several times a day with the opportunity for off lead running. Otherwise he may develop problem behaviours. These gentle, sweet natured dogs are generally well behaved. However, excess energy build up can easily cause destructive or even aggressive behaviour, to a certain extent.

Many dog behaviour problems can be remedied very quickly when the daily walks are increased in time and intensity. Behaviour can also change significantly when the dog's food is changed (food causing allergies or just poor food quality lacking necessary nutrients). But many of the most problematic behaviours stem from a lack of suitable exercise. Such behavioural problems can include: hyperactivity, excessive barking, digging, chewing, chasing, racing about the house, ripping things up, potentially knocking furniture or people over, causing an injury to either you or themselves.

Under exercised dogs are likely to become restless, tense, agitated, displaying heightened, aggressive behaviour relating to food, toys, barking at the slightest thing etc. The thing to realise is that this is not the dogs fault, as they are reacting out of frustration to not having a suitable outlet for their pent up energy. In addition to behavioural problems, a lack of adequate exercise is also likely to result in him losing muscle tone, becoming lazy and possibly becoming overweight or obese, resulting in a gradual deterioration of health.

If you are out at work for a full day then why not consider a doggy day care or professional dog walker for your Labrador dog. The dog also cannot be expected to hold it in all day if they need to urinate or defecate. A good professional canine caretaker will wear your dog out and meet his care and social needs all at once.

Puppy exercise

Please be aware that Labrador puppies along with other puppy breeds, need to be broken in gently to exercise, as their bones are soft whilst they are still growing. Your regular, long walks will begin when your puppy is several months old.

Puppy exercise should involve gentle short walks; the UK Kennel club advises;

"Puppies need much less exercise than fully-grown dogs. If you over-exercise a growing puppy you can overtire it and damage its developing joints, causing early arthritis. A good rule of thumb is a ratio of five minutes exercise per month of age (up to twice a day) until the puppy is fully grown, i.e. 15 minutes (up to twice a day) when three months old, 20 minutes when four months old etc. Once they are fully grown, they can go out for much longer.

It is important that puppies and dogs go out for exercise every day in a safe and secure area, or they may become frustrated. Time spent in the garden (however large) is no substitute for exploring new environments and socialising with other dogs. (Make sure your puppy is trained to recall so that you are confident that he will return to you

when called)".

How much daily exercise is enough?

So are you aware of how much daily exercise this breed will need to keep him happy, healthy and burn off pent up energy?

Opinions differ but it is generally considered that at least an hour, preferably two, brisk walking per day, with some off lead running, is necessary for most gundog breeds. It is preferable that this is split into half an hour or so in the morning and the same in the evening.

Opinions differ, but an off lead run is considered more beneficial to them than a long walk.

A breed requiring a lot of exercise such as a Labrador needs an actual off lead run of over a mile per day, either free running in a field or park, or whilst jogging with yourself. This would probably be the equivalent of 1 ½ to 2 hours of brisk lead walking.

A 10 minute off lead run several times a day for pups and a 20 minute off lead run morning and evening for adults, should be included as part of their daily exercise. Jogging or running in a safe area will encourage the dog to follow you and to run harder than if you leave him to it.

CHAPTER NINETEEN:

PARASITES, WORMS AND COMMON ILLNESSES

This chapter deals with the unfortunate subject of parasites and common illnesses that can affect your Labrador. Please do not skip this chapter as it is important that you are aware of these parasites and conditions and can therefore deal with their treatment and prevention.

1.) PARASITIC WORMS

A huge concern within the digestive process are parasites.

Worms are known as internal parasites of which there are plenty that can affect the Labrador dog and Labrador puppies. It may surprise you to know, but puppies are actually born with worms present. Having purchased from a reputable breeder, your puppy is bound to have already been wormed. You should check when this was, and the dose and type used, which will indicate when he needs worming next. Please do not neglect regular worming whether a puppy or adult as these parasites can seriously affect their health and in some cases lead to death. Also be very careful and stick to correct doses, as this can cause intestinal damage and again at worse lead to a fatality.

A.) ROUNDWORMS

The most common worm type is the roundworm, of which there are a few variations. Symptoms of a roundworm infection include itchiness in the anus area, worms in the dog's faeces and loss of condition.

A mother dog can pass roundworms on to her puppies. All Labrador puppies, bred and raised well, should be wormed properly by the breeder before being sent to their new homes. Worms usually live in the dog's digestive system and some are actually symptom-less. Others can have serious consequences for the health of the Labrador dog.

Hookworm and whipworm are also roundworm types that cause pain and digestive upset in dogs. The hookworm grips onto the stomach wall causing constant and severe discomfort to the dog.

B.) TAPEWORMS

The tapeworm is a type of parasite which can sit in the intestine without doing any damage, other than consuming nutrients that your dog should be consuming. They will also grow to a large size throughout the intestinal tract. The tapeworm reproduces by shedding parts of its long and segmented body, which is passed with the faeces or drops from the anus of the dog. The tapeworm is happy to live in the digestive system of both dogs and people. Again the main problem here is that it will consume a considerable amount of ingested food and obviously grow as a result. As you can imagine, your dog will not be getting sufficient nutrients and will suffer as a result.

Basic worming tablets will keep the chance of infection under control. As a routine these should be administered about every 3 months. However, some worming tablets can be administered once a month. In some cases, they are combined with flea treatment, obviously depending on the product you use. Be careful that you are giving your dog the correct dosage. This is usually gauged by kilo weight of your dog. Also be aware that different brands suggest a different number of tablets. This is probably because of the size or potency of each tablet.

C.) LUNGWORMS/HEART-WORMS

The other type of worm, and one which has serious consequences, is the lungworm/heartworm.

The larvae for this type of worm, when it gets into the body, migrates to either the lung or heart of the animal, hence the name. It then quickly breeds to fill the respective major organ with worms, as illustrated above. By the time that the symptoms of this type of infestation appears, the damage to either the heart or lungs will be well underway.

Symptoms are excessive coughing and loss of heart or lung function. This parasite type is becoming more common, and currently being diagnosed in geographical areas where it has not previously been seen.

The larvae of this parasite enters the body via a mosquito bite or ingestion. Dogs that eat slugs, snails and their eggs are particularly susceptible to an infestation of heart or lungworm.

This quick spreading infection, has necessitated preventative medication. If you are in an area that is high risk, I would strongly urge you to consult with your veterinarian about preventive measures.

As a matter of routine, you are strongly advised to check with your vet, the general type of worms your dog may be susceptible to for your area. Worming tablets can be bought at pet stores and many general stores seem to stock these now. However, be aware that like flea treatments, not all worming treatments are as affective as they should be. Be advised by your vet if you are in any doubt. Once again, always make sure you choose the correct type and dosage for both your dogs size and age.

2.) EXTERNAL PARASITES – FLEAS AND OTHER SUCKERS

The other type of parasite that can potentially affect your Labrador dog is the external parasite.

A.) FLEAS

Fleas generally seek out their host, quite often jumping from dog to dog. They then burrow within the dogs fur and feed off the dogs blood. Unfortunately they stay, reproduce and cause our dogs all sorts of problems.

Symptoms of fleas are grit like dirt that turns red in water and a profusion of itchy bites. Please be aware that fleas can transmit tapeworms.

Many vets will advise that chemical treatment will need to occur every few months as a preventative measure. This is usually in the form of a spot on treatment applied to the back of the dog's neck. Many vets as well as experienced dog people will also assert that you should automatically assume that your dog will be affected by some level of flea infestation. You should therefore not wait for an infestation, but treat as a matter of routine.

Today there are advances in flea and tick control. Always contact your vet as to the best products to use. Some products are much stronger than others, so it's really important to try and choose a formula that is not harmful to your Labrador. There are plenty of flea and tick products that are natural and environmentally friendly. These will repel and kill fleas, ticks and mosquitos with a natural botanical formula like geraniol and eugenol. Sprinkling borax powder, around the home is a known flea killer. However, salt is known to do a similar job. Again, avoid direct contact of the animal as this can dry the skin and possibly have a toxic affect. Other natural remedies often recommended include lemongrass, citronella, cedar wood, neem etc. Have a look on YouTube for some useful videos on alternative natural flea remedies.

B.) TICKS

Ticks can be found anywhere on a Labrador, but are mostly found on the neck, chest, and between the toes. They are often found in the US, but also present in many other global areas. Ticks will transmit Rocky Mountain spotted fever, tick paralysis, Lyme disease, babesiosis, and tick fever. (Erlichiosis)

Ticks are a completely different type of parasite. They do not live on the dog but simply wander onto the animal in order to feed then drop off when full.

Ticks do not differentiate and will happily bite people, sheep, deer and cattle alongside dogs. They are usually only around in the summer months, but in areas of plentiful wildlife or farming environments they come in force during the warm weather, particularly when the grass gets long.

To remove a tick it is important not to squeeze its body whilst it feeds. This can cause the stomach contents and innards to be pushed into your dog's body. It is also important not to attempt to pull the tick off the dog. This can leave the head under the dog's skin even if you remove the body. If the head is left attached, this can still easily lead to an infection. If this happens, seek veterinary attention without delay.

Pet stores sell small hooks which can be placed between the tick's body and your dog's skin for careful removal. If correctly used they will safely remove the parasite completely.

I would suggest either getting a friend or vet, who has experience of how to remove ticks to help you, or watch a step by step video from YouTube.

C.) MITES

Mites are everywhere. Generally they do us no harm, yet some can cause problems for the Labrador dog, particularly the mange mite.

Mange mites burrow under the skin of the dog and cause itchiness and general hair loss. Left untreated the mange mite will affect the general health of the animal and result in eventual baldness.

The immune system of the dog is severely affected by the presence of mange mites. If not treated, the seemingly simple mange infestation will be fatal.

Any dog that is suspected of carrying mange mites should be treated by conventional veterinary medicine. The condition can be really difficult to eradicate, and the course of treatment may be long and slow.

D.) EAR MITES

Ear mites cannot be seen by the human eye but are easily visible with the use of a microscope. These little mites grow and reproduce in the dog's ear and create a very smelly brown discharge. Ear mites are usually easily treated with drops. **http://www.vetstreet.com/care/chronic-otitis-chronic-ear-infection-in-dogs**

3.) OTHER COMMON ILLNESSES

Labrador health is something that every owner of the breed should be aware of. Dogs get sick sometimes, they have off days, and they are susceptible to passing bugs, just as we are.

To have a basic understanding of the way that these conditions affect the body of your dog, will put you in the best position to help him.

A.) DIARRHOEA

Diarrhoea is a common occurrence and not normally one to worry too much about. If your Labrador dog does display symptoms you can simply withhold his food for 24 hours, to allow the stomach and bowels to rest, then re-introduce it gradually.

If the following symptoms occur, then it is important to visit your veterinary surgeon as soon as possible;

The dog has eaten something potentially toxic such as chocolate or artificial sweetener; The dog is lethargic or staggering; The dog's gums are very pale or very dark red; When pinched, the back of the dogs neck does not spring back into place; this is a common sign of dehydration; The condition does not clear up within a few days; The dog is passing blood.

B.) VOMITING

Dogs vomit by choice, so a one off incident is usually nothing much to worry about. You will see them eating grass for instance, and then sometime later you may notice a pile of chewed up grass and mucous/stomach contents. Although eating grass doesn't always lead a dog to vomit, it may be one of the reasons you may see them vomit. It is generally thought they may vomit if they feel ill and need to empty their stomach, much the same as we may need to vomit and then feel much better afterwards.

Yet if the following circumstances are associated with vomiting, then the dog should be taken along to the veterinarian;

The dog could have been exposed to poisons; The dog's airway is obstructed either alongside or as a result of vomiting; The dog has not long been chewing a bone or toy that could possibly be stuck in his digestive system.

You should always consult a vet immediately if any of the previous conditions seem too severe to ignore or you are otherwise concerned or worried.

You know your dog better than anyone else. If you are overly worried, then it is a good idea to listen to those concerns. Your Labrador dog's health may depend on your instinct at some point in your lives together.

The following is a brief summary of parasites commonly affecting dogs, which can also be passed on to humans:

Toxocariasis (toxocarosis) – This can typically be caused by human ingestion of contaminated soil via roundworm parasite eggs passed through dog faeces.

Giardiasis – Giardia intestinalis This again is a parasite present in dog faeces that can potentially contaminate drinking water.

Lyme disease – Obviously Humans can receive tick bites, the ticks having previously bitten an infected dog.

Ringworm – An infected dog can easily pass this fungal skin infection to humans during contact.

Tapeworm – It is possible for example during a picnic, to ingest contaminated food from grass with tapeworm eggs or larvae present. Similarly a dog can easily drink from a pond where there is similar contamination.

Hookworm (Zoonotic) (Ancylostoma caninum, Ancylostoma braziliense, Uncinaria stenocephala). Contaminated soil is a common source for the spread of the Hookworm. It is also most often noted in young puppies via the mother's milk.

Consequently this can be spread through their faeces. It is also possible for this to be contracted through the top layer of human skin whether broken or not.

Roundworm (Toxocara spp.) Once again this is most often noted in young puppies via the mother's milk. Human infection can take place if coming into contact with infected faeces or by accidental ingestion.

Cryptosporidiosis (Cryptosporidium spp.) This is a parasitic disease passed via contaminated food or water.

Echinococcosis (Echinococcus spp.) This is a specific tapeworm and once again the disease can be passed via contaminated food or water.

Leishmaniasis (Leishmania spp.) This is a disease that is transmitted by sand flies.

Rocky Mountain Spotted Fever (Rickettsia rickettsii) Ticks are responsible for this disease. Once again it is typically passed from an infected dog to people.

Sarcoptic Mange (Sarcoptes scabeii), It is possible, although unlikely, that a mange infection can occur if a person has direct contact with an infected dog.

CHAPTER TWENTY:

KEEPING YOUR LABRADOR HEALTHY

The most important thing you can do to keep your Labrador healthy is to provide him with a healthy nutritious diet, and adequate daily exercise. However, even if you give your dog a healthy diet and a safe environment, he may still be prone to developing certain health problems. Familiarising yourself with the health problems to which this breed is prone will help you to identify them at the earliest point. Hopefully, you can then provide your dog, via your vet, with the necessary

treatment before a condition gets out of hand. In this chapter you will find valuable information about Labrador diseases, vaccination information and pet insurance.

PLEASE NOTE: The following is intended for informational purposes only, to inform you of potential diseases that can affect the Labrador. You should always seek professional advice and instruction from your vet and certainly never ignore or attempt to treat any condition without such advice.

Although you will read here about a number of diseases and illnesses that a Labrador can be susceptible to, please do not assume that the Labrador is bound to contract all or any of these diseases. There are also a number of diseases not mentioned here that at some time Labradors have been reported with a low frequency of the disease. You can read veterinary guides on certain breeds and you will find, in the case of some dogs, pages of diseases that at some time a particular breed, or specific dog has been affected by. Do not worry unduly about this as most dogs will get only a few mentioned and some, none at all.

1.) COMMON LABRADOR HEALTH PROBLEMS

Again all dogs are prone to developing certain diseases and congenital conditions can be passed from the parent dogs to the puppies. In this respect dogs intended for breeding and otherwise, should be regularly examined and DNA tested where appropriate for hips, knees, eye, ears and thyroid etc.

In relatively minor health cases, because many conditions affect the eyes, ears, and skin, it is advisable to keep these clean and dirt free on a regular basis. More details will be included in the section on grooming.

The following diseases and disorders listed, have been known to affect the Labrador to varying degrees:

COMMON INHERITED DISEASES

- Centro Nuclear Myopathy (CNM)
- Cystinuria
- Elbow Dysplasia
- Exercise Induced Collapse (EIC)
- Hip Dysplasia
- Narcolepsy
- Patella Luxation
- Progressive Retinal Atrophy (PRA)
- retinal dysplasia
- Tricuspid Valve Dysplasia

POSSIBLE PREDISPOSITION TO THE FOLLOWING DISEASES:

- Allergic dermatitis
- Cataracts
- Diabetes Mellitus
- Distichiasis/Trichiasis
- Epilepsy
- Gastric Torsion (bloat)
- Glaucoma
- Haemophilia A (Factor VIII deficiency)
- Histiocytic Sarcoma/ Histiocytosis
- Hypertrophic Osteodystrophy (HOD)
- Hypothyroidism
- Immune Mediated Hemolytic Anemia (IMHA)
- Osteochondritis Dessicans (OCD)
- Osteosarcoma
- von Willebrand's Disease

The following have been noted to affect the Labrador, sometimes in rare and isolated cases: These additional diseases are as follows, but are not described here:

Acral Lick Dermatitis; Acquired Laryngeal Paralysis; Atrioventricular Block; Central Axonopathy; Cerebellar Abiotrophy; Cervical Vertebral Instability; Cleft Lip/Palate; Corneal Dystrophy; Cranial Cruciate Ligament Rupture (ACL); Craniomandibular osteopathy (CMO); Chronic Hepatitis; Degenerative Myelopathy; Digital Squamous Cell Carcinoma (SCC); Dwarfism; Ectopic Ureter; Entropion/Ectropion; Fanconi Syndrome; Fibrinoid Leukodystrophy; Follicular Dysplasia; Hemophilia B (Factor IX deficiency); Hypoglycemia; Hypotrichosis; Iridociliary Epithelial Tumors; Limbal Melanoma; Lingual Squamous Cell Carcinoma (SCC); Lymphedema; Malignant Hyperthermia; Megaesophagus; Microphthalmia; Micropapilla; Mucinosis; Muscular Dystrophy; Myelodysplasia; Myoclonus; Mytubular Myopathy; Neuroaxonal Dystrophy; Neuronal Ceroid Lipofuscinosis (NCL); Optic Nerve Coloboma; Optic Nerve Hypoplasia; Panosteitis; Persistent Pupillary Membranes; Seasonal Flank Alopecia; Sebaceous Adenitis; Silica Urolithiasis; Spongiform Leukodystrophy; Supernumerary Teeth; Tetralogy of Fallot; Vitamin A Responsive Dermatosis; Vitiligo.

Available genetic tests which a breeder should carry out routinely include:

Hereditary cataract (HC) (annual testing); Glaucoma (G) (annual testing); Multi-focal retinal dysplasia (MRD); Progressive Retinal Atrophy (PRA) (annual testing) (PRA prcd/GR_PRA1 and GR_PRA2); other annual CERF eye examinations; Dwarfism (RD/OSD); Exercise Induced Collapse (EIC); Centronuclear Myopathy (CNM); Cystinuria; Haemophilia A and B; Narcolepsy; von Willebrand's disease (vWD); Muscular Dystrophy (MD); OFA Hips; Elbows; Patella; Cardiac evaluation; Thyroid profiling.

Once again, when buying from a litter of puppies it is important that the breeder confirms that there have been no historical incidences of aggression, tendencies towards dominance, epileptic seizures, thyroid problems, allergies, cases of vWD, etc.

In addition, 'The Kennel Club UK' conducted two surveys in 2004 and 2014 respectively. Although the sample of dogs used in the survey was a relatively small representation, it still makes for interesting reading. You can view the full surveys for the Labrador at the following links:

2014

http://www.thekennelclub.org.uk/pedigreebreedhealthsurvey

https://www.thekennelclub.org.uk/me-dia/749523/labrador_retriever.pdf

2004

http://www.thekennelclub.org.uk/for-vets-and-researchers/purebred-breed-health-survey-2004/

https://www.thekennelclub.org.uk/me-dia/16574/labrador%20retriever.pdf

Once again, please do not be overwhelmed by the preceding list. As with any breed, at some point a case will arise which only represents a very small percentage of the population, with perhaps a 1 or 2% frequency of dogs being affected. So again, please do not assume that your dog will suffer all of those diseases, and perhaps it will be none of them.

In the following pages you will receive an overview of most of the diseases listed. Some of the diseases are quite common and treatable or at least manageable. However, some conditions have a fatal consequence. Fortunately certain diseases can be DNA health tested. Again this highlights the importance of only ever buying health-tested dogs from reputable sources.

The following diseases are listed firstly in the order presented for Common Inherited Diseases. Diseases are then presented in alphabetical order. This is merely for ease of searching and is not listed in order of importance, severity or frequency.

Common Inherited Diseases

Centronuclear Myopathy (CNM)

This disease usually affects puppies less than 6 months of age and manifests as a weakness in the muscle due to a deficiency of muscle fibres. There is usually a progressive deterioration from around 2 months of age until an affected puppy has great difficulty moving. In the worst case scenario, a puppy may never recover. However affected cases have been known in some dogs upwards of 9 years of age but these dogs generally need ongoing medical attention due to related secondary conditions such as respiratory illness etc.

Symptoms

Reduced muscle tone, muscle weakness, abnormality of the normal posture, stiffened, hopping gait (usually the first sign of the disorder, progressing to a general weakened state), indifference and intolerance to exercise, exposure to cold temperatures can cause collapse

Cause

The cause relates to an autosomal recessive genetic disorder. Being autosomal, an abnormal gene has to be passed on by both parents. If only one parent has the defective gene and the other is clear, the likelihood is that the puppy may be a carrier of the gene, but will probably not be affected by the disease. This also means that such as puppy could also pass the disorder on to any of its potential offspring. In this respect carriers of the gene should never be part of a breeding program. It is also very important when purchasing a puppy that you obtain proof that both parents have been DNA tested as 'clear' of (CNM)

Diagnosis

Although physical symptoms can indicate the condition, the only really reliable diagnosis is through a DNA test. Scans such as x-rays would be used to determine the condition of muscle deterioration, for example the oesophagus. Where the oesophagus is affected, this can lead to conditions such as megaesophagus, which in turn can lead to regurgitation and inhalation of food, pneumonia etc.

Treatment

Although research into the condition is ongoing, unfortunately there is no known cure at present that can reverse the process or repair damaged muscle tissue. Where it is possible to treat and manage the condition, this is for the rest of the dogs life. As the condition is exacerbated by cold temperature, when out on walks it is advisable to provide coats and other types of warm clothing for the dog to wear. Ability to exercise is likely to be restricted, but should still be encouraged. Swimming may be desirable for the dog, but may be a risk in some deep waters. Some owners provide the dog opportunities to swim by applying a life jacket and safety line in case of difficulty.

CYSTINURIA

Cystine is an amino acid which is a byproduct of protein metabolism. Under normal circumstances cystine is filtered in the kidneys before being absorbed back into the blood stream.

If a dog has the condition cystinuria the kidneys fail to reabsorb the cystine and it instead passes directly into the urine.

In turn, an excess of cystine can lead to stones being formed in the urinary tract.

The condition is an autosomal recessive genetic disorder, meaning that both parents would need to be carriers of the defected gene for it to be passed on to a puppy and for the puppy to be affected by the condition.

Both male and females can be affected, but males may be affected more rapidly and intensely.

Symptoms

Blood in the urine, visible crystal deposits in the urine, an obvious inability and discomfort whilst trying to pass urine. The urine may also have a distinctive rotten egg pungent odour, due to the presence of sulphur in cistine.

Diagnosis

Other than the aforementioned symptoms, a urine test known as a nitroprusside test is often used to determine the cystinuria condition. A DNA test also offers a conclusive diagnosis.

Treatment

Because of the potential severity of the condition such as a ruptured bladder and kidney failure, immediate veterinary intervention is necessary. This is likely to involve surgery to remove the stones or crystals. Ongoing management will include providing a low protein diet as well as regular visits to the vet to assess and monitor the status of the condition. It is important to note that although crystals and stones can be removed, it is possible for them to redevelop. It is also important to keep to a special low protein diet which is likely to help in controlling the condition.

Any dog diagnosed as a carrier of cystinuria should never be part of a breeding program.

ELBOW DYSPLASIA

Degeneration or abnormal cell, tissue or bone growth of the elbow joint is the principal cause of Elbow Dysplasia. The condition is a common cause of lameness and elbow pain. Onset can occur at any age, but usually occurs before 12 months of age with clinical signs and a diagnosis made approximately 4 months to one and a half years of age. The same condition affects both sexes, but there is one type of Elbow Dysplasia that affects the male but not the female.

Symptoms

Older dogs can show signs of discomfort and lameness as a result of joint degeneration. Lameness can also occur persistently or only occasionally, usually intensified by exercise. Quite often the movements will appear stiff and worsen whilst in a state of rest after exercise. Pain and discomfort will be apparent when flexing the elbow joint. Normal flexing range will also be reduced. Where degeneration of the joint is the principal cause grating and creaking of the joint will be typical with any kind of movement. It is also common for the dog to hold the affected leg up, either stationary or whilst attempting to move. Fluid build up in the joint area may also occur.

Causes

Principally caused genetically, but can also occur due to a nutritional imbalance or be developmental. Adults with a history of the condition should never be part of a breeding program. Puppies are at risk if overfed, as this can result in rapid growth spurts likely to increase the chances of conditions such as Elbow Dysplasia developing.

Diagnosis

A physical veterinary examination and x-rays will ascertain whether trauma, infection, tumour (cancerous or otherwise), or arthritis is the cause. As both limbs are typically affected, both legs are usually examined. MRI or CT scans may also be necessary. Laboratory testing of any fluid present is likely. An arthroscopic examination of the internal joint may also be needed.

Treatment

Surgery offers the best solution and the prognosis is usually good. Treatments are likely to be administered to control the pain, decrease swelling, protect cartilage etc. Physical therapy is also likely to build movement and strength, as activity should be restricted for a number of weeks after surgery. Annual check ups are usually advisable to assess the status of the cartilage and joint.

EXERCISE INDUCED COLLAPSE (EIC)

The condition of (EIC) basically affects the nervous system during exercise. It results in an affected dog losing muscle control. In less severe cases, (EIC) may only occur occasionally. The condition is usually induced by an increase in exercise, temperature and excitement. Under normal circumstances the dog will need to have been exercising or in a state of excitement for some time to induce an attack. Onset can affect either sex and can occur at any age. But it is more common between the ages of 6 months and 3 years.

Cause

The condition is caused by a defective gene. It is an autosomal recessive disorder which means that both parents will need to be carriers of the abnormal gene, and in turn pass this on to a litter of puppies. Such puppies are then likely to be affected by the condition. However, if only one parent is a carrier and the other is clear, there is a strong probability that the puppy will also be a carrier but will not necessarily be affected by the disease itself.

Symptoms

Muscle weakness; loss of coordination; increased body temperature (in the past, before the condition was specifically identified, heat stroke was often misdiagnosed for (EIC)). Leg weakness and collapse can occur at any time during intense exercise, in some cases after only a few minutes. The condition can affect dogs in different ways, with some collapsing after very limited exercise. An attack is likely to start with a quivering or rocking motion, leading to an unsteadiness and collapse of the hind limbs. This can result in the affected dog continuing activity unhampered, limping or dragging themselves forward or a total inability to move. Attacks can last for a few minutes, up to 30 minutes. The most severe cases can result in death following an attack.

Diagnosis

The most reliable diagnosis is via a DNA test.

Treatment

In many cases an affected dog will still be able to lead a normal life. It is important however, to monitor which types of activities and the circumstances triggering the collapse. In general, low levels of excitement and relatively calm exercise, is unlikely to trigger an episode. Strenuous activity however, can easily trigger the condition very quickly. Such activities include normal hunting activity, intense training, dog sports, agility, field trials, hunt tests, retrieving games etc.

Please remember that it is possible for an affected dog to die during or immediately after strenuous exercise. In order to limit an affected dogs activity, it will be useful to think in terms of them as a house dog, and restrict exercise to leash walking only, limited, supervised or no off leash running. Exercise should be stopped the instant the dog starts to seem unsteady.

HIP DYSPLASIA

Hip dysplasia is a musculoskeletal issue seen in many dogs but it is particularly common in large and medium-sized breeds. This condition is characterised by a malformation of the hip joint, which causes the femur to pop in and out of the socket. This causes painful wear and tear and osteoarthritis. Most dogs that suffer from this condition are born with normal hips. However, various factors result in the soft tissues around the hip developing in an abnormal way, which then affects the joint itself.

This condition affects dogs of all ages. In severe cases, puppies just a few months old may begin showing signs of pain or discomfort related to hip dysplasia. These symptoms are most likely to occur during and after exercise, and the condition may worsen to the point that normal daily activity becomes painful. If the dog does not receive treatment, the condition will progress to the point that the dog becomes lame and unable to walk. In most cases, symptoms of hip dysplasia do not develop until middle age or in the later years of life.

Symptoms

Closely linked to arthritis. Altered gait whilst walking or running. Inability to fully extend or flex their back legs. Bunny hop-like gait. Trouble navigating stairs. Generally very sore or stiff getting up if lying down for a period of time. Lethargy and unwillingness to play or engage in other physical activity.

Treatment

Primarily inherited by dogs with a genetic predisposition. Dietary changes, anti-inflammatory medications, and supplements may help your dog to deal with the pain and they might slow the progression of the disease. Surgery is the most permanent and effective treatment. Surgery possibly re-aligns the bones and joints or completely replaces the hip. Surgery can also be done to remove the femoral head and to replace it with a pseudo-joint.

NARCOLEPSY

Narcolepsy is a disorder of the nervous system which affects dogs by a sudden weakness and sleep episode. Episodes are generally short lived and eventually disappear naturally. Fortunately the condition is not life threatening or fatal in itself. However, it does mean affected dogs should be supervised, particularly outside, to avoid any circumstances potentially putting them at risk. For example an attack could occur whilst the dog is swimming, and a consequent risk of them drowning. An episode could also occur in a dog park where other dogs can become hostile to anything strange and attempt to attack your dog.

An episode can last for a number of seconds upwards of half an hour or more. Although an attack may appear quite serious or distressing to see, the dog is not in any kind of pain or suffering.

Causes

The cause is not known but is considered to be either hereditary, a nerve disorder or some other bodily malfunction.

Symptoms

Unusually sleepy during the day, lack of energy, rapid onset, loss of consciousness, muscle twitching, whimpering whilst asleep, REM, are all typical. The condition is not known to be related to other underlying disorders.

With an otherwise healthy, normal dog, upon examination, neurological and physical responses will generally be normal.

The condition can occur during any activity such as exercising, eating, playing or when otherwise in a state of excitement or emotion.

A typical episode involves the dog suddenly, without any warning signs, collapsing on its stomach or side. The dog seems to be in a deep sleep, eyes closed with 'rapid eye movement'. An affected dog can be awoken by sudden loud noise or physical contact.

Diagnosis

A complete blood count, urinalysis, and an electrolyte panel are likely to flag up any other underlying cause. A DNA test is available which will conclusively confirm the condition.

Treatment

It may be possible for a vet to administer medication which may help to control the duration and frequency, but it is not really possible to stop or prevent an attack. However, if there is a specific trigger behind an attack such as certain activities, food, a particular time of day etc, it will be possible to eliminate those triggers and therefore reduce the frequency. If an attack otherwise occurs, at least you can be on hand to supervise the dog, or if possible, wake him.

PATELLA LUXATION

Patella luxation is a condition in which the dog's kneecap (patella) becomes dislocated from is normal anatomic position.

Symptoms

Depends on the severity of the condition as well as the amount of degenerative arthritis the dog has. The dog may yelp in pain and might hold up the leg for a few minutes, hopping or skipping on the other three. Once the quadricep muscles relax, the patella usually slips back into place on its own, and the dog can resume normal movement. The more frequently this occurs, the more arthritis the dog is likely to develop.

Cause

Genetic malformation or trauma. Genetic onset is likely within four months of birth. Trauma-related patella luxation can occur at any point in the dog's life.

Diagnosis

Physical examination to test for kneecap movement. Also possible x-rays and a fluid sample taken from the joint to test for increased levels of mononuclear cells.

Treatment

Medicinal treatments are typically ineffective. Surgery to correct the structure and movement of the kneecap is successful in 90% of cases

PROGRESSIVE RETINAL ATROPHY

Progressive Retinal Atrophy (PRA), is an inherited condition affecting the retina that leads to blindness in dogs. There are several different forms of PRA, which are differentiated by the age of onset and the rate of progression. In dogs with PRA, the retinas either exhibit arrested development, also called retinal dysplasia, or early photoreceptor degeneration.

Symptoms

Develops within 2 months of birth with the possibility of complete blindness within a year. Dogs having retinal degeneration are usually affected between one year and eight years after birth and the symptoms progress more slowly.

PRA does not cause the dog pain and there is usually no change in the outward appearance of the eye. Although, in some cases, the lens of the eye may become cloudy or opaque. Behavioural changes occur as a loss of vision develops. This can result in bumping into objects, reluctance to go down stairs or difficulty seeing in the dark. Progression can result in a dilation of the pupils

and an increased reflection of light from the eye.

Diagnosis

Ophthalmic examination as well as other tests.

Treatment

Unfortunately, there is no affective cure. As progression is generally slow, the dog has time to adapt to changes in vision before becoming completely blind. A CERF genetic health test is available. Dogs testing positive for PRA are obviously not recommended for breeding purposes.

RETINAL DYSPLASIA

In general Retinal Dysplasia is a hereditary condition, although other factors may be responsible.

However, as a preventative measure, dogs with a history of the condition should not be part of a breeding program. There is no known cure, and although it does affect the vision, it does not cause pain, nor is the condition progressive. However, in severe cases blindness and secondary problems can occur, such as cataracts or the more serious glaucoma.

Causes

The retina is formed of two layers. When these do not develop simultaneously, it causes folds and creases to form in the tissue. Vitamin deficiency, eye damage, viral infections, etc. are also thought to be potential causes. The herpes virus can be passed from an infected bitch, to the puppies during pregnancy, which is also considered to be a possible cause.

Diagnosis

The condition is generally not visible with the naked eye. The first sign of a problem is therefore likely to occur if the dog shows signs of their vision being affected, such as bumping into objects, etc.

A thorough investigation by a veterinary Ophthalmologist will confirm the condition.

Treatment

Again, this is a lifelong condition and considered irreversible, and therefore there is currently know known cure. However, providing a more serious secondary condition does not develop an affected dog can live a full life with very few problems.

Tricuspid Valve Dysplasia (TVD)

Tricuspid Valve Dysplasia is an inherited condition and relates to a malformed tricuspid valve within the heart. The disorder is otherwise known as 'Atrioventricular Valve Dysplasia' (AVD). The normal function of the tricuspid valve is to regulate blood flow. When the valve is malformed, the valve either does not close properly, allowing back flow of blood, or if there is a narrowing, restricts normal flow, which in turn affects normal functioning and flow of blood to other bodily parts. An enlarged heart muscle can occur if restriction causes the heart to work harder than normal. Left untreated the condition can have fatal consequences.

Symptoms

Stunted growth; audible breathing; a heat murmur or rapid heart beat; exercise intolerance, panting or fainting due to insufficient oxygen in the blood stream; swelling of the abdomen due to an accumulation of fluid

Diagnosis

A complete blood count, and urinalysis are typical initial tests carried out. Exploratory scans such as x-rays, echocardiographs, electrocardiographs will determine the physical status of any abnormalities, enlargement, dilation or narrowing and consequent blood flow.

Treatment

Although heart surgery is possible, in severe cases this is generally considered high risk and therefore not feasible. For less severe cases, medication can be prescribed to help manage the symptoms such as reducing blood pressure and the potential for heart failure. Diuretics are usually administered to reduce fluid retention. It would usually be recommended that a low sodium diet and restricted exercise be adhered to. Treatment and assessment is usually ongoing. Studies are ongoing to identify the defective gene in order to make available a DNA test for suspected carriers.

As this is a genetic condition, dogs diagnosed with the disease should never be part of a breeding program.

A to Z of diseases the Labrador is potentially predisposed to.

Atopic (allergic dermatitis)

Atopic dermatitis is simply another name for skin allergies . The condition of your dog's skin is like a window to his inner health. If your dog doesn't appear healthy on the outside, there is probably something wrong on the inside.

Symptoms

Hair loss, scratching, frequent licking, rubbing the body on objects, rashes, blisters, hot spots, lesions, diarrhoea or vomiting.

Causes

Pollen, dust, mold, dander, cigarette smoke, fleas/flea products, perfumes, fabrics, and certain food ingredients.

Diagnosis

Skin symptoms will require a veterinary diagnosis. Food allergies typically involve switching to an allergen-free dog food formula for 10 to 12 weeks. Followed by a systematic introduction of potential allergens. If tested positive, it is simply a matter of removing this from your dog's diet.

Obviously certain allergens cannot be easily removed such as preventing your dog from coming into contact with pollen or dust. Similar to humans, Antihistamines may help to manage symptoms. Fatty acids in the diet might help to improve your dog's skin and coat condition. Severe cases may require treatment with a corticosteroid medication.

Cataracts

Typically inherited, although some cataracts are the result of another disease such as Diabetes Mellitus or Progressive Retinal Atrophy. A cataract is the darkening or clouding of the lens in the dog's eye resulting from an accumulation of proteins. There are three classifications to describe the age of onset for cataracts. Congenital (present from birth), juvenile (develops at a young age), or senile (develops later in life). There are also different levels of cataracts based on how much of the lens it covers.

Symptoms

A change in eye colour, normally to a light blue, white, or grey.

Inflammation, inside or around the eye.

Other symptoms include squinting, rubbing the eye, bumping into objects, and other signs of vision loss.

Cataracts that are caused by genetic factors cannot be prevented but those caused by other diseases can be dealt with by managing the primary condition.

Diagnosis

Physical examination by your vet, with possible referral to a veterinary ophthalmologist.

Treatment

Although not always necessary, surgery is the only way to permanently remove cataracts. In addition the cause is unknown, so any cataract, whether hereditary or otherwise, should be checked out by a vet. This is a serious condition that can cause blindness. It is therefore important that annual routine examinations take place to hopefully detect possible hereditary cataracts in the early stages.

DIABETES MELLITUS

Diabetes is a condition in which the pancreas doesn't produce enough insulin to regulate and process glucose from your dog's diet. This condition tends to develop in middle-aged and senior dogs as a result of several factors including weight gain, heredity, inflammation, steroidal medications, and certain viral diseases the dog has had.

Symptoms

Increased thirst, increased urination, increased appetite, and unexplained weight loss. Weakness, lethargy, depression, dehydration are also possible.

In some cases Diabetes may lead to secondary complications such as cataracts or vision abnormalities, urinary tract infections and kidney

disease, seizure or convulsions, coma, and even death. Diabetes is not a condition you should take lightly if your dog develops it.

Diagnosis

Dogs with Diabetes are typically diagnosed between the ages of 4 and 14 years, the average being between 5 and 10 years. Female dogs are twice as likely to develop Diabetes as male dogs, though the reason for this is unknown. Diabetes is largely diagnosed through its symptoms, though a number of diagnostic tests may be performed to confirm the diagnosis. Blood and urine tests can be performed to test for insulin insufficiency or resistance as well as hyperglycemia.

Treatment

The most effective treatment for Diabetes is dietary modification, especially if the dog is overweight or obese. For the most part, dogs with Diabetes require a diet that is higher in fibre than usual to help reduce glucose absorption into the bloodstream. Dogs should be fed multiple small meals per day, possibly accompanied by an insulin injection. Insulin injections can be performed at home, but you should have your veterinarian show you how to properly administer the injection before you try it yourself. With dietary modification and insulin injections, Diabetes is a very manageable disease in dogs.

DISTICHIASIS/TRICHIASIS

Distichiasis and Trichiasis, are basically eyelash disorders. In the case of Distichiasis an eyelash growth is seen in an un-natural part of the eyelid. Trichiasis occurs as an in-growing eyelash. Both cases become problematic if the lash makes contact with the conjunctiva or cornea, which in turn can cause damage.

Both conditions can affect the dog at any age, but is typically noted in younger dogs.

Symptoms

Distichiasis; stiffened eyelash, irritation causing the dog to attempt to rub it, twitching eyelid, excess tears, the cornea develops increased sized blood vessels, ulceration of the cornea, the iris colour may change,

Trichiasis: the iris colour may change, the eyes tend to swell, twitching eyelid, excess tears.

Cause

Typically hereditary

Diagnosis

Physical examination will ascertain which disorder is present. A number of tests including a 'Schirmer tear test' will confirm the extent of tear production. A fluorescein stain is also generally used over the eye to show up possible cornea ulcers. In addition, a test to determine the fluid pressure in the eye is also likely.

Treatment

With Trichiasis, corrective surgery may be required. In minor cases it may be possible to clip the hair to allow temporary relief from irritation.

In the case of Distichiasis corrective treatment may not be necessary depending on the location of hair growth. In minor cases it may be possible to pluck the hairs, but surgery is more likely to offer a permanent solution.

EPILEPSY

This condition is very serious and is the most common neurological condition seen in dogs. It can affect as much as 5% of the canine population. Epilepsy is not actually a single disease. A diagnosis of epilepsy generally refers to any of a number of conditions characterised by recurring seizures. Seizure conditions in dogs can be genetically inherited, caused by anatomical abnormalities in the brain, or they may stem from an unknown cause in some cases.

Symptoms

Involuntary muscle movements or motor seizures, which affect localised areas.

An automatism is a type of motor seizure, which often looks like a voluntary behaviour like chewing or barking. Non-motor seizures do happen in dogs but they are more difficult to detect as they often involve the perception of a sensory stimulus that isn't actually present. You may therefore observe the dog biting at nonexistent flies or staring off into space. An accurate, specific diagnosis

will be required, as seizures can also be caused by brain tumours, blows to the head, distemper, and even liver disease. It is also considered to be linked to 'rage syndrome' in Cocker Spaniels.

Treatment

Unfortunately, there is no cure for canine epilepsy but there are a variety of treatment options available to help control the disease. Anti-epileptic drugs like potassium bromide, phenobarbital, and felbamate are commonly administered to reduce seizure activity. Research is still being conducted regarding the causes of canine epilepsy, both inherited and acquired, in order to make treatment options more effective.

GASTRIC TORSION

Also known as bloat, gastric torsion is a condition that commonly affects medium to large-breed dogs. This condition occurs when the dog's stomach dilates (swells) and then it rotates on its short axis. It can result in a number of serious conditions such as pressure within the abdomen, progressive distension of the stomach, and damage to the cardiovascular system. Decreased perfusion (passage of fluid) may also occur which could lead to damage to the body's cells and a potential for organ failure.

Symptoms

Depression, anxiety, pale gums, appearing sluggish, a pained expression, distended or swollen abdomen, abdominal pain, pacing restlessly, shallow, laboured breathing, unable to stand in later stages of bloat and possible collapse, excessive drooling, vomiting and dry heaving. As the condition progresses the dog may also experience an increased heart rate and a weak pulse. Do not assume that any or all of the symptoms are indicative of torsion. However, as always, seek veterinary assistance without delay if you suspect gastric torsion.

The causes of this condition are largely unknown, but it is considered to be hereditary. It is therefore highly recommended that dogs with a history of the condition should not be used for breeding.

Treatment

Because gastric torsion can quickly escalate and lead to emergency conditions, it is essential that you seek treatment as soon as you suspect the condition. Hospitalisation is generally required, especially if your dog is experiencing cardiovascular symptoms. Once the heart problems have been treated, the pressure in the abdomen will be released through orogastric intubation. After this happens, surgery may be performed to correct the position of the stomach. Additional treatments may be required in some cases to correct additional organ damage.

As a preventive measure it is probably best to feed your dog small meals on elevated dog bowls. Also restrict access to lots of water after vigorous exercise or immediately after and before feeding. Try resting your dog after he has eaten.

GLAUCOMA

Occurrence due to an increase of fluid pressure in the eyeball. In severe acute cases if not treated as an emergency within 24 hours, it can lead to blindness.

Signs and symptoms

Swollen eyeball that clouds over and becomes painful. Occurrence is typically after an injury, lens cataract or dislocation.

Treatment

Again the condition should be treated with immediate effect and may require urgent surgery or medication.

HAEMOPHILIA A (FACTOR VIII DEFICIENCY)

Haemophilia is basically a condition whereby the blood does not clot properly. It is not a common disorder and is typically inherited, mainly affecting males. Mild cases often go undetected throughout a dogs entire life, whereas severe cases often show up during puppyhood.

Symptoms

Again depending on the severity, mild cases may only be apparent during surgery when bleeding may be excessive. When cases are severe, symptoms include: significant bruising, sudden and uncontrollable bleeding from the nose or the gums during tooth loss. Bleeding can also occur within the gastrointestinal tract and bruising may be apparent under the skin and in the joints after activity. Less common cases can include bleeding in the airways or lungs with consequent breathing difficulties. Paralysis may occur if bleeding affects the spinal cord. In extreme cases, without intervention, a simple trauma can lead to excessive blood loss and consequently sudden death.

Diagnosis

In suspected cases, blood testing will be carried out to measure the extent of the clotting factor and consequent dysfunction.

Treatment

Unfortunately there is currently no known cure. Blood transfusions may be carried out on a periodic basis. Transfusions may also be carried out before and after surgery. It goes without saying that avoiding situations where traumas may cause bleeding should be adhered to. This may involve keeping an excitable dog calm, removing hard objects (furniture etc), in the house that are easily bumped into, minimising rough play with other dogs etc. Being on hand to monitor the dog incase of injury, may be necessary to prevent any significant blood loss. As with many problematic cases, affected dogs should never be part of a breeding program.

Although there is currently no cure for affected dogs there is a genetic blood test which can identify the defect. This is very significant in relation to breeding, and no carrier of the disease should ever be part of a breeding program.

HISTIOCYTIC SARCOMA

Histiocytic Sarcoma is considered rare in most breeds but has a relatively high frequency in breeds including the Labrador. Histiocytic sarcomas are generally aggressive and invasive, typically destroying tissue surrounding a tumour, as well as spreading throughout the body.

Organs usually affected include bone marrow, the spleen, brain, joints, lymph nodes, lungs and skin. In certain cases multiple organs can be affected.

Cause

Unfortunately the cause at present is not known.

Symptoms

In general symptoms can include weight loss and consequently anorexia as well as lack of energy. It also depends on which organs are affected and consequent deterioration of specific organs, which obviously affects their normal functioning. For example affected joints will typically involve difficulty with normal movement such as limping. Affected lungs will manifest with difficulty breathing or coughing.

Diagnosis

In most cases a cytology (needle aspiration) or biopsy of the affected tissue and laboratory analysis will confirm the cancer. As there is a risk of spreading cancerous cells throughout the body as the needle is withdrawn, other tests may carried out initially. This may include a full blood count, ultrasound, radiographs etc. Such testing should show any typical spreading to other parts of the body.

Treatment

Surgical removal of any affected tissue, or Radiation/Chemotherapy, are the usual methods of treatment. Unfortunately, where joints are affected, amputation may be necessary as a last resort. In less severe cases Radiation/Chemotherapy therapy may effectively treat the cancer.

Prognosis

If the cancer is caught at an early stage, treatment and consequent survival rates are generally good. If the cancer is particularly aggressive, and has already spread, unfortunately many cases generally do not respond well to therapy. However, individual cases have had relative success to treatment.

HYPERTROPHIC OSTEODYSTROPHY (HOD)

Hypertrophic Osteodystrophy is non infectious, and typically affects the front legs of large breed puppies. Onset is usually between the ages of 2 and 8 months. The structure of the long bone is made up of the 'diaphyses' (the main shaft); the end part of the bone, which grows is known as the 'epiphysis' ; in between those two structures is a conical part known as the 'metaphysis'. The disorder basically occurs when the 'metaphysis' becomes inflamed and develops bony deposits. This in turn causes a widening of the metaphysis. A decrease in blood flow to the metaphysis also leads to a failure of bone formation (ossification).

Cause

At present the cause of the condition remains unknown although a number of possible causes have been speculated. Sources have suggested that excessive calcium supplementation is a possible cause. In a number of cases HOD has also occurred almost immediately after a vaccination. Incidences have commonly occurred in certain breeds leading to the theory that the condition may be hereditary.

Symptoms

Mild or severe lameness; inability to stand; limb shaking; obvious reluctance to apply weight to the affected limb; arching of the spine; Ocular and nasal discharge; Depressive state with an indifference to engage in activity; Warm, swollen limbs; High temperature upwards of 106° F; Lack of appetite and weight loss; Dehydration; Diarrhoea and in some cases pneumonia

In mild cases symptoms can occur and disappear with no further occurrence. In more serious cases the condition can recur with many episodes.

Diagnosis

Physical examination; chemical blood profile; urinalysis; radiograph imaging of affected limbs. Chest (Thoracic) radiograph in suspected cases of pneumonia.

Treatment

Unfortunately at present there is no known cure. In mild cases recovery can occur naturally which can be over a few days or weeks. In severe cases affected limbs can be rendered permanently bowed. Anti inflammatory medication may be prescribed to treat symptoms of pain.

Managing the condition should involve restricted activity such as leash walking with limited to no off leash running. Confined, padded sleeping areas should be provided.

It goes without saying that as the cause may be genetic, dogs diagnosed with the condition, mild or otherwise, should never be part of a breeding program.

HYPOTHYROIDISM

Caused by a deficiency in thyroid hormones. The thyroid is an essential gland in the body, which produces a variety of different hormones that play a role in your dog's metabolism. Reduced production of T3 and T4 hormones (liothyronine and levothyroxine) results in hypothyroidism. Most commonly affects dogs between 4 and 10 years of age. Ironically, spaying is generally recommended as a preventative measure for various diseases, However, spayed/neutered dogs are more at-risk for hypothyroidism than intact dogs.

Symptoms

Lethargy, weakness, mental dullness, unexplained weight gain, hair loss, poor hair growth, scaling, recurring skin infections, intolerance to cold and seizures.

Causes

Iodine deficiency, cancer, etc. and is heredity. It can also be an after-effect of certain medical treatments, even surgery.

Diagnosis

Extensive testing may be required.

Treatment

Typically involves medication and some form of dietary modification. Medical treatments involve synthetic hormone supplements or other medications. Dietary modifications recommended for hypothyroidism include a low-fat diet, especially during the initial phase of therapy. Most dogs respond to treatment for this condition within a few weeks.

IMMUNE MEDIATED ANEMIA

Also known as Immune Mediated Hemolytic Anemia (IMHA), it is a very serious, life threatening condition. The disease occurs when the bodies own immune systems attacks and destroys its own blood cells. As the red blood cells are destroyed complications arise such as jaundice and anaemia, due to an inability of the body to produce sufficient replacement cells. The disease can occur at any time generally between the ages of 1 and 12. Females are also considered to be at a greater risk than males of contracting the disease.

Symptoms

Lethargy; General weakened state and possibly fainting; Lack of interest in activity; Appetite loss; Vomiting and diarrhoea; Increased breathing and heart rate; An increased thirst can occur and consequent urination increase; Feverish; Painful joints; Haemorrhaging can result in darkened faeces, spots, patches, bruises or other skin discolouration.

Causes

A number of causes can be responsible such as: infections, adverse reaction to drugs such as antibiotics, or vaccinations, heart-worms, tumours among other possible causes.

Diagnosis

Physical examination; blood and urine tests; x rays, ultrasound or echocardiographs to examine the status of organs such as the liver, kidney, heart, lungs, etc. Bone marrow samples may also be needed.

Treatment

The condition can be a very serious, even life threatening and will probably require hospitalisation with emergency treatment. Treatment endeavours to arrest further destruction of blood cells, generally stabilising the system. This can include fluid therapy, blood transfusion, possible surgery such as spleen removal. Again suspected cases should seek veterinary attention without delay.

OSTEOCHONDRITIS DISSECANS (OCD)

This condition is basically a deficiency of normal bone growth. In normal bone growth a process known as 'endochondral ossification' occurs whereby excess cartilage is naturally replaced by bone. The pathological disorder Osteochondrosis Dissecans (OCD) prevents this natural process from taking place.

Symptoms

Sudden or gradual lameness involving one or several limbs. Swollen joints; painful limbs particularly through movement; lack of muscle tone; inability to stand normally on affected limb; exacerbated by exercise.

Cause

The exact cause of the condition is not absolutely certain, but generally the disorder seems to be as a result of insufficient blood supply to the bone. Consequently, this results in an excess of cartilage and an absence of bone formation. Evidence also seems to suggest potential nutritional deficiency and a genetic association.

Diagnosis

A physical examination will initially determine which limbs are affected. An initial blood and chemical profile is likely as well as a urinalysis. But these are generally used to ascertain the general health of the dog and not necessarily confirm a diagnosis. Radiographs, X-rays, CT and MRI scans will confirm abnormal joints and any internal lesions. Fluid samples may also be taken, to rule out infections likely to be causing lameness not related to (OCD)

Treatment

Confirmation of the presence of OCD will necessitate corrective surgery. Administration of pain relief and anti-inflammatory medication is also likely.

In less severe cases, medications are available which arrest cartilage degeneration and damage. Upon successful surgery and or medication, advice will be given to limit exercise. Annual check ups are likely to monitor the condition. How well a patient recovers and the quality of life, is dependent on the severity and extent of the condition. Many dogs live a normal life, others are restricted. Restricted exercise can also lead to weight gain, further exacerbating the condition. In such cases a careful diet will be required to avoid obesity.

As there is a potential that the disorder can be genetically passed on, a dog diagnosed with OCD should never be part of a breeding program.

OSTEOSARCOMA

Osteosarcoma is the most common form of bone cancer in dogs. Bone cancer occurs more frequently in larger breeds. It is an aggressive cancer, rapidly spreading throughout the body.

Symptoms

Symptoms can include swelling of the limbs and joints, lameness and pain. Other symptoms may involve weight loss, anorexia, lack of energy, growth masses, localised inflammation of the affected area.

Cause

Although it is frequently associated with larger breeds, this cancer can affect any breed of dog and studies have not linked specifics of gender or genetics. In this respect there is no way of guarding against or preventing the disease.

Diagnosis

X-rays of the affected area will determine the extent of the tumour and other body parts affected. CAT scans, biopsies, blood tests etc, may also be required to confirm the cancer.

Treatment

Although there are treatment options, unfortunately the long term prognosis of a diagnosed bone cancer, is generally poor. Surgical removal of affected areas or amputation may be necessary to remove cancerous tumours. Chemotherapy is usually administered post surgery or as a specific treatment, but generally carries with it a number of side affects. Any such treatments require ongoing tests and evaluations to monitor blood counts. Scans and X-rays will confirm whether the cancer is in remission. Medications are likely to be prescribed for pain management and reduction of possible inflammation.

von Willebrand's Disease

Also sometimes shortened to vWD; von Willebrand's disease is a type of blood disorder. This disease is caused by a deficiency of von Willebrand Factor (vWF) in the blood. vWF is a type of adhesive glycoprotein which is required to facilitate the normal binding of platelets at blood vessel injury sites. Essentially, vWF is required for normal blood clotting.

Von Willebrand's Disease in dogs is similar to haemophilia in humans and it can lead to excessive bleeding following even minor injuries. This condition is autosomal which means it is not linked to a particular sex. Both males and females develop the disease with equal frequency. There are three types of vWD. The more severe forms (2 and 3) are recessive and the milder form (1) is either recessive or incompletely dominant.

The symptoms of von Willebrand's Disease include spontaneous haemorrhage including nosebleeds, bloody faeces, bloody urine, bleeding gums, and vaginal bleeding. Other symptoms may include bruising, prolonged bleeding after injury or surgery, and blood loss anaemia. This disease is caused by a genetic mutation that impairs the synthesis, release, and stability of von Willebrand Factor. Diagnosis of vWD involves a physical exam as well as blood chemical profiles, blood count, and urinalysis. Platelet counts may be taken as well. Treatment for vWD often involves blood transfusion to increase the vWF supply in the blood.

2) Additional Labrador Allergy Information

Allergy sufferers

Although dogs can be a problem for allergy sufferers, cats are more likely to cause a reaction. Certain breeds are described as being hypoallergenic, which is a coat type that doesn't cause allergic reactions. However, the truth of the matter is that no dog is completely hypoallergenic. It was originally thought that the hair caused allergic reaction. But in actual fact, the dead, dry skin flakes, or dander is the main cause of an allergic reaction. To a certain extent, allergens are also found in urine and saliva.

Minimal shedding breeds, such as those with a single shorter coat are considered to be the best options for allergy sufferers.

Dog allergies can be problematic, and any dog can be prone to or become allergic to anything from the dust in the home to grains in his diet.

Wheat Allergies

Wheat and grain allergy can cause so many health problems that grain free dog food is actually becoming quite a common product and many pet stores have at least one available variety, if not multiple types. What is wheat allergy though, and what problems can it cause Labrador dogs and their puppies? Wheat related health problems in dogs are actually split into three different reactions; wheat allergy, gluten allergy and gluten intolerance. Each has a slightly different reaction on the body, all with equal detriment.

In short, wheat in a dog's diet can lead to a number of different allergy related symptoms of varying severity. Take a look;

Itchy skin; Open sores; Ear infections; Breathing problems; Hives; Itching of the mouth or throat; Itchy and watery eyes; General itchiness; Dry skin; Lack of coat condition and dandruff; Loose bowel movements (diarrhoea); Nasal congestion; Rash; Skin swelling; Vomiting.

Gluten sensitivity is a reaction specific to gluten, found within wheat, symptoms include;

Changes in behaviour; Pain; Muscle cramps; Weight loss; Fatigue.

The biology behind allergic reactions, in very simple terms, is that a substance or foreign body attacks the immune system of the dog. When the dog is eating a diet high in something that he is allergic to, the body has to constantly fight the introduction of the substance in the body. This leaves the dog's immune system weakened and less able to cope with other infections and illnesses. Although wheat is one of the major factors in dog food allergy, there are many more. Ingredients in dog food range vastly dependent on the brand. Additionally they can include bright colours (to appeal to you, the dog owner) unnatural flavours and shocking chemical preservatives.

3) PREVENTING ILLNESS –– VACCINATIONS

Though you may not be able to prevent your Labrador from developing certain inherited conditions if he already has a genetic predisposition, there are certain diseases you can prevent with vaccinations. During the first few weeks of life, your Labrador puppy relies on the antibodies he receives from his mother's milk to fend off infection and illness. Once his own immune system develops however, you will be able to administer vaccines to prevent certain diseases such as canine distemper, parvovirus, and rabies.

Vaccinations for dogs can be divided into two categories: core vaccines, and non-core vaccines. Core vaccines are those that every dog should receive. Non-core vaccines are administered based on your dog's level of risk. Depending on where you live and how often your Labrador comes into contact with other dogs, you may not need to administer any non-core vaccines. According to the AVMA, recommended core vaccines for dogs include: distemper, canine adenovirus, canine parvovirus, and rabies. Non-core vaccines include: coronavirus, leptospirosis, Bordetella bronchiseptica, canine para-influenza, and Borrelia burgdorferi. You will need to speak to your veterinarian about non-core vaccines to determine which ones your Labrador does and doesn't need.

The rabies vaccine can be very stressful for dogs and unfortunately, it is necessary in the United States due to the prevalence of rabies in wild animals. Rabies has been eradicated in the U.K. so dogs living in this area will not need rabies vaccines. It is important to note, however, that some US states require an annual rabies vaccine, so be sure to check with your local council regarding requirements in your area. In any case, do not administer a rabies vaccine less than one month before or after a combination vaccine.

Your veterinarian will be able to provide you with specific vaccination recommendations for your Labrador

Please note: Titre testing is commonly practiced to establish whether a dog that has been immunised, is in need of a booster for a specific vaccine. This is carried out by a simple laboratory blood test. If sufficient antibodies are present, then there is no need to vaccinate with that specific vaccine. Please note that regular, unnecessary vaccinating can have an adverse affect on your dog's health. It would also constitute a waste of money.

Also please remember that vaccinations for your puppy are vital if you wish to protect him against horrific, life threatening diseases. Please bear in mind that your puppy is at risk until his vaccination injections are complete, and usually a week after that. It is therefore important that he does not come into direct contact with other dogs as well as potentially infected faeces and urine.

What is the procedure for the vaccinations programme?

- In the UK a puppy is generally vaccinated at 7 to 8 weeks followed by a booster 2 weeks later.
- It is usually advisable that they are still at risk until after another week, so three weeks in total; they then receive an annual booster (subject to titre tested mentioned previously).
- In this case, if the puppy receives his first jab at 8 weeks old, he can potentially be free to socialise at 11 weeks of age.
- Vaccination schedules in the U.S.A. are a little different.
- Again a puppy will start a course of vaccinations at 6 to 8 weeks of age.
- A minimum of 3 separate vaccinations will be administered, usually at 3 to 4 week intervals with a final dose given at 16 weeks of age.
- So obviously in the case of USA vaccinations, 16 weeks is realistically the soonest your puppy should be free to socialise. This does also depend on what your vet advises as being a safe time after their final jab.
- Once your puppy has finished his vaccination schedule and your vet has given the all clear for him to safely go outside again, then socialisation can continue relatively risk free.

Further information can be found at the following web links:

USA links

http://pets.webmd.com/dogs/
guide/routine-vaccinations-puppies-
dogs

http://www.peteducation.com/article.
cfm?c=2+2115&aid=950

UK links

http://www.thekennelclub.org.uk/get-
ting-a-dog-or-puppy/general-advice-
about-caring-for-your-new-puppy-or-
dog/general-puppy-health/

http://www.rspca.org.uk/
adviceandwelfare/pets/general/vacci-
nating

http://www.pets4homes.co.uk/pet-
advice/puppy-vaccinations-how-when-
and-why.html

4) PET INSURANCE – DO YOU NEED IT

Many new dog owners wonder whether pet insurance is a good option or whether it is a waste of money. The truth of the matter is that it is different in different cases. Pet insurance does for your pet what health insurance does for you; it helps to mitigate your out-of-pocket costs by providing coverage for certain services. While health insurance for humans covers all kinds of health care including preventive care, disease treatment, and accident coverage, pet insurance is a little more limited. Some pet insurance plans only cover accidents while others cover illnesses. Some plans cover certain preventive care options like spay/neuter surgery or vaccinations, but generally only during a puppy's first year.

The costs for pet insurance plans vary from one company to another and from one plan to another. Pet insurance works in a very different way than health insurance when it comes to payment. With a health insurance plan you might be asked to pay a co-payment to your doctor when you

visit his office but the health plan will forward the remaining payment directly to the provider. With a pet insurance plan you will generally be required to pay for the treatment up-front and then submit a claim to receive reimbursement for costs up to 90%. The actual amount a pet insurance plan will cover varies from one plan to another and it may depend on the deductible you select as well.

Just as you would with a health insurance plan, having a pet insurance plan requires you to pay a monthly premium. As long as you remain current with those payments, however, you are eligible to receive benefits from the plan. Again keep in mind however, that most pet insurance plans have some kind of deductible in place. A deductible is a set amount that you must pay out-of-pocket before the plan will offer reimbursement for covered services. In many cases, pet insurance plans are useful only for large expenses such as cancer treatments that you normally might not be able to cover at a moment's notice. It is not, however, generally cost-effective for things like annual vet exams and vaccinations.

Unless you opt for a recommended plan, perhaps from your vet, please do a Google search, shop around and always read the small print.

CHAPTER TWENTY ONE:

LABRADOR BEHAVIOUR PROBLEMS

In this area of the book we will look at potential behaviour problems that the Labrador may develop. Like people, dogs have their own specific personalities. The behaviour that the Labrador displays is partly based on his nature, and mostly a result of the nurturing effect that life has bestowed on him so far. Most canine problems can be halted before they get too severe, or even modified into manageable acts. It is important to have an understanding

of behaviour before trying to make any changes.

Please Note: With the exception of food related problems and some physiological disorders, most of these behaviour are simply a symptom of boredom, lack of mental stimulation and a lack of exercise. More often than not, when these matters are addressed, many behaviour problems disappear.

Also please be aware that puppy mills and other bad breeding practices, have been known to breed dogs that have a number of serious issues. These include dogs that can be neurotic and aggressive with a tendency to bite, as well as a host of serious physical health issues.

As with physical health issues, the following behavioural disorders have been noted in some dogs of this breed. This may be of a relatively small frequency. You should therefore not be overly concerned about your dog developing a number of these conditions. Your dog may not be affected by any of them, but again, forewarned is forearmed.

1) DEALING WITH COMMON BEHAVIOUR PROBLEMS

It is not fair to generalise, as two dogs of the same breed could be either high maintenance or no trouble at all. As previously noted however, if your dog doesn't get enough exercise or attention he is likely to develop problem behaviours which in serious cases may require professional training to correct.

Much of what follows will go against the the general descriptions you will read for most Labradors as perfect, placid easy-going dogs. However, unfortunately these problems have occurred in certain cases.

Possessiveness, resource guarding, jumping up, digging etc are all possibilities. Aggressive, nasty behaviour has also been noted in certain puppy farmed dogs or through other irresponsible breeding practices. Similar problems can occur with temperament, behavioural issues of puppy farmed dogs such as biting, aggression towards other dogs, people, territorial aggression etc. Such dogs can also be prone to timidity, fearfulness, submissive urination fawning and grovelling.

Bad, irresponsible breeding has also unfortunately resulted in dogs with health problems and shortened lives.

Labradors can also be moderately excitable, although not to the extent that this would be deemed a problem.

However, enthusiastic mouthing and licking of hands and faces often occurs, particularly as a puppy and adolescent.

Being relatively jowly, can lead them to being slobberers. As carrying objects in their mouths is a regular occurrence, it is advisable to therefore provide plenty of toys and other objects that you do not mind covered in spit. He may also be inclined to chew items other than his toys, so you will need to be mindful of what items you leave lying around.

Also expect toys or other items to be carried, presented to you or otherwise dropped everywhere.

Labradors tend to be glutenous, so strict diets are a must as ad lib feeding will see a dog quickly becoming overweight, particularly if he does not receive adequate exercise.

Labradors are another of the so called 'velcro breeds', wishing to be by their owners side. This along with pestering for attention can be annoying for some people.

Although generally considered to be attentive and alert, some can also be easily distracted by scents etc, whilst out on walks. Their strong scenting ability can also lead them to wander if they pick up an interesting scent. It is therefore imperative that off lead exercise is only carried out in safe areas, away from busy roads. In this respect, early training for control and obedience is a must. A secure fenced yard or garden is also a must as he will be inclined to escape and wander given the chance.

Lead pulling, and the dog taking the owner for a walk, can also be an issue if the dog is not taught basic obedience to prevent this.

What you first of all need to understand before you try to tackle any behaviour problem, is that many behaviours that you might consider problematic are actually natural behaviours for your dog. For example, chewing is a very natural way for puppies to learn about their world. They also do it to ease the pain of teething or to alleviate boredom, tension or anxiety. When your puppy fulfils his need to chew by gnawing on an expensive pair of shoes, is when the behaviour becomes a problem. The best way to deal with problem behaviours is not to teach your puppy to avoid the behaviour altogether but to channel that behaviour toward a more appropriate outlet. So in this case, it is a simple matter of providing plenty of chew toys, and not allowing him access to anything you do not wish chewed. Below you will find tips for dealing with some of the most common behaviour problems potentially affecting this breed:

The following is presented in alphabetical order. It is not meant to indicate problems in any order of importance or severity.

A) AGGRESSION

Aggression is one of, if not the most commonly reported disorders affecting dogs and their owners. In the U.S.A for example, it is estimated that between 3 and 5 million dog bites are reported annually. Many of these affect children and are of a serious nature, in some cases fatal. Aggression between other dogs is also a common problem.

Aggression is a broad ranging problem and can include incidences relating to the following: resource guarding relating to food or general possessiveness; fear; defence; territorial; familiar and unfamiliar people; familiar and unfamiliar dogs; other causes of an idiopathic nature such as epilepsy.

Important note: Many 'minor' cases of aggression can be dealt with by following a program of behaviour modification at home. However, for more serious cases it is highly recommended that you consult a dog behaviour specialist, perhaps via your vet.

AGGRESSION WITH OTHER DOGS

Main causes

Imposed restrictions such as fences, leashes or being chained up. This in turn prevents a dogs natural access to other dogs, in order to greet and socialise normally. This can typically occur during a puppies 12 to 16 week 'critical period'.

In some cases dogs are encouraged to be hostile and suspicious of strangers in an attempt to make them 'guard dogs' or 'watchdogs'. The dog that is chained up, becomes more aggressive. This is similar to the situation when out on lead walks as owners pull or jerk the dog away from another dog walker, further exacerbating the aggression.

Punishment or threat based training techniques can also exacerbate aggression. Conversely it can create submissive or fear responses.

Preventative measures

Correct and adequate socialisation is the most obvious remedy for this problem. Correctly socialised dogs are highly unlikely to experience problems. However, that is not to say that under socialised or hostile dogs will not attempt to attack your dog. Again, refer to chapter 13 for more detail.

Controlling the problem

A dog that has a tendency for aggression towards other dogs, might not entirely lose the tendency. However, it is possible to modify and desensitise the behaviour with the following techniques:

- A reliable well trained 'recall', is a very important factor here.
- Use of a training leash, around 5 meters to give him greater freedom.
- Try and maintain a slack leash by allowing him to safely wander, but train him to regularly come back to you. Gradually expose him to other dogs in order to condition him coming back to you, in preference to going to the other dog.
- Do not display hostility towards another dog that you may wish to usher away from your dog. This can often trigger aggression from your dog.

- As with any training, avoid acknowledging unacceptable behaviour simply by ignoring the behaviour.
- Castration in males can lessen aggressive tendencies but this is not 100%.

Aggression towards adults and children

IMPORTANT:

For obvious reasons of safety, if this is a problem, you should seek professional help. Your vet will be able to diagnose a possible medical cause that may require medication. Otherwise for behaviour problems, help should come from either an experienced dog trainer or behaviourist.

Gundogs in general are not known for aggression towards people, but can become aggressive if mishandled.

Please again refer to the previous chapters 11 for introducing your dog to children, and chapter 13 for socialisation.

A Note on Growling

It is important to know your own dog, where growling is concerned. Take a look at the scenario within which the growl occurs. Observe your dog's body language and the signs that show how he must be feeling, before deciding why your dog may be growling.

Generally in the dog world, growling is an early warning system that something is not right. The growl from an aggressive dog can be delivered seconds before a bite. If a dog growls at your approach or attention, then it is a request to be left alone. You should adhere to that, for the dog has very few methods of communicating his wishes.

Dog growling during play and tug games is actually common. So if your Labrador growls when he is playing, it is probably him expressing himself rather than a display of aggression. Although it can sound pretty fierce, play based growling is usually nothing to worry about.

B) ATTENTION SEEKING: WHINING, BEGGING, BARKING, PAWING ETC.

Unfortunately, in many cases this problems starts when the dog is a cute, adorable puppy. It is actually normal behaviour for a young puppy to seek care and assurance from their adult carers, whether human or their mother.

However, it is important that the puppy learns to become an adult and not depend or rely on us to baby them.

It is easy to unwittingly teach a dog to seek attention with the following:

Constantly lifting the puppy up, cuddling and carrying him; Giving into him barking, whining, pawing etc, and attempting to pacify him by giving him a treat; Stroking him if he licks, paws or conducts any other unwanted behaviour; Even pushing him down or away is giving him attention; During meal times, giving him food from the table when he sits and begs; Encouraging him to jump up and stroking him when he does.

Of course it is beneficial to you and your dog that you should stroke, cuddle, pet him etc. However, this has to be done on your terms. In other words only doing so if and when he is not pawing, barking, whining etc. This should hopefully reassure him that you will stroke him, but not when he whines, barks or paws.

Preventing the problem:

We unwittingly reinforce these unwanted behaviours by indulging and giving into the behaviour, therefore reinforcing, rather than ignoring the behaviour. If you do not mind these behaviours then fine, but otherwise it is not advisable to indulge the dog by stroking or praising him when he persistently carries out potentially annoying behaviours.

Make sure he is getting plenty of exercise and play time during the day. In other words, alleviating boredom and getting your attention.

It is very Important to avoid confusing the dog. The only realistic way to achieve this is for every person who comes into contact with the dog to stick to a few simple rules.

Do not feed your dog treats from the table. Even if this is very occasional, you are still encouraging or reinforcing him to continue begging.

Occasionally you may have to temporarily leave your dog in the yard or garden or a room in the house (of course this assumes you are also in the house). If he starts whining, barking or pawing at the door, only let him back in when he stops those behaviours.

He may come to you when you are busy doing something else, and start pawing, whining, jumping up or barking. Again, do not give into him, but simply ignore this by turning or walking away, perhaps into another room and close the door. Wait for a few seconds until your Labrador stops the attention seeking, then return to the room and pet him calmly. Repeat this sequence every time your dog whines, paws, barks at you, and he will eventually learn that these behaviours do not earn him your attention.

If he seems to be relying on you, or pestering you all the time, another dog may be the answer or involve other people in walking him or playing games.

Do not be overly protective, keeping him away from situations that he needs to be exposed to. Give him the freedom to 'safely' explore and discover his surroundings. Socialisation should give him many opportunities to confront unusual situations.

c) BARKING

Dogs can easily become victims of poisoning, from what you may consider as malicious neighbours who are annoyed with a dog that incessantly barks or comes into their garden digging up flower beds, harassing the cat, defecating etc. It is usually against council regulations to allow dog fouling and incessant barking. Obviously your neighbours have a right to enjoy their home environments in peace.

Dog barking can be a useful warning or deterrent for would be intruders, but can be problematic if this becomes habitual or excessive. Certain guard dog breeds are selected for the specific purpose of barking to warn off intruders. The unfortunate downside to this, is the dog that reacts and barks at the slightest thing and consequently cause problems with neighbours.

Please consider the problems you may encounter with neighbours and local councils if you live in a built up urban area or apartment block. You can control barking to an extent whilst you are home, but if the dog is on its own for large parts of the day, you will not know until you receive a complaint. Certain local authorities can impose warnings if complaints are made or even court orders enforcing action from the dog owner and fines or bans for non compliance.

Why dogs bark

A key reason dogs bark is through boredom. Please refer to the section on boredom that follows.

Dogs that habitually bark, do so for a variety of reasons such as fear; asking to be let inside the house; through separation anxiety when alone or because they derive pleasure from the act.

It is also thought that excessive barking is strongly linked with how reactive the dog is. Terriers are a typical example and again this is related to their excitability levels, activity or hyperactivity levels, snappy and affection seeking.

In most cases a breed that is relatively unreactive is unlikely to bark. An exception to this is a low reactive breed such as a Beagle, a breed that is expected to bark as part of hunting, letting hunters on horseback know which direction the fox is heading.

Preventing a problem:

Once you have addressed possible problems associated with boredom, the following should help. You will often find that if you leave your dog out in a fenced yard or garden, he is likely to hear sounds that trigger him to bark. The obvious solution to this is to bring him back into the house.

The easiest way to teach your dog to stop barking if you are present, is actually to teach him to bark on command first.

For this you will need to have a friend stand outside your front door and to ring the doorbell.

Get your Labrador's attention and give him the cue word 'speak' > As soon as you give the command, have your friend ring the doorbell to get your dog to bark > When he barks, praise him excitedly and reward him with a treat.

After a few repetitions, your dog should start barking on command before the doorbell rings when you issue the 'speak' cue word.

Once your dog learns to respond to you by barking on command, you can then teach him a 'hush' command. Give your Labrador the 'speak' command and let him bark a few times before telling him 'hush'. When he stops barking, praise him excitedly and reward him with a treat.

Repeat this sequence several times until your Labrador gets the hang of barking when you say 'speak' and stopping when you say 'hush'. Labradors are an intelligent breed that will be eager to please, so this shouldn't take too many repetitions.

So to recap, first teach the dog to bark and add a command ('Speak/Bark') to it. Next, start to reinforce the short pauses between barks and add a command ('Hush/Quiet') to THEM. The dog will soon learn that the pauses are rewarded too. Therefore he is rewarded for being quiet as well as when he barks. It may seem odd that you are teaching the dog to bark, the very thing you are trying to avoid. This is merely for exercise or control purposes as you would otherwise have to wait for your dog to start barking before implementing a stop barking command.

The command word you use could also be 'quiet' or 'be quiet', rather than 'hush'. It is important that your timing is correct as you want him to know at what point he receives a treat for being quiet. Again, once he is barking on cue and being quiet on cue, stop rewarding him for barking. So you will no longer reward the barking, but you ARE rewarding him being 'quiet'. From now on, when he barks, issue the 'hush' cue and treat him when he immediately stops. Of course, it is unlikely that you will stop the natural impulse for him to bark, but at least now, you should be able to quickly stop him.

d) Biting (fear or otherwise)

Biting is an inherently natural thing for any dog to do. The Wolf for example, during the hunting process, has to bite in order to survive. This is most notable when either killing prey to eat, or attacking an 'enemy' Wolf straying into their territory. It is therefore unsurprising that the dog has inherited this tendency. Dogs naturally explore and investigate using their mouths. Movement can also trigger the game of chasing and biting.

Although the media reports many cases of dog bites, these are not always the so called dangerous dog breeds such as the Staffordshire/Pitbull types, Rottweilers etc. Smaller dog breeds including terriers, Sporting/Gundogs etc are also breeds that have been linked with dog bites. Arguably Labradors are a breed who can be indifferent to obedience training and children and if not properly handled have a predisposition to become hostile or even bite.

Also see sections (a), (f), (i), (q), (r), (s), (v)

Preventative measures

Bite inhibition is something that the puppy has to learn. This is not to be confused with teething which generally involves biting on relatively hard objects to relieve the discomfort of teething.

As previously noted elsewhere, providing plenty of chew toys and restricting access to any item likely to be chewed, is the first step.

Be aware that a playful puppy or dog may react to your movements or clothing likely to move; loose clothing and shoelaces are a prime target.

e) Boredom

Lack of exercise, mental stimulation, attention, being restricted to the house, yard or garden for extended periods, are all reasons dogs become bored. Signs that a dog is bored include, digging, attempting to jump your boundary fence, destroy furnishings and other items etc.

Feral or stray dogs have the freedom to roam and so are highly unlikely to develop symptoms of boredom. Obviously letting your dog roam the streets is not the answer. Dogs need similar mental and physical outlets to us, and to deny them this would be akin to being imprisoned, in solitary confinement.

Preventing the problem:

Provide opportunities for him to explore his environment out on walks and 'safe area' off lead runs on a daily basis.

Be prepared for him to keep stopping to sniff where other dogs have been and to scent mark. This is often more important to the dog. So it is very important that you allow him this time, and do not drag him away.

Be aware that his hunting instinct does not disappear just because he is well fed and not hungry. He will therefore be keen to follow the scent of another animal.

Allow him the opportunity to meet other dogs. It is important to note that unless another dog is hostile and dog aggressive, most dogs are generally well behaved when not restricted by a leash.

Human interaction is also very important. Leaving a dog home alone all day is never a good idea. If possible take the dog to work, or employ a dog sitter or ask a neighbour, friend or family member to keep him company and take him for walks etc.

Long leashes, between 3 and 5 meters in length, allow the dog to safely wander. You also minimise lead pulling. However, be careful near busy roads as your dog could easily wander into the road. Be careful with retractable leads as many have a breaking strain of 30 to 40kg. The pulling power of most dogs is considerably more than their actual weight. So if a dog suddenly lunges, perhaps having seen a cat, the retractable can easily snap.

F) CHASING

All dogs have a prey drive to varying degrees, which in some cases is very strong, in others hardly noticeable. Breeds such as the Terrier, Gundog, Hound etc have a strong instinctive prey drive that was particularly useful for hunting centuries ago and to a certain extent to this day.

However in most cases it can be a problematic trait as dogs chase cats, cyclists, rabbits, livestock etc. Dogs that have a strong tendency to chase need to be de-sensitised with lots of socialisation and exposure to such triggers. Training may also be necessary for them to resist the temptation to chase. As a last resort, the dog may have to be kept on a lead or kept away from situations and locations likely to trigger a chase.

Older dogs moving into a new home can also be a problem with small pets such as guinea pigs, cats, rabbits or even smaller dogs.

Most Sporting/Gundogs are an inquisitive breed and will want to investigate anything unusual. If let off the lead this could well involve chasing after small animals or following scents.

It is important to be generally aware of certain consequences of chasing behaviour that could affect any dog. Chasing wildlife, livestock or similar animals, can be a problem with most dog breeds. Just as other animals are easy targets, so are cars, pedestrians and bikes. Chasing behaviour can also be a very dangerous game with potential fatal consequences. In the UK for example, a farmer is

legally entitled to shoot a dog chasing his livestock.

The steps that we take to reform chasing behaviour are similar to those which we use for social fear. It is a gradual process of teaching the dog to stay relaxed with the trigger at a distance. Eventually you build the dog's capacity to be near the trigger whilst he also stays relaxed and controlled.

It's important to focus on your dog's behaviour carefully, and reinforce every time he looks towards you instead of at the trigger. If you can master this art alone, then your control over the behaviour of your Labrador dog will improve dramatically.

The law and your dog

Included in the following resources you will find the sort of information that may be applicable to you, depending on your global location. The document includes keeping your dog on a leash under certain circumstances including country walks.

A short 16 page PDF document produced by The Kennel Club UK, will give you basic information regarding the law and your dog.

The Kennel Club UK

https://www.thekennelclub.org.uk/ media/8277/law.pdf

Additionally do a Google search using a search term such as [the law and dogs], for more information. Obviously this is applicable if you are searching in the UK, simply add your location 'USA' etc for specific laws and legislations where you live.

Preventing the problem:

Again, socialisation and de-sensitising the dog from anything likely to trigger a chase response will probably be necessary. Ideally this should take place when still puppies, particularly during their critical period. Older dogs however, can be exposed in the same way, but results may take longer.

Once a dog has given chase, this becomes their reward or reinforcement and is often difficult to suppress or change. It therefore becomes necessary to use training and control measures.

Fortunately much of gundog training is designed to suppress the natural instinct to give chase. A reliable 'stop' and 'recall' command is very important preliminary requirement, as well as basic obedience of 'sit' and 'stay'. Once these training commands are reliable, you are then ready to start exposing your dog to situations likely to trigger a chase.

Whenever introducing your dog to unfamiliar animals, it is vital that you attach a long training leash of about 5 meters, in case he gives chase, possibly across a busy road.

If you are likely to exercise your dog in the countryside you should ideally introduce your dog to the type of farm animals or horses he is likely to encounter as follows:

Approach the animals at a distance with his training leash attached. Allow slack on the lead, but do not give him 2 or 3 meters incase he decides to chase. He could cause himself a neck injury if he comes to an abrupt halt.

1. Once you are reasonably close, provided he has not reacted by barking or lunging on the leash, get him to sit and stay for a few moments. Give him a treat and lots of praise occasionally to reward him for remaining calm.

2. Now move closer repeating (2). If at any point he loses control and attempts to chase, as (1), make sure he does not have too much slack. He should pull up short after a few feet anyway, at which point ask him to sit.

3. If you have taught him the 'stop' command, blow the stop whistle if his body language suggests he is about to give chase. You can also use the verbal cue, 'no' or 'ah ah' at the same time.

4. Once he is again calm, continue to slowly move forward. It is important that you praise and reward him when he is calm, and don't give in to him chasing.

You should be able to use the same procedure if chasing cyclists or joggers is a problem. In this case I would firstly advise asking a friend to cycle or jog by. Again, begin at a distance and gradually move closer. Reward him when he remains calm, and ensure you hold his leash securely so he cannot suddenly take off. Other domestic animals such as cats can be dealt with in a similar way.

G) CHEWING

The simplest way of preventing your Labrador from chewing items you do not want chewed, is to make sure that he has plenty of chew toys available. Many dogs also chew on items out of boredom, so ensuring that your Labrador gets enough exercise and play time, will also help to prevent him from chewing on things around the house. If chewing does become a problem all you need to do is replace the item your dog is chewing on with one of his toys (swapping). Ideally you would have taken care of such items in your initial puppy proofing stage. However, we can't always be present or be sure which items he will chew and which he will ignore. You are therefore better off keeping every potential chewable item that you wish to keep intact, out of his reach.

If after this you still find your Labrador has found something you had forgotten about and is chewing on it, do not make a fuss about this, or show displeasure, but simply say 'NO' or 'leave', and take the object away. Immediately replace the object with your dog's favourite toy, then praise him when he starts chewing on it. Eventually your Labrador will learn what he is and is not allowed to chew on around the house.

H) DESTRUCTIVENESS

Unfortunately many dogs have been euthanised due to a lack of understanding as to why they are chewing or destroying household furnishings. Again this is a symptom of insufficient exercise, lack of mental stimulation and general boredom. The dogs are not necessarily being delinquents, they are merely acting out of frustration at not having an outlet for pent up energy.

Tug of war games are often encouraged as a good game to play with our dogs. However, it is also thought that this encourages destructive activities such as tugging or ripping curtains, washing hanging out to dry and other hanging objects.

Preventing the problem:

In the first instance make sure that the dog is getting enough exercise, mental stimulation with games and general attention. Additionally refer to the advice for the boredom problem.

Ensure he has a large array of chew and other toys to keep him preoccupied.

Avoid games which encourage the behaviour such as tug of war. Retrieving is an excellent alternative that will burn off energy as well as mentally stimulate him. Throwing a stick or ball has a similar effect. You could also try activities such as 'scent work'. These activities are also ideal for dog owners whose mobility may be an issue.

Again referring back to proofing your house. If you have to leave him unattended for however short a time, it may be necessary to restrict access to rooms such as your lounge where he may be tempted to destroy your sofa etc.

i) DOMINANCE

The general perception of gundog breeds, is that they were selectively bred to work with and tolerate other dogs. Typically these other dogs may not have been part of that particular dogs social group. However, this is a generalisation and individual cases can result in dogs that do not necessarily fit that mould. It is therefore possible that dominance, possessiveness and aggression can occur with any individual dog within a breed group.

Dominance/Status

In most cases a dog will be a member of a number of social groups. A first group will no doubt include humans within the immediate family and then a wider circle of friends and neighbours. A second group may possibly include other dogs living in the household.

A hierarchy or pecking order will typically occur when two or more dogs share the same household. A puppy will probably be submissive or subordinate to an adult. However, once the puppy matures and gains strength the status can easily change. Two or more adults may live harmoniously without conflict, or a dominance, submissive 'game playing' may take place.

What is important is in these situations is that we remain in control of any potential conflicts. Such conflicts can easily escalate into aggressive behaviour which could be dangerous to the dogs as well as human family members.

Preventing the problem:

Preventing a competitive environment is important here. If it is possible to leave toys, gnarl bones lying around, have plenty spread over a wide area. This will avoid a central focus for one dog to

guard and create a potential conflict.

Also become the controller of the resources. It will therefore be necessary to allow play time with toys. However, if confrontations occur, remove all of them until things have calmed down. The dogs should hopefully learn that the toys are a reward for good behaviour and unacceptable behaviour results in their removal.

The dogs as a group may well establish a 'pecking order' between themselves. However, it is important to not favour any in particular to prevent any jealousies occurring.

Teaching cooperation and group harmony:

Each dog should already be well experienced with the 'recall' and 'sit'

1. Call the dogs together and ask them for a 'sit' and 'stay' > Once they are all sat facing you, randomly and quickly give each one a piece of food.
2. Walk away > 'recall' them > ask for a 'sit' and 'stay' > once they all comply > give each a piece of food.
3. Repeat this several times and on a regular basis. If at any point they attempt to jostle, compete or show any aggression towards the other, ignore the behaviour and walk away. Then repeat the steps until they harmoniously obey the command and patiently wait for each other to receive a food treat.

Try and keep them all together so that they work as a unit and see the benefit of each others company. This will teach the dog that cooperation will get a reward, competing with each other will not.

Dominance aggression

IMPORTANT: In severe aggressive cases it is important to consult with a professional behaviourist/trainer. Quite often the context of the situation can be too specific to make a general 'one solution fits all cases'.

Modification of mild cases would normally involve a variety of solutions. For example if any kind of handling elicits a growl, it would be necessary to gradually introduce the dog, probably giving treats to make the experience pleasant for the dog.

If the dog attempts to guard or possess a particular toy, the couch, access to these should be denied.

This type of aggression occurs when, for example two dogs are in conflict for the control of a resource. It can also occur if a dogs perceived social status is challenged. As well as other dogs, this aggressive response can be directed towards humans. This is often more noticeable towards immediate family members rather than strangers. Dogs can challenge human members of the family, such as when the dog is asked to move from the couch.

In such cases it is important that the owner of the dog becomes the keeper or controller of the resources. It may be necessary to teach the dog to regularly give up or swap their toys or other objects the dog may wish to guard. The dog also needs to regularly comply with the basic control commands 'sit', 'come', 'stay', 'stop', 'heel', 'down' etc.

The aggression can range from subtle posturing, growling to full on biting. The occurrence of this type of behaviour is usually from one year old as the dog starts to mature, but it can occur sooner. The behaviour can occur with either sex whether neutered or not, but commonly occurs with un-neutered males.

Dominance and possessiveness

The extent to which a dog will react to an item he wishes to possess, depends on the value they place on the item. It can also depend on how the dog views the 'status' of the other dog or human, as to whether he will challenge them. In the same respect a dog may react depending on historical experiences of previous conflicts.

At its very basic level, food is seen as valuable in order to survive. But the same instinct to posses does not necessarily apply to all elements necessary for survival. Water is probably more important for their survival as they can survive without food much longer than water. However, dogs rarely if ever fight over water. But dogs can become obsessive about items such as toys, balls, nylon gnarl bones, a favourite bed, couch or other sleeping area etc.

If the dog feels one of their valuable resources is about to be taken away, they may threaten and possibly attack. You will typically see the dog stiffen, growl, snarl, bare their teeth, snap, bite etc.

Preventing the problem:

It is important to never use physical reprimands, shout or otherwise raise your voice, as it is likely to worsen the situation. For example, the dog may growl before you physically remove him from the sofa. However, next time the dog may have learned that growling does not work so they may snarl or snap.

It is easier to condition a puppy to relinquish or swap an item. Than it is for an adult. This is best approached by getting him used to early retrieves. That is, he willingly gives up an item in exchange for lots of praise or food.

Getting him off the sofa:

Teaching a dog to come away from a sofa is best achieved by encouraging him with a food.

1. With a piece of food in your hand, place this to your dogs nose, but not allowing him to take it.
2. Now lure him by gradually pulling your hand away from his nose towards the floor. If he seems reluctant, try his favourite toy or other item. If he is particularly reluctant you could also try placing a piece of food on the sofa for him to take. Once he has taken this, place another piece on the floor, which hopefully he will jump down to take.
3. The moment he jumps down use the command word 'down' or 'off' if 'down' confuses him, and he lies down on the sofa > give him lots of praise when he jumps down. It may also be necessary to place an object on the sofa so that he cannot jump straight back on again.
4. Practice this as often as necessary, with food at first and then just using the 'down'/'off', and perhaps luring with your hand, but without food.

Once you have a controlled response from him, it is your choice whether you occasionally allow him back on the sofa. As long as you can easily get him off if you have to.

Getting him to give up an item (swapping):

This can be carried out a number of ways. Usually swapping is used to take an item off him, such as a shoe, and replace this with a toy or gnarl bone.

This is best approached by first of all having a toy, chew or gnarl bone to hand and a piece of food.

1. Offer the item (toy, gnarl bone) to him, which hopefully he will take, but keep hold of the item.
2. Now with the food in the other hand, present this to him and at the same time use the word 'leave' or 'give'.
3. As soon as the dog releases the item, give him the food and offer lots of praise.
4. Practice this a number of times so that the dog is conditioned to handing over items they are in possession of. Gradually phase out giving food and offer praise only.

Swapping an item the dog already has:

This assumes that the dog already has an item that he is playing with or chewing on.

1. Take another item, toy or gnarl bone in one hand and show this to him. He may immediately drop the item he has and take the item you are offering.
2. If not, as you show the toy, slowly move your hand towards the shoe or other item the dog has. Avoid any sudden movements as this may encourage him to snap.
3. Gently take hold of the item and use the word 'leave' or 'give'. Hopefully he will let go of that and take the item you are offering. If not, try the previous exercise with food.

Regularly practice this exercise so that he gets used to relinquishing items and does not become possessive.

Possessiveness around food:

Be very careful with possession problems relating to food. You are advised to consult a professional behaviourist/trainer with any kind of aggressive response from the dog.

However, in mild cases you can try the following:

A similar exercise is described in the section on resource guarding.

1. At feeding time, take his food bowl with food and hold this high enough so the dog cannot take it, usually just above the dogs nose level.
2. Take a few pieces of food from the bowl and offer this to him. Be careful that he doesn't snatch. Now take the bowl away from his nose, possibly standing up for a few seconds.
3. Return the bowl to him but place this at his nose level, again so that he cannot immediately help himself. Once again offer a few pieces then take it away for a few seconds.
4. Now return the bowl to him, but just below his nose level. Do not allow him to help himself, but feed a few pieces as before, them remove the bowl for a few seconds.
5. Continue repeating this in 3 to 6 inch increments, gradually getting lower to the ground. Eventually you should be able to place the bowl on the ground.

By this point your dog should be conditioned to accepting you as part of his feeding, and not wish to possess or guard the food.

You can also practice adding pieces of meat as the dog is eating. They will therefore be further encouraged that your visit has a positive outcome.

You should be cautious about proceeding like this with an adult, possibly rescue dog. It is often useful to practice feeding the dog on neutral ground where he would not normally be fed. This can be your yard or garden. Do not place all of his food in his bowl, but spread or scatter this around the yard or garden. For the purposes of this exercise it is advisable to use a basic dry kibble food.

As the dog is eating, approach him and offer pieces of cooked meat. Again the idea is that he gets used to your presence as part of feeding. Also with the food spread out, he does not have a single focus point to guard, which he would have with a food bowl.

Practice this each day during feeding times, until he is relaxed with your presence. Gradually scatter the food in a smaller area until you can place it in a small pile. You should then be able to put the entire meal in his bowl.

If you have two dogs that resource guard, quite often the most straightforward solution is to feed them separately, perhaps in separate rooms.

J) ESCAPING AND ROAMING

Escaping can take the form of digging under the boundary fence, or attempting to jump or climb over.

It is an offence in certain countries to let a dog roam the streets. In such cases a dog must be kept on a lead in designated areas, but in particular on public highways where dogs could be a hazard to motorists. But some owners still allow their dogs to roam the streets, harassing people or other animals.

Once again, this can occur simply because the dog is; under exercised, under stimulated and generally bored. It also relates to his innate desire to investigate and explore his surrounding area. It generally involves him wishing to be free from the confinement of his immediate, less stimulating surroundings. A common reason why dogs escape and roam also occurs when a bitch is in season. A dog will instinctively wish to escape and pursue a bitch in season. But bitches are also known to escape for the same reason, in order to fulfil and instinctive urge to mate.

Preventing the problem:

In the first instance the fence should be at least 6ft to 8ft high. It may also be necessary to modify the base, by placing paving slabs around the perimeter. In extreme cases you could also try digging a trench of approximately 1 to 2ft deep and sinking a wire mesh or similar barrier. In other words, even if he attempts to dig out he will be prevented by the barrier.

K) FUSSY/PICKY EATERS

If your adult or puppy seems off their food for no apparent reason, you should consult with your vet. The vet can then diagnose whether or not there is a medical reason for this.

However, if the puppy does not appear ill, it is worth noting that a major reason for this problem, is 'over feeding' the dog or puppy. Most dogs will eat as much daily nutrients and calories as his body needs, then stop. If you continue presenting him with more than he needs, this may then result in him, either showing a disinterest or picking and choosing what he eats, or attempting to bury or hide food.

If you are having problems with your puppies picky eating, consider the following:

- At 8 weeks of age, a puppy can be fed 3 meals per day. Unless of course the breeder has fed perhaps 4 times per day with a specific diet. In which case, you need to stick to that for a few weeks then aim to reduce this to 3 per day.

- At 12 weeks old a puppy can realistically be fed twice per day. At 4 months of age, this can further be reduced to a single meal per day. Although many dog owners prefer to feed two meals.

- You should however, proceed with caution. The puppy is still growing and underfeeding can be as detrimental as overfeeding, potentially causing problems of stunted growth through malnutrition etc.

Feeding is discussed in much more detail in chapter 14. But basically feeding is simply a matter of providing the correct amount per day, divided by the number of meals per day.

With the correct amount in his food bowl, place this down on the floor for him to start eating. If he does not finish it, then leave it with him for approximately 10 minutes. After which time, take this away, refrigerate if necessary and provide this next time. Have to hand his full ration for next time, but be prepared to let him finish the food he previously left. You can then add half of the new ration, again if he finishes this, add the rest. make sure you are providing enough for his current weight.

A mistake some people make is to tempt the dog with a different food. Again, if your dog generally has a healthy appetite and suddenly stops eating for no apparent reason for a couple of days, you can assume there is a problem and you should consult with a vet.

Feeding can be a bit of a juggling act based on a number of variables including: metabolic rate; activity level; the richness of the food etc. Unless you make a scientific analysis of these variables each day you are unlikely to get it exactly right each time. It is therefore easier to take into consideration what he normally eats, then expect him to want slightly more or less each time.

L) GLUTTONY

Some dogs will happily leave food when they are full and not return to eat until they feel hungry again. However, a gluttonous dog, will tend to gorge themselves regardless. Gluttony can be a similar condition to scavenging, if a dog has been conditioned to never know when their next meal is coming from, it can become mentally engrained to eat as much as possible, whenever possible.

If your dog is given palatable food that he particularly likes, he will perhaps eat more than he needs if an unlimited supply is presented to him. This in turn can easily lead to obesity, if he is not burning off those extra calories through exercise or other activities. This is why it is important to match his intake with his ideal weight, factoring in his activity level. Obesity is a serious problem in terms of shortening a dogs life and potentially causing illnesses such as heart disease, diabetes and even cancer.

With some dogs, even though they may be obese, begging and gluttony can be habit forming. However, if a dog looks underweight, it will be necessary to rule out a possible medical problem such as a parasite infestation, before drawing any conclusions. It will also be necessary to confirm the nutritional value of the food and determine whether or not the dog may be suffering a nutritional deficiency.

Increased appetite can be caused by any one of a number of physiological conditions including: Cushing's disease, hyperthyroidism, diabetes, intestinal worms, an overgrowth of bacteria etc. Ultimately many of these conditions lead to an inefficiency in digesting food or absorbing nutrients.

Research has also taken place, leading scientists to believe that there is a genetic connection, (a gene known as POMC), with appetite and obesity in certain breeds such as certain retrievers.

Preventing the problem:

You may wish to consult with your vet or a canine nutritionist to establish what calories and dietary needs your dog needs every day.

Stick to a feeding schedule including the same diet, in the correct quantity. Also feed at the same times per day, so that your dog gets used to only eating at certain times. In addition, get into the habit allowing him time to eat, but as soon as he walks away, leave the dish down 5 or 10 minutes, then take it away until the next day.

Do not be tempted to chop and change foods or tempt him with treats all of the time, unless of course he earns them. Also remember that it is important to cut down and phase out food treats, beyond initial training.

If the reason is psychological, it may be because something has changed in the household, initiating an anxious response. This could include a new dog, which perhaps makes him eat more, particularly if he feels his food resource is threatened.

If there have been no obvious changes in the household recently, then the most likely cause of your dog's increased hunger is a physical problem. This may also be the case if there have been changes, but the methods above show no results after a week or two.

M) HOWLING

Some dogs howl for a variety of reasons such as when hearing sirens or perhaps as part of being left home alone.

Although it is common for Wolves to howl, it is less common in dogs. It is commonly thought Wolves howl in order to resume contact when separated from other members of the pack. The reason dogs howl is not as clear cut, however it can occur when they are isolated. There does seem to be a connection with separation anxiety. But again, howling often occurs if the dog hears an unusual sound. In some cases sound frequencies not apparent humans can trigger howling.

There isn't a great deal you can do if your dog suddenly starts howling at passing fire engines or ambulances. However, if you are present then the easiest solution is to interrupt the howling by calling your dog or issuing a 'no' or 'ah ah'. Please see the section on separation anxiety if you suspect this may be a symptom once you leave the house.

N) HYPERSEXUAL

This generally involves some sort of sexual behaviour such as mounting. The behaviour is often seen in dominant male dogs, but bitches to a certain extent are also known to mount other dogs. Intact females in season can often demonstrate mounting, and be mounted by other females. Obviously the pheromone which bitches give off when in season will play havoc with males.

Mounting of humans often occurs if a dog is an only dog within the family. Neutering does not necessarily correct this behaviour as established mounting behaviour can become a habit, rather than hormonal.

Preventing the problem:

It is advisable to keep dogs away from bitches in season. However, this is not always possible as the scent can carry and cause problems with howling, escaping, loss of appetite etc.

The action of mounting is similar to jumping up. It is therefore advisable to use the solution to the jumping up problem. It is also advisable to anticipate mounting and use commands such as 'sit', 'down', 'stay' etc.

If the dog should attempt to mount you or someone else, again use the control commands of 'sit', 'down', 'stay' etc. You can also simply turn or walk away.

As always, the unwanted behaviour should be ignored. Similarly the dog should be praised when they stop the unwanted behaviour and comply with one of the commands.

Diversion tactics are also useful, such as engaging the dog in a trick, game or retrieve.

It is also important that the scent of a bitch in season, does not find its way into your house or on your clothes. Disinfect household areas and wash clothes if this is the case.

Destruction of furnishings and other items can often relate to these items having scents on them. However, this could also relate to the dogs frustration due to boredom and lack of exercise and attention. Getting angry with the dog when this happens is not the answer. This actually gives the dog attention for the wrong reasons, as they are likely to repeat the destructive behaviour in order to get the attention they crave.

O) HYPERACTIVE; OVERLY ENTHUSIASTIC; EXCITABLE

Excitable behaviour is often evident when you are about to go on a walk. The dog begins to bark excitedly, spin in circles, rush back and forth etc.

Preventing the problem:

Quite often, high energy, easily bored breeds display this type of behaviour. So first and foremost, enough exercise and mental stimulation is a necessary requirement. All of the recommended training in chapters 15 & 16, as well as off lead runs will certainly help.

Socialisation is vital as it is necessary to desensitise the dog from triggers that he is unfamiliar with and likely to overly stimulate him.

As you can imagine, any stimulating game is also likely to trigger excitability. Games of tug or teasing fetch games etc, can also easily trigger excitability.

It may be necessary to remain relaxed and calm when interacting with him. Also control commands such as 'sit', 'stay', 'stop' etc are important to pacify him if things start to get out of hand.

However, be aware that any kind of restless behaviour may also be due to pain or discomfort. In this case you should not hesitate in getting him checked out with your vet.

P) JUMPING UP

The first thing to note is that jumping up is something we humans inadvertently teach and encourage a puppy to do. This occurs in the early days of bonding and playing with a small puppy. As the puppy grows in size and strength the puppy obviously continues the behaviour. It also becomes an appropriate (to the dog) means of greeting you after an absence. It is also their way of expressing how happy and excited they are at the prospect of being fed or going for a walk. Children quite often trigger and encourage this excitability with their actions.

When your Labrador is a cute and cuddly puppy it can be tempting to reward him with pets and cuddles when he crawls into your lap or jumps up at your legs. When your Labrador grows up, he expects you to react in the same way to this behaviour because you have reinforced it.

Preventing the problem:

Don't be tempted to push the dog away as this just becomes a good game for the dog. Pushing the dog away also becomes a means of getting attention. Cruel, physical deterrents should also be avoided at all costs. In the past, techniques were used such as kneeing or punching the dogs chest; hitting their nose; squeezing the front paws; standing on their feet; squirting water at them etc. The dog would also invariably be shouted at.

Quite often when a dog jumps up, many people instinctively hold out their hands to stop the dog. The best approach is to get into the habit of turning your back, the moment he jumps up. He may try again, but will soon realise, the only way you acknowledge him is when he greets you without jumping up.

With this in mind it is better to prevent this, or teach this not to occur when your dog is still a young puppy. Of course for someone acquiring an older dog, this is never possible.

For a young puppy it is simply a matter of ignoring the jumping behaviour and obviously not encouraging it.

Teaching the 'sit', 'stand', 'down' and 'stay' as soon as possible, teaches the puppy the correct, well behaved manner of greeting you. By asking for these commands you can then legitimately give him a treat as a reward.

However, very early conditioning can be achieved by pre-empting your puppy approaching you. Before he gets chance to jump up, have a treat in your hand and hold this to his nose as he gets close enough. This will act as a focus, so be careful not to raise your hand, encouraging him to jump up. Once you get him to remain calm and not jumping up, you can then give him the treat.

If jumping up at doors is a problem, it may be necessary to have an internal baby gate or similar barrier to discourage him from immediately jumping at the door.

Jumping up on other people:

To teach your Labrador not to jump up on other people, you may need to enlist the help of a friend.

1. Have your friend stand outside the front door to your house and get them to ring the doorbell. This should get your Labrador excited.
2. After ringing the doorbell, have your friend enter the house. When your Labrador jumps up, your friend should place their hands behind their back and ignore the dog for a few seconds before turning around and leaving again.
3. After a few repetitions of this, have your friend give your Labrador the 'Sit' command. If he complies, allow your friend to calmly pet the dog for a few seconds before leaving again.

Repeat this sequence several times until your Labrador remains calm when the doorbell rings. It may take quite a few repetitions to recondition your dog against jumping up, but with consistency you can make it happen.

Q) MOUTHING

Mouthing is a common means by which puppies explore their environment. It is part of the rough and tumble of play. However, it becomes a problem if the puppy plays a little too rough and the mouthing turns into a nip or a bite. Pups learn bite inhibition from the mother and litter-mates when they mouth a little too keenly and consequently gets reprimanded. It is also important that human play interaction can unwittingly encourage the same mouthing problem.

The problem is worse if the puppy becomes the adult who has not learned bite inhibition. As you can imagine, the adult dog is a lot stronger and capable of inflicting serious damage. Play mouthing can easily lead to aggressive biting. You should consult a qualified professional canine behaviourist if you suspect any kind of aggression problem.

In less serious cases you can manage this by not engaging or encouraging the dog if he starts chewing your hand fingers and generally play mouthing.

Preventing the problem:

As with other problems that need a verbal correction, you can simply raise your voice and give a sharp 'ah ah', 'No' or 'ouch'. Do not be tempted to tap the dog on the nose or use any other physical reprimand.

Ignoring the behaviour is also advised. You simply disengage from the play, stand up and either turn away or walk away. If he is persistent and follows you, it may be necessary to leave the room, and perhaps employ a baby gate so that he can see you, but cannot physically touch you. If he starts to bark or whine, again do not give into this until he stops, when you can re-engage with him.

It is also useful to practice swapping, that is substituting your hand for one of his toys.

Basic obedience commands of 'sit', 'leave' 'stay' etc also calm things down. These should as always be rewarded so that he learns to differentiate between when he gets rewarded for good behaviour, a 'sit' and ignored for unacceptable behaviour, you ignoring him, or verbally letting him know it is not acceptable.

Also use these simple procedures if he mouths your feet or legs.

Engaging in play activities is a very important aspect of bonding, so it is not advisable to stop engaging with him. But he needs to be able to play in a gentle manner and remain well behaved by applying the previous techniques or similar ones.

R) NEUROTIC AND AGGRESSIVE

A common reason for neurotic behaviour again relates to general boredom, lack of exercise, lack of mental stimulation etc.

Neurotic behaviours can include: being pre-occupied with imaginary objects; compulsive, excessive barking for no obvious reason; obsessive pacing of boundaries; pica (eating and swallowing non food objects); chasing his tail; constant licking and chewing of body parts (self mutilation); destruction; aggression.

Preventing the problem:

If there is a boredom issue due to lack of exercise etc, you should deal with this regardless (see the section on boredom). Quite often dogs

in prolonged confinement have to make work for themselves such as pacing of whirling, tail chasing.

However, it is also important to consult with your vet to rule out any medical reason as to why the behaviour may be occurring. This could be a brain injury, brain tumour, genetic, food sensitivity, a chemical imbalance such as endocrine etc.

S) OVERPROTECTIVE

This is a form of aggressive behaviour relating to the dogs perceived territory. It can involve the dog being hostile to guests and other visitors to your house, leaving the owner concerned about a potential dog bite or attack.

It is also a leadership issue, which means that the dog may feel the need to take charge of a situation, if he does not feel that you are there to take charge. Dogs like to feel safe and secure in their environment and rely on a leader to provide this. It is therefore up to us humans to be in charge.

Some dogs can be clever at manipulating their owner. You will typically see this when the dog barks for you to open a door, get out of bed to let him out in the morning (unless of course he is generally desperate to relieve himself), stroke him etc. You will also typically find that he will obey you if and when he feels like it. Under these circumstances he may perceive himself as being in charge, the leader.

Preventing the problem:

A good place to start in order to avoid this, is to routinely issue basic commands. You should also only reward him when you have asked for a particular command. This will mean that if he initiates a sit or performs any other taught command, he should not be rewarded. It is necessary to ignore this unwanted manipulative behaviour, otherwise you will be reinforcing him leading you into giving him a reward.

You also need to be aware of what triggers him into taking charge. This can be if someone knocks at the door or rings the doorbell; he hears your front gate open, or a visitor walk down your pathway.

Preferably you need to act as soon as you hear one of the triggers. You ideally want to avoid him reacting by jumping up or starting to bark, otherwise it will be difficult to stop him as it quickly escalates into a barking frenzy. You therefore need to redirect this, take charge and get him to 'sit', 'come', 'stay', 'wait' or whatever. You could also try redirecting the behaviour at this point, by engaging him in a game of fetch or throwing one of his toys.

Be aware that overprotective dogs can often favour a particular member of the family who perhaps gives the dog a lot more attention. This can then lead the dog to be protective of that person. It is therefore very important that in order to avoid any conflicts, all family members should take a relatively equal role in handling the dog. This will entail each family member being involved in training and issuing him with basic obedience commands in order to earn praise or treats.

It is also worth noting, that dogs who display aggressive tendencies such as snarling or growling, often react positively (tail wagging, relaxed etc) when you react in a humorous way towards him. This can involve laughing, or generally behaving in a lighthearted, jovial manner towards him, similar to how you might talk to a baby. Physical punishments and threats will only promote an aggressive response from the dog. Only positive reinforcements (non physical) methods should ever be used.

Caution: In serious cases of aggression, or if you are in any doubt about the seriousness of a case, you are advised to consult with a professional behaviourist/trainer.

T) PICA

Pica is a condition whereby a dog craves and ingests non-food objects. The condition may relate to an underlying medical cause or a behavioural issue. If diagnosis relates to a medical issue then it is a simple matter of treating the medical cause. If a behavioural problem is indicated, it may be necessary to modify the dogs' behaviour.

Symptoms

Items that the dog may eat, is not limited and can include soil, rocks, plastic, rubber, chemicals such as soap etc. The gastrointestinal tract is principally affected, should an item be swallowed, beyond chewing. Symptoms largely depend upon the substance. If this is relatively toxic there may be a general lethargic, weakened state. Other symptoms may include vomiting, diarrhoea etc.

Causes

Again, pica can be caused by either a behavioural issue, or any of a number of medical conditions.

Medical issues can include: neurological, thyroid, bowel disease, parasites of the intestine, anaemia, malnutrition, hunger, a vitamin deficiency.

Overfeeding and underfeeding can also be a reason. The diet in all cases should produce firm stools and certainly not loose or soft. If not, the diet may be at fault and will need changing.

Diagnosis

Initial investigations by your vet will establish whether there is a behavioural or medical reason. In addition to a physical examination it will be necessary to provide information about the dogs environment, diet, appetite etc. The vet will of course treat an underlying medical issue. They should also be able to advise you of your best course of action, if pica occurs because of a behavioural condition.

U) PULLING ON THE LEAD

Leash pulling or straining should never be a problem if you have followed the basic obedience techniques of 'heel', 'recall' and 'stop'.

Without this control, a dog will resort to its instinctive desire to sniff, scent mark, hunt, chase etc. The problem arises when we attach a lead and expect a dog to do the preceding at our pace, not theirs. We are unlikely to be able to go fast enough for the dog.

Once we lose control of the dog, it becomes a problem taking them out in public. This in turn leads to the dog not having a sufficient outlet to burn off pent up energy, because it is not getting sufficient exercise. The dog is largely kept indoors or the yard, boredom sets in, destructive behaviour ensues and a whole vicious circle can occur.

As heeling is best taught off lead as well as on, what we often find is that the dog responds much better if he feels he is not restrained by a short leash. In public areas therefore it is beneficial to utilise a long training leash of about 5 to 10 meters. You can then allow him the freedom he desires. It also allows you plenty of time to practice recalling him if he decides to take off.

v) RESOURCE GUARDING, OBJECTS, PEOPLE AND PLACES

Again the thing to realise here is that guarding food is a natural survival instinct for all dogs. However, it can be a potentially serious problem if the dog snaps at or bites anyone coming too close.

Resource guarding is something that any dog can develop, but it is usually as a result of a past learning experience. A dog that has been truly hungry for instance is likely to develop resource guarding of food which may settle when the dog feels secure.

When a dog is scared of losing a resource he may be reactive to anyone who approaches the resource. He may growl or even bite. To then approach the dog and focus on the resource, is doing nothing more than intensifying the fear. Therefore, the dog is likely to be more aggressive, not less.

When resource guarding is based on fear, confrontation is the last thing that will end the behaviour. Fear aggression is actually a major reason for a dog to bite.

Preventing a problem:

A puppy is easy to condition or train to accept us near the food bowl. Unfortunately an adult, possibly rescue dog will be more difficult to cure.

An adult dog:

If you have an adult rescue dog and this is a problem, you are advised to consult with a dog trainer/behaviourist. In relatively safe cases, it is possible to condition him to you being associated with feeding. This is easily done by scattering some pieces of kibble in an approximate 6 feet circle. By doing this you are diffusing the focal point of a food dish to a much wider area. You should next proceed with caution. As he is eating, walk into this area and drop small pieces of a favourite food, cooked meat or cheese etc. It is important to condition him to your presence like this, so don't get too close at first.

It is then a question of repeating this on a regular basis, at the same time reduce the area you scatter the food. Eventually you will be able

to simply place the food in the bowl, whilst you are close by. Again, never take anything for granted.

It may also be necessary to change his normal feeding location, perhaps to a part of your yard or garden. This will be important if he is associating a particular room with feeding.

A puppy

A puppy however, can be taught from day one to accept you feeding him from the bowl.

It is a simple matter of feeding him from the dog bowl.

Once he is used to this, place a bowl of dry kibble down, then allow the dog to eat.

Now with some small pieces of cooked meat, start to periodically drop these in whilst he is eating. This should indicate to the puppy that you are providing him with something even better. He will therefore welcome you around the food bowl. Remember to offer lots of praise and encouragement.

w) SCAVENGING FOR FOOD

Scavenging and stealing food are similar problems. This is relative to opportunism, which is a natural trait all dogs are capable of. The dog may scent something edible on an off lead run, or he may raid a garbage bin that he believes contains something edible.

Preventing the problem:

For off lead opportunism, you will have to rely on a good 'stop' and 'recall', or get to him as soon as you can. Around the house it will be necessary to purchase child or dog proof bins that are lockable or not easily opened.

You will also have no doubt taught your dog the 'leave' command or a variation of it. You can therefore put this to good use in all situations where you catch him in the act.

x) STEALING FOOD

Once again, the simple fact of the matter is that dogs are opportunists who instinctively take whatever is presented to them. What we may call theft, is a survival mechanism to the dog. If a dog is hungry, he will not be concerned about morality, right and wrong, guilt or remorse.

Preventing the problem:

As with many problem behaviours, it is a question of pre-empting the dogs likelihood to take the opportunity that is presented. So in the same way that you should not leave items lying around for the dog to find and chew, you should not leave food within reaching distance.

Y) SEPARATION ANXIETY

The strong bonding and desire to please people is an overriding reason the Sporting/Gundog has been such a success in the field and family home. This lack of independence and the desire to be with you most of the time however can cause a number of problems such as separation anxiety. The dog can become needy to the extent that he looks for attention for example by following family members around the house. For this reason the Sporting/Gundog is not an ideal choice for families who are away from home for large parts of the day or do not have alternatives such as pet sitters/walkers.

Separation anxiety typically occurs when a dog fears being alone to the point of becoming severely stressed or distressed.

It is currently thought to be for one of an unknown number of reasons. There are two types of separation anxiety, amid other undefined reasons for the disorder. These are fear of unexpected noises or over attachment to the owner.

It is often suggested that two dogs will provide a good human substitute and alleviate the problem of separation anxiety. However, it is debatable, and some would argue that there is no evidence that two dogs together will still not suffer separation anxiety. Having said that, dogs do become attached to each other and when separated, display signs of distress such as pining, howling, whining etc. So I would say that two dogs together do add mutual comfort to a certain extent. But two or more dogs can still display a type of anxiety which seems to be linked specifically with the absence of human presence from the home. As every dog is an individual, so is their experience when suffering from separation anxiety.

Some suffer greatly and become destructive to themselves and their surroundings. Others simply become sad and depressed when left alone. They leave no trace of the stress, thus leaving owners unaware that anxiety occurred at all during the dog's alone time.

The actual anxiety becomes a phobia and can become so severe that the dog develops serious stress related behaviours causing poor health, self-harm and obsessive worrying about being left alone.

Preventing the problem:

To prevent separation anxiety in your own dog you have a number of options. The best one, if you are leaving your dog regularly, is to employ a willing neighbour or relative to periodically check in on your dog. Alternatively, consider employing a doggy day caretaker or similar canine professional. This usually takes the form of a canine crèche area or similar and is wonderful for meeting the dog's mental and physical needs alongside ensuring the dog is not alone regularly for long periods of time.

A dog walker is the minimum provision that a full time, at home dog, should have when everyone is out at work all day.

Once again, the other possibility here is having two dogs. Companionship can make all the difference, whereby the dogs keep each other company and entertained. However, this doesn't always work and some dogs can still become overwhelmed with separation anxiety, resulting in the aforementioned negative behaviours.

If separation anxiety becomes a real problem, a local dog behaviourist may be the answer. They can observe your dog and create a modification program to try and alleviate his stressed reaction to being alone. This can work really well when carried out carefully.

For extra tips and guidance, see chapter 12 from section (7) on crate training.

Z) SOILING IN THE HOUSE

As long as the recommendations in chapter 12 have been applied, you should not experience further problems.

However, problems can and do occur even after successful toilet training. If a problem does occur at any time it is first of all necessary to establish whether this is due to a behavioural or physical problem. Usually if an adult suddenly starts soiling in the house, there would generally be a physical cause, such as cancer or urinary infection, bladder stone, hormones etc. The problem may also relate to a problem with diarrhoea, possibly due to food poisoning or a bacterial/viral intestine infection. In all cases it would require a consultation with a vet to diagnose the possible condition and medically treat the problem.

If you have acquired an adult, possibly rescue dog, you may experience soiling in the house simply because the dog has not been taught otherwise. If this is the case it will require that you start from the beginning of chapter 12, toilet training him as if he were a puppy.

Submissive urination

As the name suggests, the dog will lie on his side and literally wet (pee) himself. In some cases the dog may defecate or empty the anal glands. This is a fear response designed to prevent aggression or to give in to the perceived dominance of another dog, or in some cases a person. This can typically occur if the dog has been harshly treated during training or otherwise. It is therefore common in rescue dogs. It can become a habitual trigger to defuse an anticipated attack. It is a typical response of timid, shy, anxious sensitive breeds.

Preventing the problem:

Harsh punishment based methods should never be used.

It is important to treat any urination the same as any other toilet accident by not acknowledging it and simply cleaning the mess up.

We may wish to reassure a dog who is acting submissively by patting them. However, it is advisable to refrain from this as the dog can easily view this as a dominant, aggressive act on your part. Similarly avoid standing or looming over the dog as again this can be perceived as a threat. It is therefore better to crouch down, approach him side ways on and avoid eye contact, when moving towards him.

Be aware of the dog displaying avoidance behaviour such as cowering, and be careful not to inadvertently acknowledge this. The 'recall' command is a very useful technique in this respect

as it requires that the dog is encouraged to come back to you, resulting in a food reward and lots of praise. Other basic commands will also build his confidence as you reward and praise him.

It may also be necessary to involve other family members or friends if other people evoke a submissive response.

Early socialisation is very important to prevent this problem. The dog should therefore be exposed to many positive experiences in order to build his confidence.

Excitement based urination:

Initial greeting can also initiate urination due to excitement. This usually occurs if the adult or puppy is expected to spend prolonged periods of time on their own. They then become excited when you return and in some, not all cases, urinate in the process.

In such cases you may have to ignore the puppy, not engaging with him for a few minutes. This will allow him to calm down in his own time and negate his need to urinate.

You can also train him to greet you with greater control using a few pieces of food.

If your front door is your first point of contact with the puppy, upon returning, have to hand a couple of pieces of food.

1. As you open the door, as soon as the puppy jumps up or rushes over, make sure that the first thing the puppy greets is your hand with the food in it.

2. Hold this to his nose and ask for a 'sit' or 'stand' to establish control. If he at any point urinates then do not acknowledge this, and certainly do not give him the food treat.

3. Simply step back > then come forward again with the treat to his nose > ask for the 'sit' or 'stand'. Once again provided he does not urinate, give him the treat and offer lots of praise.

Practice like this until he greets you each time without urinating. You can then ask for a 'sit' or 'stand' as soon as you greet him each day.

Tips to help the situation:

» His overexcitement will diminish if he has regular contact throughout the day. So if you are away for extended periods, arrange for someone to visit every hour or so.

» Ensure that he gets regular walks, safe off lead runs and play time each day.

» Do not encourage the puppy if he is already excited. It is best to remain calm and still until he calms down. Touching or stroking him is also likely to excite him more.

» As with any toilet accident, do not make a fuss or get angry, and certainly do not physically punish him. Simply clean up the mess and things will soon settle down.

Fears and Phobias

Whether they have lived in a safe home since puppy-hood, or were raised in a different environment, any dog can develop fear behaviours. Fireworks, thunder, travel, other animals and people are some examples of why your dog can become afraid.

A dog that is fearful has a very distinct body language. He will tuck his tail below his hind quarters and cower. He may try to leave the situation and look away from the frightening stimulus. It is vital that a scared dog is never cornered.

A scared or worried dog will often display calming signals. Some calming signals include yawning; a stressed dog will yawn frequently.

The yawning response is often mistaken for tiredness by an uninformed human. However, once you know what to look for, it is easily recognisable. Licking his lips; a calming signal and stress response, can take the form of a single nose lick or more. Sniffing the ground is a 'leave me alone, I am invisible' plea.

Your job as the owner of a fearful dog is to neither ignore nor encourage the fear. Be aware

of the situations in which your dog feels threatened and gently build him up by gradually exposing him to the trigger and de-sensitising him. Introduce new and worrying situations gradually, and amalgamate them with rewards such as playing with a toy or receiving a treat for relaxed behaviour.

A very important point is to never over sympathise with your dog as this can reinforce the fear. If he gets too much attention when he is afraid, he will either repeat the behaviour for the attention, or even worse think that the stimulus is a threat which you too recognise. If he sees that the stimulus doesn't concern you, then your dog will learn that it shouldn't concern him either.

A scared dog should never be cornered or forced to accept attention. If he is, then he will become more scared, growl and possibly even snap. It is better to help him relax around people without them paying him any attention, than to push him into a negative reaction.

If the fear has an environmental cause, for instance fireworks, then it is worth trying a natural remedy to appease your dog's fear. Rescue remedy which can be bought in most chemists/drug stores, is suitable for short-term treatment of a worried dog. Your vet may also be able to suggest something to get your dog through difficult times such as on bonfire night or New Year's Eve, when there are a lot of fireworks.

Once again, problem behaviours can arise despite your best efforts at initial obedience training and setting ground rules. However, in the same way that a child can push boundaries so can puppies and adult dogs. Of course this should not be tolerated. The following chapter will provide detailed steps to follow for potential behaviour problems that may occur. If these do not seem to be working it is advisable to contact a dog trainer who may have experience of a particular problem. In the worst case scenario, it may be necessary to contact a canine behaviourist who will analyse any underlying causes.

You may wish to initially consult with your vet who can make a referral. Alternatively you can browse the links below for a behaviour professional.

Canine Behaviourist links USA:

The Association of Animal Behavior Professionals (AABP)
http://www.associationofanimalbehaviorprofessionals.com/

The Pet Professional Guild
https://petprofessionalguild.com/

The International Association of Animal Behavior Consultants
https://iaabc.org/consultants

Certified Applied Animal Behaviorists
http://corecaab.org/owners/

http://www.animalbehaviorsociety.org/web/applied-behavior-caab-directory.php

You may also find useful information at the following:

American College of Veterinary Behaviorists
http://www.dacvb.org/about/member-directory/

American Veterinary Medical Association
https://www.avma.org/Pages/home.aspx
Association of Companion Animal Behavior Counselors
http://www.animalbehaviorcounselors.org/

Canine Behaviourist links UK:

Association of Pet Behaviour Counsellors (APBC)
http://www.apbc.org.uk/

The Animal Behaviour Training Council (ABTC)
http://www.abtcouncil.org.uk/clinical-animal-behaviourists.html
Certified Clinical Animal Behaviourists (CCABs)
http://www.asab.org/ccab-register/

The Canine Behaviour & Training Society (formerly the UK Registry Of Canine Behaviourists
https://www.tcbts.co.uk/

CHAPTER TWENTY TWO:

CARING FOR YOUR SENIOR LABRADOR

When you first bring home your Labrador puppy, it's difficult to imagine that in only 12 to 15 years later, you will have to say goodbye.

This chapter covers what to expect in your dogs senior years and how to best care for him.

1) THE SENIOR LABRADOR

All dog breeds approach old age in the same way, but at different times, depending on their breed and size. Smaller dog breeds tend to live longer. Some dog breeds are still jumping agility courses at 13 years of age. Again, depending on the size, many other purebred dogs may only live to 8 or 9 years of age. Keep in mind that good health begins during puppy-hood and lasts a lifetime.

Your Labrador has most likely been your best friend for life. You've both shared so many experiences. Your Labrador will depend on you throughout his life. You've made a commitment to take care of him from puppy-hood to the end. Bare in mind that your Labrador will change as he ages. His body and natural exuberance may sometimes allow you to forget his age. Then one day you'll look into your Labrador's eyes and notice his silvery face, and stiffened gait. He'll most likely sleep longer, and may be less eager to play. As your Labrador nears his ten or twelve year mark, he may start slowing down on his walks. Getting your Labrador to live comfortably during his senior years need not be a challenge, but needs to be well-prepared for.

A) Caring for your Senior Labrador

Most Labradors will show signs of ageing by greying of the coat and usually around the eyes and face. They may have a dull, flaky coat, loss of hair, slowness of gait and enjoying the family couch more than usual. Activities like running, jumping, eating and retrieving will become more difficult for him. That said, other activities like sleeping, barking, and a repetition of habits may increase. Your Labrador will want to spend more time with you, and will go to the front door more often when you are leaving.

As your Labrador ages, he'll need certain therapeutic and medical preventative strategies. Your veterinarian will advise you on special nutritional counselling, veterinary visits and screening sessions for your senior Labrador. A senior-care Labrador program will include all of these.

Veterinarians will determine your Labrador's health by doing blood smears for a complete blood count, which will include the following:

Serum chemistry profile with electrolytes; Urinalysis; Blood pressure check; Electrocardiogram; Ocular tonometry (pressure of the eyeball); Dental prophylaxis.

Extensive, regular screenings for senior Labradors are recommended well before you begin to see the symptoms of ageing, again such as slower movement and disinterest in play and other activities.

By following this preventative program, you will not only increase your Labrador's chance of a longer life, but you'll also make his life so much more comfortable. There may be so many physical changes like loss of sight through cataracts, arthritis, kidney problems, liver failure, and other possible degenerative diseases. Adding to that you may notice some behavioural changes related to ageing. Labradors suffering from hearing and eyesight loss, dental pain or arthritis may often become aggressive because of the constant pain that they have to live with. Labradors that are near deaf or blind may also be startled more easily at the slightest environmental changes. Do your best not to move furniture around in your home, and to keep things as they are, as this can be unsettling for them. Senior Labradors suffering from senility may do many unusual things, and will often become impatient.

B) House Soiling Accidents

These are associated with loss of bladder control, kidney problems, loss of mobility, loss of sphincter control, physiological brain changes, and reaction to new medications. Your older Labrador will need more support than ever, especially doing his toilet business.

Avoid feeding your senior Labrador too many unhealthy treats. Obesity is a common problem in older dogs as they naturally become less active. Additional weight will put extra stress on his joints and his body's vital organs. Some breeders suggest supplementing meals with high fibre foods that are also low in calories. You are also advised to ask your veterinarian for any special prescription diets that may best suit the needs of your senior Labrador.

C) Every Day Tips

Be consistent with your schedule and do not change the way things are in your home. Doors that have always remained open should stay that way. Leave his favourite couch in the same place.

Never punish or use harsh tones against your senior Labrador for anything at all. Protect your Labrador, and foresee his reactions to any environmental changes. Pay special attention to his immediate needs such as going to the toilet, pain levels and eating habits. Visit your veterinarian often and work together on providing your senior Labrador with the best of care. Keep your Labrador company as often as possible. Be mindful of the fact that your Labrador does not understand why he's losing his sight or hearing. It is therefore important to be very patient and understanding. The world may seem to be a strange place to him right now. Comfort him frequently, and try to leave a family member with him when you go out. Your Labrador will appreciate the companionship. Also be aware that older Labradors may not be able to wait until morning to go outdoors. Provide him with alternatives such as puppy pads or spread out newspaper, to relieve himself on during the night/ early hours. Above all, expect this as a normal everyday occurrence and the fact that you will have to clear up any mess made.

Be consistent with your schedule and do not change the way things are in your home. Doors that have always remained open should stay that way. Leave his favourite couch in the same place.

D) KEEPING A DIARY

You may wish to keep a diary to note the day-to-day record of how your Labrador is feeling and whether he is eating, drinking and walking. As a dog owner you are able to observe all your Labrador's activities, and record how your Labrador feels and behaves.

E) CHECK LIST OF QUESTIONS ABOUT YOUR AGEING LABRADORS CONDITION

- Is your Labrador still happy to see you and how does he respond? Is it with his usual wag or does he seem to be less responsive than normal?
- Record his respiratory rate each evening when your Labrador is resting peacefully. Record the breaths taken per minute.
- Does he still come to you when called? What is his reaction to you being there? Record the levels of anxiety and pain. When he wags his tail or walks to you.
- Can your Labrador still walk? Does he still get up and come to you? How far can he walk until he tires?

- How much pain does your Labrador seem to have? Does he have many episodes of pain? Does he yelp when handled or display signs of aggression when handled?
- Does your Labrador eat if presented with his favourite foods? Does your Labrador pick at his food or refuse to try some?
- Does your Labrador still drink fluids? How much fluid per day/week? Take note of how much fluid intake he has per day.
- Is your Labrador defecating, and how often does this occur? Are all his faeces normal?
- Is any disease/illness worsening or improving?
- Weigh your Labrador every day or every week. If he is losing weight, how much weight is your Labrador losing each week or month? Weight is an important indicator of health.

F) IS THERE AN EMERGENCY HEALTH DETERIORATION STAGE?

Your Labrador could suffer from an acute situation that is related to their condition. These chronic or acute episodes of disease related deterioration require immediate veterinary treatment. Some internal cancers will present themselves with haemorrhaging and states of severe shock and collapse. Congestive heart failure results in distressed breathing and pulmonary oedema. Labradors with renal failure, for example, will start vomiting blood and go into shock.

G) SYMPTOMS OF PAIN IN YOUR SENIOR OR TERMINALLY ILL LABRADOR

It is always devastating when medical treatment does not work. But it's also important to think about the potential suffering of your Labrador and how he was before the illness or injury. So as to determine whether your Labrador is in pain or not, veterinarians and most importantly Labrador owners need to have a way to determine a Labradors' pain and pain threshold.

Typical symptoms are as follows:

Whimpering, whining and yelping when touched; Your Labrador yelps when he tries to get from point A to point B; He shows obvious difficulty in moving about; Your Labrador is often depressed, and does not want to interact with other animals or people in the household; Sleeplessness, listlessness and hiding under the bed or in dark places; Your Labrador is squinting which is typical for head and eye pain in animals. Some dogs will squint both eyes when experiencing head pain; Your Labrador has an elevated heart rate; Your Labrador injures himself by attacking or injuring the pain inflicted area; Chattering of the teeth is suggestive of mouth pain and dental pain, but is also indicative of shock, overall trauma and pain throughout the body; Your Labrador is drooling excessively. This could be indicative of pain and trauma.

2) TIME TO SAY GOODBYE!

If you are lucky, those 12 to 15 years or so, are what you get; a number of years that feel so very short. Nonetheless, mercifully, although we are aware of the unfair discrepancy between our dogs' lifespan and ours, we always somehow manage to push aside this fact; that is, until we are facing the very end with our dogs.

The heartbreaking decision to "put down" or euthanise your dog is an issue frequently faced by pet parents and veterinarians. You will never be prepared for this day. Putting your Labrador to sleep is an extremely difficult and upsetting decision that you will need to make with your veterinarian. As a Labrador owner, you will usually be making this decision when your Labrador goes through one or more life-threatening symptoms that will force you to seek veterinary help immediately.

If the prognosis indicates that the end is near and that your Labrador is in great pain, euthanasia may be the right choice. It is a difficult and heartbreaking decision for any dog lover. But if the dog is suffering then it is cruel to prolong their agony.

3) WHAT IS EUTHANASIA

Just the thought of euthanasia/putting your Labrador to sleep is enough to make anyone cringe.

There are varying opinions regarding this final decision. What are the rights and wrongs? Are we actually helping our dogs or being selfish? Do we have the right to end a life?

Euthanasia refers to the planned and painless death of a dog that is suffering from a painful condition, or who is old and cannot walk, cannot see or unable to control his bodily functions. It is typically carried out with an overdose of an anaesthetic.

The process of euthanasia takes a matter of seconds. Once the injection takes place it quickly enters the blood stream and the dog goes to sleep. The overdose suppresses the heart and brain function, in turn causing an instant loss of consciousness and therefore, pain. The animal dies peacefully whilst asleep.

The difficult decision to euthanise your senior or sick Labrador is never an easy one, and one that may take a while for you to come to terms with. This time is usually stressful for you and your family. If this is a first time in dealing with the death of a loved one, you'll need your family by you.

4) WHAT HAPPENS AFTERWARDS

I know many vets who will give the owner of their beloved pet, the option to take them away and bury them in a quiet area of their own garden. This may well be a favourite spot that your Labrador frequented. You are generally advised to dig a hole deep enough to avoid the problem of foxes or similar predators, digging the body up.

If your Labrador is buried in a pet cemetery, or in your garden, it's also a good idea to plant a special tree or place a stone over the site. A few dog owners prefer to leave their deceased dogs at the veterinary clinic. Today, many pet parents opt for individual cremation. Your veterinarian can help to arrange the cremation service, and will also be able to advise you on where to find a suitable pet cemetery.

Most dog owners have given a considerable amount of thought as to what makes a fitting tribute to honour our dogs. There's no better way to do this than by commissioning a great portrait of your Labrador. This simple act will keep your memories alive and bring you happiness when time has healed your pain. After spending over a decade

together sharing life's most special moments, you'll be able to recall your Labrador's most happy, crazy and sometimes most peaceful moments with a portrait. Professional studio photos are also a great alternative to this. After some time you may miss not having your friend around. You may perhaps wish to give a loving home to another Labrador.

Obviously you are not attempting to replace your friend, but have such love for the breed or dogs in general, that this seems a natural thing to consider. Many dog owners breed one litter of pups for this very reason. In that way they keep the generation of their beloved dogs intact.

Adopting a Labrador from a rescue is another excellent option. Perhaps you may want to adopt a different breed so that you'll not make comparisons. Most dog owners will usually choose the same breed because they understand and love the temperament. Perhaps the best thing that you can do for yourself as well as your departed Labrador will be to adopt another Labrador.

" If there are no dogs in heaven, then when I die I want to go where they went."
-Will Rogers

CHAPTER TWENTY THREE:

WEEK BY WEEK PUPPY DEVELOPMENT & CARE GUIDE: 8 WEEKS OLD TO 1 YEAR AND BEYOND

This chapter intends to summarise and show you week by week what you can expect in the general caring of your Labrador.

Learning and development stages

The general behaviour of any puppy in the very early stages of development, focuses on them learning through play and interaction. Additionally behaviour intended to gain attention, cleaning, grooming, nutrition and warmth etc, initially from the mother via yelping, whining, nuzzling etc. With the exception of a few involuntary movements, they are mostly reacting to a stimulus that makes them uncomfortable or restless.

Three weeks of age until approximately 12 weeks of age is the most impressionable stage when a puppy forms lasting impressions of its environment including people and other dogs. Reputable breeders recognise this period as essential in terms of socialisation. Conversely puppy farms disregard the importance of this confining the mother and puppies in cramped spaces or cages. Consequently the puppies never receive the socialisation and the opportunity to form relationships which is essential to avoid the risk of starting life with fear related and other behaviour problems. Many behaviourists assert that such dogs although improving significantly once they are able to live with a loving family in an optimum social environment, never fully lose the handicap of a lack of early socialisation. It cannot be said often enough, early socialisation must involve many and varied experiences with lots of different dogs, people of all ages, animate and inanimate objects etc.

The juvenile period ranges from twelve weeks to six months whereby previously learned behaviours become more fixed. The juvenile period is arguably an optimum stage whereby good behaviour can be encouraged and undesirable behaviour can be changed. After the juvenile period, the dog progresses to adulthood where behavioural changes become more difficult.

Birth to 2 weeks (neonatal)

At this stage the puppies are completely dependent on the mother for food, warmth, protection, safety, care, hygiene, grooming etc. They can feel, taste, suckle and nuzzle but their ability to regulate their own temperature, to hear or see are not developed. They will learn to cope with mild stresses such as when the mother temporarily leaves them alone and exposed to lower temperatures. It is also beneficial to introduce them to human contact by regular handling.

2 to 4 weeks (Transitional period)

At this point their senses develop with eyes and ears opening and they begin to respond to the consequent external stimuli of light and movement. Awareness of their mother, litter mates, human contact and general environment becomes stronger. Their physicality and motor skills develop and strengthen as well as the mother initiating weaning with her regurgitating food for them to eat. They begin to explore, play, interact, learn and remember via interaction with their mother and litter mates. This is one of a number of vital periods that must be experienced with the mother and litter mates. The breeder should be introducing them to new stimuli such as new scents, playing surfaces, obstacles etc. The puppies should also be regularly handled, examined, massaged, stroked, groomed etc, through additional human contact.

4 to 16 weeks old (socialisation)

At 4 weeks and beyond Gundogs will benefit from the introduction of loud, potentially disturbing noises which they would have to become accustomed to if hunting with gunshot. There is therefore no need to worry about accidental banging and clattering noises going on around them. At this stage puppies are ready for complex learning experiences with sufficiently developed senses. Learning about bite inhibition and compromising with their mother and litter mates will occur. It is very important that they are exposed to as much human contact as possible. It is usually recommended after their final vaccination shots that they start being introduced to the local environment.

This will include short walks and runs, opportunities to retrieve objects, obstacles to climb, concrete steps etc,

Birth to maturity lifecycle

At Birth: The puppy is born deaf, blind and toothless, but with limited senses of taste, scent and touch, which allow the puppy to detect the mother and to suckle.

At 7 days: By approximately the end of the first week, the puppy will be spending most of its time sleeping. Approximately 10% will be spent suckling. The pup has very little limb strength and is relatively helpless. The mother carries out the ancestral throwback trait of licking the anus and genitals to stimulate defecation and urination. This act is considered a survival instinct against predators who would otherwise pick up the scent of a litter.

At 14 days: The front leg strength develops and whereas previously the puppy would only be able to crawl, they now begin to sit up. Between 7 and 10 days the eyes begin to open, but vision is limited. Approximately 10 to 15 days the puppy will be able to see. At around 14 days the ear canal opens and the puppy is able to hear. Also around this time, the first adult roundworms will be passed.

At 21 days: Strength and reflexes in the rear end at around 21 days, enable the puppy to stand and start moving about on all fours. The primary milk teeth generally appear between 14 and 21 days. At approximately 18 days the puppy will begin to make play movements and vocalise with barks/yelps. By 21 days they are able to urinate and defecate unaided.

At 28 days: At approximately 28 days they should have full vision, be playing with litter mates, be walking and running, be eating from a dish. The mother at this point spends less time with the puppies. She will however, be on hand to break up fights, console injured pups and correct excessive biting (bite inhibition). Weaning usually starts around 4 weeks and should be a gradual process over a couple of weeks, fully weaned by about 7 weeks.

http://pets.webmd.com/dogs/weaning-puppies-what-do

At 42 days: Development of coordination, balance, reflexes, strength and confidence will continue. As they gain confidence, they begin to explore more. At approximately 35 days the hearing will be more acute and they will be actively playing with toys. By about 40 days they will be playing more constructively, with mouth and paw skills developing.

At 56 days (7 to 8 week period): By now, the breeder should have socialised the puppy to a vast amount of household experiences and noises. This includes household appliances, exposure to children and different adults, regular handling, grooming etc. By 8 weeks the nervous system has matured, and with early socialisation and weaning completed, they are now able to go to new homes.

At 126 days (8 to 18 weeks): Voluntary control of defecation and urination will start around 10 to 12 weeks of age. This is important to note as success with toilet training will be possible, but any prolonged crate training before 12 weeks will be difficult to achieve. By 4 to 6 months of age however, they should have full voluntary control. Continuing with socialisation is very important from 8 weeks.

At 4 to 6 months: With correct adequate socialisation, having being completed previously, particularly during the 'critical period' (up to 16 weeks of age), the puppy will continue to grow in confidence and independence and be now testing his limits of permitted behavior.

12 months: At one year old, the young dog is not physically or mentally mature. However, they are considered an adult in terms of height and sexual maturity. From this age they gradually gain muscle mass and so broaden out proportionally.

18 months to 2 years: During this time they become more emotionally mature

The following check list should ideally be consulted a week before your puppies arrival. It is then hoped to give you an action plan to follow for each day.

WEEK 1: (8 WEEKS OLD)

Important check list of things to do during the week:

- Make sure you have his food available and familiarise yourself with how much he needs per meal
- Work out the times you will feed him such as 7 – 8am, 11am - 12 noon, 3 – 4pm, and 7 – 8pm.
- Ensure his bed is in place and that you have his water bowl ready and filled with water. Again please remember to keep this topped up with fresh, clean water at all times.
- Have news paper or puppy pads ready for his toilet training routine
- Have scales ready to weigh him
- Make sure he is eating his meals and check that his faeces look normal; reasonably solid, no runny diarrhoea or unusual discharge.
- Check whether he needs flea and worming treatment. Make a note on your calendar if you haven't already
- Check the dates for his initial vaccination shots if these have not already been initiated by the breeder
- Start brushing/combing him at least once or twice per week
- Allow for some play time/exercise in the yard, garden or room in the house

The first day home

You should hopefully have prepared everything necessary for his arrival, so that you can simply and safely introduce him to his new home.

As soon as you arrive home, take the puppy into your back yard/garden and allow him to wander about and to hopefully do his toilet business. Give him at least 5 minutes or so, then pick him up and take him back inside the house.

Take him to his bed area and again allow him to explore, settle and sleep if he wants

Weighing the puppy. Although it is not vital, it is a good idea to start weighing your puppy as soon as you can, and keep a record of this. He will be naturally growing and this will be quite rapid initially. You will need to ensure that he is gaining weight on a weekly basis and contact your vet if you notice a lack a growth or any other abnormalities.

From day one and the first week you should simply allow the puppy the freedom to settle in and bond with the family. Most puppies will want to be with you and therefore follow you everywhere. It is a good idea to have his bed where ever you are likely to spend most of the day, assuming that you or someone else will be at home most of the day.

Your puppy should be fit and healthy when you pick him up, but keep an eye on him in case he suddenly develops an illness. Obviously if this is the case, contact your vet without delay. For peace of mind some dog owners prefer to make an appointment as soon as possible anyway to let the vet check them over.

Training

You should ideally familiarise yourself with the Initial Obedience Training chapter. Although you will be busy bonding with your puppy the first week, you should be getting him used to initial 'recall' and 'retrieve' etc.

Housebreaking routine

Consult the previous chapter on toilet training, but this will provide a general summary of what to expect.

Toilet training involves taking the puppy, or encouraging him outside as often as possible. This is usually after he has had a drink, eaten, having woken from a sleep, first thing in the morning, last thing at night and any time you notice him sniffing the ground, circling etc. In most cases however, it is necessary to build in a routine of taking him out up to every hour, but more usually every half hour. If he has a toilet accidents before the hour, reduce this to every half or three quarters of an hour. Remember to praise him and offer a treat every time he successfully does his toilet business outside in the yard/garden. Under no circumstance punish or shout at him for any accident inside the house. This will only frighten him and possibly induce a phobia relating to doing his toilet business. Ignore the accident, clean up the mess and be more vigilant next time.

Feeding

Puppies usually require their daily food intake split into four equal meals. It is best to keep to a regular routine morning, noon, tea time and early evening. Hopefully you have purchased the food recommended by the breeder, even if they provide a few days supply.

Fleas

Again you should have enquired with your vet as to the best flea treatment for your puppy. Unless the breeder has already administered flea treatment treat as soon as possible.

You should find that if you stick to a regular flea treatment you should be able to keep fleas under control. However at any other time be aware if you notice any of the following:

If you notice any obvious scratching, check the coat for fleas, bites, black specks which could be an indication of flea droppings.

Exercise at 8 weeks old

Obviously the puppy is still growing and his joints and bones will be vulnerable to injury or breakages. It is therefore important to restrict exercise, play time and general physical activity.

Socialisation

Unfamiliar surroundings

This initial period will be a big upheaval for a young puppy newly separated from his mother, litter mates and his old surroundings. Do not worry too much if he appears nervous or anxious. Simply give him lots of fuss and attention and again if he wants to hide in his crate or elsewhere don't worry as he is just attempting to cope with the situation. It is all perfectly natural and he will soon adjust and settle.

WEEK 2: (9 WEEKS OLD)

Important check list of things to do during the week:

- Remember to have his food available and how much he needs per meal
- Stick to the times you are intending to fee again for example 7 – 8am, 11am - 12 noon, 3 – 4pm, and 7 – 8pm.
- His bed will already be in place, but again please remember to keep his water bowl topped up with fresh, clean water at all times.
- Have news paper or puppy pads ready for his toilet training routine
- Have scales ready to weigh him

- Familiarise yourself with the procedure for giving him a health check and carry this out
- Have his collar and leash to hand ready to introduce this as part of his leash walking
- Make sure he is eating his meals and check that his faeces look normal; reasonably solid, no runny diarrhoea or unusual discharge
- Remember to brush/comb him at least once or twice per week
- Allow for some play time/exercise in the yard, garden or room in the house

You should notice by week two a much more happy confident puppy. His routine should remain much the same as week 1, feeding, toilet training etc.

Taking his weight

You will probably notice a change in his growth by the second week. Again weigh him on the first day of week two and write this down, making a comparison with day one of week one.

IMPORTANT: 8 to 16 weeks of age (the critical period)

Please refer back to the chapter on socialisation and his vaccinations.

Socialisation it very important during this period in order for him to develop into a happy, confident, un-fearful young dog. It is during this period that he should be introduced to as many experiences as possible. This should include different sights, sounds, smells, people and age groups, different animals, varied environments (quiet countryside, noisy pedestrian areas etc).

It is important to be with him at all times to offer lots of encouragement, praise and a treat particularly if he reacts calmly and without fear.

There are no breed specific guarantees regarding whether they will act fearful, or confident and friendly. It is very much down to the individual.

Weekly routine health check

Similarly to weighing your puppy on a weekly basis, it is also a very good idea to get into the habit of giving them a check up yourself.

You are obviously looking for any signs of illness or abnormal swellings on the body.

Lightly stroke/massage each part of his body in turn starting around their head; look in his ears, eyes, nostrils; lift his lips and check his teeth and gums; check each leg, paws, pads; run your hands along their back, sides, tummy; finally check their tail, lifting this to check the anus and genitals.

Training

You should ideally have already familiarised yourself with the Initial Obedience Training chapter. As well as the collar and leash information you should start introducing him to early recall and retrieve around the house. There is also nothing to stop you introducing the basis of 'sit', 'down', 'stay' etc.

Introducing the collar and leash

In addition, check the chapter on Initial Obedience Training:

Some people introduce the collar and lead from week 1 at 8 weeks old. It is not vital, but it is advisable to start his introduction by week 2, 9 weeks of age. Most puppies react to a collar as it is uncomfortable when they are not used to it.

1. On a daily basis, put the collar on for short periods of time and allow him to wander around the house, yard or garden.
2. Ignore any protestations and after five or ten minutes remove the collar, enthusiastically praise him and offer a treat.
3. Repeat this a number of times throughout the day
4. Always try to be present as you do not want him getting snagged or caught on something, potentially choking him
5. Now attach a lead to the collar and let the puppy wander around, trailing the lead.
6. Move in opposite directions and call him to you with a 'this way', 'here' or 'come'. This is his first introduction to the 'recall'.
7. When he comes to you offer lots of praise and a treat.

Initial walk with leash

Following on from the previous, you now want to offer some sort of resistance. He will need to get used to walking on the lead when you take him for his walks.

1. As before with his collar and lead attached let him wander.
2. Recall him to you > when he comes back, say 'good boy' > and this time pick the lead up.
3. Let him try and wander but stand still without saying anything.
4. He is bound to try pulling away > Again stand firm and say 'this way' or 'here' > Do not try and pull him away, but wait for him to move towards you > when he does, say 'good boy' and then start walking away.
5. Hopefully he will follow and go as far as you can before he pulls back on the leash.
6. If he does, again stand firm saying 'this way' or 'here'.
7. Again when he comes to you, say 'good boy' and walk as far as you can.
8. Once you have done this several times offer lots of praise and a treat
9. Remove the leash and let him freely wander again

Socialisation and fear

There are bound to be noises, people, animals or other situations and objects that may cause some fear during his socialisation period. You should never punish, scold or attempt to correct his reaction. A useful tip is to anticipate a fear response and immediately distract the puppy by moving away and calling him to you, in other words distract him. Then immediately praise and reward with a treat. He will soon associate being rewarded with coming to you and not the fearful trigger.

During this socialisation it is important to let him freely explore your house, garden, yard and eventually beyond this. It is also important to stay close by to monitor his reactions and again keep him safe.

Other considerations

He needs to get into a routine of sleeping at set times

Don't forget to practice his Weekly routine health check

Make sure he is eating his meals and check that his faeces look normal; reasonably solid, no runny diarrhoea or unusual discharge

WEEK 3: (10 WEEKS OLD)

Important check list of things to do during the week:

- Remember his food routine from the previous weeks.
- Stick to the times as per previous weeks.
- Please remember to keep his water bowl topped up with fresh, clean water at all times.
- Have news paper or puppy pads ready for his toilet training routine.
- Have scales ready to weigh him and keep a record of the measurement.
- Remember to give him a health check.
- Continue his collar and leash training.
- Make sure he is eating his meals and check that his faeces look normal; reasonably solid, no runny diarrhoea or unusual discharge.

Chew toys should ideally be available from week 1. However, you may notice him becoming more troubled by teething at this time, so make sure he has plenty of suitable chew toys.

- » Remember to brush/comb him at least once or twice per week.

- » Allow for some play time/exercise in the yard, garden or room in the house.

Teething/chewing

You will hopefully have purchased a number of chew toys for your puppy before he arrived. The desire to chew can occur early on and indeed bite inhibition is something the mother and other litter mates will kerb whilst still part of the litter.

Similarly to an adult baby, teething can be troublesome for a young puppy. They will need to alleviate the pain and discomfort of teething by chewing on hard objects. In the absence of hard chew toys, the puppy will seek out alternatives such as shoes, furniture etc. You are therefore strongly advised to ensure the puppy has a number of chew toys for this purpose. However, be aware that even with a supply of chew toys they can become bored and generally do not discriminate when looking for things to chew. So if you wish to keep expensive shoes etc intact, make sure you keep these out of reached.

Bite inhibition

Although biting will have been discouraged in the litter this will not stop some puppies from playfully attempting to chew your hand. Bite inhibition should be discouraged from day one. It is therefore important to pull your hand away and vocalise with a firm 'No', to let the puppy know they should not do this. Do not be tempted to hit the puppy, not even a tap.

Energy

Again not unlike children, a puppy at this age will be full of energy and excitability. They have a tendency to madly rush about to the point of exhaustion, at which point they will wish to sleep until the next burst. During periods of excitement they can suddenly relieve themselves, so again be vigilant of this. If you notice him suddenly squat, don't shout but give a firm 'No', pick him up and take him into the yard/garden, allowing them to do their toilet business there.

Dominant behaviour

Around this time it is not uncommon for the puppy to start feeling his feet and gain in confidence. He may therefore show signs of dominance by barking, growling, snarling and other behaviour designed to get your attention. In this case it is best to simply ignore the behaviour and walk away. Don't be tempted to indulge him or otherwise acknowledge this.

Check list reminders

You will hopefully have been instructed from the breeder of any vaccinations or parasite treatments already carried out. It is advisable to write any vaccination or treatment dates on a wall calendar that you can quickly refer to and take the appropriate action.

Taking his weight

Don't forget to weigh him again on the first day of week three and again write this down, making a comparison with day one of week two.

WEEK 4: (11 WEEKS OLD)

Refer to the information to follow regarding his food routine. Basically you have been feeding 4 meals per day, now is a good time to reduce this to 3, but increase the amount for each portion.

The new feeding times will reflect the fact that he now has three meals spread throughout the day. So for example the first one can be between 7 and 8am, then between 1 and 2pm and a final meal between 7 and 8 pm. You may have to be flexible on those timings, depending on your availability and lifestyle. However, try and be as near to that sort of schedule as you can.

- Always remember to keep his water bowl topped up with fresh, clean water at all times.
- Have news paper or puppy pads ready for his toilet training routine.
- Have scales ready to weigh him, again making a note and comparing the previous week.
- Don't forget his health check.
- Continue his collar and leash training.
- Make sure he is eating his meals and check that his faeces look normal; reasonably solid, no runny diarrhoea or unusual discharge.
- Make sure he has plenty of suitable chew toys available.
- Remember to brush/comb him at least once or twice per week.
- Allow for some play time/exercise in the yard, garden or room in the house.

Growth and development

The puppy is still growing and developing and in order to avoid muscle, bone or ligament injury it is best to prevent him from becoming overexcited. It is normal around this age for him to start losing milk teeth so do not be alarmed if you notice a small tooth on his bedding or the floor.

Socialisation and behaviour

His socialisation around the house should continue. It is important to continue your normal household routine; vacuuming, switching on appliances etc. It depends on the personality of the puppy and he may be either indifferent or fearful to anything unusual. It is also important to keep him exposed to anything that makes him anxious as he needs to become 'de-sensitised' to fearful triggers. This certainly does not mean that you should literally take hold of him and make him face it. This is likely to terrify him and potentially have a long term psychological effect. It is therefore best to remain calm and reassure him but don't give in to this fear and attempt to protect or hide him away from it. Generally encourage him towards the thing he fears, all the while saying, 'come on', 'its alright', or words to that effect.

Play

The puppy will be naturally playful, but any play sessions with the family or other dogs should be monitored. You do not want things to get too rough or boisterous, and again be aware of biting which again should be corrected with a firm 'No'.

Toilet training

He should be getting used to the house-training routine by now. But do not neglect taking him out first thing in the morning, last thing at night, after each meal, having woken from sleep or any time he looks as if he is about to do his toilet business.

Planning a socialisation programme

For obvious reasons it is generally considered to be inadvisable to expose a puppy to potentially life threatening diseases until he has completed his final vaccinations. It is also generally considered that a puppy should be sufficiently socialised before the end of their 'critical period' usually at 12 to 16 weeks of age. Again refer to the chapter on socialisation.

Feeding

As you will be reducing his meals from 4 to 3 per day, be aware that an upset tummy can occur as a result of any changes of diet. Hopefully this will not happen if you change the times you feed which again ideally should be early morning, mid day, early evening.

Leash training and socialisation

This follows on from the leash training started during the previous week. Ideally you should be aiming to have your puppy leash trained for when he can safely socialise out and about. Again, it important that he is comfortable being led on his lead without pulling. So it is advisable to carry on practicing leash walking around the yard/garden in order to make the transition as smooth as possible, in preparation for this. It is not vital that he is walking at 'heel' which will be covered later, but comfortable being led and not pulling or holding back.

WEEK 5: (12 WEEKS OLD)

- Make sure you are sticking to his 3 meals per day, and ensure his bowel movements are normal and regular
- Stick to the feeding times as per previous weeks. Always remember that it is better if your puppy keeps to a routine.
- Always remember to keep his water bowl topped up with fresh, clean water at all times.
- Have news paper or puppy pads ready for his toilet training routine.
- Have scales ready to weigh him.
- Don't forget his health check.
- Continue his collar and leash training.
- Make sure he is eating his meals and check that his faeces look normal; reasonably solid, no runny diarrhoea or unusual discharge.
- Make sure he has plenty of suitable chew toys available.

- Remember to brush/comb him at least once or twice per week.
- Allow for some play time/exercise in the yard, garden or room in the house.

Leash walking

If your puppy has completed his vaccination shots (this will only apply if you are following a UK, schedule. However, for the US or anywhere else, bear this information in mind for when your puppy finishes his schedule at approximately 16 weeks of age) and your vet has advised you that he is now safe to interact with other dogs, then start taking him out walking either around your neighbouring area or perhaps a dog park or local field. Again refer to the socialisation chapter for specific information.

His bones and ligaments are now stronger and he will have movement similar to a grown adult. However, as he is still growing and developing, walking should be restricted to 2 or 3 short walks and the odd romp in the garden, but nothing overly energetic. As a rule of thumb the larger the dog breed, the less exercise they will need or should have. If you go to an open space, be sure to attach a long training lead or attach a long retractable lead in case he goes running off.

Tooth loss

Again, you may notice milk teeth loss as the new teeth emerge, which is normal between the ages of 12 and 16 weeks old.

Socialisation and anxiety

As you may now be introducing new and potentially frightening experiences, be mindful that he is likely to act fearful. Again it is best to remain calm and reassuring, but do not make a fuss or attempt to hide him. If you are walking near busy roads, vehicles will seem large, added to this the noise and fast movement, it may take some getting used to.

It is important at this stage to put the socialisation action plan into motion. The same old people and locations are not adequate for this. New locations, sights, sounds, objects; people of all ages, shapes, sizes, personalities etc.

Training

At this age, a big obstacle is holding the puppies attention for longer than 10 minutes. They have a limited attention span and tendency to become easily bored at this age, concentrate training sessions to short 5 or 10 minutes gradually pushing this to 15 minutes at a time.

Bonding

He should be closer to everyone now and will be keen to please you and start behaving appropriately.

Home alone

We cover also cover this to a certain extent in the section on crate training.

Some trainers advise training the puppy to be home alone for short periods each day after the first week at 9 weeks old. However, it is advisable, in order to avoid separation anxiety, to start this no later than 12 weeks of age.

It is normal for any dog to pine or fret if they have been used to human company to suddenly be left on their own. They have no idea if or when you will be coming back. For this reason get him used to you leaving for short periods.

Set this up as follows:

1. It is best to confine him to the one room they sleep in along with his bed and his crate if you are using one. The crate covered in a blanket with the door left open can offer a comforting retreat. Also leave toys and an item or items of clothing with your scent on. It is also a good idea to have the radio switched on as the music and talking, will be a distraction from the silence. Do not forget to leave water and perhaps a few treats.
2. Start by saying something like ' I won't be long' then closing the door for 10 seconds.
3. Provided he does not whine or bark, open the door again giving him lots of praise and offer a treat. If at any point he starts to whine or bark, only go back into the room once he stops. Otherwise it will

become a habit that if he whines or barks you will return, and he may continue this if left for any length of time

4. Now repeat (2) and (3), but increase the time to 20 seconds then 30, then 40 and so on. Once you reach a minute, increase the time by minutes, so 1 minute, then 2 then 3 etc.

This training may sound long winded, but the repetition of this routine will soon accustom him to expecting you to return once you leave.

Nail clipping

Once your dog is regularly walking on pavements or running about a concrete yard his nails will probably not need clipping. You should still check them in case they become overgrown, particularly if you a scraping or tapping sound.

WEEK 6: (13 WEEKS OLD)

Keep following the checklist routine for the previous weeks. It will not be listed from now on, unless you are reminded about changing a specific aspect such as cutting his feeding down.

General condition

Weighing your puppy in the initial stages can be a useful indication that he is gaining weight. However, it is also a good idea to make visual and physical checks. As part of the weekly health check, take note of the puppy's body shape. It is obviously important that he is neither over nor underweight. Common sense will no doubt tell you whether he looks too thin with an obvious visible rib cage or obese, no ribs showing and obviously fat or barrel shaped.

A useful link showing illustrations from underweight to obese can be found at the following:

https://www.purina.co.uk/dogs/health-and-nutrition/exercise-and-weight-management/dog-body-condition-tool

It is therefore important that he receives a correct calorie intake and increase or decrease his food intake accordingly. Also, relate this to any increase in exercise and other activity likely to burn more calories.

Be aware that an underweight condition may be as a result of worms or other internal parasite. If after a couple of weeks, an increase or decrease in food intake does not show improvement then it is important to consult your vet for a check up.

Growing confidence

At this stage in his socialisation development, providing he has not experienced anything fearful or traumatic, most puppies will be confident expanding their experiences.

Mentally, he should be getting stronger and be in need of more mental stimulation either training or social experiences. At this age he is also likely to start pushing boundaries. Your usual well behaved puppy may start to misbehave. This can manifest in him wilfully ignoring you as he starts to please himself.

Regular routines

Once again, dogs like to know where they stand and therefore respond well to routines. These should include the following:

» Times of day when they know you will not be in the house, in order to avoid separation anxiety.

» Regular feeding times.

» Times when they know it is time for them to sleep when you go to bed.

» Exercise, play time and training times at approximately the same time per day.

Limits

As well as keeping to routines and letting him know where he stands you should also be very careful how you reward behaviours. During formal training you usually reward behaviour you want repeated and ignore behaviour you don't want repeating.

Problems can occur when you are playing and generally giving him attention. As puppies you will feel the need to encourage them by petting, stroking and saying 'good boy' etc. But if they start to misbehave, chew your hand or whatever, it is important to stop this. Encouraging the behaviour is obviously seen as rewarding to the puppy and they will continue.

Obedience training

Basic training, 'sit', 'stay' etc, should be improving by now providing you are continuing this on a daily basis. Regular repetition is a must, in order to keep him focused, reliable and well behaved.

Motivation

By regularly interacting with your dog through play and general interaction, you will soon find out what his is motivated by. This is very important in terms of rewards for training and general obedience. He will either be motivated by playing a certain game, being allowed to play with a favourite toy, or like most dogs, by food, and in some cases a favourite food.

Bite inhibition

Play mouthing or biting is inevitable for most puppies to varying degrees whilst they are teething. This is another area where you need to be very careful not to reward such behaviour. You either need to stand up and walk away, or give a firm 'No', certainly no praising or trying to make a game of it.

WEEK 7: (14 WEEKS OLD)

As usual, make sure you are following the checklist of routines to carry out each week.

Although these may happen sooner or later, as he grows in size and confidence, you may experience the following behaviours:

Jumping up

Ignoring this behaviour by turning away as he jumps up usually has the desired effect of not rewarding the behaviour or acknowledging it as acceptable. If you can anticipate him jumping up, move toward him invading his space and taking away his momentum.

Manic exuberance

Over excitement is a problem that is started as a puppy, but can easily continue into adulthood.

This usually happens when the dog anticipates a walk, or game etc. Again it is best to ignore the behaviour and not continue until they are calm. Please be aware that you are not ignoring him if you maintain eye contact with him. Therefore to make the ignoring more effective always break eye contact.

New socialisation experiences

Please note: if you are based anywhere where he will still be undergoing his vaccinations, socialisation may have only taken place under strict conditions. It is a risk to expose your puppy to infected areas until after his 16 week vaccination program is complete.

For anywhere else, the following may apply.

When exposing your puppy to any new experiences always remember to put him on a lead. It is unlikely you will have reliable control over his actions until he has de-sensitised from stimuli likely to cause either a fight (curiosity) or flight response.

WEEK 8: (15 WEEKS OLD)

As usual, make sure you are following the checklist of routines to carry out each week.

Growth and development

Up until 15 weeks of age you will have gradually noticed your puppy getting bigger and stronger in terms of bone and muscle growth. After 15 weeks you will probably notice things starting to slow down. His calorie intake and therefore food needs will also reach a plateau.

However it should be noted that he may still eat everything put in front of him. You should therefore be careful not to over feed, as he probably does not need as much food as he is willing and able to eat. Obviously cut down his daily food intake if he starts to look overweight.

Children and puppy play

Allowing children to interact with puppies from day one is usually recommended as long as this is always supervised. Usually by 15 weeks of age he has learned or is learning bite inhibition and that biting or nipping is not acceptable. However, if a puppy gets too excited during play nipping, play biting or mouthing can still occur.

If this happens as always give a firm 'No', end the game by ignoring him or walking away until he has calmed down. These are all procedures that should be practiced by you and your children.

Testing your leadership

As your puppy begins to gain confidence he may test your authority and leadership. This can happen sooner or later but is common around this age. It is always wise to assert your authority by being firm and letting him remember that you control the resources; food, attention, play toys etc. This is not about you been a dictator, but about retaining good manners and behaviour. He should also realise that any misbehaviour will result in you taking these resources away. Again it is simply a question of rewarding acceptable behaviour and ignoring anything unacceptable.

Resource guarding

This again is about you controlling the resources. It can occur over anything the dog wishes to possess and in extreme cases involves food which can lead to serious fights. If however your puppy takes a fancy to your best pair of shoes it is best to practice 'swapping'. Again, this is simply distracting him with one of his toys which hopefully he takes once he drops your shoes or other item. Never physically punish 'bad behaviour' but practice ignoring it.

Avoiding destructive behaviour

As a reminder, the biggest reasons for bad or destructive behaviour is a lack of general attention, exercise and mental stimulation.

On a daily basis it is therefore your responsibility to provide the following:

Sufficient exercise, preferably off lead running in a safe area; Walking several times per day; Taking time each day to play games of tug, fetch etc; Training; Agility and tricks; A varied assortment of soft, hard and puzzle toys (the previous activities should also provide much needed mental stimulation)

WEEK 9: (16 WEEKS OLD)

Make sure you are following the checklist of routines to carry out each week.

Weight

If you have been weighing your puppy on a weekly basis you may realise that at 16 weeks he is approximately half of his expected adult weight.

Bladder-control and house-training

As a young puppy he will have found it difficult to hold his bladder for more than an hour. At this age he should be able to hold it without needing to urinate between 3 and 5 hours. However, it is important to not get complacent as accidents are likely to happen if you do not take note of when he last did his toilet business and when he is likely to need to go again. As a matter of routine, plan to let him out for 5 minutes or so at least every 3 hours.

Continued socialisation

If you are in the U.S.A or other locations with a vaccination schedule up to 16 weeks of age, you may be safe to begin socialisation anywhere. However, as always check with your vet beforehand.

Similarly to the previous week and since you started socialising, endeavour to expose him to new experiences.

Household pets

If you have other pets, you may suddenly notice that the puppy at this age reacts differently towards them. This is generally as their senses and perceptions become more acute. What he may have ignored before may suddenly be an object of interest. This is important for breeds with a strong prey instinct. Pet cats, guinea pigs, rabbits etc may suddenly be vulnerable to an attack or an episode of chasing. He may of course react with fear or friendliness toward them. However, to be safe, carefully monitor his behaviour and supervise any interactions or let him observe whilst the pet is caged. Or in the case of a cat, the cat has an obvious escape route.

Dominant behaviour

Touched on previously, this is a trait which can occur by now. Unlike other unwanted behaviour this is best not ignored, but tell him 'No' if he starts to show any wilfulness or dominance towards anyone.

Grooming

As a reminder, in many cases extensive trimming, bathing etc is only required occasionally, every one to two months or so. However, on a daily basis it is a good idea to at least give a good brush and comb to prevent a build up of mats or loose hair, and to generally keep the coat healthy. It is also a good idea to coincide this with his weekly health check. Don't forget to check for signs of fleas or droppings, perhaps using a fine flea comb.

House proof evaluation

It is also important as the puppy grows to go over the routine you initially did before his arrival. Things that were safely out of his reach as a small puppy may now be reachable and may need moving or readjusting. As he is no doubt stronger and more active he could also potentially bump into objects that a young puppy would be unable to do, smashing or knocking them over. Food or harmful substances again should be kept out of reach.

WEEK 10: (17 WEEKS OLD)

Make sure you are following the checklist of routines to carry out each week.

Teething

At around this time his new teeth will begin to emerge. His gums will become irritable during this process and he will seek out opportunities to chew on hard objects. It will therefore be necessary to ensure he has a variety of chew toys hard and soft.

Exercise

You will no doubt notice he is more energetic at this stage

Confidence and curiosity

As his confidence grows, so will his desire to explore his surroundings. It is important to keep him safe and anticipate potential hazards when out in public. If in doubt keep him on a long training lead that you can easily follow and catch if he takes off and fails to respond.

Fear and socialising

Once again increase his exposure to new experiences. Be mindful that he may become fearful and as usual it is best to not give into this by being overly protective. This increased fear aspect may be more prevalent in puppies that have just started properly socialising after their final vaccination jab at 16 weeks old.

House-training

Even though his house-training will be relatively reliable by now, do not take it for granted that accidents will never happen. Keep a routine of letting him out at regular intervals of at least 2 to 3 hours or so. Once again, accidents should never be punished.

Mental stimulation

He will respond and benefit well from you engaging him in one or two new mental stimulation games.

There are a number of useful books on the subject. Without wishing to recommend any in particular I would suggest doing a search on Amazon for search terms [dog tricks] or [dog games].

Obedience training

Hopefully you will be continuing with new training or revising skills already covered.

Food intake

Again, it is important to physically appraise your puppy and make sure he neither too fat nor too thin.

WEEK 11: (18 WEEKS OLD)

Make sure you are following the checklist of routines to carry out each week.

Once again the puppy will require fewer calories than before and it is not unusual for him to start leaving part of his meal. In this respect it is not necessarily an indication that he is ill. You should therefore not worry unduly. Unless of course you suspect an illness, in which case do not hesitate to consult your vet for a check up.

However, muscle growth is a significant factor at this stage. It is therefore important that your puppy is receiving sufficient levels of protein in the form of good quality food.

Male puppies

At this stage males are beginning to sexually develop, with an increase in testosterone and consequent sexual behaviour.

Separation anxiety

Many people do not like the idea of crate training. However it is important that puppies are trained as early as possible to sleep remotely from you in some respect (this was covered in WEEK 5, but you can start this earlier). This may be utilising a crate or it could be confining him to the kitchen or other room. He needs to feel comfortable sleeping or generally being alone otherwise he may develop fear responses such as separation anxiety if he is not with you all the time.

Individual character

The puppy will have matured mentally at this stage and will be displaying more of his natural adult personality.

Independence

In the same way that children gradually gain independence from their parents, so the puppy will begin to venture and be keen meet new potential playmates. This will usually take place where other dog walkers frequent such as parks, local recreation fields or pavement walking. This will be a strong temptation for any dog to rush off to greet other dogs. Do not therefore trust him off lead until you have trained a reliable recall.

Changing his collar

You may find at this stage that he has outgrown his collar; in which case it is advisable to take him to your local pet store and get them to size him for a new one.

WEEK 12: (19 WEEKS OLD)

Make sure you are following the checklist of routines to carry out each week.

In a similar way to previous weeks, growth and weight gain will be slowing down as he reaches maturity.

Adult coat

During puppyhood his coat will have been softer and by this age you may see signs of his adult coat coming through. Continue with regular grooming

Pecking order

His natural adolescence will see him pushing boundaries whether this is with you or other pets.

Growth and fear

In a similar way to human teenagers, growth can involve anxieties, fear and aggression. If this happens with your dog, accept this as a phase that he is likely to grow out of.

Feeding

At this stage it is a good idea to review his diet. He will have been on a diet suitable for a growing puppy. But again although muscle growth will continue to a certain extent, as his growth generally slows, he will need less protein than before.

Exercise

As with all exercise up to this point, long extended walks of three miles or more should be avoided. He will be getting stronger muscle and bone wise but is still vulnerable to injury. In this respect keep walks short and frequent.

Try and make sure that he has the opportunity to socialise and play with other dogs. You may wish to organise a group of other dog owners, join an organised group or simply meet other dog owners at a park etc.

Give him plenty of opportunities to meet dogs of different ages. In particular older dogs who will teach him appropriate behaviour and what he can and can't get away with.

WEEK 13: (20 WEEKS OLD)

Make sure you are following the checklist of routines to carry out each week.

If you have been weighing him on a regular basis, the weight that he will be at this stage should be approximately three quarters of his adult weight. His height should also be approximately three quarters of his adult height.

Teething

His gums will probably still be sore as his adult teeth are still emerging. It is important to note that certain dry dog food may be uncomfortable to eat as the hardness may jar on his sore gums. If you notice he seems off his food, try softer foods such as cooked chicken until this period subsides.

Sexual development

You should expect him to reach sexual maturity now or in the next week or so. Although his toilet training will for the most part be reliable, you will need to be aware that 'marking' behaviour in your house is a possibility, mostly males. It will therefore be necessary to be vigilant to prevent this from becoming habitual.

Training

Basic command should be solid and reliable by this point if you have been regularly practicing. You may have also started on some of the more advanced techniques.

If you have taught him routines beyond the basics, be aware that these need to be maintained with regular practice otherwise you may find he quickly forgets. As with all other aspects of maturity he will soon be mentally mature, but will not be as flexible at learning new information as he once was as a young puppy.

Continued socialisation

Again, if you have been following a socialisation plan you will be looking to add new experiences and solidify older ones.

Feeding

Up until this point you will have been feeding 3 meals per day. As his growth is slowing and he advances towards adulthood plan to cut his meals to two per day. Remember that when you reduced the number of meals from 4 to 3, it was necessary to make sure each meal is increased to keep the overall daily allowance in line with the recommended amount for his age and weight.

Cutting his meals down to 2 per day, also makes it much easier if your lifestyle dictates that you will not be around mid day as you can now feed morning and evening. If you stick to these routine times, he will invariably be ready to eat at these times.

Exercise

Remember to avoid boredom and behaviour problems by providing regular exercise and mental stimulation games.

WEEK 14: (21 WEEKS OLD)

Make sure you are following the checklist of routines to carry out each week.

He is now nearing 6 months of age and is nearing his physical and mental peak. If you have a bitch you may find she has her first season around now. Be aware that discharges (blood or otherwise) are possible, so be prepared to clean any mess up or confine her to any area that is easy to clean. Remember to not allow contact with intact males if she comes into season.

Dogs are also likely to exhibit mounting behaviour as part of their growing sexual maturity. In this respect they are capable of fathering a litter of puppies.

Again, be vigilant about catching them scent marking.

WEEK 15: (22 WEEKS OLD)

Make sure you are following the checklist of routines to carry out each week.

Bathing and teeth cleaning

Regular grooming is something you will have been doing on a regular basis since he arrived. However, bathing and teeth cleaning may not have been actioned as yet.

Intermediate training

Again, if you have not continued training him beyond basic obedience, you may wish to consider intermediate to advance training now. Many owners do not train their dog beyond basic obedience. This is fine but the puppy will benefit a great deal from further training procedures that will keep him mentally stimulated.

Having said that, please be aware that too much physical and mental stimulation can do more harm than good if he is not getting sufficient rest and sleep as well.

WEEK 16: (23 WEEKS OLD)

Make sure you are following the checklist of routines to carry out each week.

By this stage things will hopefully be going smoothly in terms of training, feeding and all other routines.

WEEK 17: (24 WEEKS OLD)

Make sure you are following the checklist of routines to carry out each week.

You may notice at this point or sooner his nails start to appear thicker and harder as his adult nails emerge. Nail clipping is something you have been doing or at least keeping an eye on as part of his regular checks and grooming. Be aware that they will be harder to cut.

Shedding

This depends on the breed but many breeds shed or 'blow' their coat twice per year. This is not dependent on seasonal changes as such but sunlight seems to play a part in the release of melatonin from the pineal gland, which causes shedding. Shedding can also occur as a result of artificial heat and light, an allergic reaction etc.

WEEK 18: (25 WEEKS OLD)

Make sure you are following the checklist of routines to carry out each week.

As he nears the six month mark he is still growing and maturing, but he will probably be at a size similar to his eventual adult size.

Problem behaviours

The ironical thing about problem behaviours is they are only a problem to us. To a dog the following are perfectly natural. However, as previously noted they are all also usually a symptom of boredom, lack of exercise or in some cases maturity, as follows:

Chewing; Digging; Resource guarding; Biting; Growling; Dominance; Fighting; Scent marking; Sexual behaviour; Roaming; Barking; Howling

It is obviously important to control or discourage these and should therefore be tackled before they get out of hand.

WEEK 19: (26 WEEKS OLD)

Make sure you are following the checklist of routines to carry out each week.

Again check your puppies general appearance and weight, ensuring they are not overweight through over feeding.

Tooth brushing

It is a good idea to start brushing their teeth as soon as possible for their oral health as well as getting him used to the routine. In the early stages his gums will have been benefiting more so as his baby teeth give way to adult teeth. Up to approximately 7 months of age his adult teeth will have come through. If you haven't already started this, it is now recommended that regular tooth brushing takes place. It is also recommended that you make available dental chews, and or raw meaty bones will be an important routine, to clean the teeth and gums.

Scavenging

A natural behaviour for dogs is scavenging and begging, which you may encounter around this time.

It is important to discourage this by not randomly giving them food other than their meals or treats for good behaviour.

Adulthood and dominance

Group hierarchy is natural for dogs as they reach adulthood and sexual maturity. They may form 'pecking orders' with other dogs, but in the absence of firm leadership from you, may also attempt to dominate you or other family members, if you let them.

The opposite of this is submissive behaviour. This is a fundamental reason why traditional dog training involving 'alpha rolls' and other techniques are a bad idea for many dogs. A lot of dogs can become fearful and lack confidence if they are subjected to such harsh training methods.

Keeping calm

During his transition towards adulthood you may find that certain socialisation encounters, make him fearful and consequently stressed. It is very important to remember to deal with these as noted before, by firstly identifying the trigger/problem and then gradually de-sensitising him.

WHAT TO EXPECT DURING THE NEXT 3 MONTHS (6 TO 9 MONTHS)

Although chewing is associated with teething, if a dog has a predisposition towards chewing, this will continue regardless. However, many dogs do exercise the need to chew around this age, specifically in conjunction with them acquiring their adult teeth. For this reason it is always important to provide chew toys as well as keep chewable valuables, shoes etc, out of reach.

Growth

Slow gradual growth will now continue towards adulthood. In most cases a six month old puppy will be approximately at their expected adult size. However, depending on the breed and the individual, adulthood usually occurs around 9 months, but can be another 6 months beyond this. His senses will also be much more acute around this age.

Hormonal issues

You may have already encountered issues associated with hormonal increases such as sexual behaviour, general aggression, resource guarding or aggression towards other dogs. It usually passes without issue, but if you get recurring problems then you may need to consider neutering. If so you are advised to consult with your vet as to your puppies suitability.

Feeding

Once again, continue to regularly check your dogs weight against the ideal weight. Also visually check for obesity or being underweight. Again, if when you feel along the rib cage you cannot feel his ribs, chances are he is overweight through over feeding.

House training

Hopefully you have been keeping to a routine of regularly letting him outside to do his toilet business. In addition, provided you have been vigilant, watching for signs of him needing to go, you should be encountering few if any 'accidents'. It is worth noting however that at this age most puppies are able, or potentially capable to hold their bladder for between 6 and 8 hours. Technically speaking he can now hold his bladder overnight, but this does not mean you will not come down to a pool of urine. It all depends if he has a drink overnight, or whether he urinated before you retire to bed.

WHAT TO EXPECT DURING THE NEXT 3 MONTHS (9 – 12 MONTHS)

Despite him nearing maturity, he is still likely to retain his puppy exuberance.

Chasing

The chase prey instinct, if this occurs, should be channelled into acceptable alternatives such as chasing balls or other toys. Although with perseverance, a reliable recall can be achieved. You do however, have to be prepared for unpredictability. Prevention is therefore often the only reliable solution to chase behaviour. In areas where rabbits, squirrels and other wildlife frequent, keep him on a long line leash unless it is safe from road traffic or other hazards, let him off leash.

Infections and disease

Ear and skin disorders are common until he has a strong, developed immune system. Parasites can take their toll in terms of weakening the immune system which is why you should treat for worms and fleas etc on a regular basis. As part of his regular health check you should also check the ears for mites or infection, and the skin for disorders.

Injury, strains and sprains

As he matures and grows in strength and confidence, so will the risk of injury. Obviously injuries can occur at any age, but will be more so the stronger and more active he becomes. Ligaments, joints and muscles are therefore susceptible to tears, strains, sprains and breakages. Do not hesitate to consult your vet if such injuries occur during any kind of activity.

1 YEAR AND BEYOND

Do not confuse muscle gain with obesity. Having reached one year he will have attained an adult physicality but may still bulk out muscle wise up to 18 months of age.

Routines which you have been following must be maintained at all times.

Be careful not to over feed, or to leave him with ad lib food and expect him to eat only as much as he needs. Some dogs are good at eating only their daily needs but others can be greedy which results in obesity issues.

CHAPTER TWENTY FOUR:

WEBSITES, MISCELLANEOUS RESOURCES & CONCLUSION

Caring for a dog can be challenging so you can probably use all the help you can get. In this chapter you will find a collection of useful resources to help you care for your Labrador. Here you will find links to suppliers for food, crates, dog beds, toys, accessories and more. You will also find links to additional resources about the Labrador Breed

Please note: Initially and for convenience, I would advise you to purchase any basics that you will need from a local supplier. You may then wish

to look at perhaps buying from internet suppliers.

The following are a few suggestions for on-line suppliers in both the USA and the UK. It is intended to give you a good start, locating various supplies that you will no doubt need. It is not intended as a definitive list, nor is the author in anyway necessarily recommending or endorsing any of these in preference to any other product or supplier. They are considered to be good suppliers, but again it is up to you to do your own research and decide who you wish to deal with.

I would also suggest doing a Google search for additional suppliers. Once you gain experience, you will no doubt have your own favourites. I would always urge you to shop around, and not necessarily go for the cheapest, particularly where feed is concerned.

Please also note that at the time of press, the following web links were working. However, from time to time, pages get changed, deleted or a supplier goes out of business. If you find these do not work, please go to the route .com or .co.uk web address. Again, the author takes no responsibility for the availability of any of these, when you the reader come to access them.

1) FOOD FOR LABRADOR'S

Providing your Labrador with a healthy diet is the key to maintaining good health. In this section you will find a collection of relevant websites for Labrador food.

UNITED STATES LINKS:

"High Endurance Adult Dog Food." Nutro Natural Choice.
https://www.nutro.com/natural-dog-food/nutro/high-endurance

"Active Care Healthy Joint Formula." Breeder's Choice.
http://www.goactivedog.com/

"Which Dog Food is Right for My Dog?" SelectSmart.com.
http://www.selectsmart.com/dogfood/

Nutro Natural Choice Medium Breed Dog Food.
https://www.nutro.com/natural-dog-food/medium-breed

Blue Buffalo – Puppy and Adult Natural Dog Food.
https://bluebuffalo.com/for-dogs/lifestage/puppy-food/

https://bluebuffalo.com/for-dogs/lifestage/adult-dog-food/

Earthborn Holistic – Puppy and Adult Natural Dog Food.
https://www.earthbornholisticpetfood.com/dog-food-formulas/holistic/puppy-vantage

https://www.earthbornholisticpetfood.com/dog-food-formulas/holistic/adult-vantage

1-800-PetMeds – Adult and Puppy Dog Foods.
http://www.1800petmeds.com/Puppy+Food-cat240006.html

http://www.1800petmeds.com/Adult+Pet+Food-cat250010.html

UNITED KINGDOM LINKS:

Burns Natural Food for Pets.
http://burnspet.co.uk/dog-food-for-active-dogs.html

"Taste of the Wild Dog Food." Taste of the Wild.
http://www.tasteofthewildpetfood.co.uk/

"Field & Trial – For Working and Active Dogs." Skinner's.
https://www.skinnerspetfoods.co.uk/product-category/field-trial-range/

"VetSpec Active Nutritional Supplement." VetSpec for Dogs.
http://www.vetspec.co.uk/shop/vetspec-active-500g/

"Active and Working Dog Food." PetPlanet.co.uk.
http://www.petplanet.co.uk/category.asp?dept_id=462

Eukanuba – Dog Food Formula.
http://www.eukanuba.co.uk/products
Canagan – Grain Free Dog Food Products.
https://www.canagan.co.uk/products.html

Iams ProActive Health
http://www.iams.co.uk/product

More Pet Foods – Small and Larger Breed Adult.
https://www.morepetfoods.co.uk/#products

"Purina Feeding Guide".
https://www.purina.co.uk/dogs/health-and-nutrition/daily-feeding-guide/tailoring-a-diet-to-your-dog
The following includes alternative suppliers and is a mixture of natural, freeze dried or dehydrated . I am not personally recommending or endorsing any in particular. However, all of the suppliers listed have been recommended by certain individuals on various forums.

Also please note that dehydrated or freeze dried foods can work out a lot more expensive than other available foods including raw.

UK

https://www.naturesmenu.co.uk/natural-dog-food/shop-by-product/superfood-crunch

http://www.orijenpetfoods.co.uk/dog-food/freeze-dried-dog-food/

http://www.naturaldogfoodcompany.com/

http://www.naturalpetproductsltd.com/ziwipeak-2/

https://www.k9natural.co.nz/where-to-buy/

http://www.chudleys.com/

https://www.wellbeloved.com/

https://www.ardengrange.com/

https://www.applaws.co.uk/product-category/dog/dry-dog-food/

USA

https://www.k9natural.co.nz/where-to-buy/

http://www.onlynaturalpet.com/products/Only-Natural-Pet-EasyRaw-Dehydrated-Dog-Food/999244.aspx

http://www.thehonestkitchen.com/

https://www.iandloveandyou.com/product-category/dog/

https://www.nrgdogproducts.com/

Please also have a look at the following website. This has links to stockists of raw feed as well as raw dehydrated food.

https://www.dogfoodadvisor.com/best-dog-foods/raw-dog-food/

There are many more similar products both online and no doubt in your local pet store. You may wish to do an additional Google search for your location along the lines of [dehydrated raw dog food] or [freeze dried raw dog food]. The important factor is that the product is either raw freeze dried or raw dehydrated.

You may be interested to read the following useful articles giving a brief overview of the dehydration/freeze dried process as well as recommendations:

https://www.whole-dog-journal.com/issues/17_9/features/Dried-and-True-Consider-Dehydrated-Dog-Foods-for-Your-Dog_21043-1.html

http://www.drsfostersmith.com/pic/article.cfm?articleid=3138

Once again if you are interested in BARF/raw feeding, I would urge you to check your local area for suppliers. However, in my experience I have often found that the equivalent product such as chicken wings and portions can be bought cheaper from the supermarket. So do not automatically assume a raw pet food supplier will be your best or cheapest option. Again, as always please shop around.

Again, please refer to the section on feeding for more detail.

2.) CRATES AND BEDS FOR LABRADOR'S

Your Labrador's crate is the place where he can retreat if he wants a nap or to take a break. In this section you will find a collection of relevant websites for dog crates and beds.

UNITED STATES LINKS:

"Crates, Carriers & Pens." Drs. Foster and Smith.
http://www.drsfostersmith.com/dog-supplies/dog-cages-crates-carriers-pens/ps/c/3307/10627

Cabela's. Search "Dog Supplies."
http://www.cabelas.com/catalog/browse/_/N-1106731

"Crates." PetSupplies.com.
http://www.petsupplies.com/dog-supplies/crates/9113/

"Crates, Gates and Containment." PetsMart.
http://www.petsmart.com/dog/crates-gates-and-containment/carriers-and-crates/

"Orvis Dog Beds." Orvis United Kingdom.
http://www.orvis.co.uk/dog-beds#close
"Dog Crates." PetPlanet.co.uk.

http://www.petplanet.co.uk/category. asp?dept_id=771

"Dog Crates and Kennels." Amazon.co.uk.
http://www.amazon.co.uk
Please search for dog crates and kennels

"Dog Beds and Bedding." Pet-Supermarket. co.uk.
https://www.pet-supermarket.co.uk/ Dog/Dog-Beds-Bedding/c/PSGB00051

3.) TOYS AND ACCESSORIES FOR LABRADORS

Having the right toys and accessories for your Labrador is very important. In this section you will find a collection of relevant websites for Labrador toys and accessories.

UNITED STATES LINKS:
"Interactive Dog Toys." Petco.
https://www.petco.com/shop/en/petcos- tore/category/dog/dog-toys

"Dog Toys." Chewy.com.
http://www.chewy.com/dog/toys-315

"Bowls & Feeders." PetSmart.
http://www.petsmart.com/ search/?q=dog+bowls+feeders

"Dog Toys." Drs. Foster and Smith.
http://www.drsfostersmith.com/dog- supplies/dog-toys/ps/c/3307/3

"Collars, Harnesses and Leashes." PetSmart.
http://www.petsmart.com/ search/?q=dog+collars-harnesses- leashes

"Dog Grooming Supplies." Drs. Foster and Smith.
http://www.drsfostersmith.com/dog- supplies/dog-grooming/ps/c/3307/5

"Dog Toys." PetPlanet.co.uk.
http://www.petplanet.co.uk/dept. asp?dept_id=16

"Dog Feeding and Watering Supplies." Amazon.co.uk.
http://www.amazon.co.uk
Please search for dog feeding and watering

"Dog Toys." VetUK.
http://www.vetuk.co.uk/dog-toys-c-439

"Toys." Battersea Dogs & Cats Home.
http://www.battersea.org.uk
Please search for toys on their site

"Dog Bowls & Feeders." Pet-Supermarket. co.uk.
https://www.pet-supermarket.co.uk/ Dog-Bowls-and-Feeders/c/PSGB00064

Pets at Play: 10 Best Dog Toys." The Independent.
http://www.independent.co.uk/extras/ indybest/house-garden/crufts-2014-in- destructible-dog-toys-9170885.html

"Dog Toys." Pet-Supermarket
http://www.pet-supermarket.co.uk/ Category/Dog_Supplies-Dog_Toys

Friendly Dog Collars.
http://www.friendlydogcollars.com/

"Dog Grooming Supplies." Pet-Supermarket.
https://www.pet-supermarket.co.uk/ Dog/Dog-Grooming/c/PSGB00058

4) GENERAL DOG CARE INFORMATION

The key to being the best Labrador owner you can be, is to learn everything there is to know about dog ownership. In this section you will find a collection of relevant websites about various aspects of dog ownership.

UNITED STATES LINKS:

"Dog Care." ASPCA.org.
https://www.aspca.org/pet-care/dog-care

"Pet Care Center: Dog." PetMD.
http://www.petmd.com/dog/petcare

"Dog Care and Behavior Tips." The Humane Society of the United States.
http://www.humanesociety.org

"Dog Diet and Nutrition." WebMD.
http://pets.webmd.com

http://pets.webmd.com/dogs/guide/diet-nutrition

UNITED KINGDOM LINKS:

"General Advice About Caring for Your New Puppy or Dog." The Kennel Club.
http://www.thekennelclub.org.uk/getting-a-dog-or-puppy/general-advice-about-caring-for-your-new-puppy-or-dog/

"Caring for the Older Dog." Blue Cross for Pets.
http://www.bluecross.org.uk/pet-advice/caring-older-dog

Battersea Dogs & Cats Home - Dog Care Advice:
https://www.battersea.org.uk/pet-advice/dog-care-advice

5) MISCELLANEOUS RESOURCES

GENERAL ORGANISATIONS USA

Labrador Retriever Club Websites
http://www.labradorretriever.com/clubwebsites.html

Keystone Labrador Retriever Club
http://www.keystonelrc.com/

The Labrador Retriever Club
http://www.thelabradorclub.com/

American Kennel Club breed information
http://www.akc.org/dog-breeds/labrador-retriever/

AKC Breed Standard
http://images.akc.org/pdf/breeds/standards/LabradorRetriever.pdf?_ga=2.32352638.1540083946.1512582652-982655679.1507657217

GENERAL ORGANISATIONS UK

The Kennel Club Find A Dog Club Breed Clubs Retriever (Labrador)
https://www.thekennelclub.org.uk/services/public/findaclub/breed/list.aspx?id=2048

Kennel Club UK Breed Standard
https://www.thekennelclub.org.uk/services/public/breed/standard.aspx?id=2048

RESOURCES; FURTHER READING AND INFORMATION

AKC Gazette:
http://www.akc.org/pubs/gazette/

http://www.dogsnaturallymagazine.com/

Animal Protection Organisations To Support Humane Society International (HSI): http://www.hsi.org

http://www.humanesociety.org/

SPCA International
http://www.spcai.org

International Animal Rescue:
http://www.internationalanimalrescue.org
International Fund For Animal Rescue (IFAW)
http://www.ifaw.org

Soi Dog Rescue:
http://www.soidog.org/en/about

PETA:
http://www.peta.org/international/

OTHER LINKS

Gundog Web Links

Gundog Web Links
http://www.gundogweblinks.co.uk/retrievers.html

The Breed Club Connection
http://www.thebreedclubconnection.com/labrador-retriever-information/labrador-retriever-breeders/

http://totallygundogs.com/

Positive Gundog Links:

https://positively.com/contributors/the-state-of-positive-gun-dog-training-who-will-take-up-the-gauntlet/

http://www.positivegundogtraining.com/resources/myths-exposed/

http://www.thelabradorsite.com/dog-training-methods/

http://www.positivegundogassociation.com/

http://www.themoderndogtrainer.net/best-approach-addressing-aversive-techniques-equipment-new-clients/

http://totallygundogs.com/what-age-should-you-start-training-your-gundog-puppy/

ADDITIONAL LINKS:
http://www.theretrieverjournal.com

http://www.pointingdogjournal.com

http://www.positivegundogsmn.com/resources--photos.html

http://totallygundogs.com/the-positive-gundogs-group/
http://www.clickertraining.com/node/1021

http://www.clickertraining.com/node/1134

http://www.patriciamcconnell.com/the-otherendoftheleash/positive-training-for-hunting-dogs

http://gundogandbirddogforums.yuku.com/

NATIONAL GUNDOG CLUBS

http://www.ahdc.org

http://www.huntingretrieverclub.org/

GENERAL HEALTH LINKS

https://www.thelabradorsite.com/health-screening-for-labrador-diseases/

https://labradorhealthclearances.weebly.com/

http://www.lab-health.co.uk/puppy.html

https://www.thekennelclub.org.uk/media/14688/dnatestsworldwide.pdf

http://www.thekennelclub.org.uk/health/

"How Will Spaying Change my Dog?" ASPCA. https://www.aspca.org/pet-care/virtual-pet-behaviorist/dog-behavior/how-will-spaying-change-my-dog

"Plans and Coverage." Veterinary Pet Insurance. http://www.petinsurance.com/plans-and-coverage.aspx

"U.S.A. Vaccination Schedules for Dogs and Puppies." PetEducation.com. http://www.peteducation.com/article.cfm?c=2+2115&aid=950

"Nutrients Your Dog Needs." ASPCA. https://www.aspca.org/pet-care/dog-care/nutrients-your-dog-needs

"What Causes Nutrient Deficiencies in Dogs?" Dog-Nutrition-Naturally.com. http://www.dog-nutrition-naturally.com/nutrient-deficiencies.html

"Your Dog's Nutritional Needs." National Research Council. http://dels.nas.edu/resources/static-assets/banr/miscellaneous/dog_nutrition_final_fix.pdf

"The Dog Food Project." http://www.dogfoodproject.com/index.php?page=main

"Canine Terminology." https://www.thekennelclub.org.uk/media/471961/glos_of_terms_rtf.pdf

http://www.akc.org/about/glossary/

http://www.gopetsamerica.com/dogs/terminology.aspx

"Getting Started Showing Your Dog." AKC.org. http://www.akc.org/events/conformation-dog-shows/getting-started-show-ing/

"How to Choose an Experienced Dog Breeder." PetMD. http://www.petmd.com/dog/care/evr_dg_breeders

"How to Find a Responsible Dog Breeder." The Humane Society of the United States. http://www.humanesociety.org/issues/puppy_mills/tips/finding_responsible_dog_breeder.html?referrer=https://www.google.com/

OTHER MISCELLANEOUS LINKS:
http://cani-cross.co.uk

https://en-gb.facebook.com/canicrossusa/

http://agilitynet.co.uk/

http://www.flyball.org

http://www.flyball.org.uk

https://apdt.com/

http://www.ahvma.org

http://www.bahvs.com/

https://www.dogwise.com/

International Association of Animal Massage & Bodywork: also Association of Water canine Therapy http://www.iaamb.org/preferred-educational-providers.php

Tellington TTouch UK: http://ttouchteam.co.uk/

FORUMS

Just Labradors The Forum http://www.justlabradors.com/forum/

The Labrador Forums UK
http://www.labradorforums.co.uk/

The Labrador Retriever Chat Forums
http://www.lab-retriever.net/board/

The Labrador Forum
https://thelabradorforum.com/

http://www.dogforum.com/

http://www.petforums.co.uk/
Arknaturals

https://arknaturals.com/

Doggie doors are also a great way to promote healthy Toilet habits. These are a great way for your dog to come and go as he pleases. Be aware that other pets and animals could enter back into your house. You would also not want to leave these open whilst you are away from the house, in case of intruders having easy access to your property. The following are a few examples, but again research as many possibilities as you can.
https://www.petdoors.com/

http://store.intl.petsafe.net/en-gb/doors/large-dog

Hopefully you have read this far and have found the contents useful, informative and inspiring. There is a lot to consider when buying any dog, and consequently to appreciate their needs. Hopefully this book reflects that. For the most part, dogs that are properly looked after with love, care and respect, will repay you with unconditional love and devotion, many times over.

The intention of the book was not to overwhelm you the reader and put you off committing to being the guardian of this fantastic Labrador breed. The intention was simply to give you as broad an appreciation as possible, so that you are fully prepared and equipped to properly look after and appreciate your new friend.

As you will realise, having read the various chapters, keeping a dog happy does not necessarily come without its problems. However, with correct awareness and training, many potential problems can be avoided. The health and welfare of your new Labrador should go without saying, so please do everything you can to provide healthy food and a safe warm environment. In essence, it doesn't take a lot to keep your dog happy and healthy.

At the very least you should be providing the following:

(i) A warm safe habitat. (ii) Healthy food and fresh water, daily. (iii) Routine health procedures such as worming, flea treatment and veterinary check-ups. (iv) Basic training and regular daily exercise. (v) As much love and attention as you can provide.

Thank you for reading and allowing me to assist you in being a loving, caring guardian for your new friend.

INDEX

Printed in Great Britain
by Amazon